KEEP YOUR HANDS OFF EIZOUKEN!

01

STORY AND ART BY

大童澄瞳
SUMITO OOWARA

CONTENTS

KEEP YOUR HANDS OFF EIZOUKEN! VOL. 1
TRANSLATED BY KUMAR SIVASUBRAMANIAN
SPECIAL THANKS FOR TRANSLATION ASSISTANCE: CHITOKU TESHIMA
LETTERING AND RETOUCH BY SUSIE LEE AND STUDIO CUTIE
EDITED BY CARL GUSTAV HORN

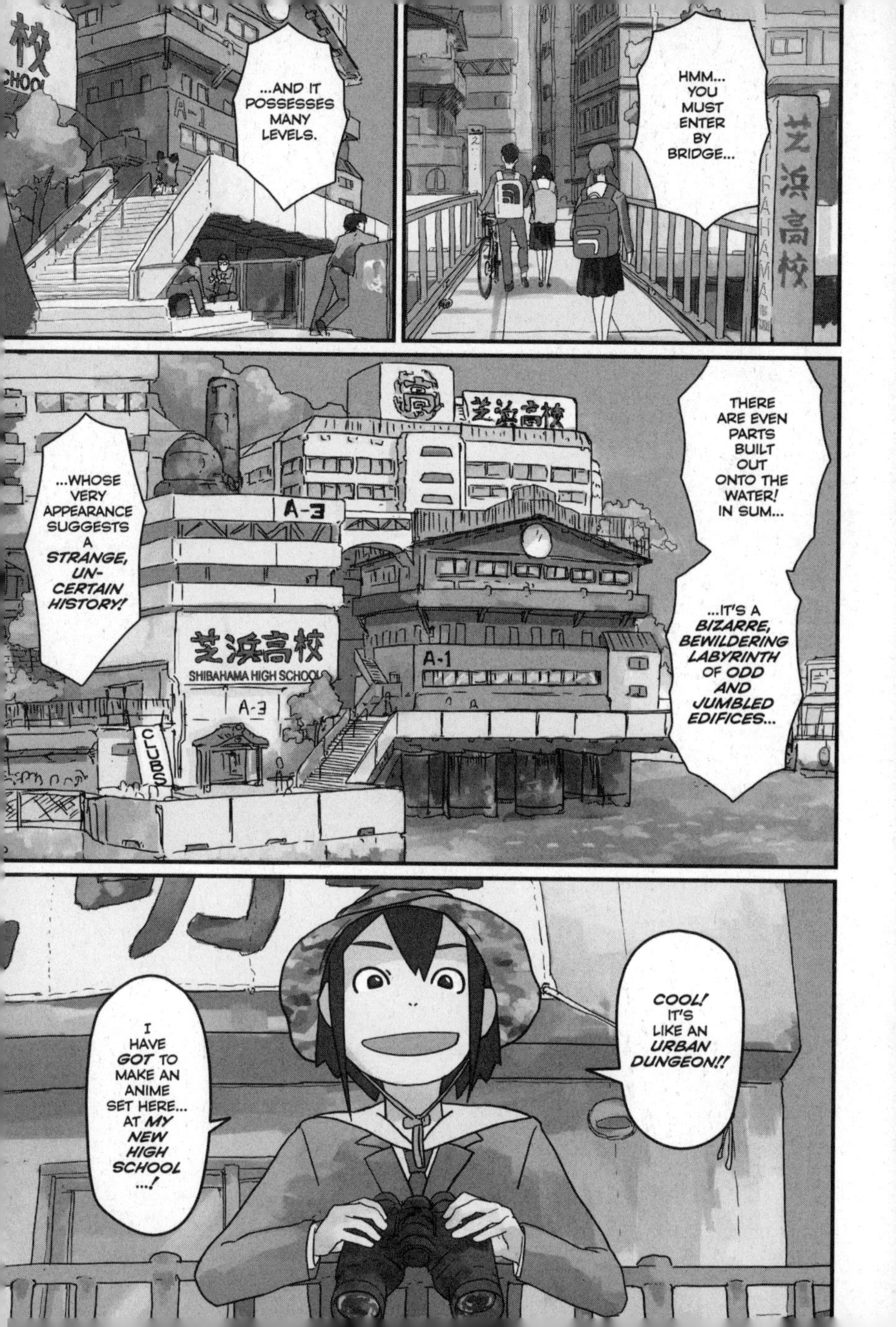
HMM... YOU MUST ENTER BY BRIDGE...
芝浜高校
...AND IT POSSESSES MANY LEVELS.
A-1
THERE ARE EVEN PARTS BUILT OUT ONTO THE WATER! IN SUM...
...IT'S A BIZARRE, BEWILDERING LABYRINTH OF ODD AND JUMBLED EDIFICES...
...WHOSE VERY APPEARANCE SUGGESTS A STRANGE, UN-CERTAIN HISTORY!
芝浜高校
A-3
A-1
芝浜高校
SHIBAHAMA HIGH SCHOOL
A-3
CLUBS
COOL! IT'S LIKE AN URBAN DUNGEON!!
I HAVE GOT TO MAKE AN ANIME SET HERE... AT MY NEW HIGH SCHOOL ...!

CHAPTER 1:
THE GREATEST WORLD

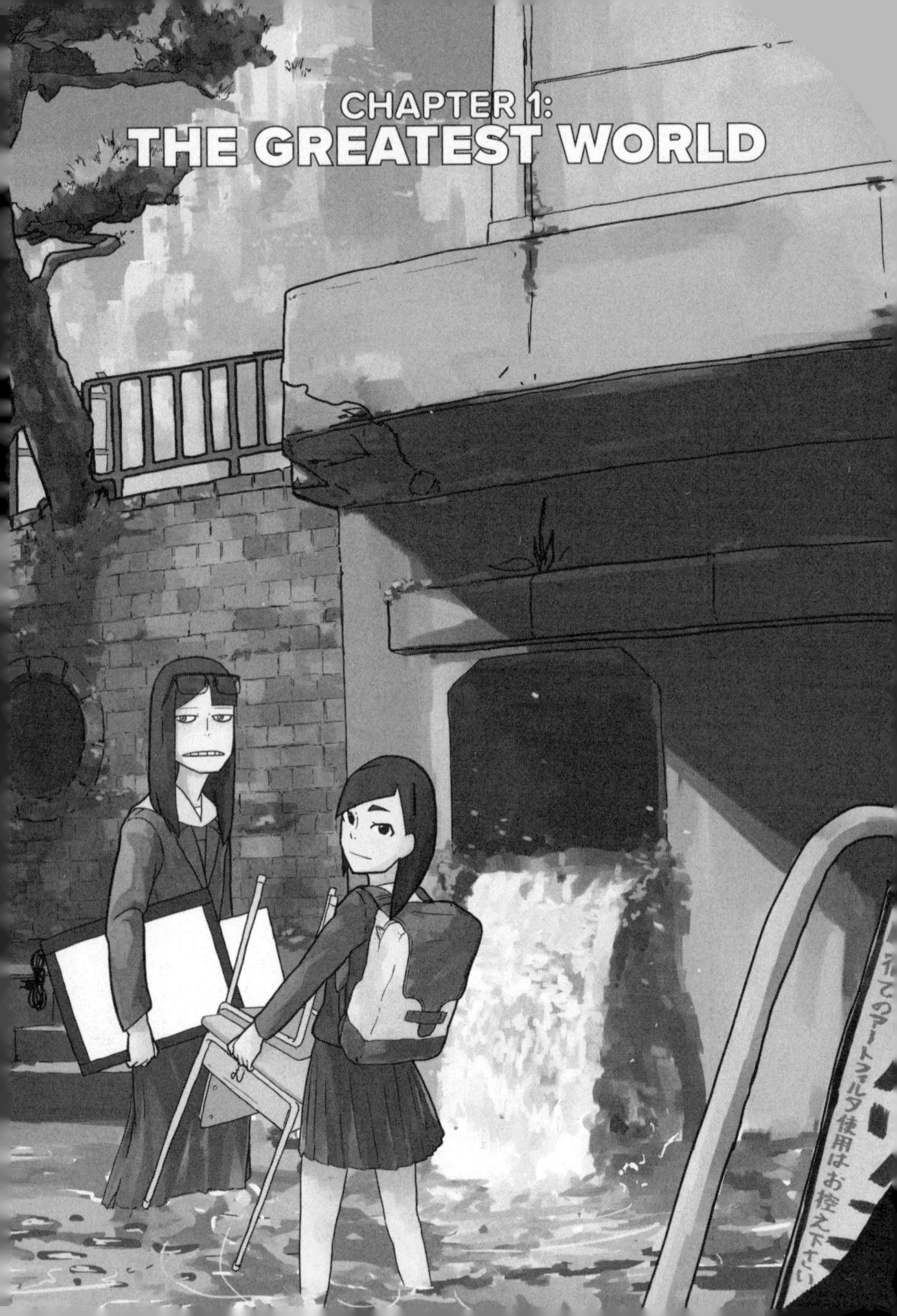
てのアートフォルタ使用はお控え下さい

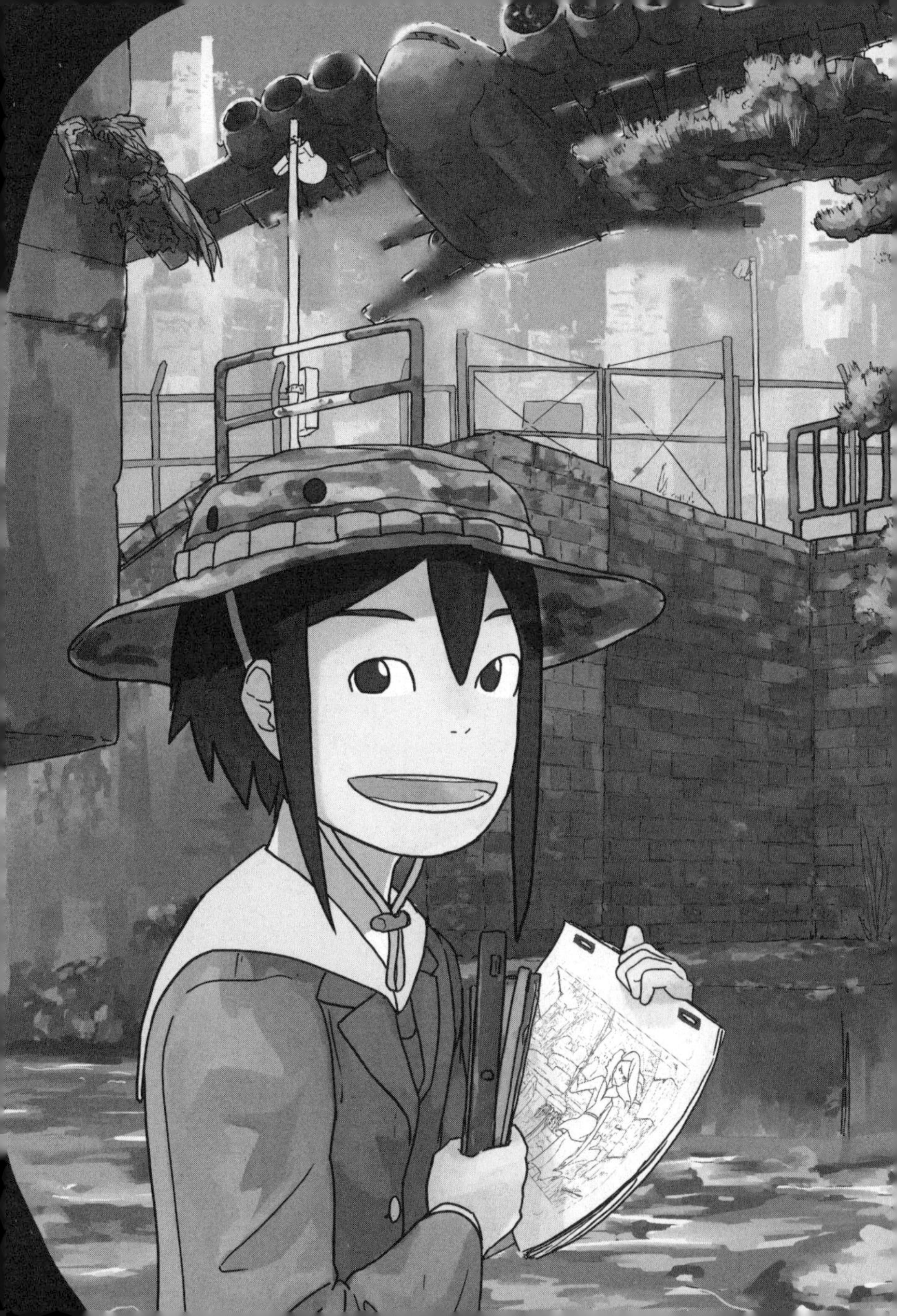

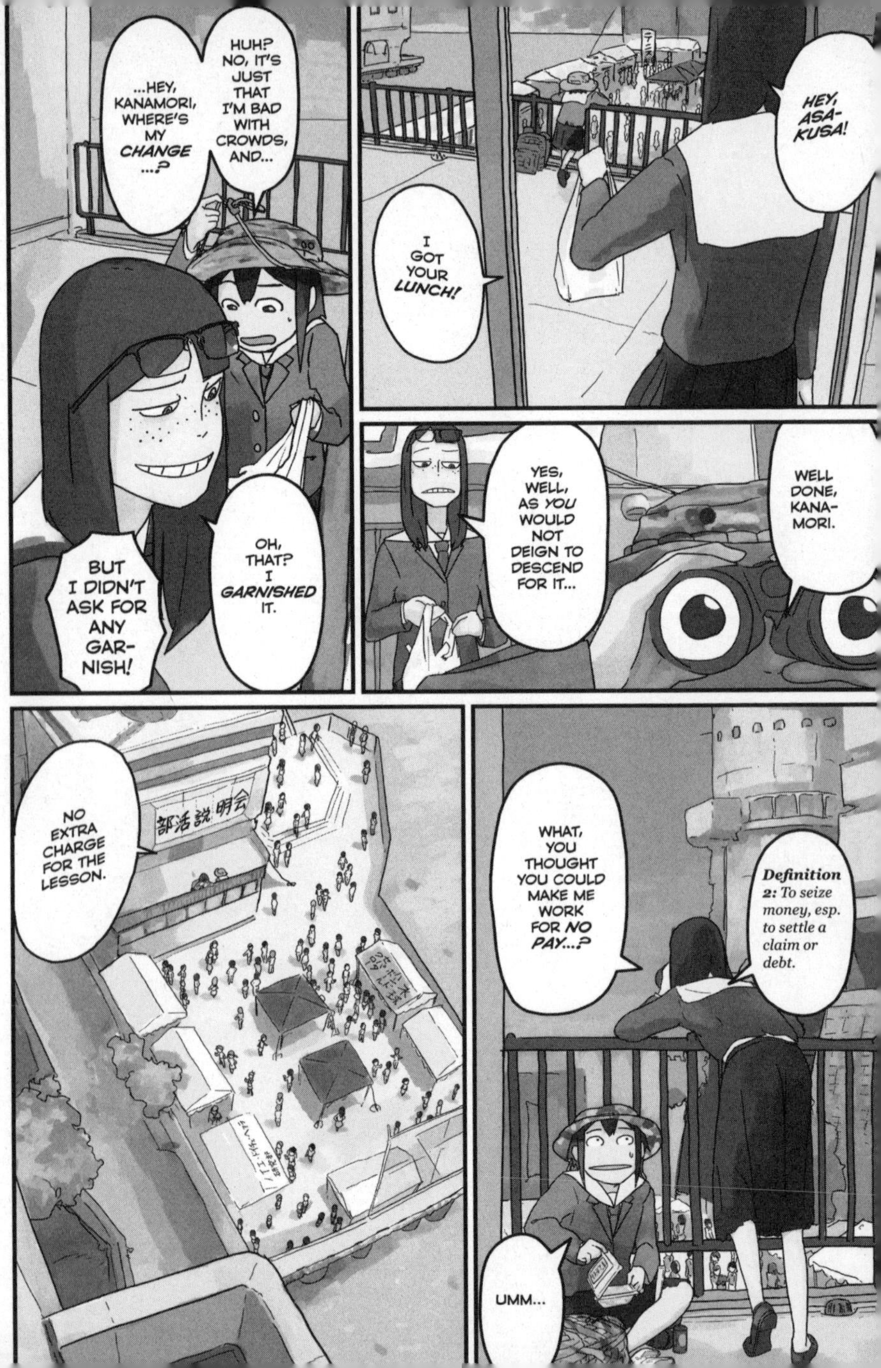
HEY, ASAKUSA!
I GOT YOUR LUNCH!
WELL DONE, KANAMORI.
YES, WELL, AS YOU WOULD NOT DEIGN TO DESCEND FOR IT...
...HEY, KANAMORI, WHERE'S MY CHANGE ...?
HUH? NO, IT'S JUST THAT I'M BAD WITH CROWDS, AND...
OH, THAT? I GARNISHED IT.
BUT I DIDN'T ASK FOR ANY GARNISH!
Definition 2: To seize money, esp. to settle a claim or debt.
WHAT, YOU THOUGHT YOU COULD MAKE ME WORK FOR NO PAY...?
UMM...
部活説明会
NO EXTRA CHARGE FOR THE LESSON.

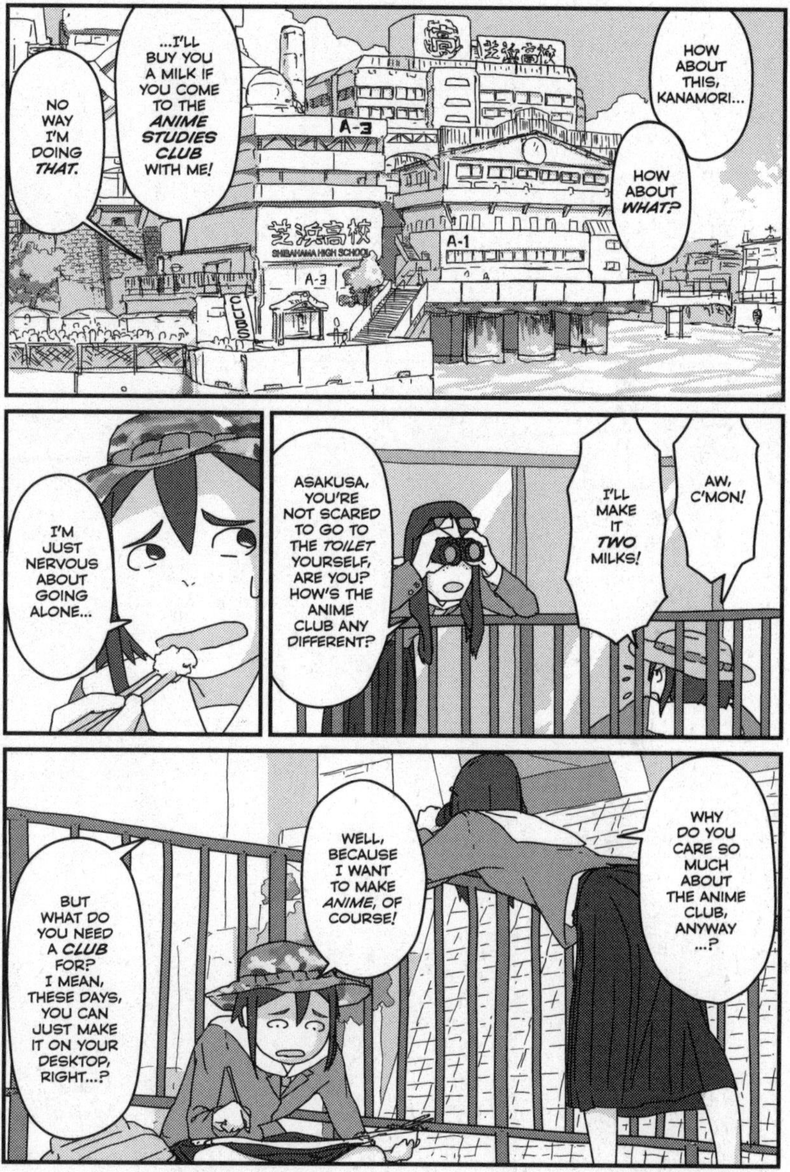
HOW ABOUT THIS, KANAMORI...
HOW ABOUT *WHAT?*
...I'LL BUY YOU A MILK IF YOU COME TO THE ***ANIME STUDIES CLUB*** WITH ME!
NO WAY I'M DOING *THAT.*
A-3
A-1
芝浜高校
SHIBAHAMA HIGH SCHOOL
CLUBS
AW, C'MON!
I'LL MAKE IT *TWO* MILKS!
ASAKUSA, YOU'RE NOT SCARED TO GO TO THE *TOILET* YOURSELF, ARE YOU? HOW'S THE ANIME CLUB ANY DIFFERENT?
I'M JUST NERVOUS ABOUT GOING ALONE...
WHY DO YOU CARE SO MUCH ABOUT THE ANIME CLUB, ANYWAY ...?
WELL, BECAUSE I WANT TO MAKE *ANIME*, OF COURSE!
BUT WHAT DO YOU NEED A *CLUB* FOR? I MEAN, THESE DAYS, YOU CAN JUST MAKE IT ON YOUR DESKTOP, RIGHT...?

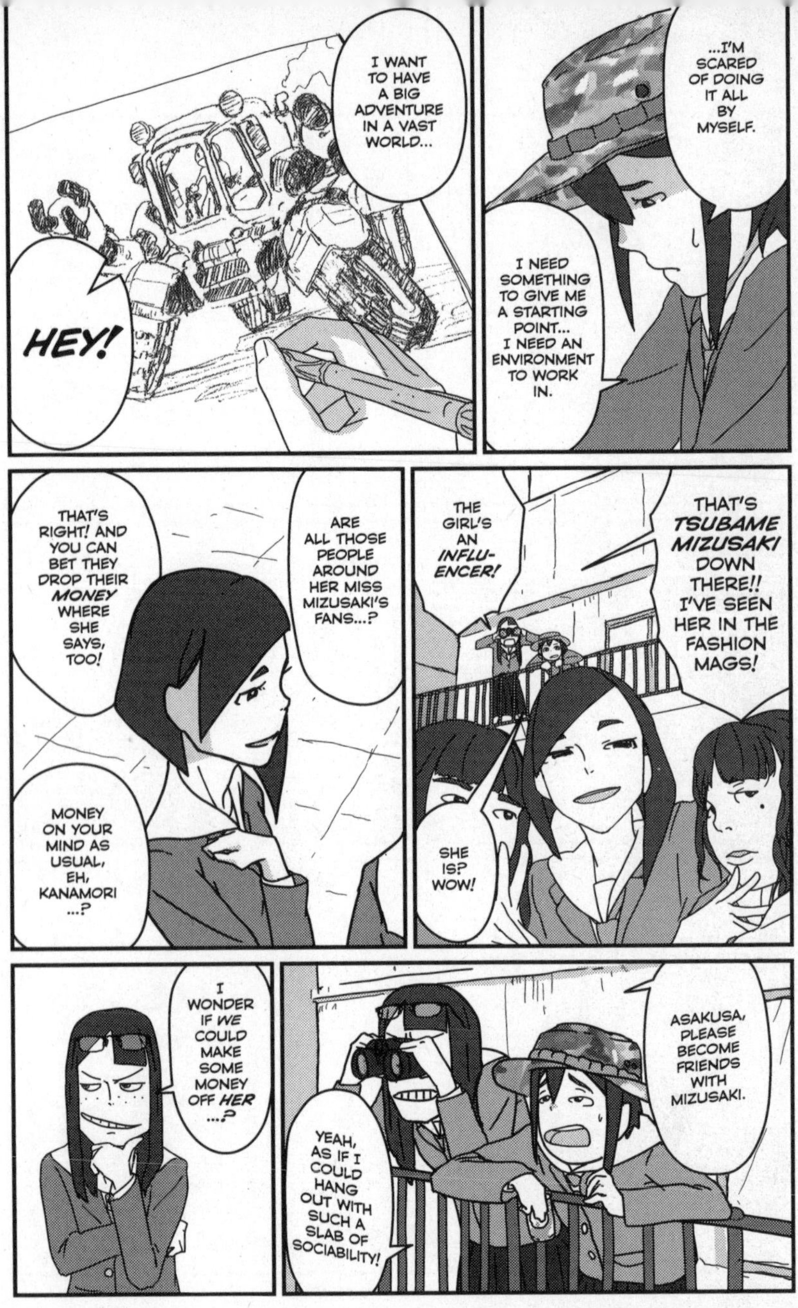
...I'M SCARED OF DOING IT ALL BY MYSELF.
I NEED SOMETHING TO GIVE ME A STARTING POINT... I NEED AN ENVIRONMENT TO WORK IN.
I WANT TO HAVE A BIG ADVENTURE IN A VAST WORLD...
HEY!
THAT'S TSUBAME MIZUSAKI DOWN THERE!! I'VE SEEN HER IN THE FASHION MAGS!
THE GIRL'S AN INFLU-ENCER!
SHE IS? WOW!
ARE ALL THOSE PEOPLE AROUND HER MISS MIZUSAKI'S FANS...?
THAT'S RIGHT! AND YOU CAN BET THEY DROP THEIR MONEY WHERE SHE SAYS, TOO!
MONEY ON YOUR MIND AS USUAL, EH, KANAMORI...?
ASAKUSA, PLEASE BECOME FRIENDS WITH MIZUSAKI.
YEAH, AS IF I COULD HANG OUT WITH SUCH A SLAB OF SOCIABILITY!
I WONDER IF WE COULD MAKE SOME MONEY OFF HER...?

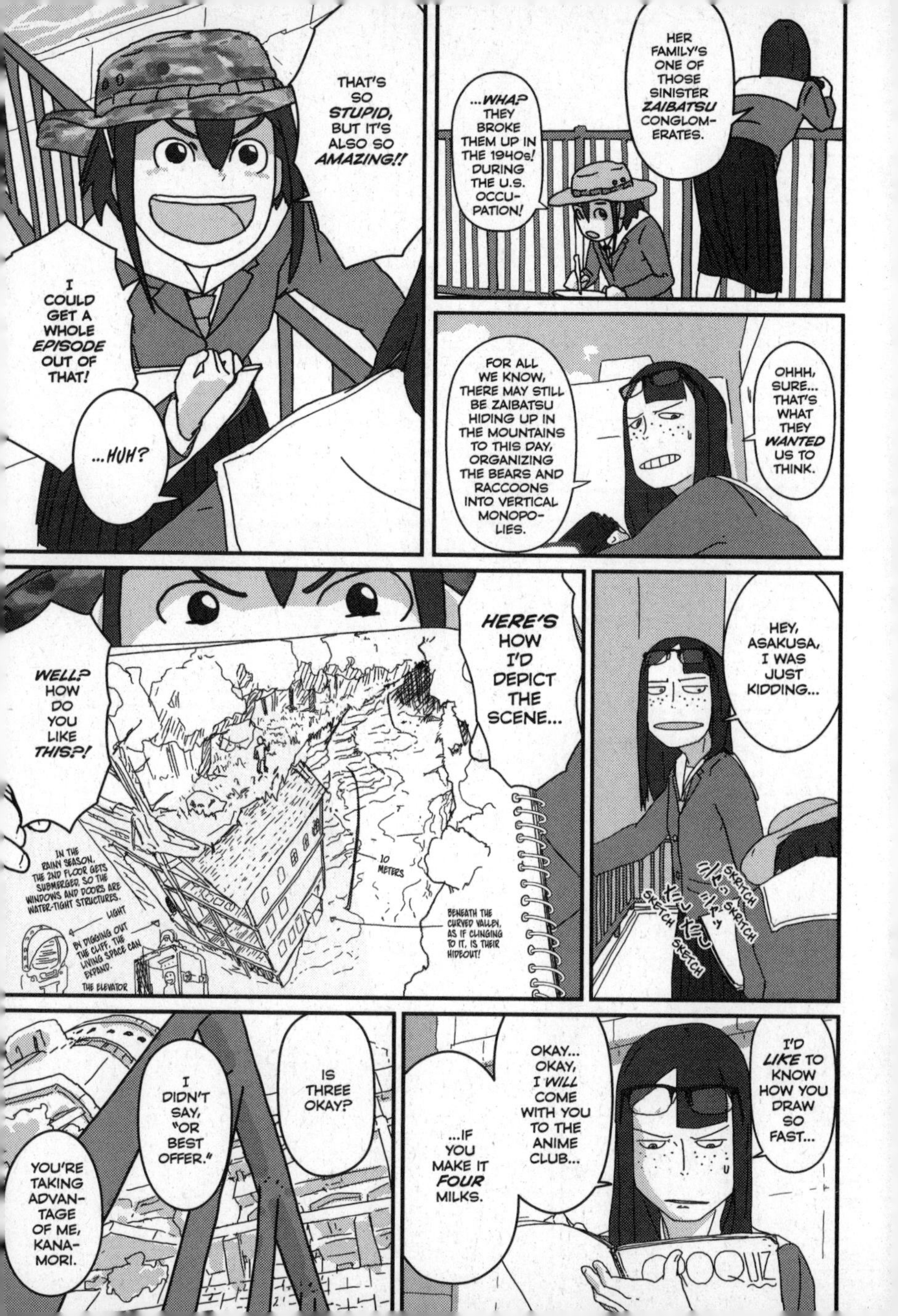
HER FAMILY'S ONE OF THOSE SINISTER ZAIBATSU CONGLOMERATES.
...WHA? THEY BROKE THEM UP IN THE 1940s! DURING THE U.S. OCCUPATION!
OHHH, SURE... THAT'S WHAT THEY WANTED US TO THINK.
FOR ALL WE KNOW, THERE MAY STILL BE ZAIBATSU HIDING UP IN THE MOUNTAINS TO THIS DAY, ORGANIZING THE BEARS AND RACCOONS INTO VERTICAL MONOPOLIES.
THAT'S SO STUPID, BUT IT'S ALSO SO AMAZING!!
I COULD GET A WHOLE EPISODE OUT OF THAT!
...HUH?
HEY, ASAKUSA, I WAS JUST KIDDING...
SKRITCH SKRITCH
SKETCH SKETCH
HERE'S HOW I'D DEPICT THE SCENE...
WELL? HOW DO YOU LIKE THIS?!
IN THE RAINY SEASON, THE 2ND FLOOR GETS SUBMERGED, SO THE WINDOWS AND DOORS ARE WATER-TIGHT STRUCTURES.
LIGHT
BY DIGGING OUT THE CLIFF, THE LIVING SPACE CAN EXPAND.
THE ELEVATOR
10 METERS
BENEATH THE CURVED VALLEY, AS IF CLINGING TO IT, IS THEIR HIDEOUT!
I'D LIKE TO KNOW HOW YOU DRAW SO FAST...
OKAY... OKAY, I WILL COME WITH YOU TO THE ANIME CLUB...
...IF YOU MAKE IT FOUR MILKS.
CROQUIZ
IS THREE OKAY?
I DIDN'T SAY, "OR BEST OFFER."
YOU'RE TAKING ADVANTAGE OF ME, KANAMORI.

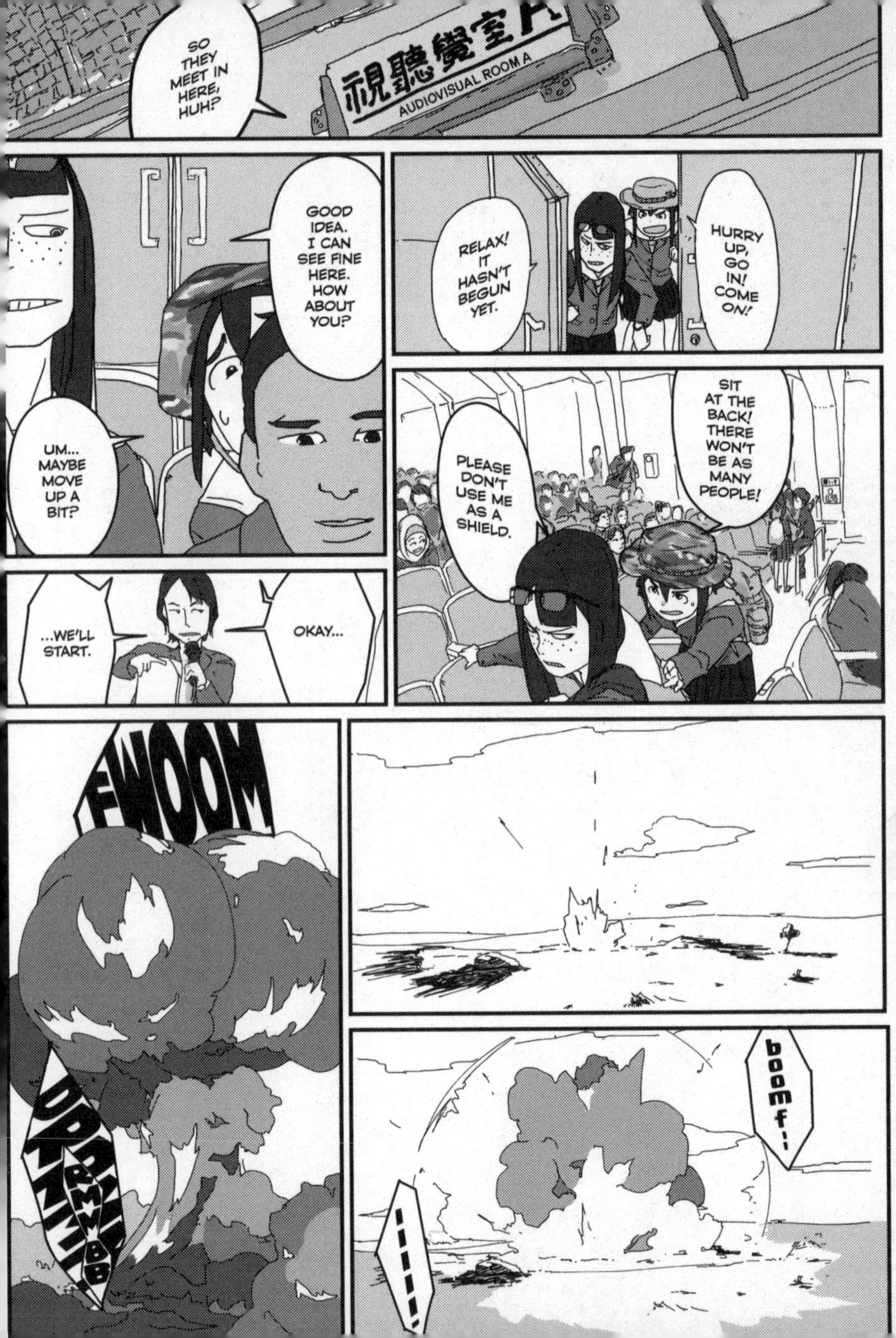
SO THEY MEET IN HERE, HUH?
視聴覺室A
AUDIOVISUAL ROOM A
HURRY UP, GO IN! COME ON!
RELAX! IT HASN'T BEGUN YET.
SIT AT THE BACK! THERE WON'T BE AS MANY PEOPLE!
PLEASE DON'T USE ME AS A SHIELD.
GOOD IDEA. I CAN SEE FINE HERE. HOW ABOUT YOU?
UM... MAYBE MOVE UP A BIT?
OKAY...
...WE'LL START.
boomf!!
!!!!!!
FWOOM

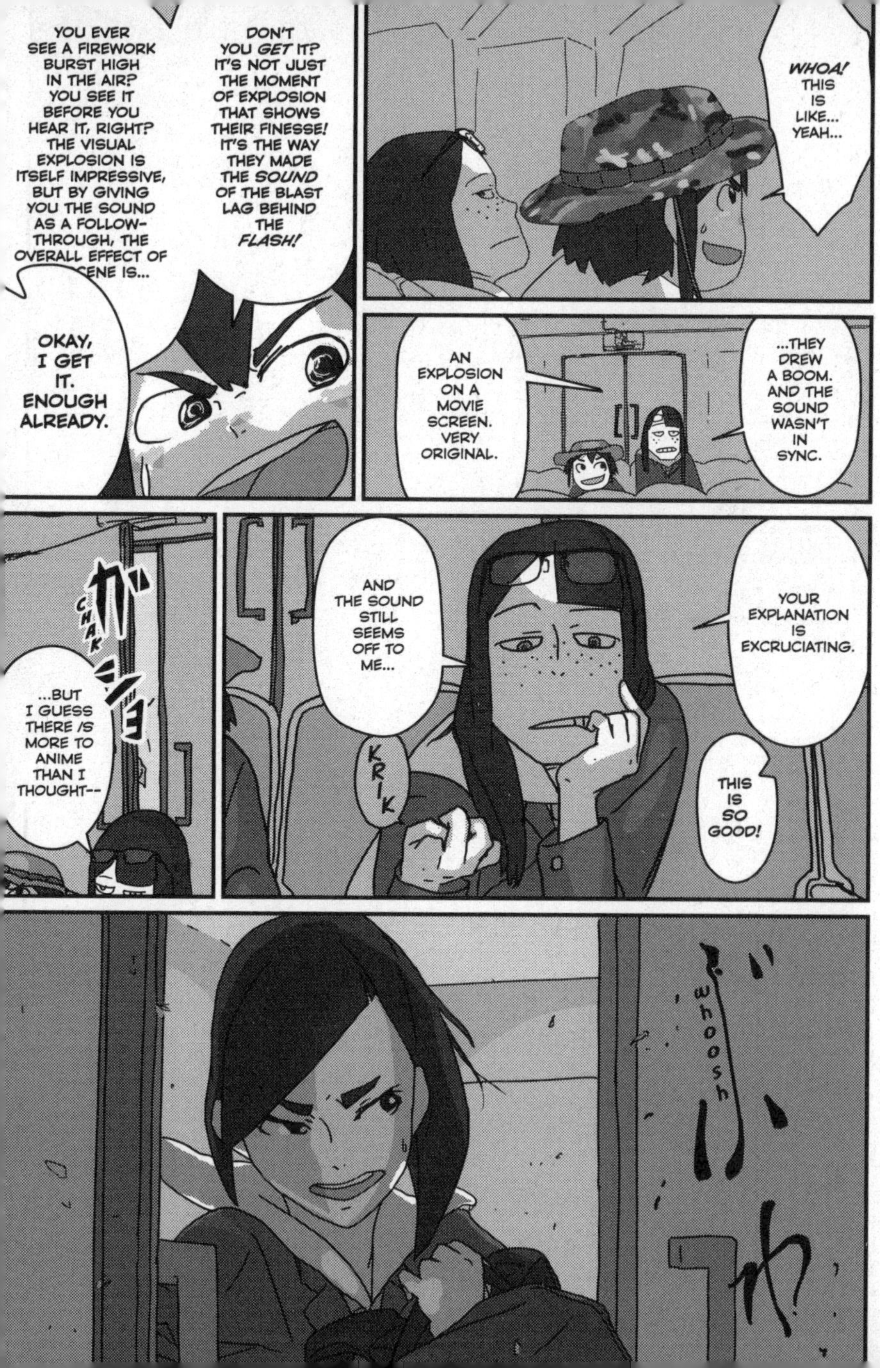
WHOA! THIS IS LIKE... YEAH...
...THEY DREW A BOOM. AND THE SOUND WASN'T IN SYNC.
AN EXPLOSION ON A MOVIE SCREEN. VERY ORIGINAL.
DON'T YOU GET IT? IT'S NOT JUST THE MOMENT OF EXPLOSION THAT SHOWS THEIR FINESSE! IT'S THE WAY THEY MADE THE SOUND OF THE BLAST LAG BEHIND THE FLASH!
YOU EVER SEE A FIREWORK BURST HIGH IN THE AIR? YOU SEE IT BEFORE YOU HEAR IT, RIGHT? THE VISUAL EXPLOSION IS ITSELF IMPRESSIVE, BUT BY GIVING YOU THE SOUND AS A FOLLOW-THROUGH, THE OVERALL EFFECT OF CENE IS...
OKAY, I GET IT. ENOUGH ALREADY.
YOUR EXPLANATION IS EXCRUCIATING.
AND THE SOUND STILL SEEMS OFF TO ME...
THIS IS SO GOOD!
KRIK
CHAK
...BUT I GUESS THERE IS MORE TO ANIME THAN I THOUGHT--
whoosh

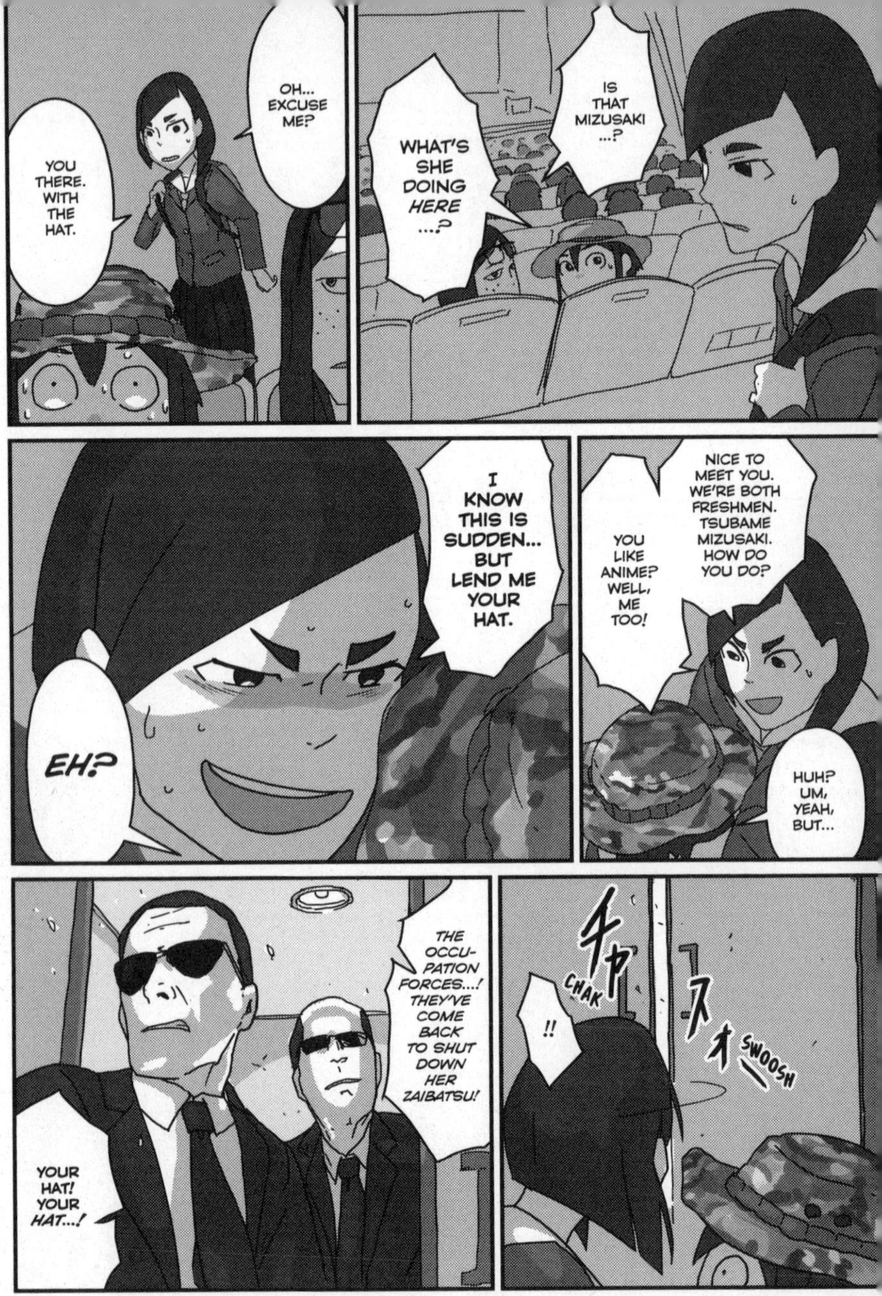
IS THAT MIZUSAKI ...?
WHAT'S SHE DOING *HERE* ...?
OH... EXCUSE ME?
YOU THERE. WITH THE HAT.
NICE TO MEET YOU. WE'RE BOTH FRESHMEN. TSUBAME MIZUSAKI. HOW DO YOU DO?
YOU LIKE ANIME? WELL, ME TOO!
HUH? UM, YEAH, BUT...
I KNOW THIS IS SUDDEN... BUT LEND ME YOUR HAT.
EH?
チャ
CHAK
!!
スオ
SWOOSH
THE OCCUPATION FORCES...! THEY'VE COME BACK TO SHUT DOWN HER ZAIBATSU!
YOUR HAT! YOUR *HAT...!*

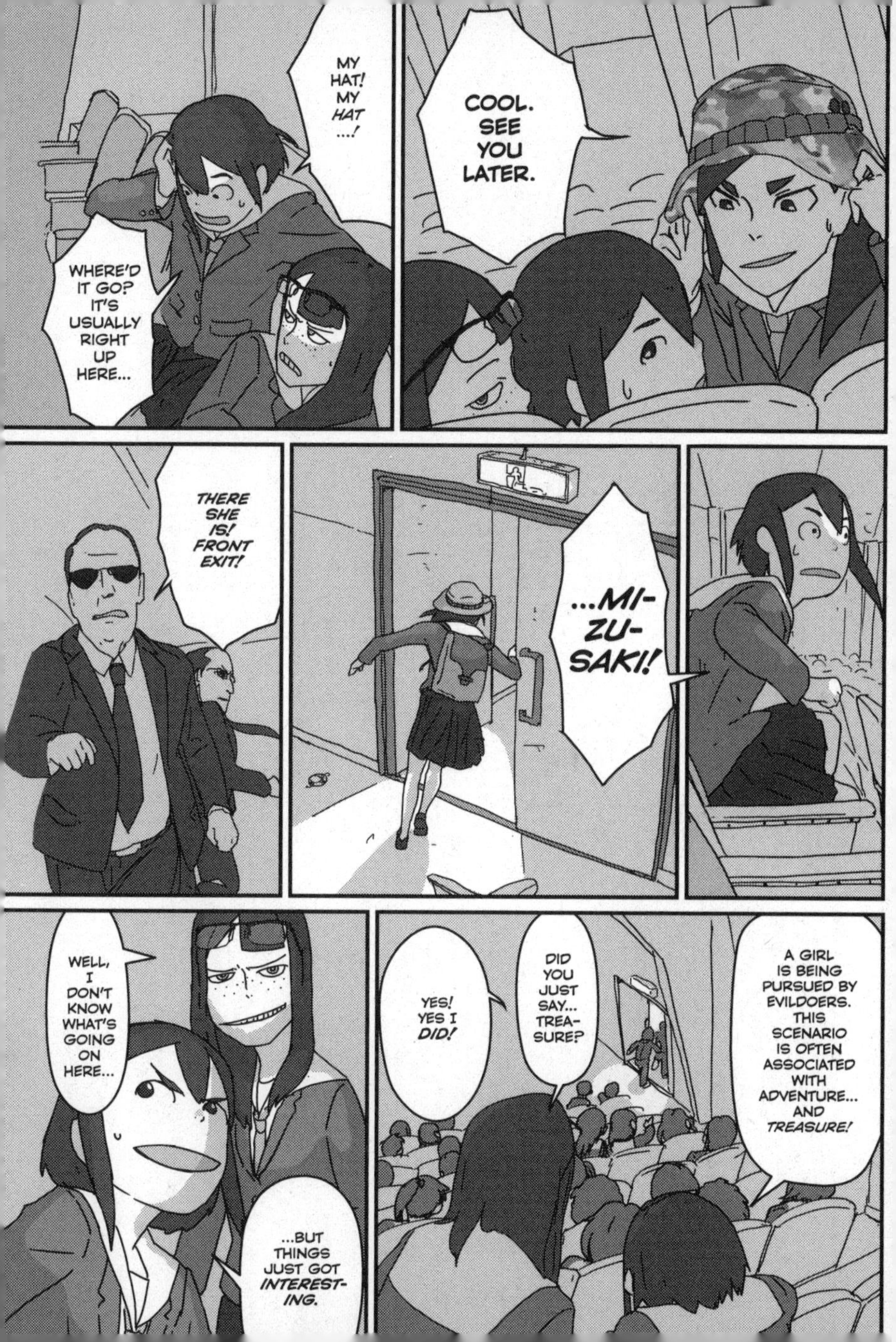
COOL. SEE YOU LATER.
MY HAT! MY HAT ...!
WHERE'D IT GO? IT'S USUALLY RIGHT UP HERE...
...MI-ZU-SAKI!
THERE SHE IS! FRONT EXIT!
A GIRL IS BEING PURSUED BY EVILDOERS. THIS SCENARIO IS OFTEN ASSOCIATED WITH ADVENTURE... AND TREASURE!
DID YOU JUST SAY... TREA-SURE?
YES! YES I DID!
WELL, I DON'T KNOW WHAT'S GOING ON HERE...
...BUT THINGS JUST GOT INTEREST-ING.

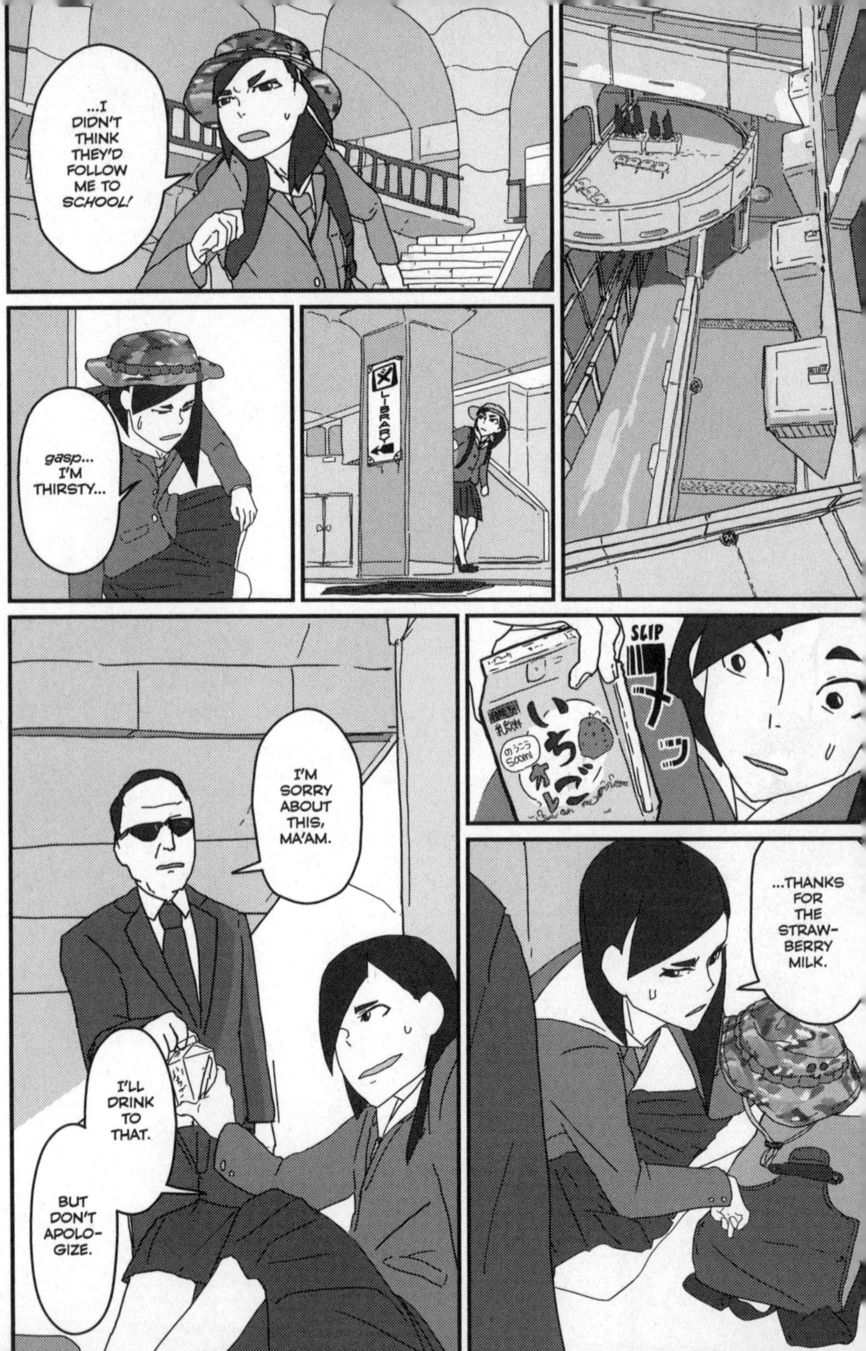
...I DIDN'T THINK THEY'D FOLLOW ME TO SCHOOL!
LIBRARY
gasp... I'M THIRSTY...
SLIP
いちご
...THANKS FOR THE STRAW-BERRY MILK.
I'M SORRY ABOUT THIS, MA'AM.
I'LL DRINK TO THAT.
BUT DON'T APOLOGIZE.

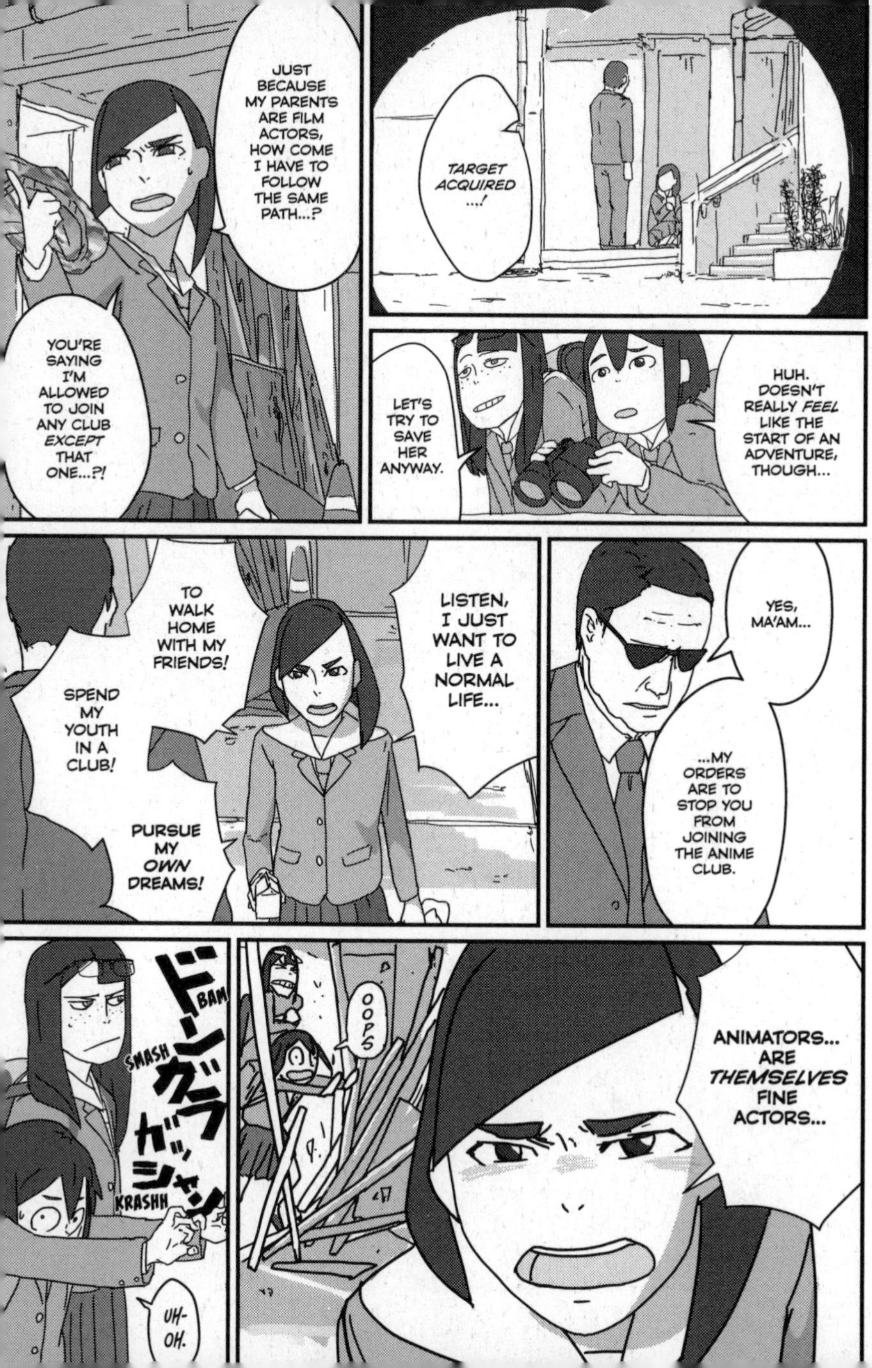

TARGET ACQUIRED ...!
HUH. DOESN'T REALLY *FEEL* LIKE THE START OF AN ADVENTURE, THOUGH...
LET'S TRY TO SAVE HER ANYWAY.
JUST BECAUSE MY PARENTS ARE FILM ACTORS, HOW COME I HAVE TO FOLLOW THE SAME PATH...?
YOU'RE SAYING I'M ALLOWED TO JOIN ANY CLUB *EXCEPT* THAT ONE...?!
YES, MA'AM...
...MY ORDERS ARE TO STOP YOU FROM JOINING THE ANIME CLUB.
LISTEN, I JUST WANT TO LIVE A NORMAL LIFE...
TO WALK HOME WITH MY FRIENDS!
SPEND MY YOUTH IN A CLUB!
PURSUE MY *OWN* DREAMS!
ANIMATORS... ARE *THEMSELVES* FINE ACTORS...
OOPS
ドン BAM
ガラ SMASH
ガッシャン KRASHH
UH-OH.

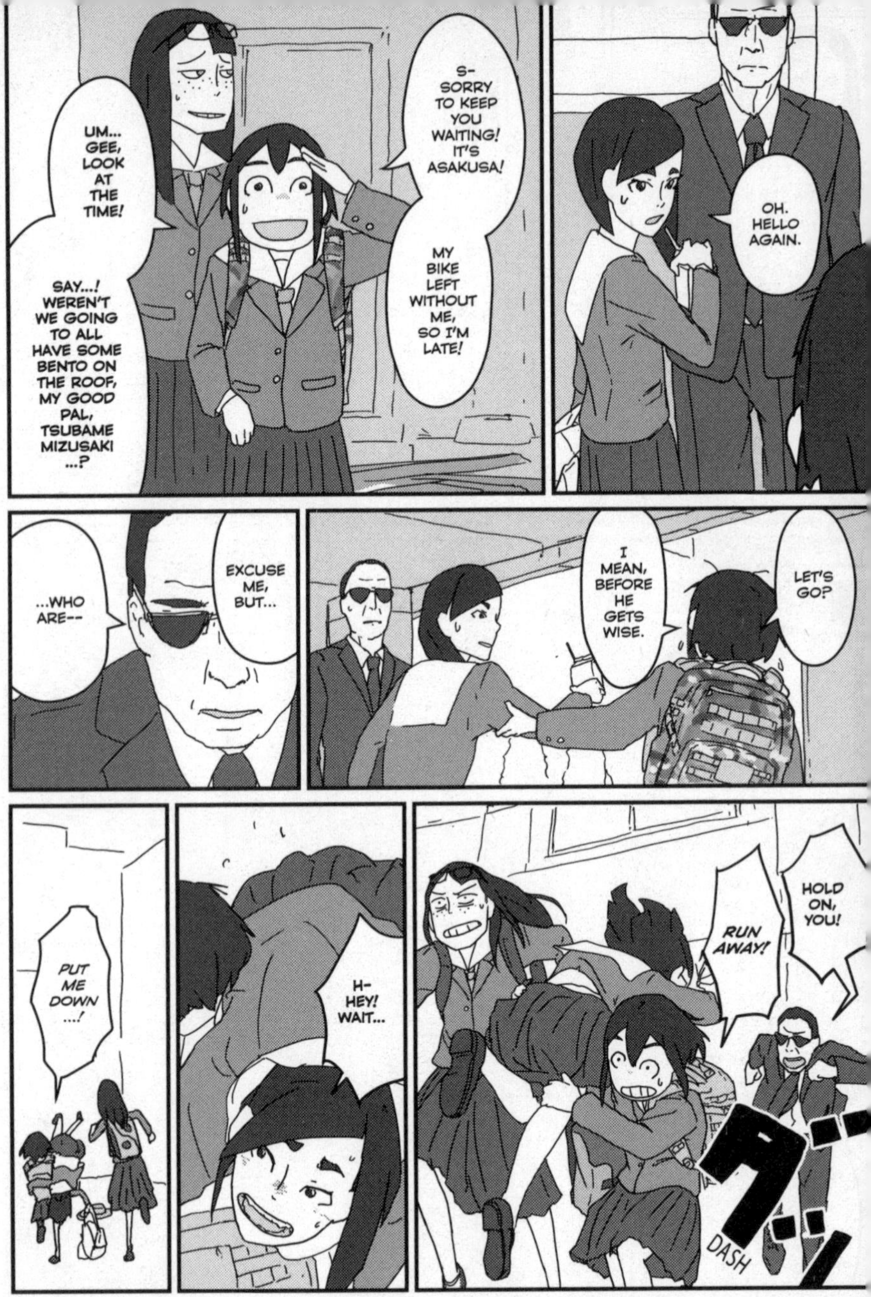
OH. HELLO AGAIN.
S-SORRY TO KEEP YOU WAITING! IT'S ASAKUSA!
MY BIKE LEFT WITHOUT ME, SO I'M LATE!
UM... GEE, LOOK AT THE TIME!
SAY...! WEREN'T WE GOING TO ALL HAVE SOME BENTO ON THE ROOF, MY GOOD PAL, TSUBAME MIZUSAKI ...?
LET'S GO?
I MEAN, BEFORE HE GETS WISE.
EXCUSE ME, BUT...
...WHO ARE--
HOLD ON, YOU!
RUN AWAY!
DASH
H-HEY! WAIT...
PUT ME DOWN ...!

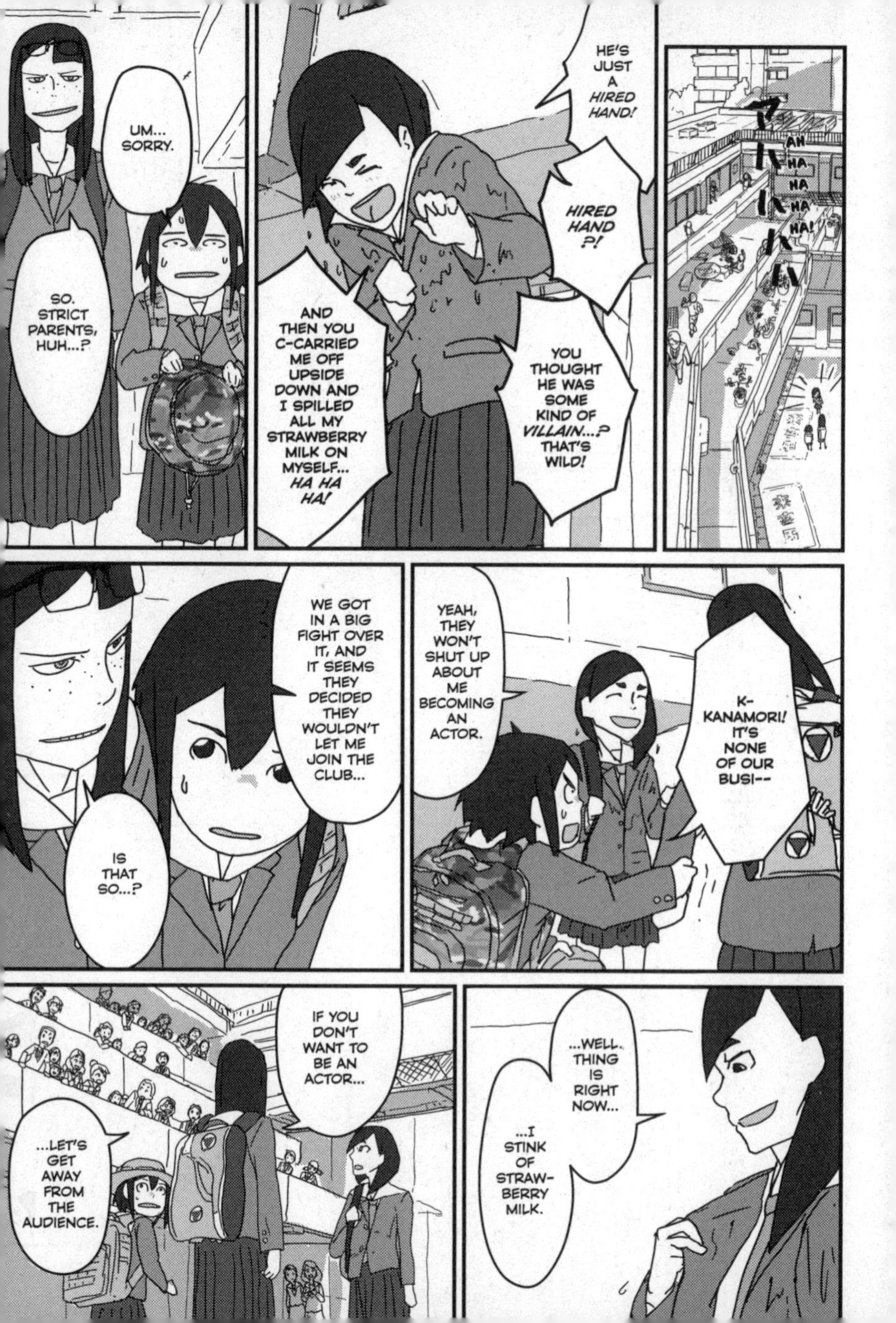
AH HA HA HA HA!
HE'S JUST A *HIRED HAND!*
HIRED HAND ?!
YOU THOUGHT HE WAS SOME KIND OF *VILLAIN...?* THAT'S WILD!
AND THEN YOU C-CARRIED ME OFF UPSIDE DOWN AND I SPILLED ALL MY STRAWBERRY MILK ON MYSELF... *HA HA HA!*
UM... SORRY.
SO. STRICT PARENTS, HUH...?
K-KANAMORI! IT'S NONE OF OUR BUSI--
YEAH, THEY WON'T SHUT UP ABOUT ME BECOMING AN ACTOR.
WE GOT IN A BIG FIGHT OVER IT, AND IT SEEMS THEY DECIDED THEY WOULDN'T LET ME JOIN THE CLUB...
IS THAT SO...?
...WELL. THING IS RIGHT NOW...
...I STINK OF STRAW-BERRY MILK.
IF YOU DON'T WANT TO BE AN ACTOR...
...LET'S GET AWAY FROM THE AUDIENCE.

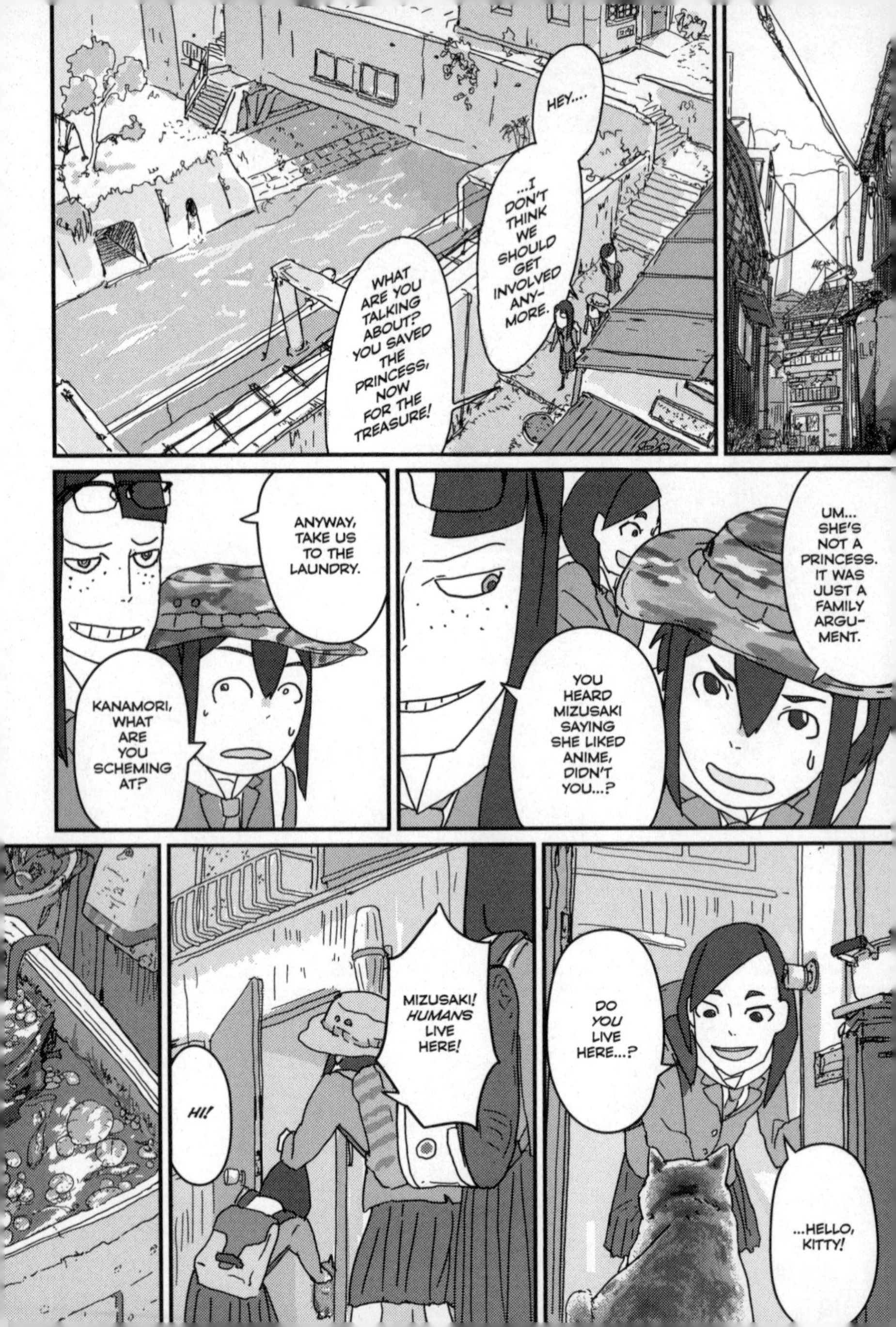
HEY....
...I DON'T THINK WE SHOULD GET INVOLVED ANY-MORE.
WHAT ARE YOU TALKING ABOUT? YOU SAVED THE PRINCESS, NOW FOR THE TREASURE!
UM... SHE'S NOT A PRINCESS. IT WAS JUST A FAMILY ARGU-MENT.
YOU HEARD MIZUSAKI SAYING SHE LIKED ANIME, DIDN'T YOU...?
ANYWAY, TAKE US TO THE LAUNDRY.
KANAMORI, WHAT ARE YOU SCHEMING AT?
DO *YOU* LIVE HERE...?
...HELLO, KITTY!
MIZUSAKI! *HUMANS* LIVE HERE!
HI!

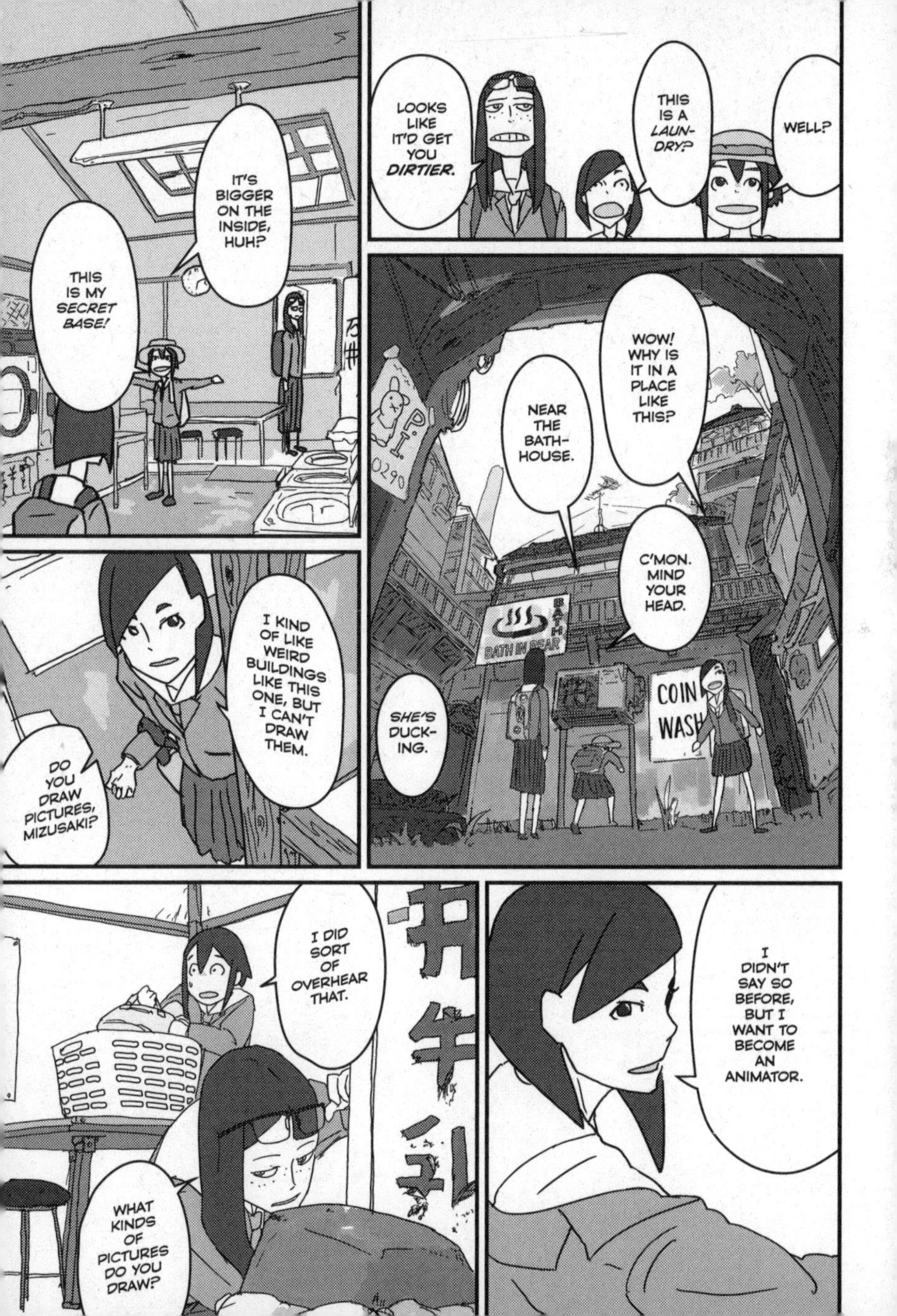
WELL?
THIS IS A *LAUNDRY?*
LOOKS LIKE IT'D GET YOU ***DIRTIER.***
WOW! WHY IS IT IN A PLACE LIKE THIS?
NEAR THE BATHHOUSE.
C'MON. MIND YOUR HEAD.
BATH
BATH IN REAR
COIN WASH
SHE'S DUCKING.
IT'S BIGGER ON THE INSIDE, HUH?
THIS IS MY *SECRET BASE!*
I KIND OF LIKE WEIRD BUILDINGS LIKE THIS ONE, BUT I CAN'T DRAW THEM.
DO YOU DRAW PICTURES, MIZUSAKI?
I DIDN'T SAY SO BEFORE, BUT I WANT TO BECOME AN ANIMATOR.
I DID SORT OF OVERHEAR THAT.
WHAT KINDS OF PICTURES DO YOU DRAW?

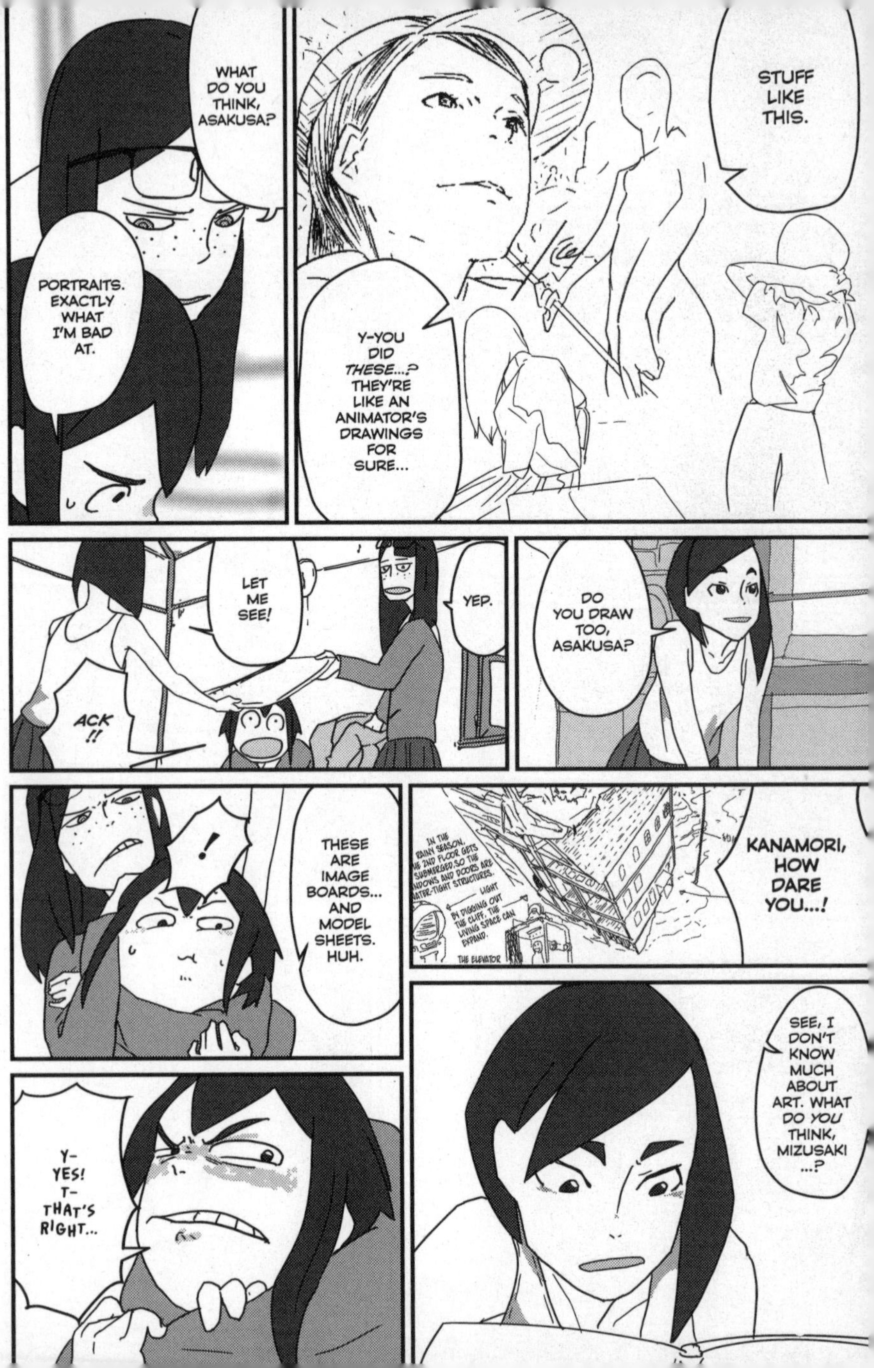
STUFF LIKE THIS.
Y-YOU DID *THESE*...? THEY'RE LIKE AN ANIMATOR'S DRAWINGS FOR SURE...
WHAT DO YOU THINK, ASAKUSA?
PORTRAITS. EXACTLY WHAT I'M BAD AT.
DO YOU DRAW TOO, ASAKUSA?
YEP.
LET ME SEE!
ACK!!
KANAMORI, HOW DARE YOU...!
IN THE RAINY SEASON, THE 2ND FLOOR GETS SUBMERGED. SO THE ANDOWS AND DOORS ARE ATER-TIGHT STRUCTURES.
LIGHT
BY DIGGING OUT THE CLIFF, THE LIVING SPACE CAN EXPAND.
THE ELEVATOR
!
THESE ARE IMAGE BOARDS... AND MODEL SHEETS. HUH.
SEE, I DON'T KNOW MUCH ABOUT ART. WHAT *DO YOU* THINK, MIZUSAKI...?
Y-YES! T-THAT'S RIGHT...

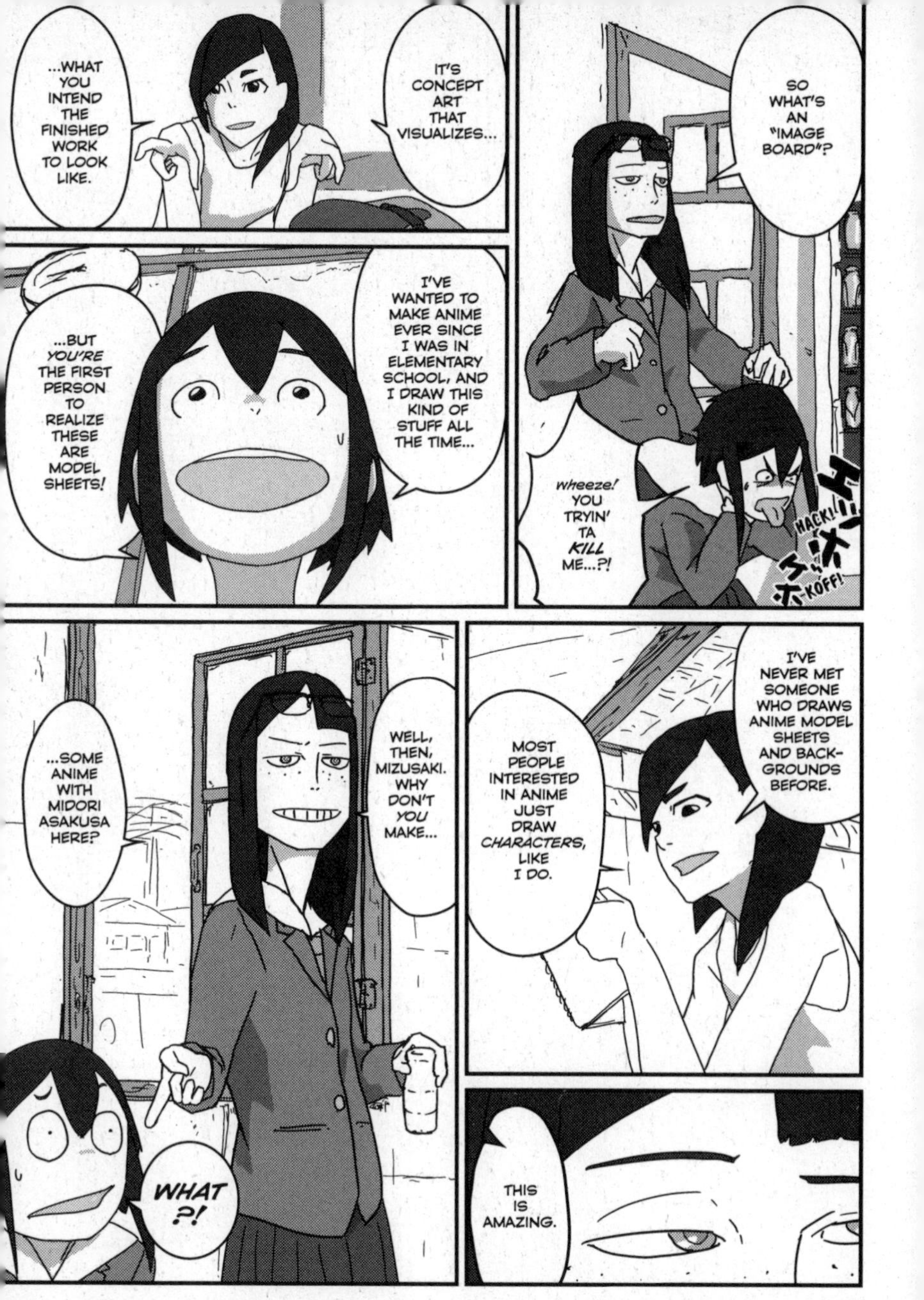
SO WHAT'S AN "IMAGE BOARD"?
Wheeze! YOU TRYIN' TA KILL ME...?!
HACK!
KOFF!
IT'S CONCEPT ART THAT VISUALIZES...
...WHAT YOU INTEND THE FINISHED WORK TO LOOK LIKE.
I'VE WANTED TO MAKE ANIME EVER SINCE I WAS IN ELEMENTARY SCHOOL, AND I DRAW THIS KIND OF STUFF ALL THE TIME...
...BUT YOU'RE THE FIRST PERSON TO REALIZE THESE ARE MODEL SHEETS!
I'VE NEVER MET SOMEONE WHO DRAWS ANIME MODEL SHEETS AND BACK-GROUNDS BEFORE.
MOST PEOPLE INTERESTED IN ANIME JUST DRAW CHARACTERS, LIKE I DO.
THIS IS AMAZING.
WELL, THEN, MIZUSAKI. WHY DON'T YOU MAKE...
...SOME ANIME WITH MIDORI ASAKUSA HERE?
WHAT ?!

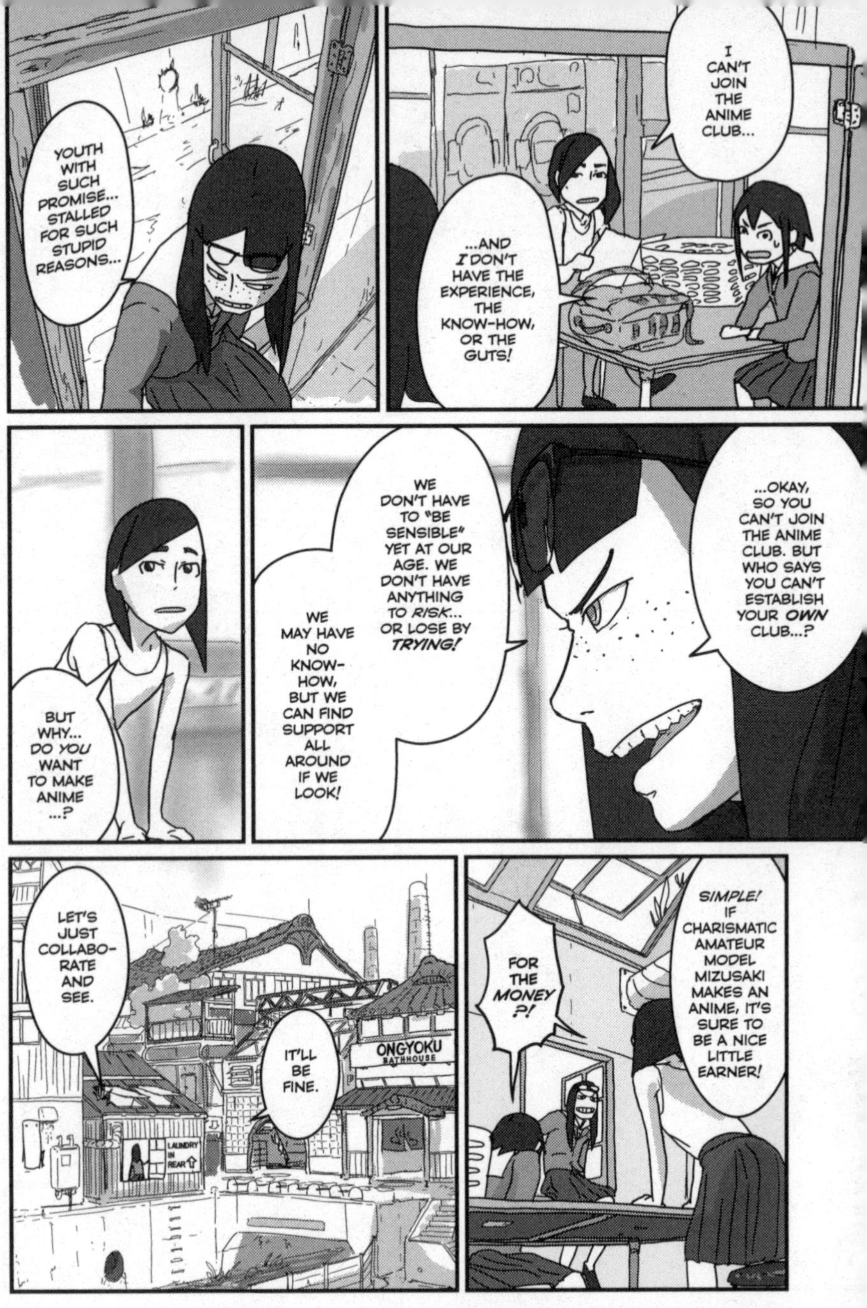
I CAN'T JOIN THE ANIME CLUB...
...AND *I* DON'T HAVE THE EXPERIENCE, THE KNOW-HOW, OR THE GUTS!
YOUTH WITH SUCH PROMISE... STALLED FOR SUCH STUPID REASONS...
...OKAY, SO YOU CAN'T JOIN THE ANIME CLUB. BUT WHO SAYS YOU CAN'T ESTABLISH YOUR *OWN* CLUB...?
WE DON'T HAVE TO "BE SENSIBLE" YET AT OUR AGE. WE DON'T HAVE ANYTHING TO *RISK*... OR LOSE BY *TRYING!*
WE MAY HAVE NO KNOW-HOW, BUT WE CAN FIND SUPPORT ALL AROUND IF WE LOOK!
BUT WHY... *DO YOU* WANT TO MAKE ANIME ...?
SIMPLE! IF CHARISMATIC AMATEUR MODEL MIZUSAKI MAKES AN ANIME, IT'S SURE TO BE A NICE LITTLE EARNER!
FOR THE *MONEY* ?!
LET'S JUST COLLABORATE AND SEE.
IT'LL BE FINE.
ONGYOKU
BATHHOUSE
LAUNDRY IN REAR

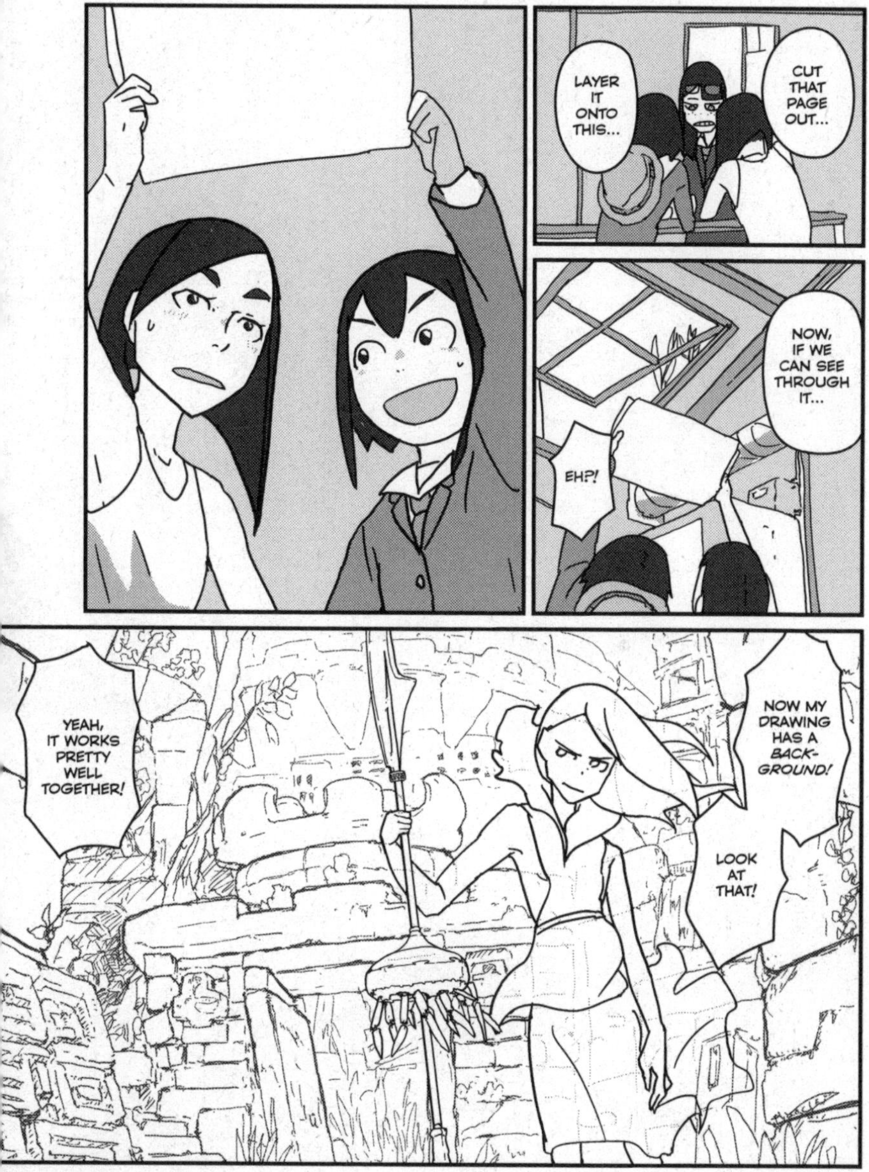
CUT THAT PAGE OUT...
LAYER IT ONTO THIS...
NOW, IF WE CAN SEE THROUGH IT...
EH?!
NOW MY DRAWING HAS A *BACK-GROUND!*
LOOK AT THAT!
YEAH, IT WORKS PRETTY WELL TOGETHER!

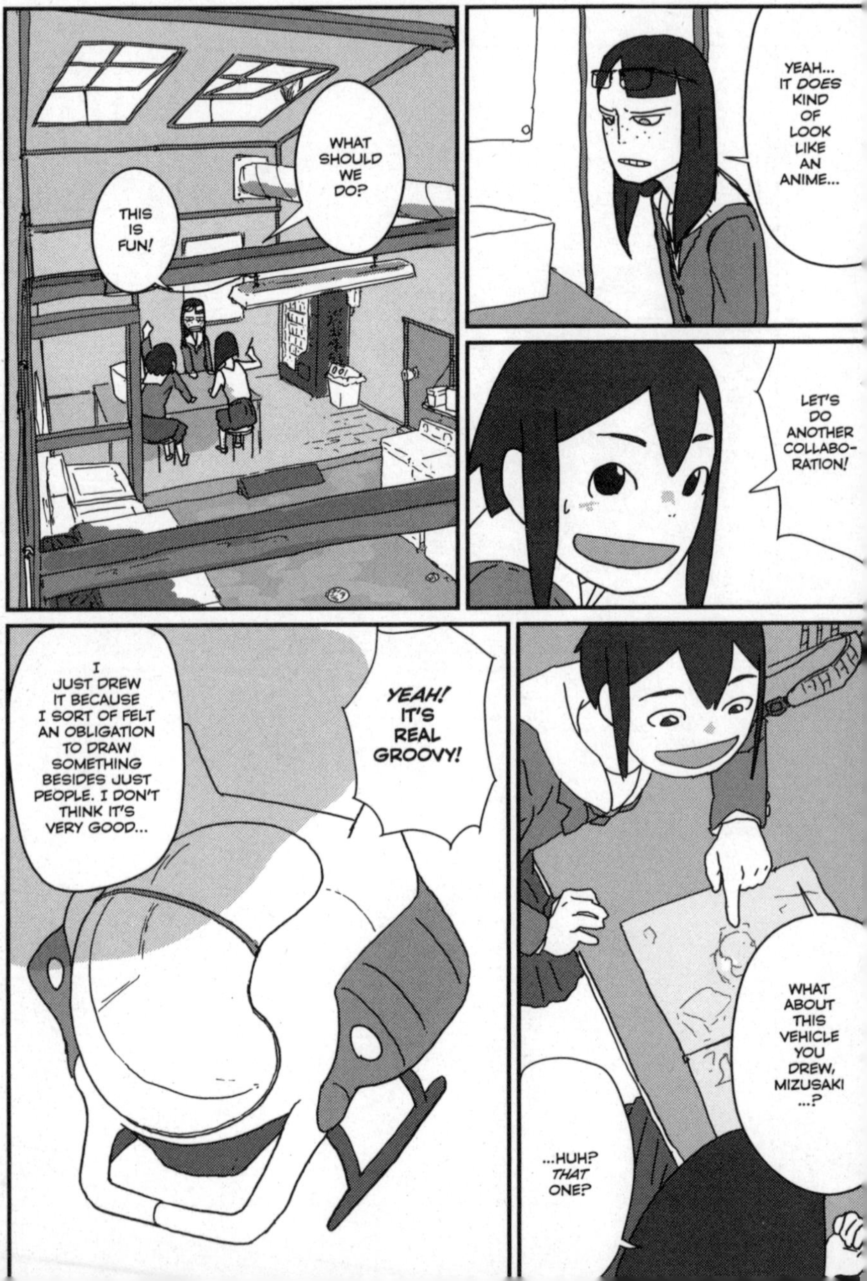

YEAH... IT *DOES* KIND OF LOOK LIKE AN ANIME...
LET'S DO ANOTHER COLLABO-RATION!
WHAT SHOULD WE DO?
THIS IS FUN!
WHAT ABOUT THIS VEHICLE YOU DREW, MIZUSAKI ...?
...HUH? *THAT* ONE?
YEAH! IT'S REAL GROOVY!
I JUST DREW IT BECAUSE I SORT OF FELT AN OBLIGATION TO DRAW SOMETHING BESIDES JUST PEOPLE. I DON'T THINK IT'S VERY GOOD...

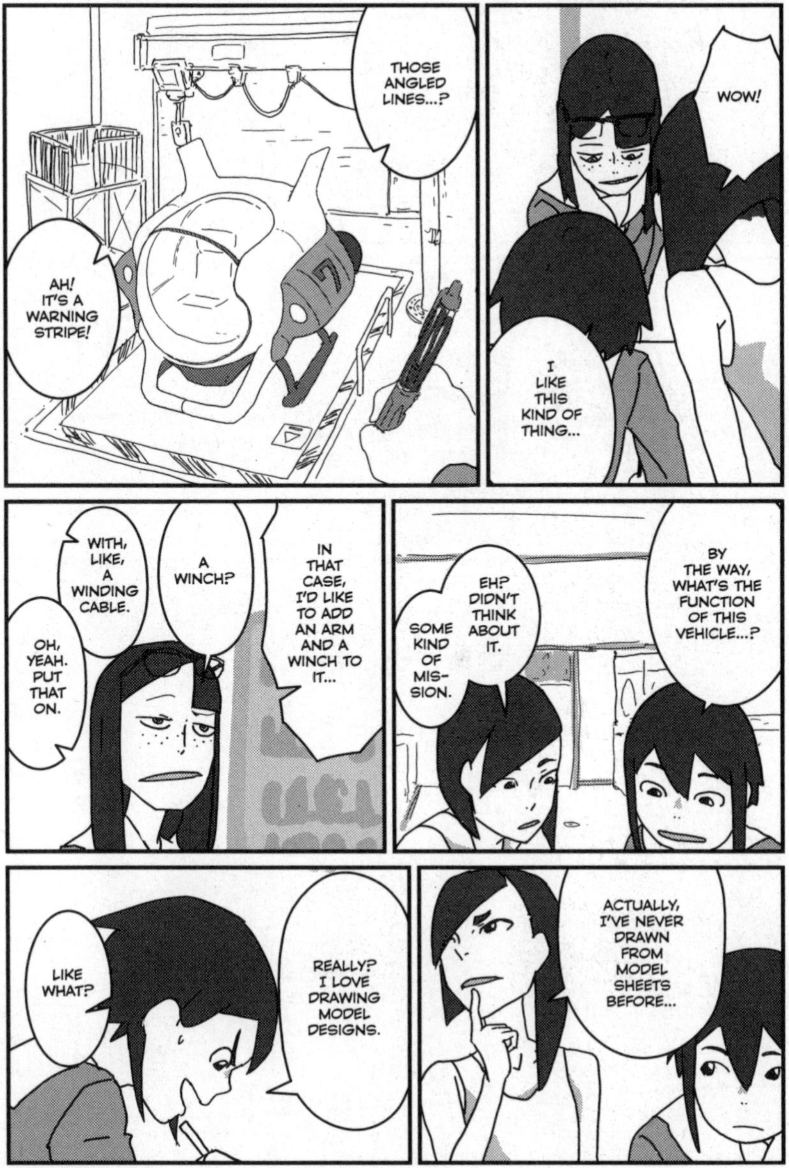
WOW!
I LIKE THIS KIND OF THING...
THOSE ANGLED LINES...?
AH! IT'S A WARNING STRIPE!
BY THE WAY, WHAT'S THE FUNCTION OF THIS VEHICLE...?
EH? DIDN'T THINK ABOUT IT.
SOME KIND OF MIS-SION.
IN THAT CASE, I'D LIKE TO ADD AN ARM AND A WINCH TO IT...
A WINCH?
WITH, LIKE, A WINDING CABLE.
OH, YEAH. PUT THAT ON.
ACTUALLY, I'VE NEVER DRAWN FROM MODEL SHEETS BEFORE...
REALLY? I LOVE DRAWING MODEL DESIGNS.
LIKE WHAT?

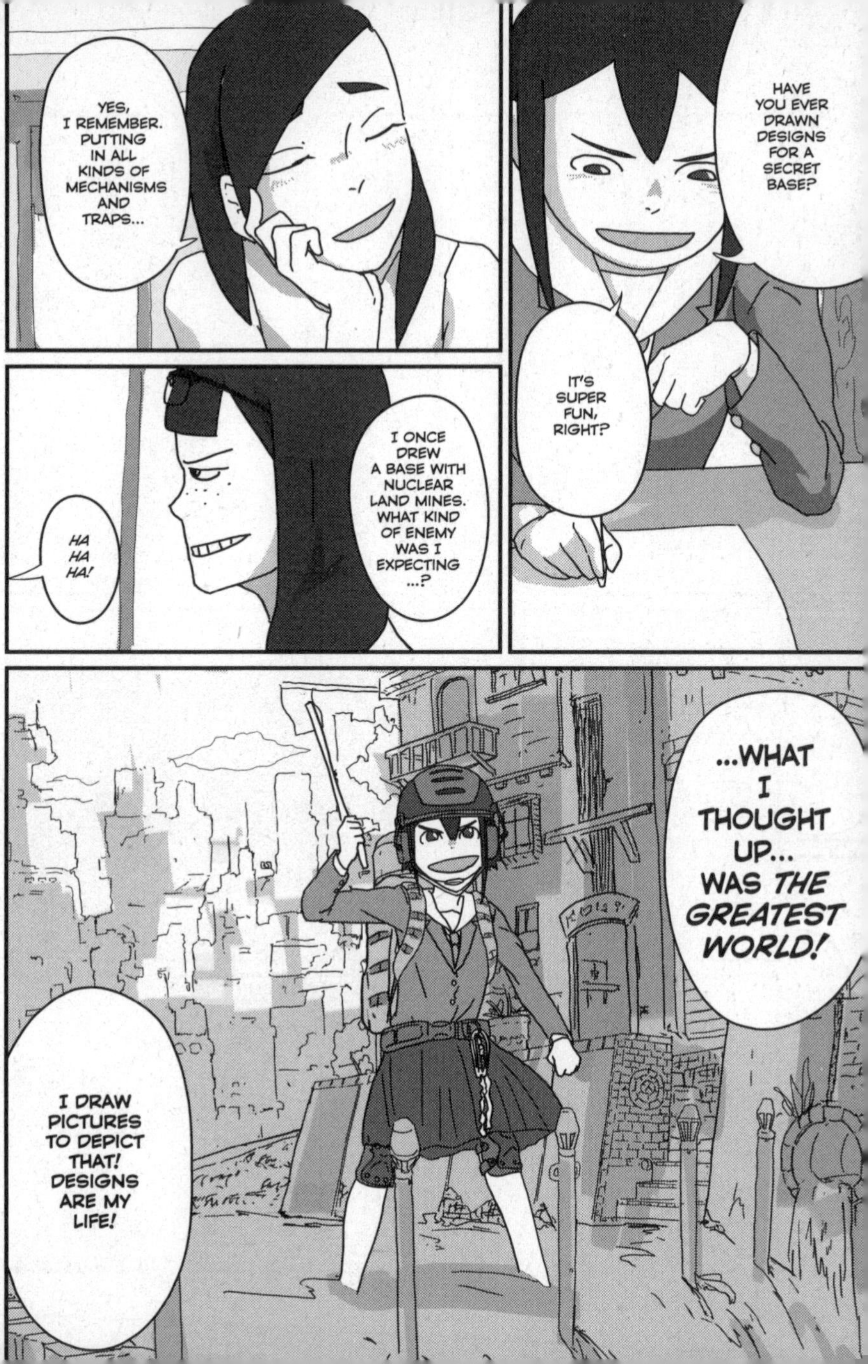
HAVE YOU EVER DRAWN DESIGNS FOR A SECRET BASE?
IT'S SUPER FUN, RIGHT?
YES, I REMEMBER. PUTTING IN ALL KINDS OF MECHANISMS AND TRAPS...
I ONCE DREW A BASE WITH NUCLEAR LAND MINES. WHAT KIND OF ENEMY WAS I EXPECTING ...?
HA HA HA!
...WHAT I THOUGHT UP... WAS *THE GREATEST WORLD!*
I DRAW PICTURES TO DEPICT THAT! DESIGNS ARE MY LIFE!

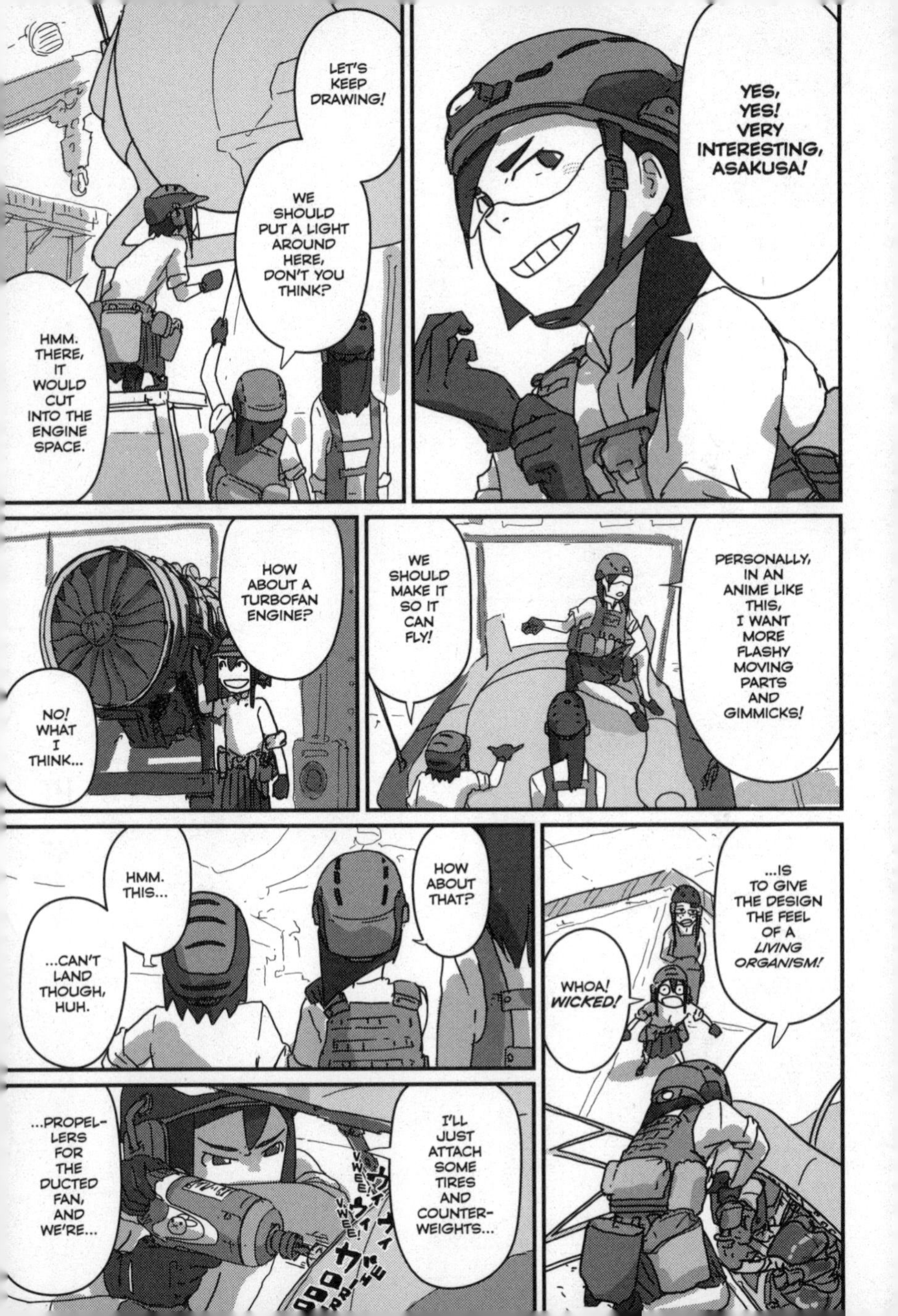
YES, YES! VERY INTERESTING, ASAKUSA!
LET'S KEEP DRAWING!
WE SHOULD PUT A LIGHT AROUND HERE, DON'T YOU THINK?
HMM. THERE, IT WOULD CUT INTO THE ENGINE SPACE.
PERSONALLY, IN AN ANIME LIKE THIS, I WANT MORE FLASHY MOVING PARTS AND GIMMICKS!
WE SHOULD MAKE IT SO IT CAN FLY!
HOW ABOUT A TURBOFAN ENGINE?
NO! WHAT I THINK...
...IS TO GIVE THE DESIGN THE FEEL OF A *LIVING ORGANISM!*
WHOA! *WICKED!*
HOW ABOUT THAT?
HMM. THIS...
...CAN'T LAND THOUGH, HUH.
I'LL JUST ATTACH SOME TIRES AND COUNTER-WEIGHTS...
...PROPEL-LERS FOR THE DUCTED FAN, AND WE'RE...
VWEE! VWEE!

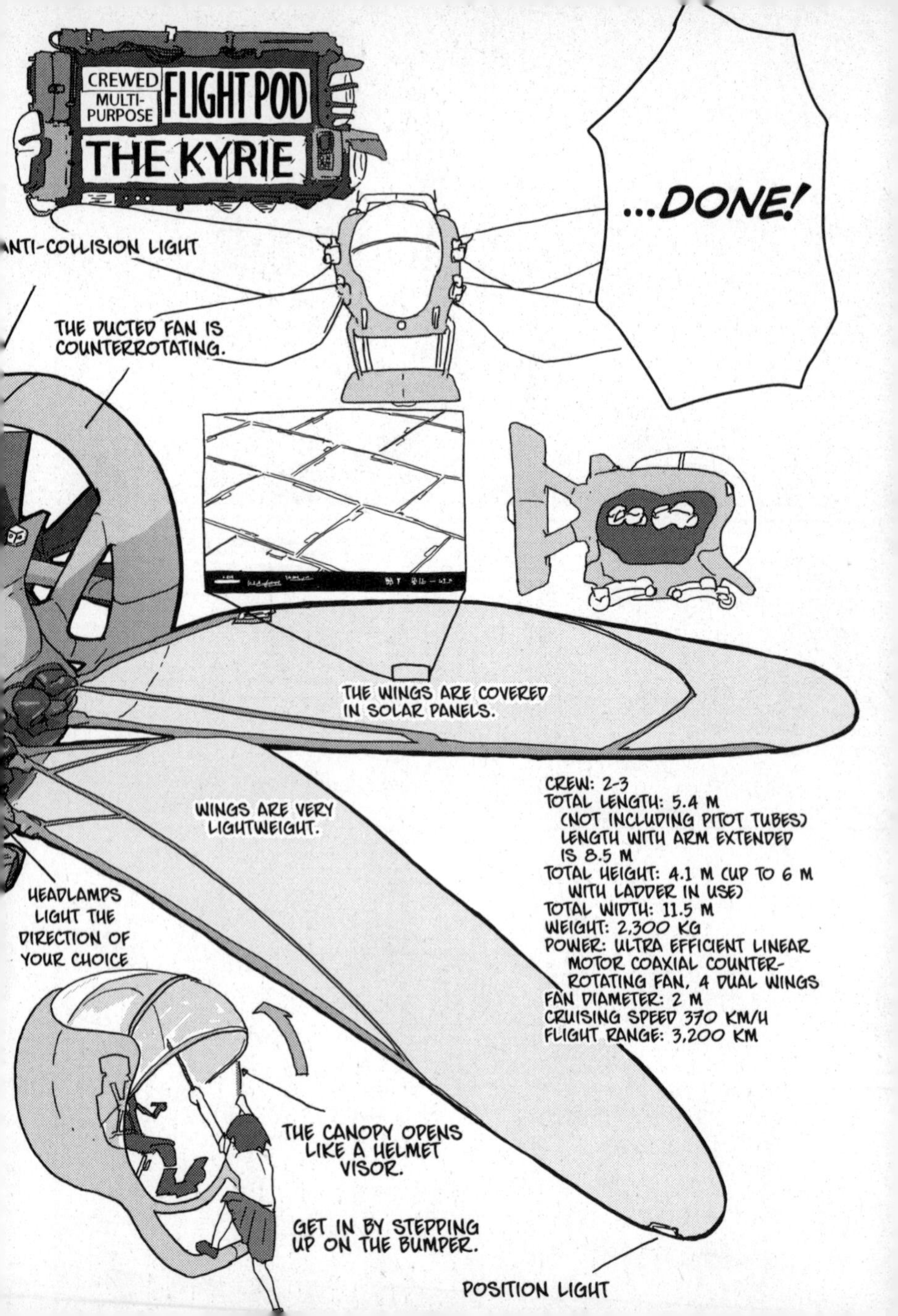
CREWED MULTI-PURPOSE FLIGHT POD
THE KYRIE
...DONE!
ANTI-COLLISION LIGHT
THE DUCTED FAN IS COUNTERROTATING.
THE WINGS ARE COVERED IN SOLAR PANELS.
WINGS ARE VERY LIGHTWEIGHT.
CREW: 2-3
TOTAL LENGTH: 5.4 M (NOT INCLUDING PITOT TUBES) LENGTH WITH ARM EXTENDED IS 8.5 M
TOTAL HEIGHT: 4.1 M (UP TO 6 M WITH LADDER IN USE)
TOTAL WIDTH: 11.5 M
WEIGHT: 2,300 KG
POWER: ULTRA EFFICIENT LINEAR MOTOR COAXIAL COUNTER-ROTATING FAN, 4 DUAL WINGS
FAN DIAMETER: 2 M
CRUISING SPEED 370 KM/H
FLIGHT RANGE: 3,200 KM
HEADLAMPS LIGHT THE DIRECTION OF YOUR CHOICE
THE CANOPY OPENS LIKE A HELMET VISOR.
GET IN BY STEPPING UP ON THE BUMPER.
POSITION LIGHT

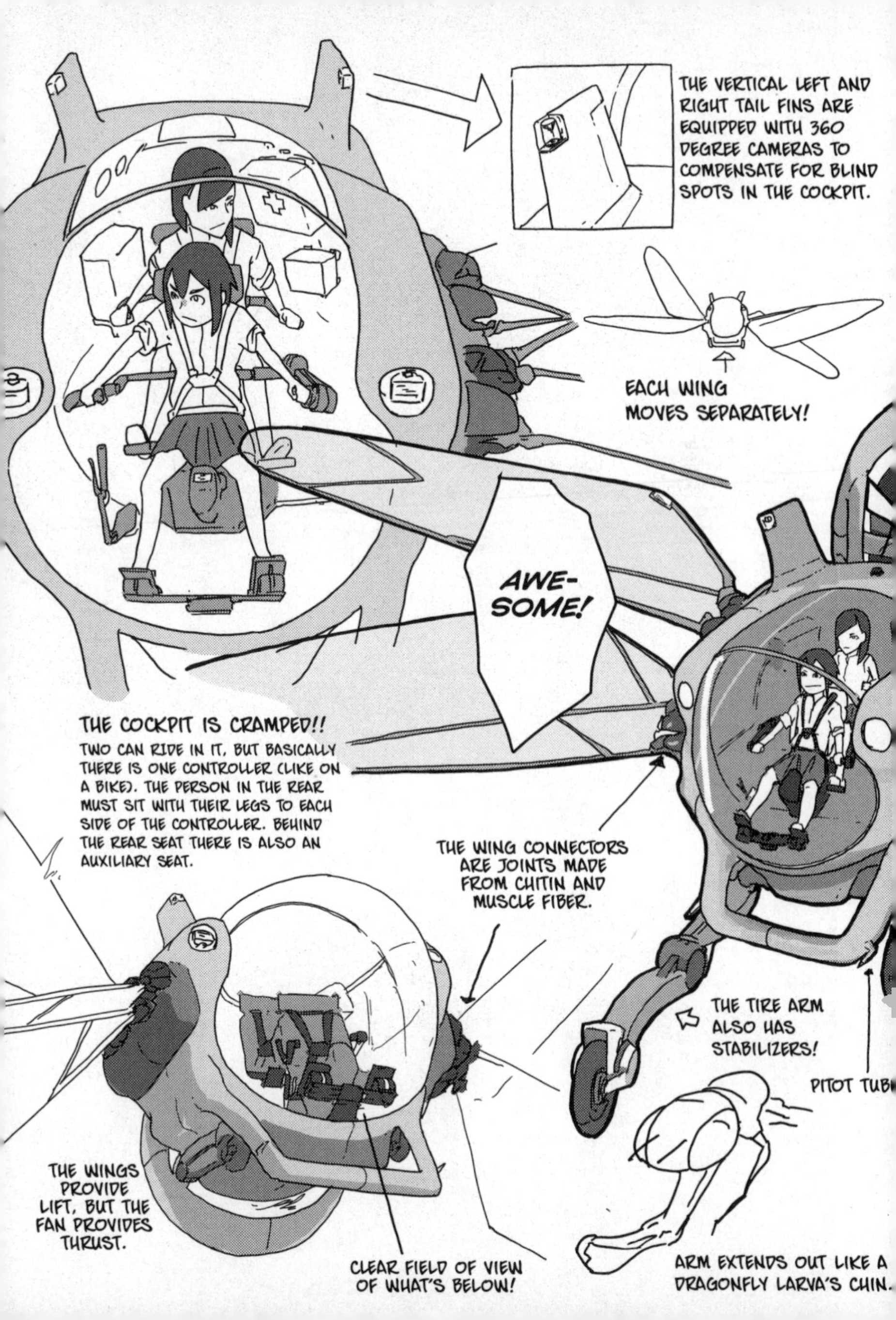
THE VERTICAL LEFT AND RIGHT TAIL FINS ARE EQUIPPED WITH 360 DEGREE CAMERAS TO COMPENSATE FOR BLIND SPOTS IN THE COCKPIT.
EACH WING MOVES SEPARATELY!
AWE-SOME!
THE COCKPIT IS CRAMPED!!
TWO CAN RIDE IN IT, BUT BASICALLY THERE IS ONE CONTROLLER (LIKE ON A BIKE). THE PERSON IN THE REAR MUST SIT WITH THEIR LEGS TO EACH SIDE OF THE CONTROLLER. BEHIND THE REAR SEAT THERE IS ALSO AN AUXILIARY SEAT.
THE WING CONNECTORS ARE JOINTS MADE FROM CHITIN AND MUSCLE FIBER.
THE TIRE ARM ALSO HAS STABILIZERS!
PITOT TUB
ARM EXTENDS OUT LIKE A DRAGONFLY LARVA'S CHIN.
CLEAR FIELD OF VIEW OF WHAT'S BELOW!
THE WINGS PROVIDE LIFT, BUT THE FAN PROVIDES THRUST.

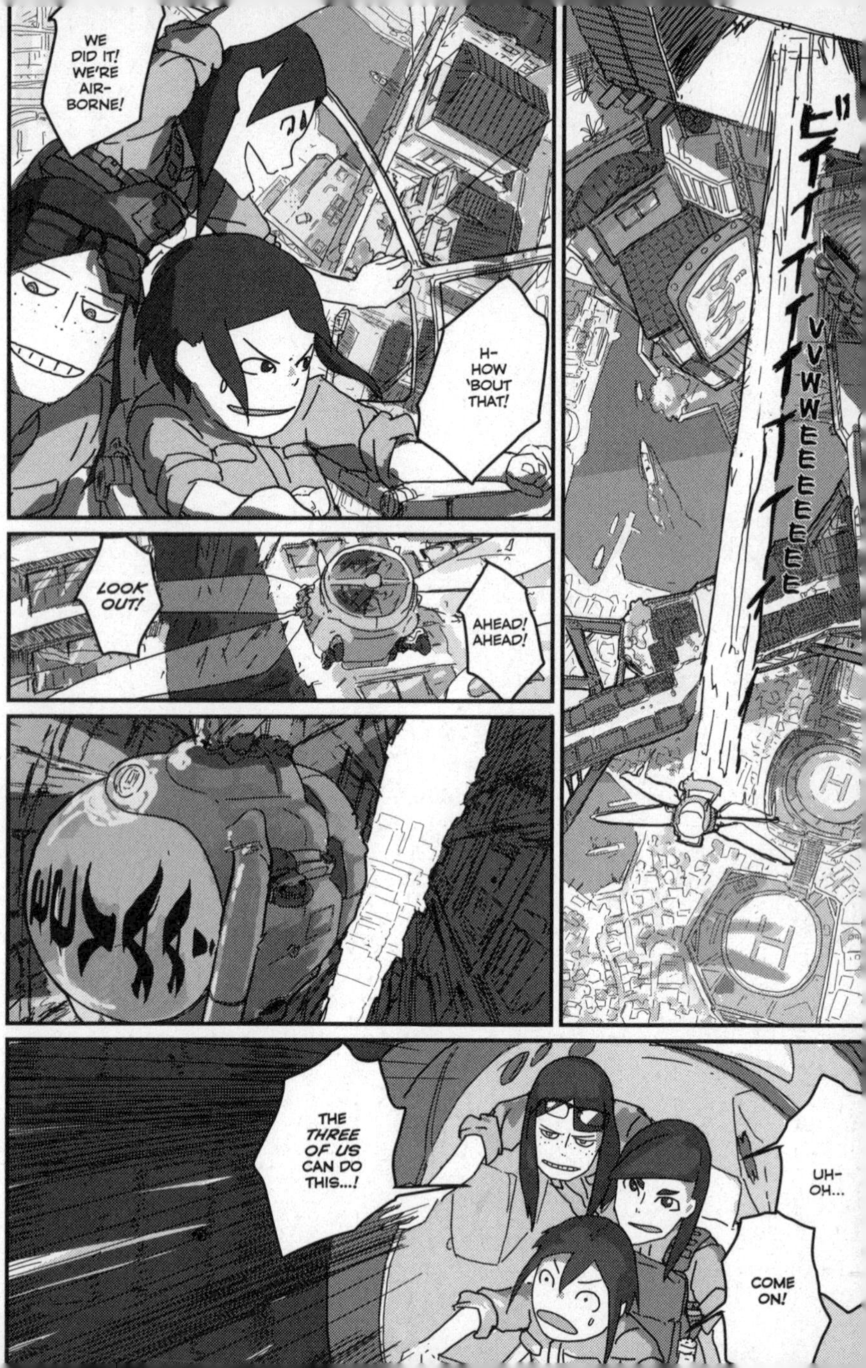
VVWWEEEEEEEE
WE DID IT! WE'RE AIR-BORNE!
H-HOW 'BOUT THAT!
AHEAD! AHEAD!
LOOK OUT!
UH-OH...
COME ON!
THE THREE OF US CAN DO THIS...!

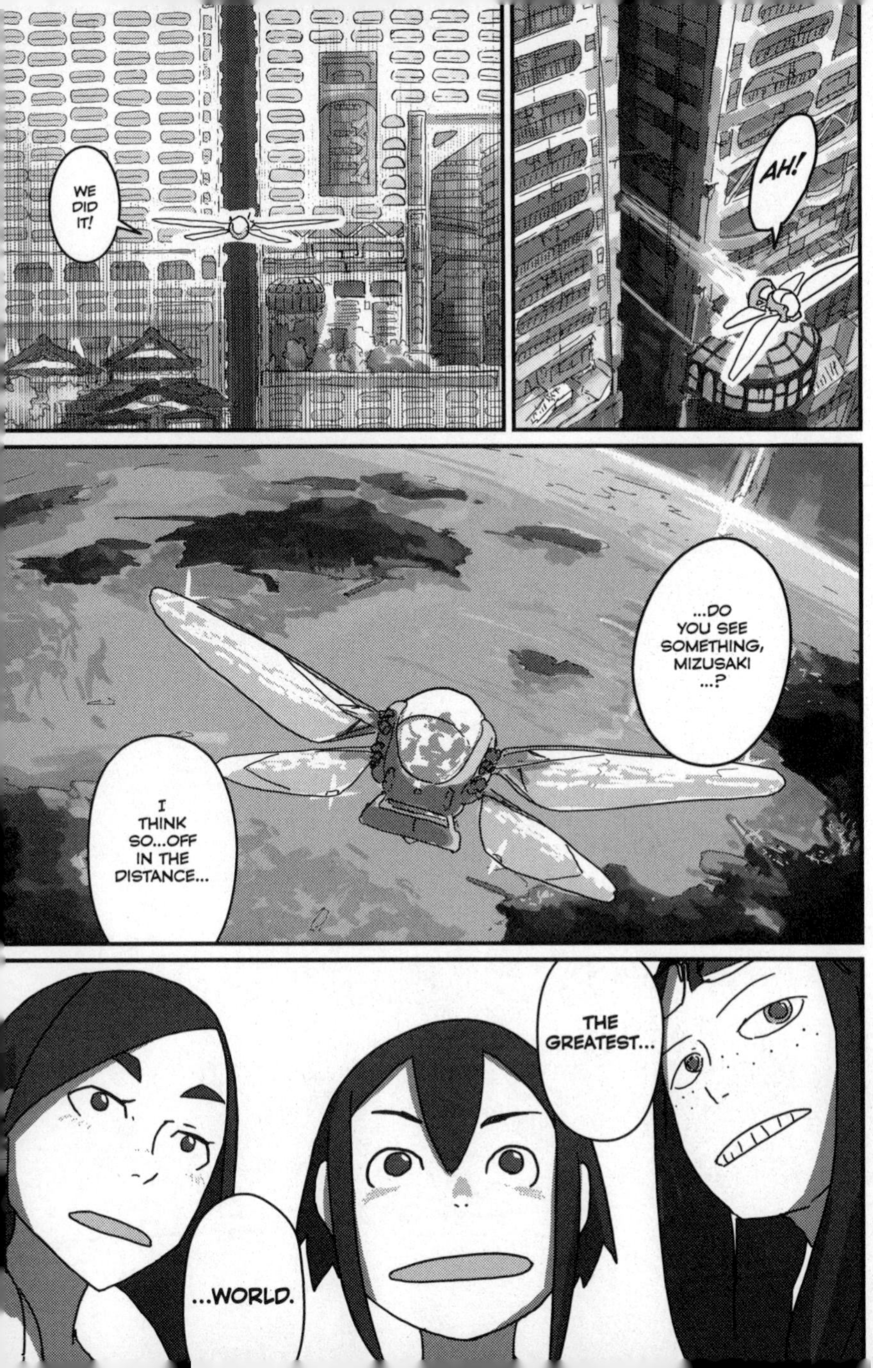
AH!
WE DID IT!
...DO YOU SEE SOMETHING, MIZUSAKI ...?
I THINK SO...OFF IN THE DISTANCE...
THE GREATEST...
...WORLD.

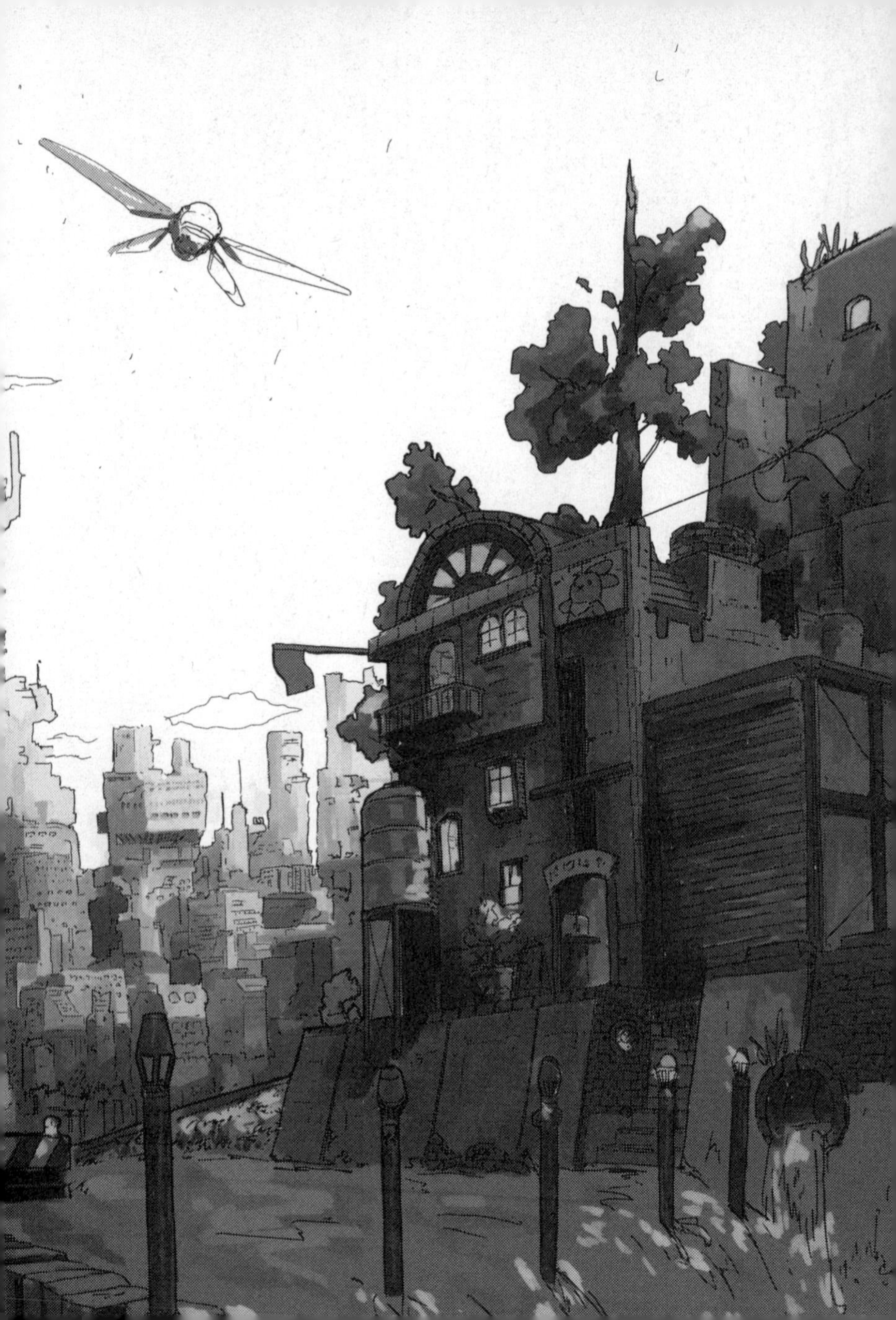

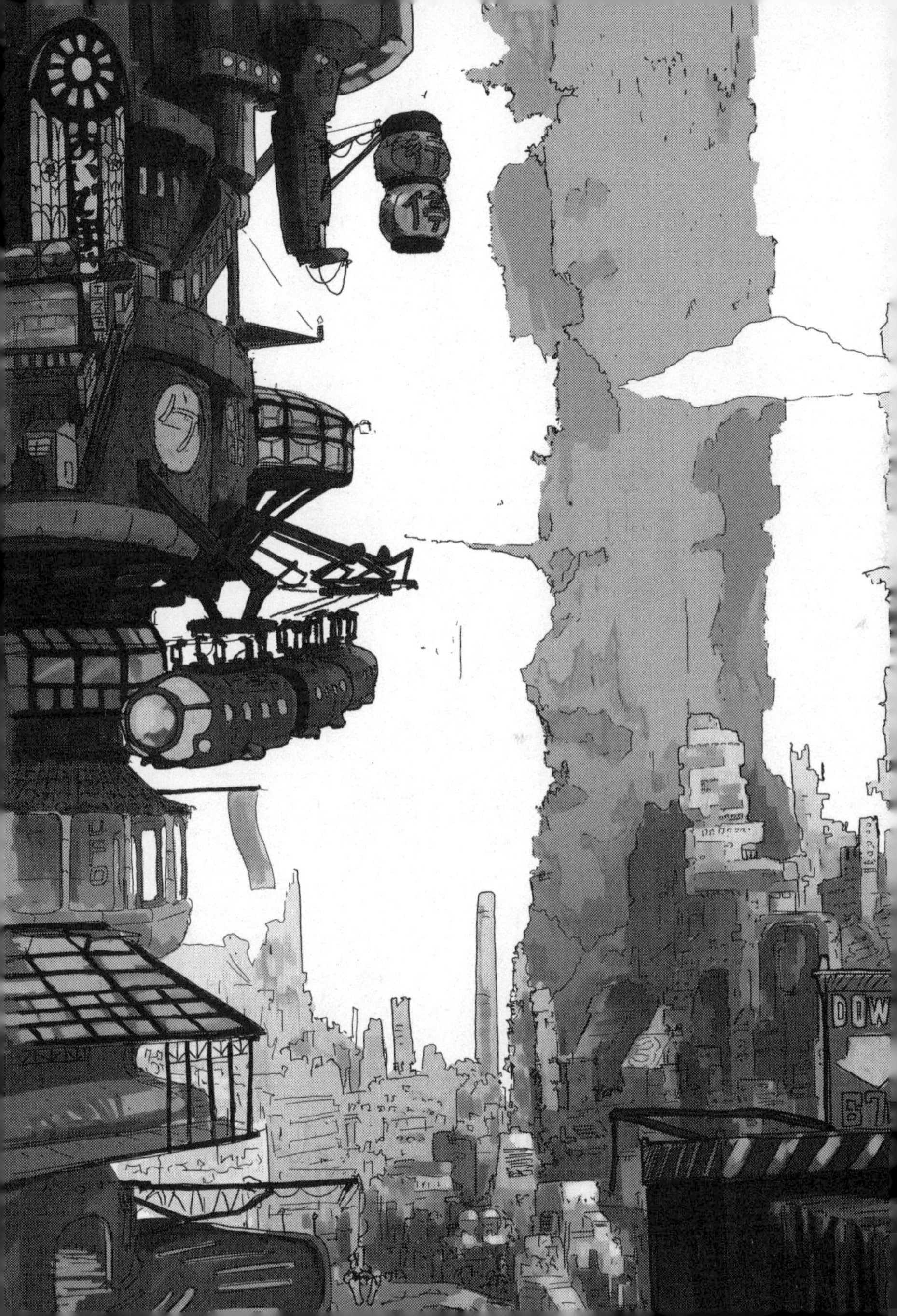
UFO
DOW

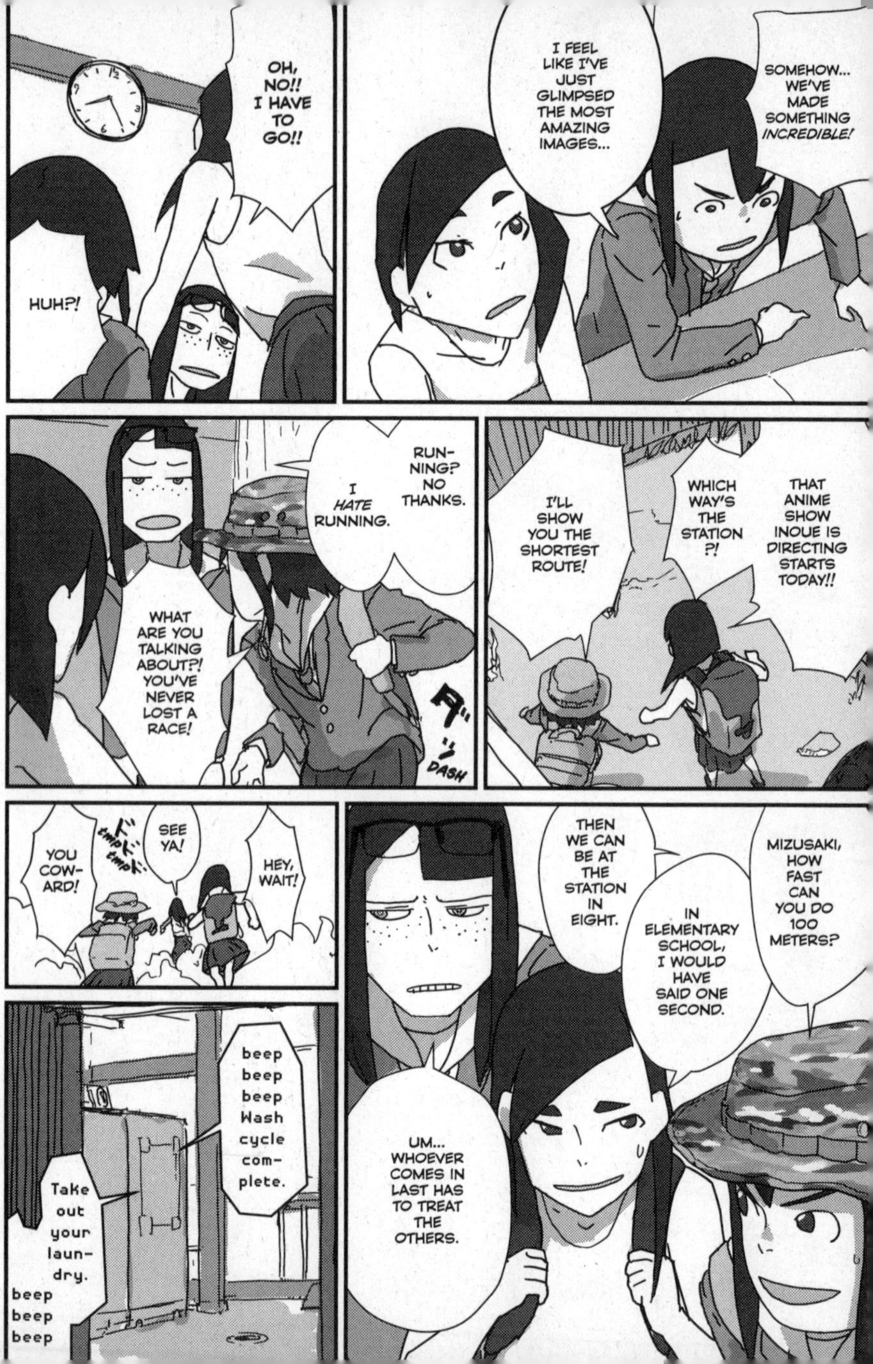
SOMEHOW... WE'VE MADE SOMETHING *INCREDIBLE!*
I FEEL LIKE I'VE JUST GLIMPSED THE MOST AMAZING IMAGES...
OH, NO!! I HAVE TO GO!!
HUH?!
THAT ANIME SHOW INOUE IS DIRECTING STARTS TODAY!!
WHICH WAY'S THE STATION ?!
I'LL SHOW YOU THE SHORTEST ROUTE!
RUN-NING? NO THANKS.
I *HATE* RUNNING.
WHAT ARE YOU TALKING ABOUT?! YOU'VE NEVER LOST A RACE!
DASH
MIZUSAKI, HOW FAST CAN YOU DO 100 METERS?
IN ELEMENTARY SCHOOL, I WOULD HAVE SAID ONE SECOND.
THEN WE CAN BE AT THE STATION IN EIGHT.
UM... WHOEVER COMES IN LAST HAS TO TREAT THE OTHERS.
HEY, WAIT!
SEE YA!
YOU COW-ARD!
tmp tmp
beep beep beep Wash cycle com-plete.
Take out your laun-dry.
beep beep beep

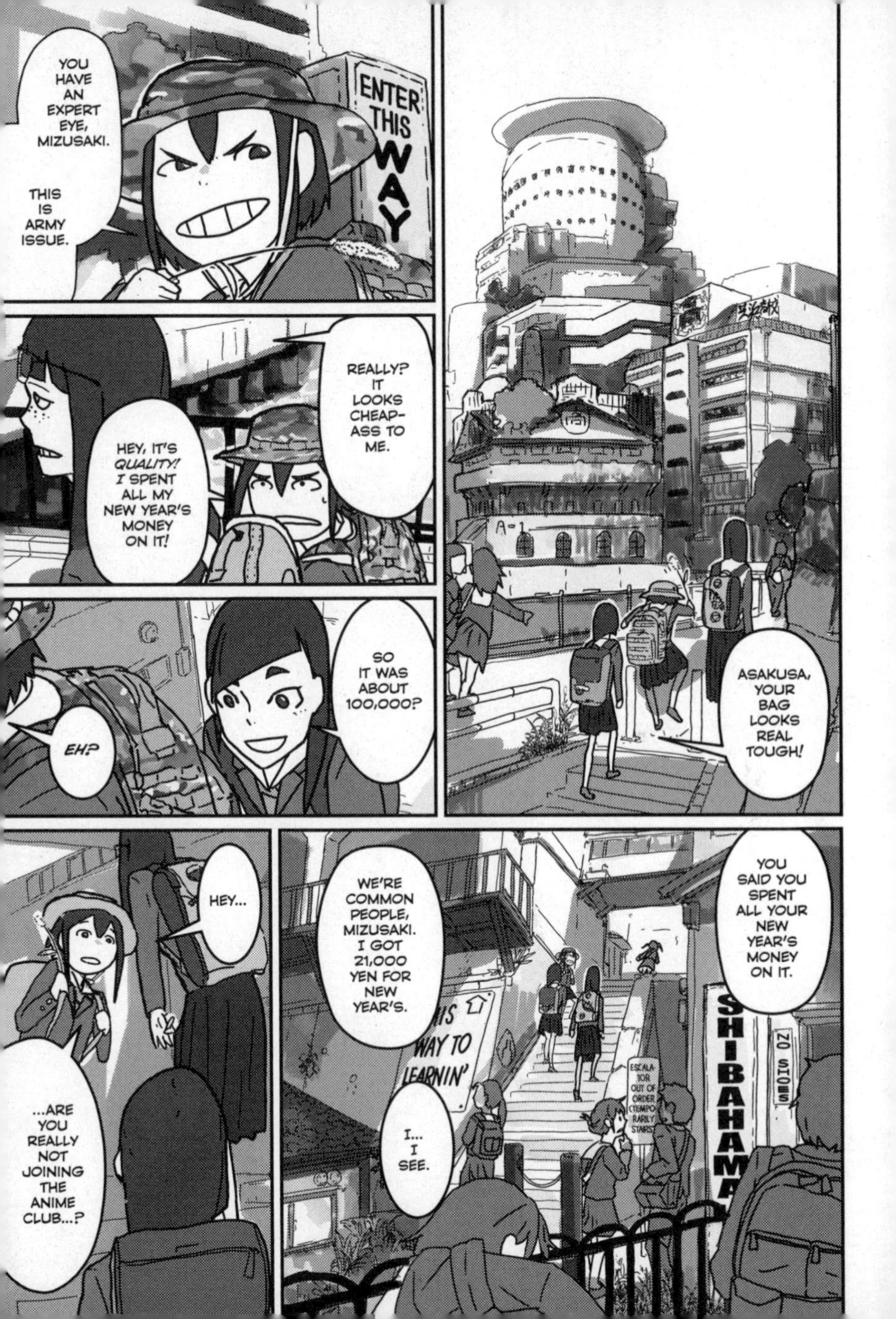
ASAKUSA, YOUR BAG LOOKS REAL TOUGH!
ENTER THIS WAY
YOU HAVE AN EXPERT EYE, MIZUSAKI.
THIS IS ARMY ISSUE.
REALLY? IT LOOKS CHEAP-ASS TO ME.
HEY, IT'S *QUALITY!* I SPENT ALL MY NEW YEAR'S MONEY ON IT!
SO IT WAS ABOUT 100,000?
EH?
YOU SAID YOU SPENT ALL YOUR NEW YEAR'S MONEY ON IT.
SHIBAHAMA
NO SHOES
ESCALATOR OUT OF ORDER (TEMPORARILY STAIRS)
WE'RE COMMON PEOPLE, MIZUSAKI. I GOT 21,000 YEN FOR NEW YEAR'S.
HIS WAY TO LEARNIN'
I... I SEE.
HEY...
...ARE YOU REALLY NOT JOINING THE ANIME CLUB...?

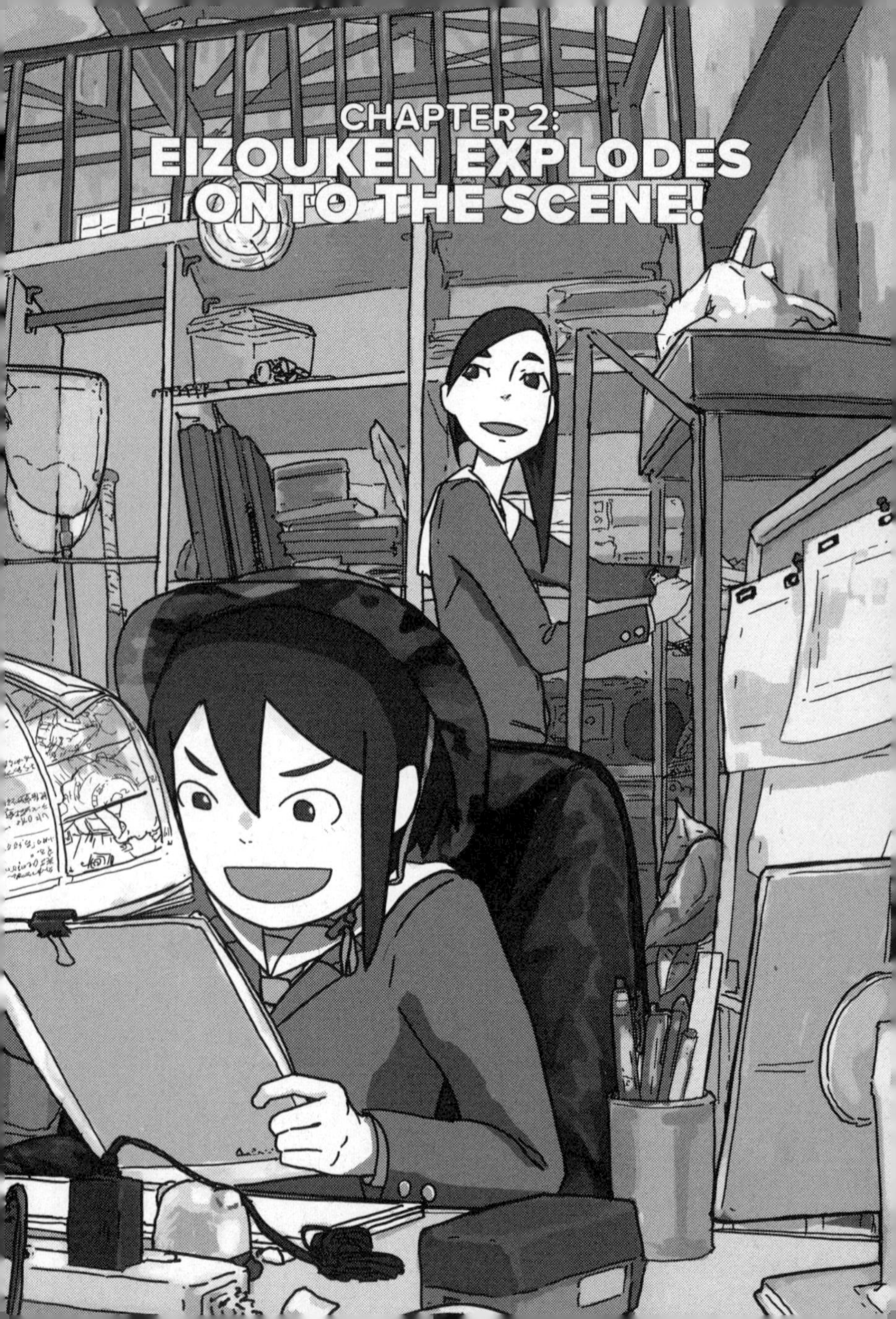
CHAPTER 2:
EIZOUKEN EXPLODES ONTO THE SCENE!

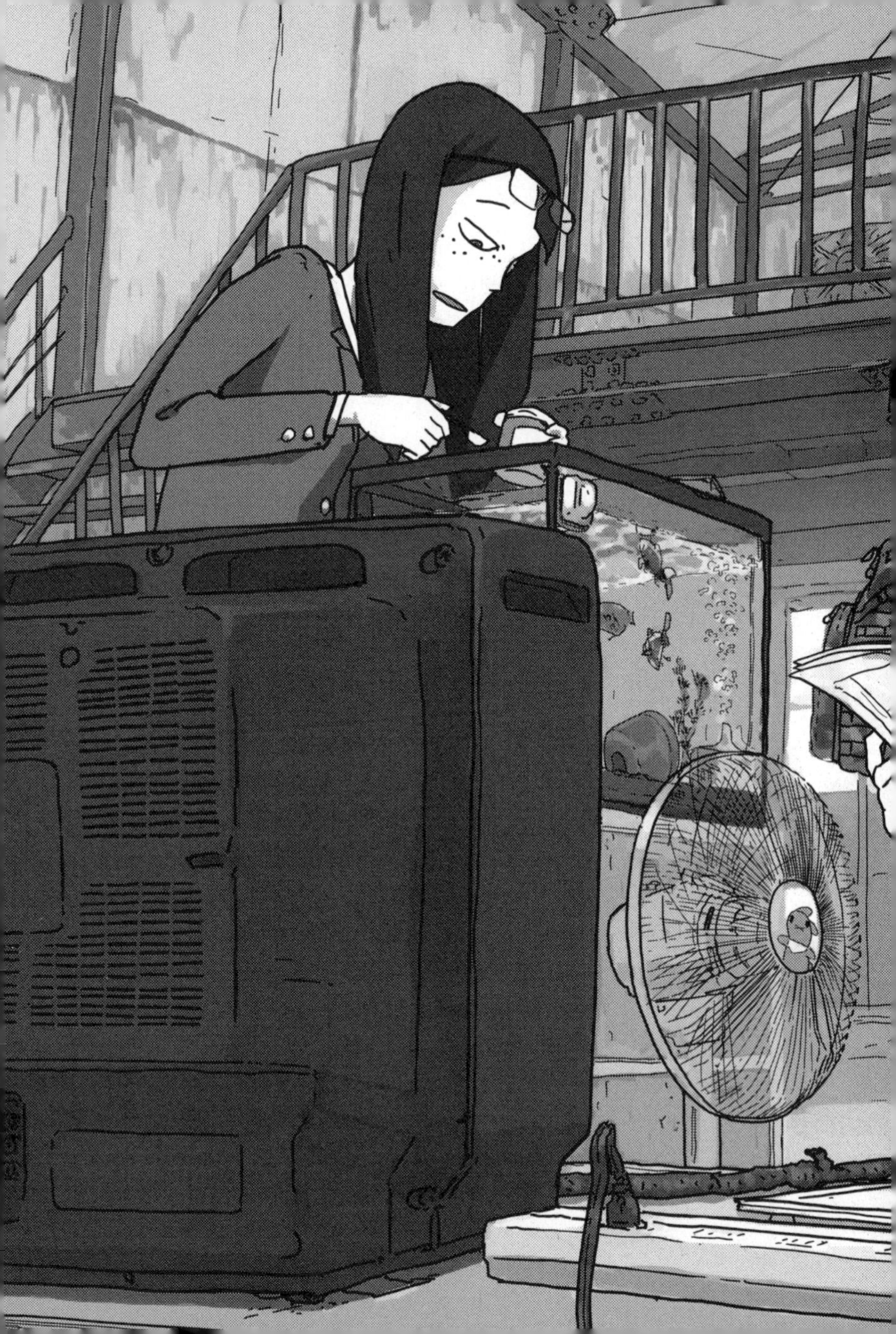

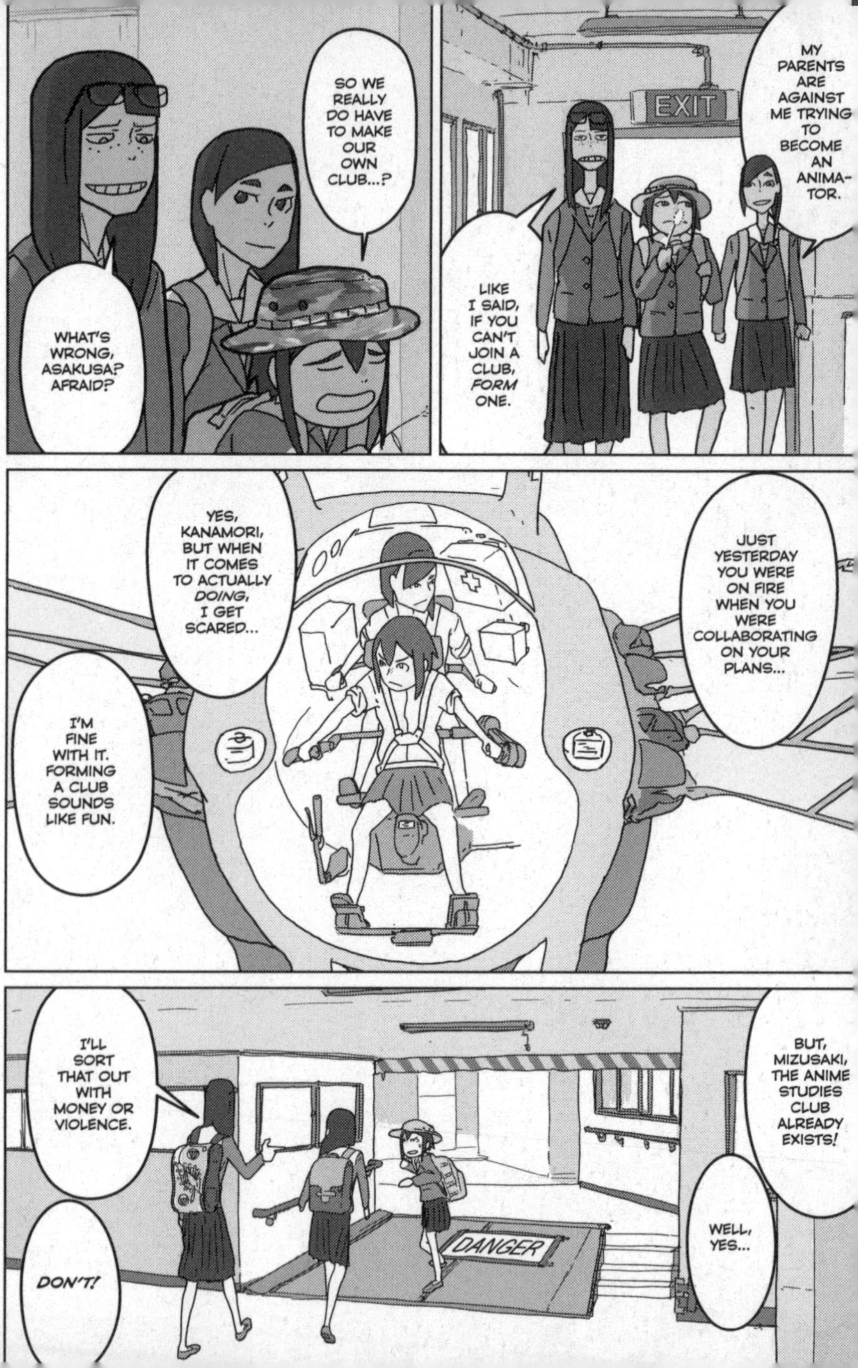
EXIT
MY PARENTS ARE AGAINST ME TRYING TO BECOME AN ANIMATOR.
LIKE I SAID, IF YOU CAN'T JOIN A CLUB, *FORM* ONE.
SO WE REALLY DO HAVE TO MAKE OUR OWN CLUB...?
WHAT'S WRONG, ASAKUSA? AFRAID?
JUST YESTERDAY YOU WERE ON FIRE WHEN YOU WERE COLLABORATING ON YOUR PLANS...
YES, KANAMORI, BUT WHEN IT COMES TO ACTUALLY *DOING*, I GET SCARED...
I'M FINE WITH IT. FORMING A CLUB SOUNDS LIKE FUN.
BUT, MIZUSAKI, THE ANIME STUDIES CLUB ALREADY EXISTS!
I'LL SORT THAT OUT WITH MONEY OR VIOLENCE.
WELL, YES...
DANGER
DON'T!

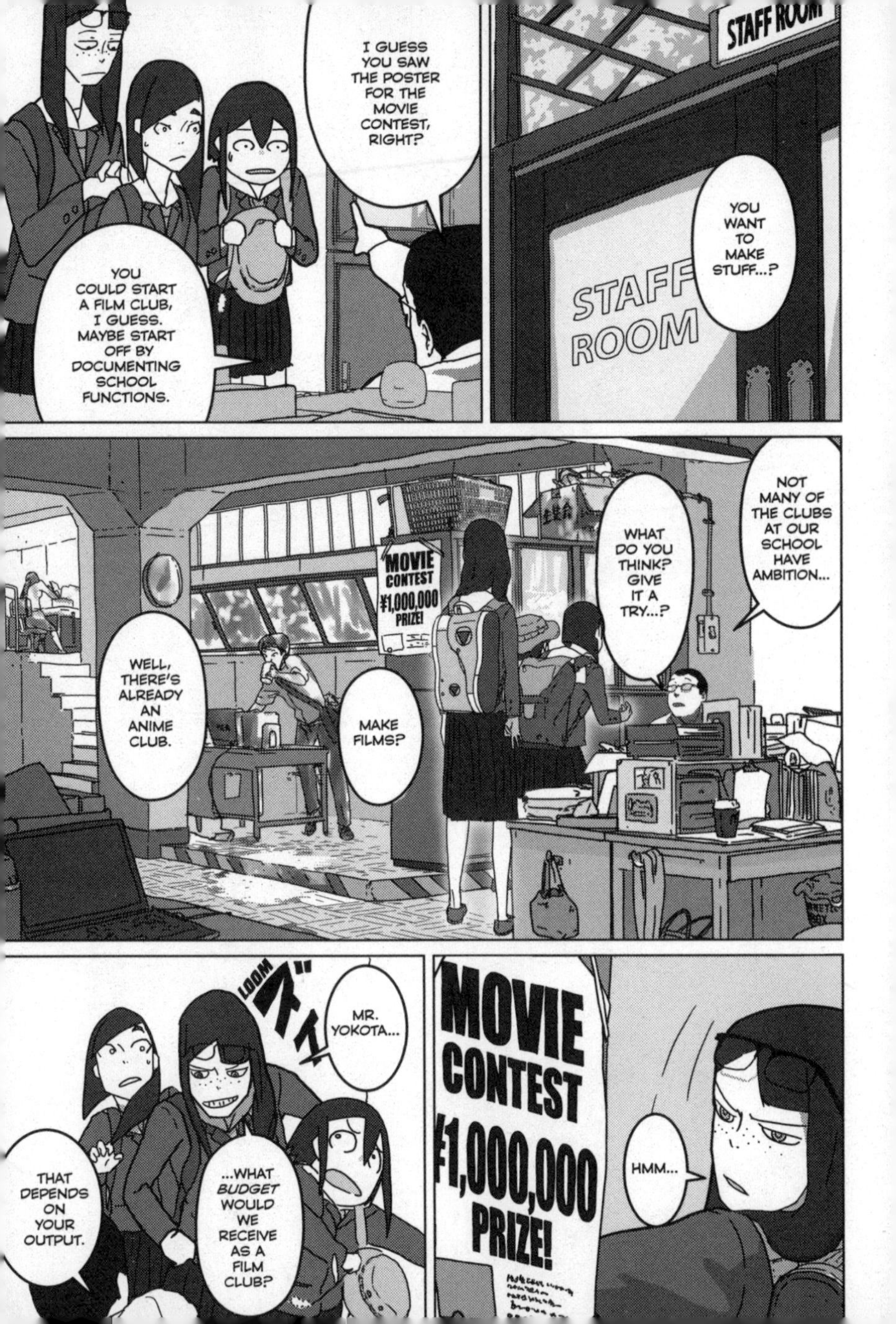
STAFF ROOM
YOU WANT TO MAKE STUFF...?
STAFF ROOM
I GUESS YOU SAW THE POSTER FOR THE MOVIE CONTEST, RIGHT?
YOU COULD START A FILM CLUB, I GUESS. MAYBE START OFF BY DOCUMENTING SCHOOL FUNCTIONS.
NOT MANY OF THE CLUBS AT OUR SCHOOL HAVE AMBITION...
WHAT DO YOU THINK? GIVE IT A TRY...?
MOVIE CONTEST ¥1,000,000 PRIZE!
MAKE FILMS?
WELL, THERE'S ALREADY AN ANIME CLUB.
MOVIE CONTEST ¥1,000,000 PRIZE!
HMM...
MR. YOKOTA...
LOOM
...WHAT *BUDGET* WOULD WE RECEIVE AS A FILM CLUB?
THAT DEPENDS ON YOUR OUTPUT.

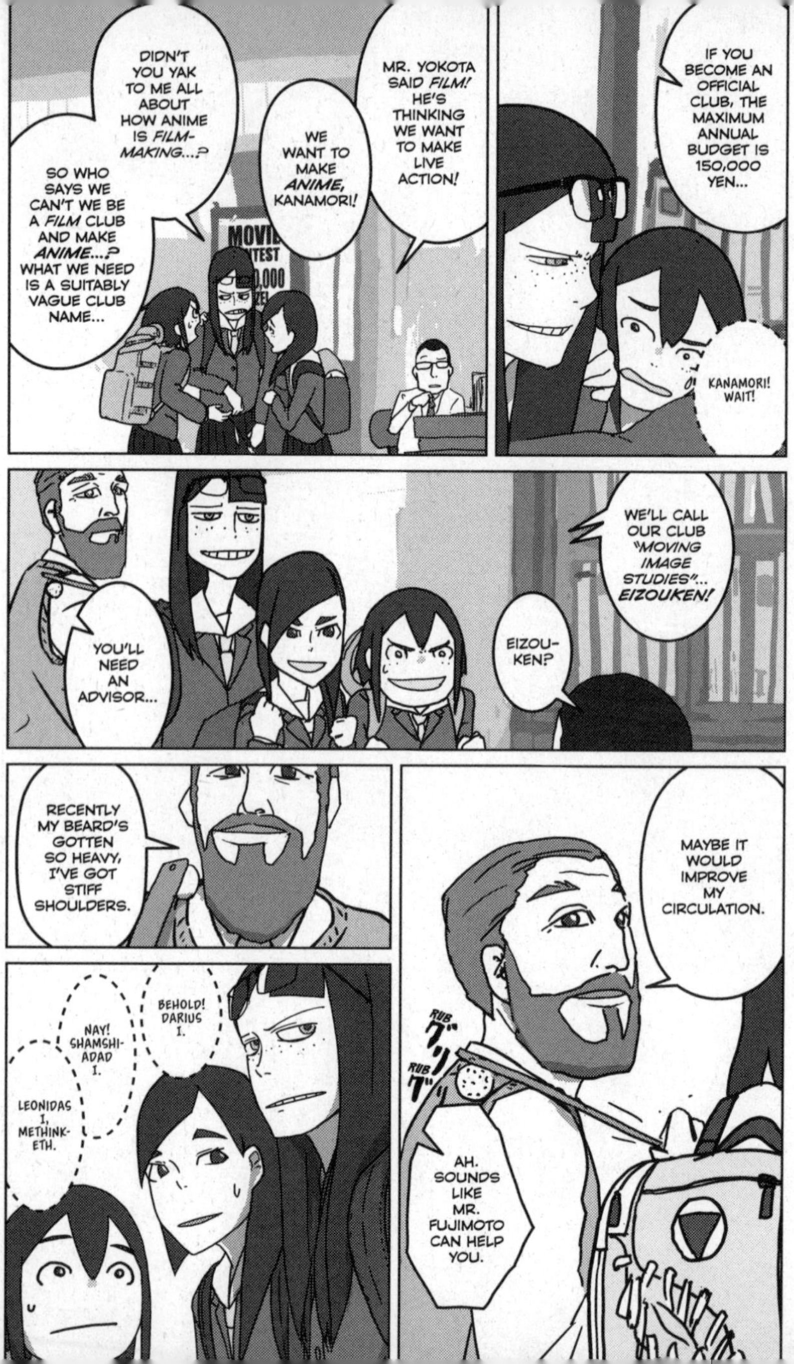
IF YOU BECOME AN OFFICIAL CLUB, THE MAXIMUM ANNUAL BUDGET IS 150,000 YEN...
KANAMORI! WAIT!
MR. YOKOTA SAID FILM! HE'S THINKING WE WANT TO MAKE LIVE ACTION!
WE WANT TO MAKE ANIME, KANAMORI!
DIDN'T YOU YAK TO ME ALL ABOUT HOW ANIME IS FILM-MAKING...?
SO WHO SAYS WE CAN'T WE BE A FILM CLUB AND MAKE ANIME...? WHAT WE NEED IS A SUITABLY VAGUE CLUB NAME...
WE'LL CALL OUR CLUB "MOVING IMAGE STUDIES"... EIZOUKEN!
EIZOU-KEN?
YOU'LL NEED AN ADVISOR...
MAYBE IT WOULD IMPROVE MY CIRCULATION.
RUB
RUB
AH. SOUNDS LIKE MR. FUJIMOTO CAN HELP YOU.
RECENTLY MY BEARD'S GOTTEN SO HEAVY, I'VE GOT STIFF SHOULDERS.
BEHOLD! DARIUS I.
NAY! SHAMSHIADAD I.
LEONIDAS I, METHINKETH.

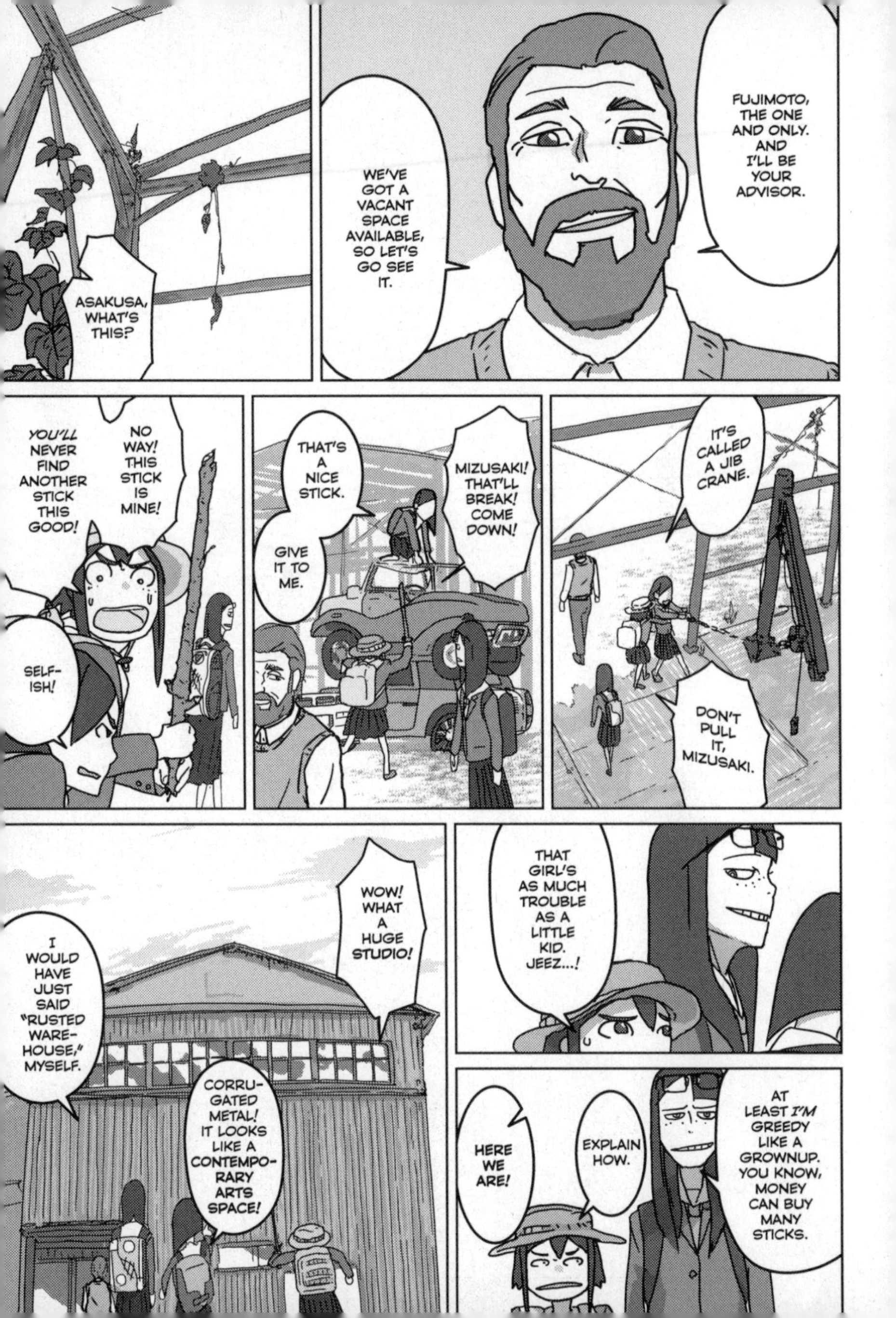
FUJIMOTO, THE ONE AND ONLY. AND I'LL BE YOUR ADVISOR.
WE'VE GOT A VACANT SPACE AVAILABLE, SO LET'S GO SEE IT.
ASAKUSA, WHAT'S THIS?
IT'S CALLED A JIB CRANE.
DON'T PULL IT, MIZUSAKI.
MIZUSAKI! THAT'LL BREAK! COME DOWN!
THAT'S A NICE STICK.
GIVE IT TO ME.
NO WAY! THIS STICK IS MINE!
YOU'LL NEVER FIND ANOTHER STICK THIS GOOD!
SELF-ISH!
THAT GIRL'S AS MUCH TROUBLE AS A LITTLE KID. JEEZ...!
AT LEAST *I'M* GREEDY LIKE A GROWNUP. YOU KNOW, MONEY CAN BUY MANY STICKS.
EXPLAIN HOW.
HERE WE ARE!
WOW! WHAT A HUGE STUDIO!
I WOULD HAVE JUST SAID "RUSTED WARE-HOUSE," MYSELF.
CORRU-GATED METAL! IT LOOKS LIKE A CONTEMPO-RARY ARTS SPACE!

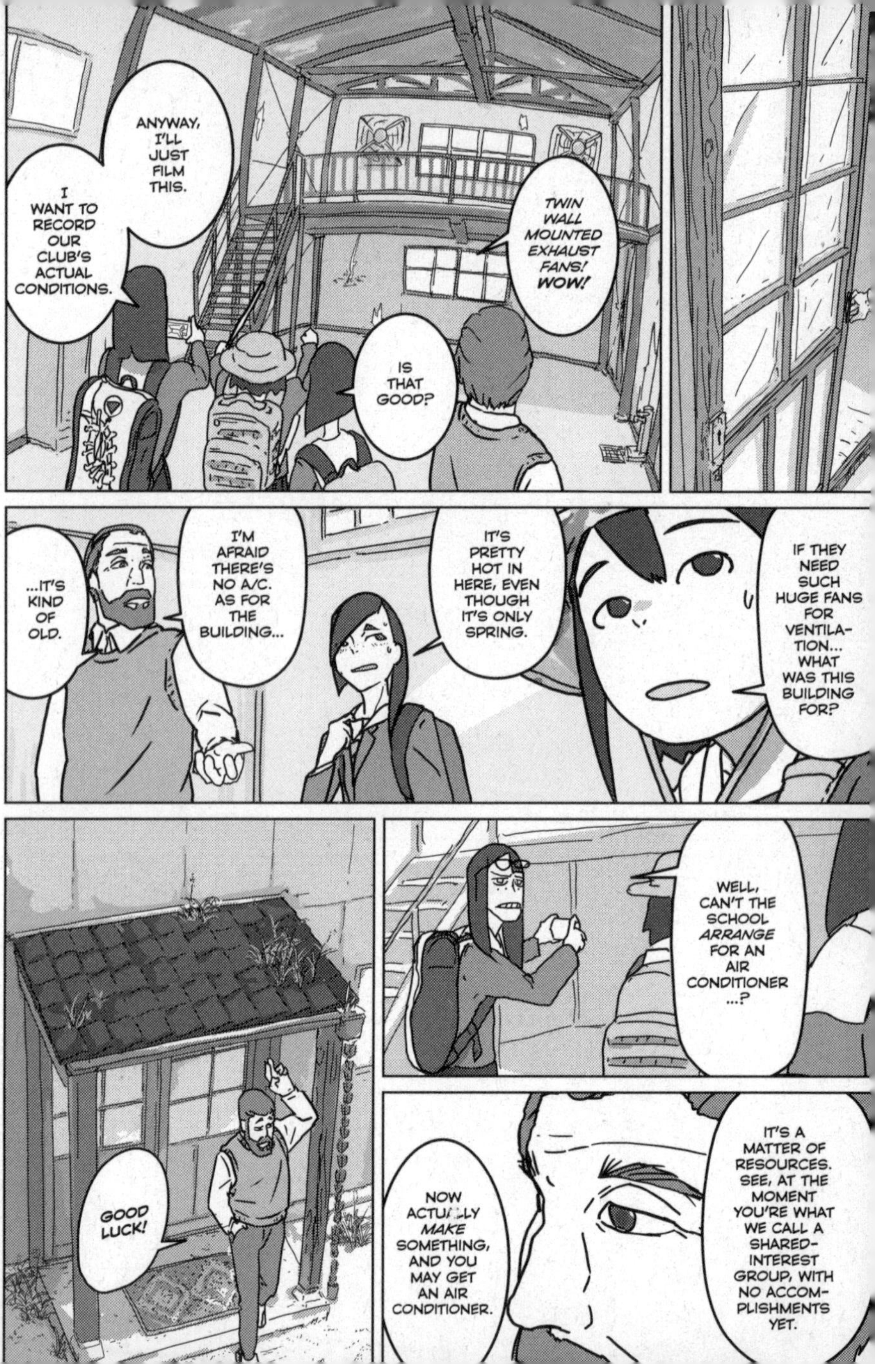
TWIN WALL MOUNTED EXHAUST FANS! WOW!
IS THAT GOOD?
ANYWAY, I'LL JUST FILM THIS.
I WANT TO RECORD OUR CLUB'S ACTUAL CONDITIONS.
IF THEY NEED SUCH HUGE FANS FOR VENTILATION... WHAT WAS THIS BUILDING FOR?
IT'S PRETTY HOT IN HERE, EVEN THOUGH IT'S ONLY SPRING.
I'M AFRAID THERE'S NO A/C. AS FOR THE BUILDING...
...IT'S KIND OF OLD.
WELL, CAN'T THE SCHOOL ARRANGE FOR AN AIR CONDITIONER ...?
IT'S A MATTER OF RESOURCES. SEE, AT THE MOMENT YOU'RE WHAT WE CALL A SHARED-INTEREST GROUP, WITH NO ACCOMPLISHMENTS YET.
NOW ACTUALLY MAKE SOMETHING, AND YOU MAY GET AN AIR CONDITIONER.
GOOD LUCK!

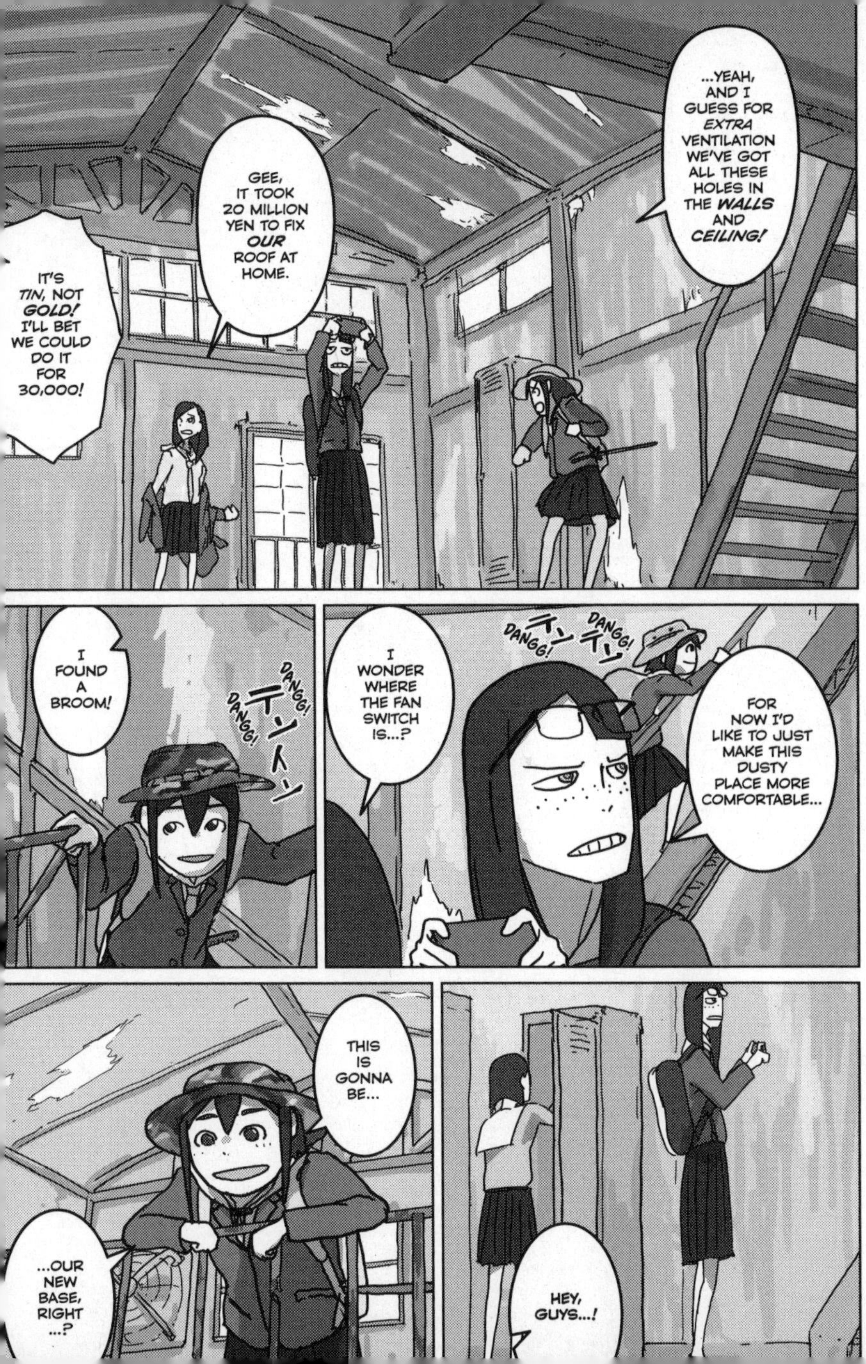
...YEAH, AND I GUESS FOR *EXTRA* VENTILATION WE'VE GOT ALL THESE HOLES IN THE ***WALLS*** AND ***CEILING!***
GEE, IT TOOK 20 MILLION YEN TO FIX ***OUR*** ROOF AT HOME.
IT'S *TIN*, NOT ***GOLD!*** I'LL BET WE COULD DO IT FOR 30,000!
DANGG! DANGG!
FOR NOW I'D LIKE TO JUST MAKE THIS DUSTY PLACE MORE COMFORTABLE...
I WONDER WHERE THE FAN SWITCH IS...?
I FOUND A BROOM!
DANGG! DANGG!
HEY, GUYS...!
THIS IS GONNA BE...
...OUR NEW BASE, RIGHT ...?

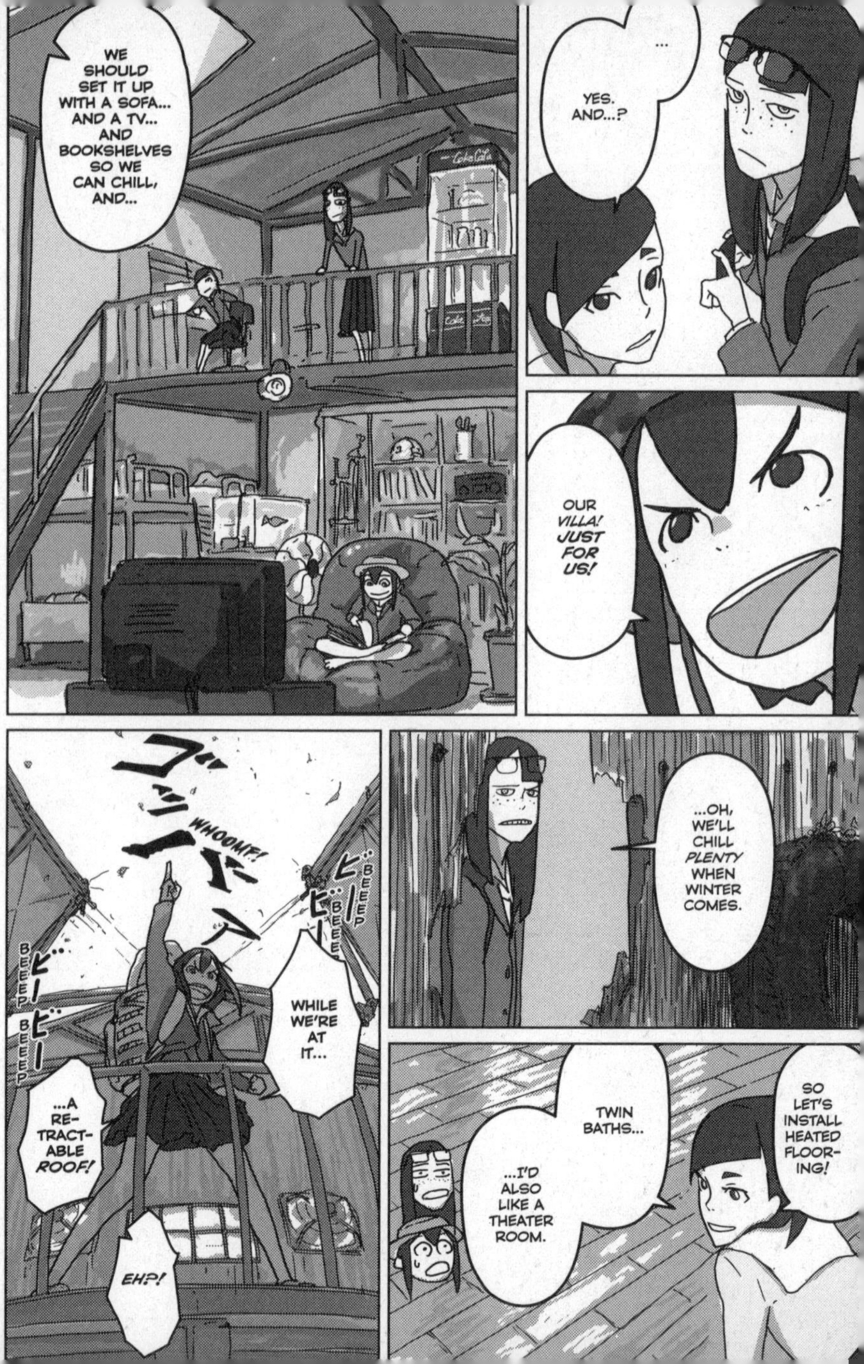
...
YES. AND...?
OUR VILLA! JUST FOR US!
WE SHOULD SET IT UP WITH A SOFA... AND A TV... AND BOOKSHELVES SO WE CAN CHILL, AND...
...OH, WE'LL CHILL PLENTY WHEN WINTER COMES.
SO LET'S INSTALL HEATED FLOORING!
TWIN BATHS...
...I'D ALSO LIKE A THEATER ROOM.
WHILE WE'RE AT IT...
...A RETRACTABLE ROOF!
WHOOMF!
BEEEP BEEEP
BEEEP BEEEP
......
EH?!

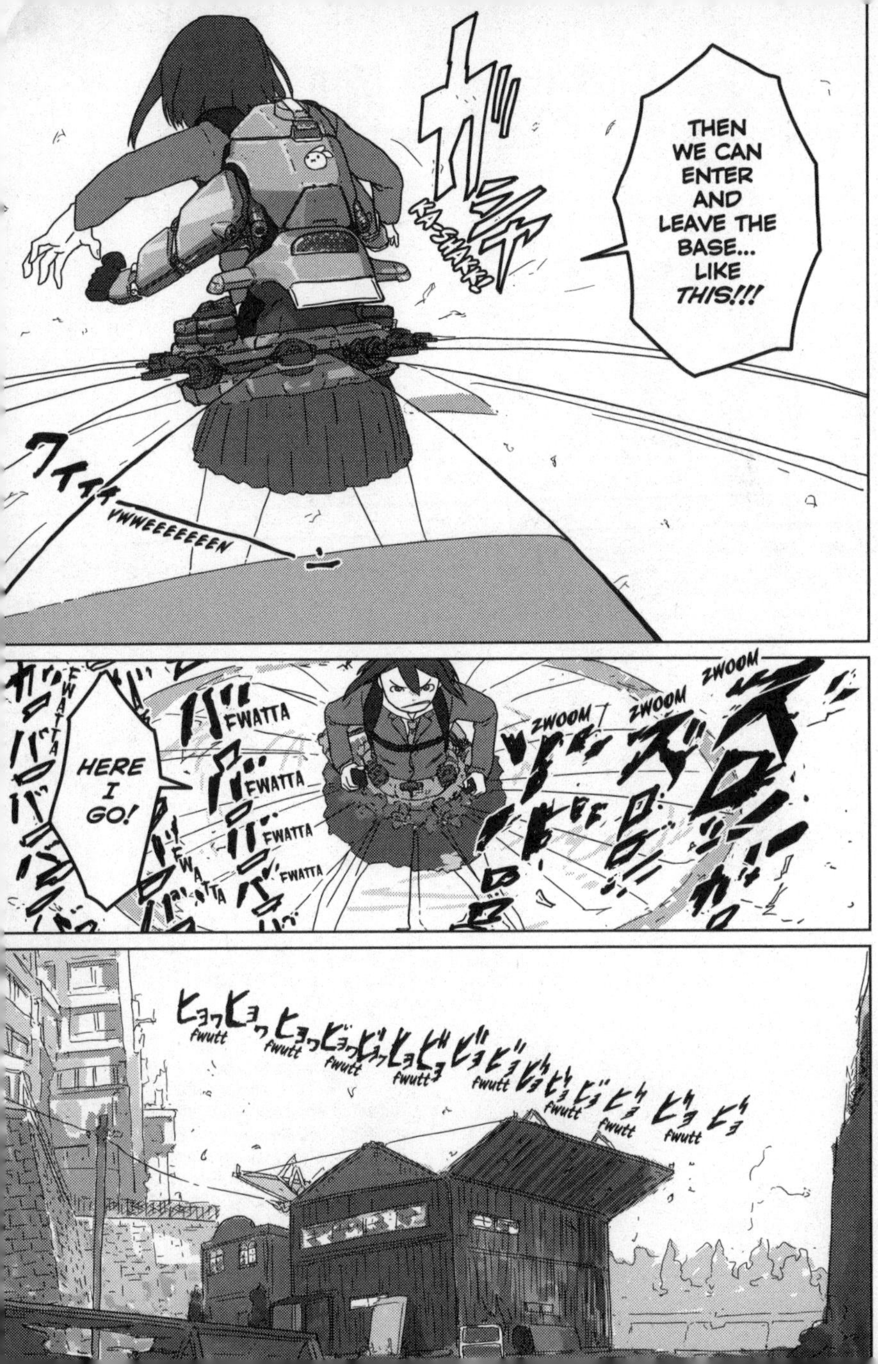
THEN WE CAN ENTER AND LEAVE THE BASE... LIKE THIS!!!
KA-SHAK!!
VWWEEEEEEEN
ZWOOM
ZWOOM
ZWOOM
FWATTA
FWATTA
FWATTA
FWATTA
HERE I GO!
FWATTA
FWATTA
fwutt
fwutt
fwutt
fwutt
fwutt
fwutt
fwutt
fwutt

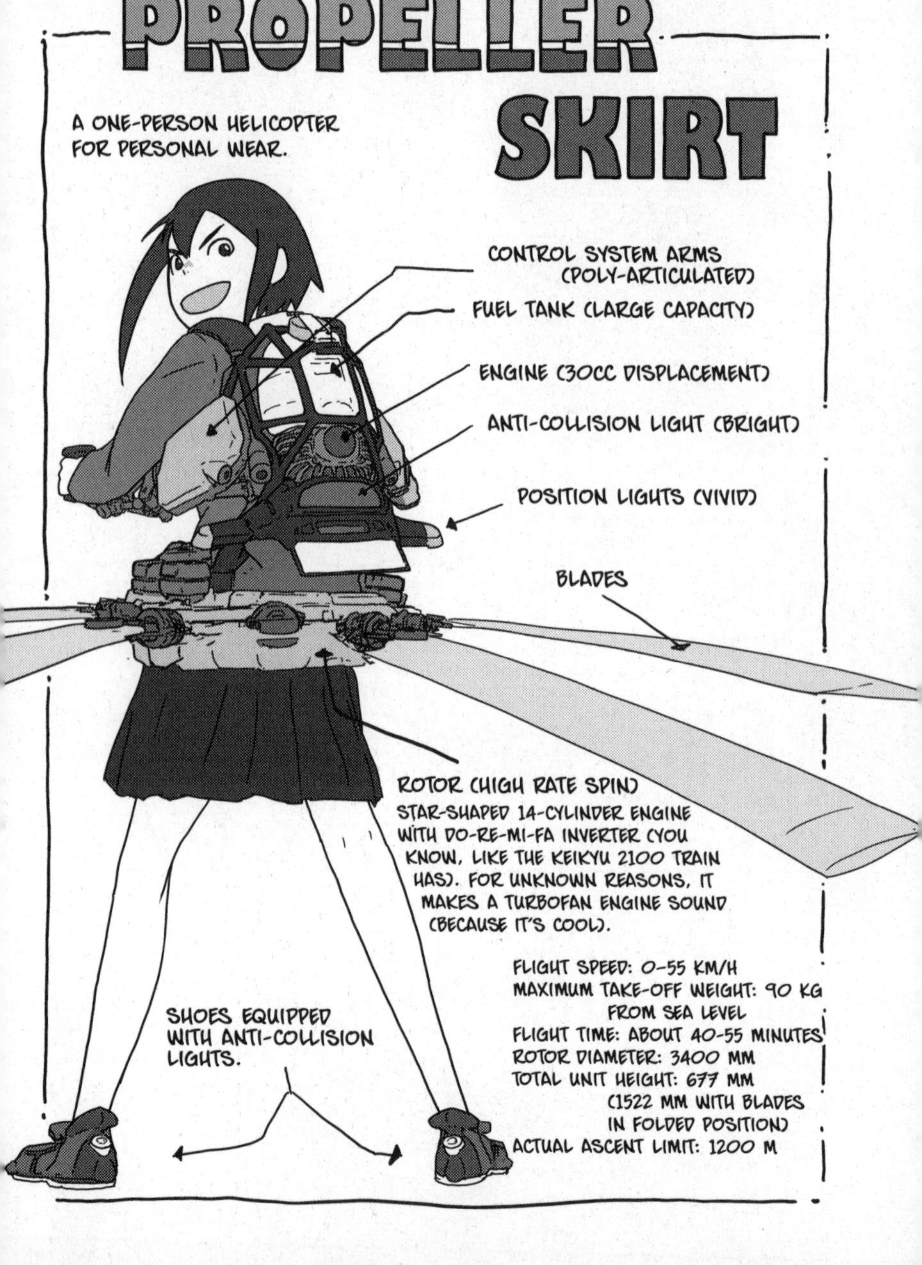
PROPELLER SKIRT
A ONE-PERSON HELICOPTER FOR PERSONAL WEAR.
CONTROL SYSTEM ARMS (POLY-ARTICULATED)
FUEL TANK (LARGE CAPACITY)
ENGINE (30CC DISPLACEMENT)
ANTI-COLLISION LIGHT (BRIGHT)
POSITION LIGHTS (VIVID)
BLADES
ROTOR (HIGH RATE SPIN)
STAR-SHAPED 14-CYLINDER ENGINE WITH DO-RE-MI-FA INVERTER (YOU KNOW, LIKE THE KEIKYU 2100 TRAIN HAS). FOR UNKNOWN REASONS, IT MAKES A TURBOFAN ENGINE SOUND (BECAUSE IT'S COOL).
FLIGHT SPEED: 0–55 KM/H
MAXIMUM TAKE-OFF WEIGHT: 90 KG FROM SEA LEVEL
FLIGHT TIME: ABOUT 40-55 MINUTES
ROTOR DIAMETER: 3400 MM
TOTAL UNIT HEIGHT: 677 MM (1522 MM WITH BLADES IN FOLDED POSITION)
ACTUAL ASCENT LIMIT: 1200 M
SHOES EQUIPPED WITH ANTI-COLLISION LIGHTS.

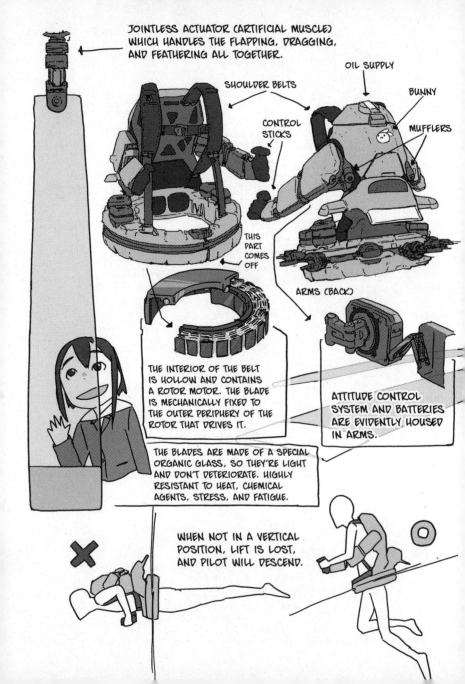

JOINTLESS ACTUATOR (ARTIFICIAL MUSCLE) WHICH HANDLES THE FLAPPING, DRAGGING, AND FEATHERING ALL TOGETHER.

OIL SUPPLY

SHOULDER BELTS

BUNNY

CONTROL STICKS

MUFFLERS

THIS PART COMES OFF

ARMS (BACK)

THE INTERIOR OF THE BELT IS HOLLOW AND CONTAINS A ROTOR MOTOR. THE BLADE IS MECHANICALLY FIXED TO THE OUTER PERIPHERY OF THE ROTOR THAT DRIVES IT.

ATTITUDE CONTROL SYSTEM AND BATTERIES ARE EVIDENTLY HOUSED IN ARMS.

THE BLADES ARE MADE OF A SPECIAL ORGANIC GLASS, SO THEY'RE LIGHT AND DON'T DETERIORATE. HIGHLY RESISTANT TO HEAT, CHEMICAL AGENTS, STRESS, AND FATIGUE.

WHEN NOT IN A VERTICAL POSITION, LIFT IS LOST, AND PILOT WILL DESCEND.

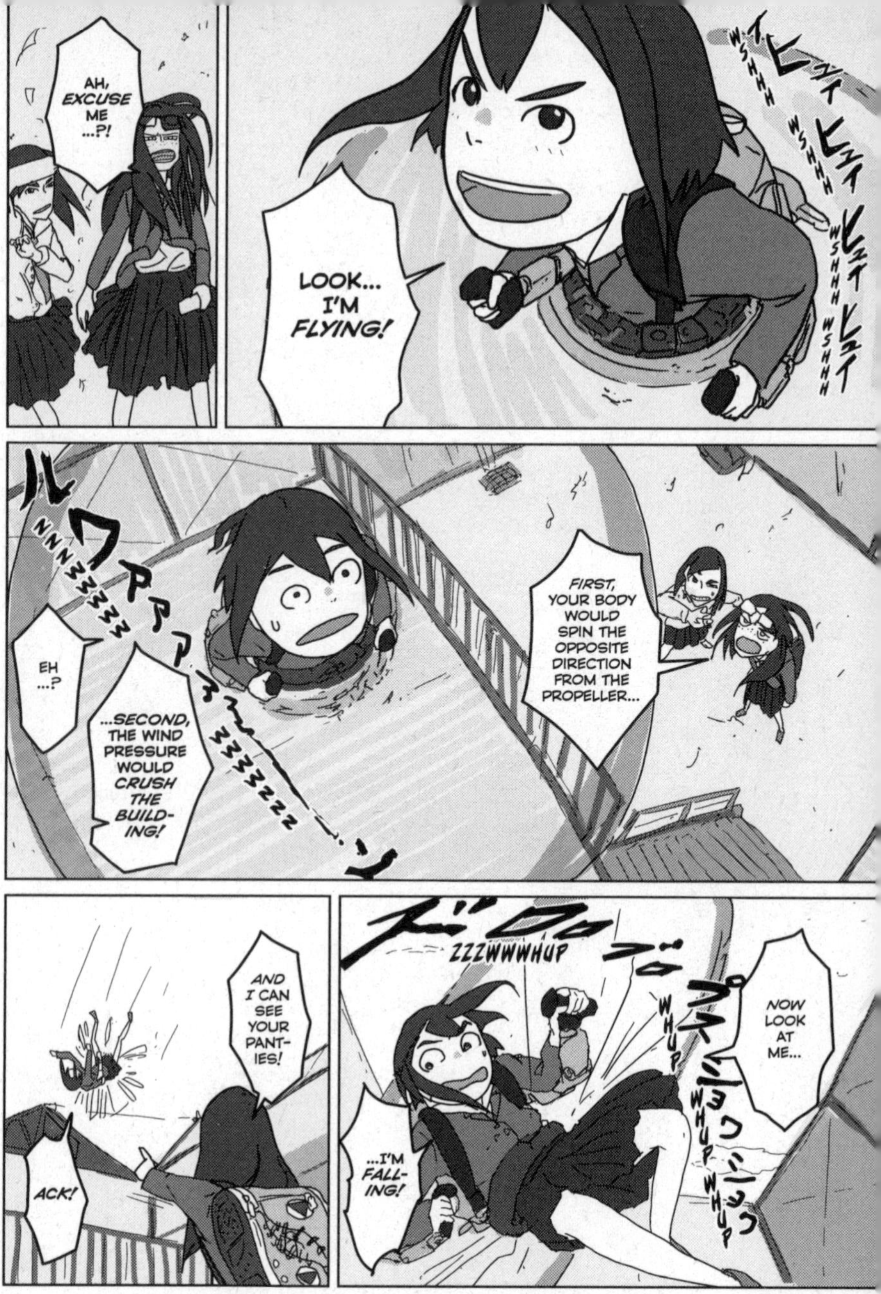
WSHHH
WSHHH
WSHHH
WSHHH
LOOK... I'M FLYING!
AH, EXCUSE ME ...?!
FIRST, YOUR BODY WOULD SPIN THE OPPOSITE DIRECTION FROM THE PROPELLER...
EH ...?
...SECOND, THE WIND PRESSURE WOULD CRUSH THE BUILDING!
NOW LOOK AT ME...
ZZZWWWHUP
WHUP WHUP WHUP
...I'M FALLING!
AND I CAN SEE YOUR PANTIES!
ACK!

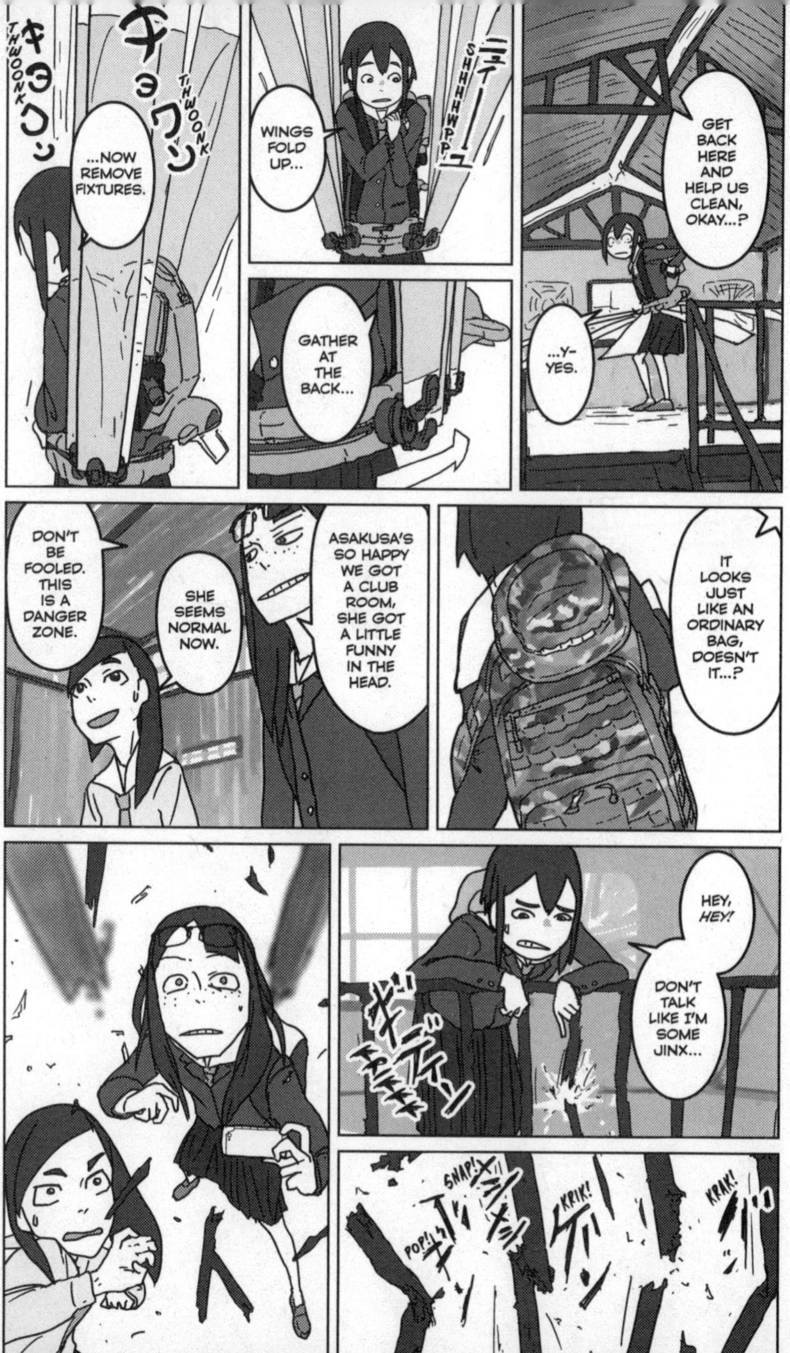
GET BACK HERE AND HELP US CLEAN, OKAY...?
...Y-YES.
SHHHHWPP
WINGS FOLD UP...
GATHER AT THE BACK...
THWOONK
THWOONK
...NOW REMOVE FIXTURES.
IT LOOKS JUST LIKE AN ORDINARY BAG, DOESN'T IT...?
ASAKUSA'S SO HAPPY WE GOT A CLUB ROOM, SHE GOT A LITTLE FUNNY IN THE HEAD.
SHE SEEMS NORMAL NOW.
DON'T BE FOOLED. THIS IS A DANGER ZONE.
HEY, *HEY!*
DON'T TALK LIKE I'M SOME JINX...
KRKKKK
KRAK!
KRIK!
SNAP!
POP!

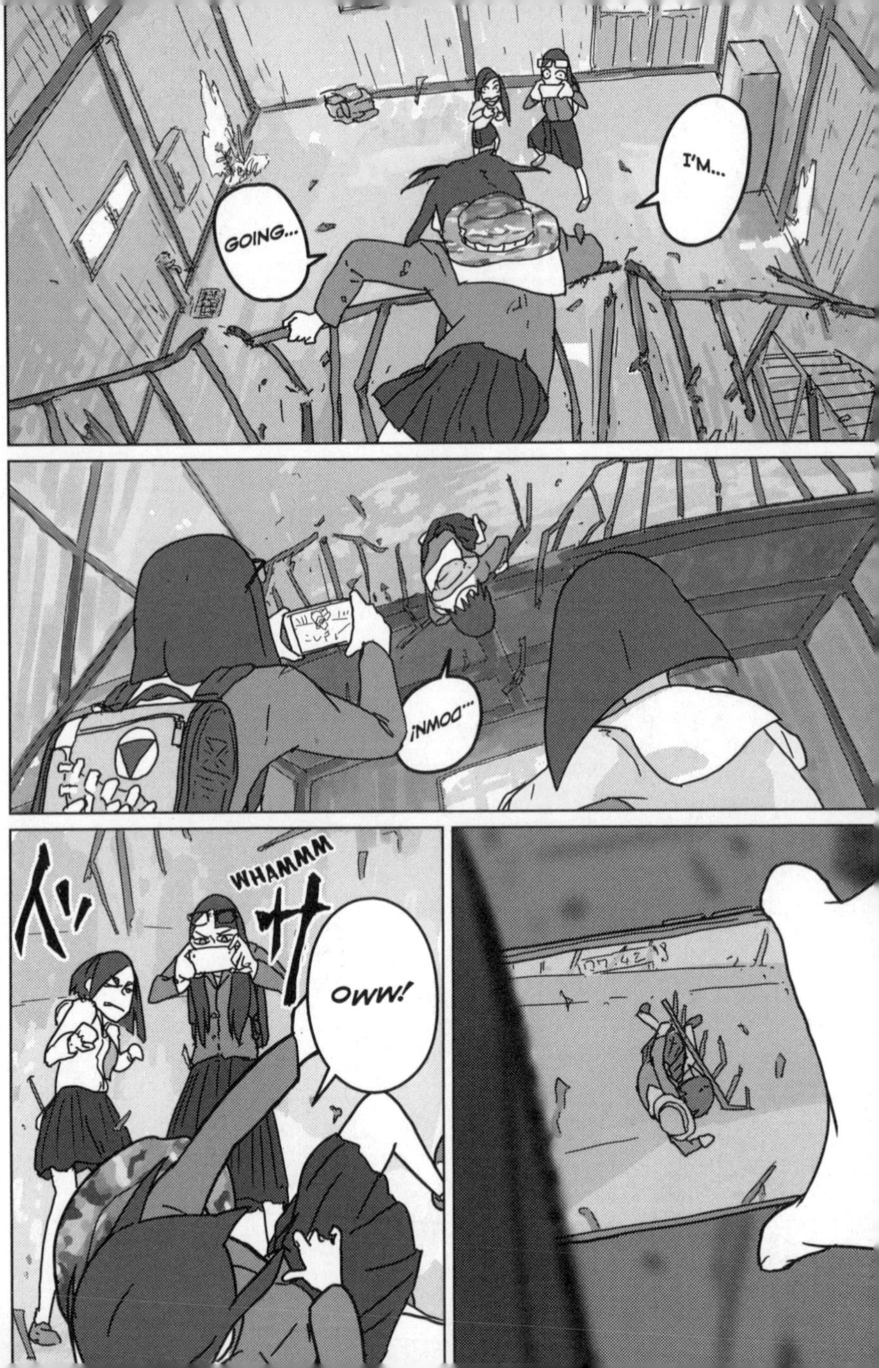
I'M...
GOING...
...DOWN!
WHAMMM
OWW!

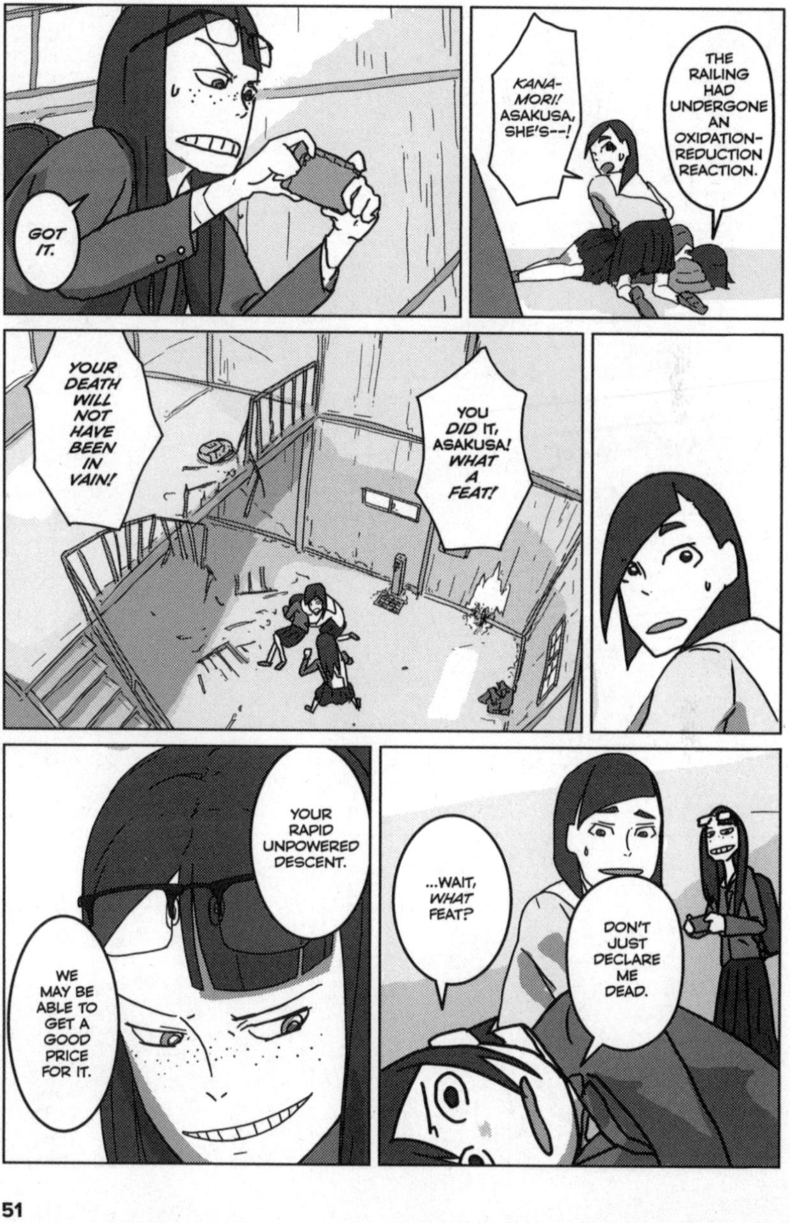
THE RAILING HAD UNDERGONE AN OXIDATION-REDUCTION REACTION.
KANA-MORI! ASAKUSA, SHE'S--!
GOT IT.
YOU DID IT, ASAKUSA! WHAT A FEAT!
YOUR DEATH WILL NOT HAVE BEEN IN VAIN!
DON'T JUST DECLARE ME DEAD.
...WAIT, WHAT FEAT?
YOUR RAPID UNPOWERED DESCENT.
WE MAY BE ABLE TO GET A GOOD PRICE FOR IT.

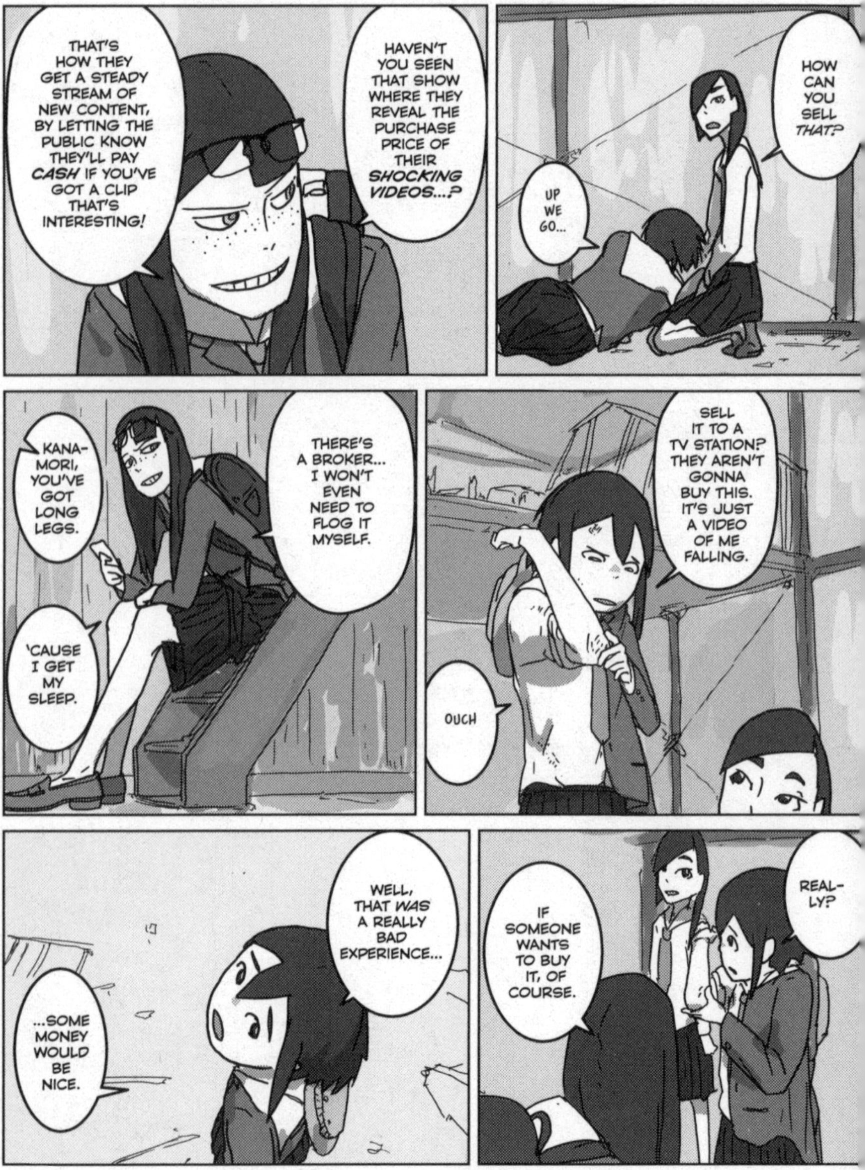
HOW CAN YOU SELL *THAT?*
UP WE GO...
HAVEN'T YOU SEEN THAT SHOW WHERE THEY REVEAL THE PURCHASE PRICE OF THEIR ***SHOCKING VIDEOS...?***
THAT'S HOW THEY GET A STEADY STREAM OF NEW CONTENT, BY LETTING THE PUBLIC KNOW THEY'LL PAY ***CASH*** IF YOU'VE GOT A CLIP THAT'S INTERESTING!
SELL IT TO A TV STATION? THEY AREN'T GONNA BUY THIS. IT'S JUST A VIDEO OF ME FALLING.
OUCH
THERE'S A BROKER... I WON'T EVEN NEED TO FLOG IT MYSELF.
KANA-MORI, YOU'VE GOT LONG LEGS.
'CAUSE I GET MY SLEEP.
REAL-LY?
IF SOMEONE WANTS TO BUY IT, OF COURSE.
WELL, THAT *WAS* A REALLY BAD EXPERIENCE...
...SOME MONEY WOULD BE NICE.

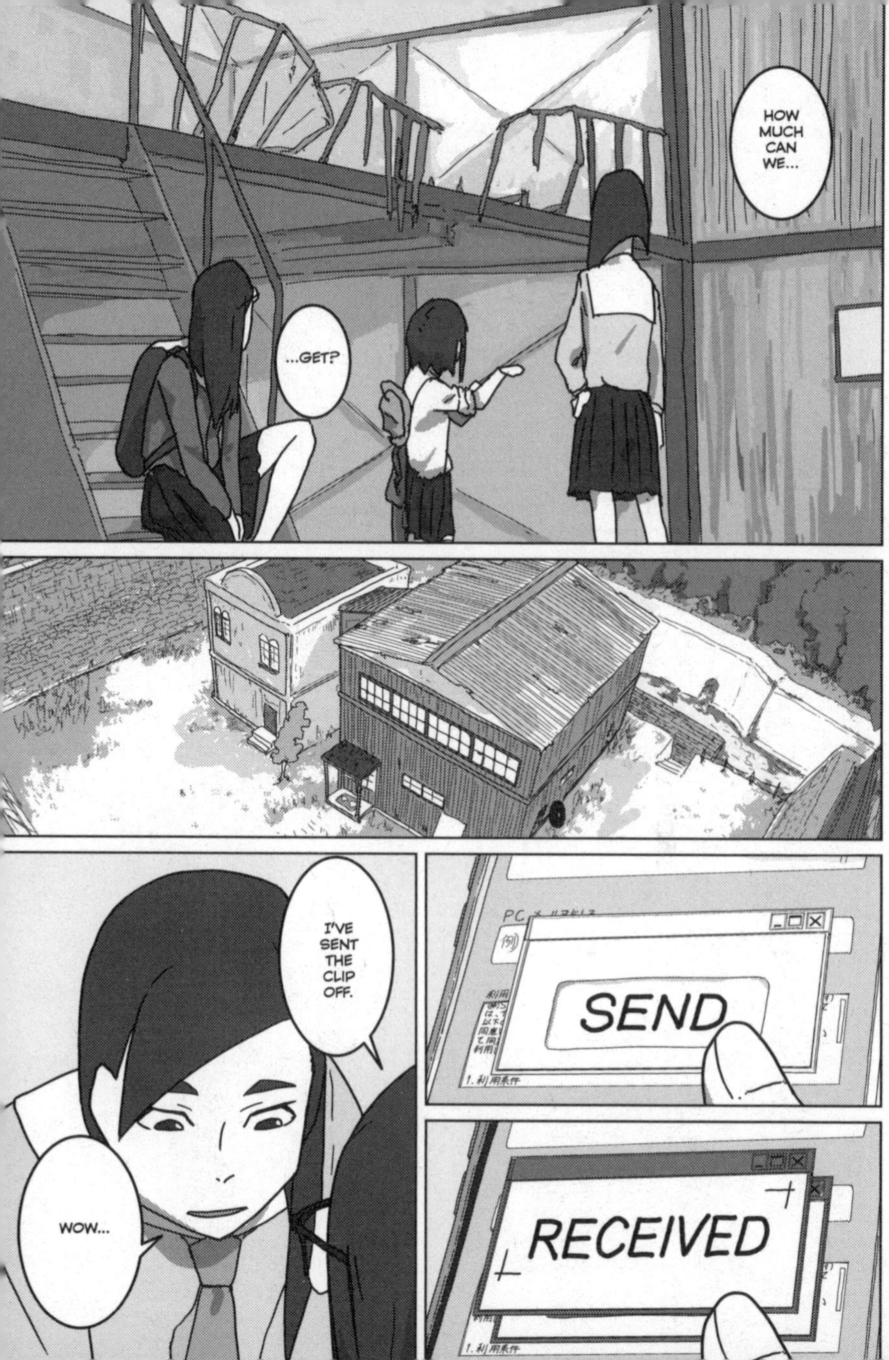
HOW MUCH CAN WE...
...GET?
SEND
RECEIVED
I'VE SENT THE CLIP OFF.
WOW...

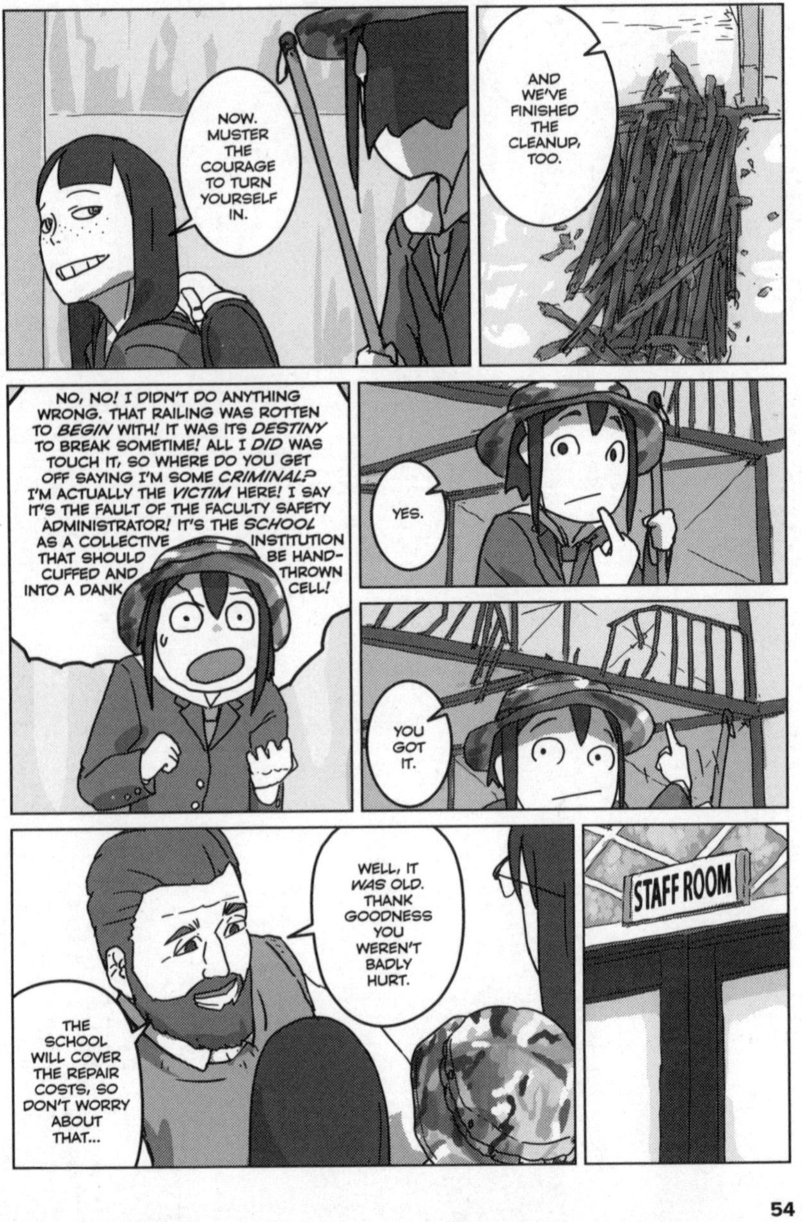
AND WE'VE FINISHED THE CLEANUP, TOO.
NOW. MUSTER THE COURAGE TO TURN YOURSELF IN.
YES.
YOU GOT IT.
NO, NO! I DIDN'T DO ANYTHING WRONG. THAT RAILING WAS ROTTEN TO *BEGIN* WITH! IT WAS ITS *DESTINY* TO BREAK SOMETIME! ALL I *DID* WAS TOUCH IT, SO WHERE DO YOU GET OFF SAYING I'M SOME *CRIMINAL*?! I'M ACTUALLY THE *VICTIM* HERE! I SAY IT'S THE FAULT OF THE FACULTY SAFETY ADMINISTRATOR! IT'S THE *SCHOOL* AS A COLLECTIVE INSTITUTION THAT SHOULD BE HAND-CUFFED AND THROWN INTO A DANK CELL!
STAFF ROOM
WELL, IT *WAS* OLD. THANK GOODNESS YOU WEREN'T BADLY HURT.
THE SCHOOL WILL COVER THE REPAIR COSTS, SO DON'T WORRY ABOUT THAT...

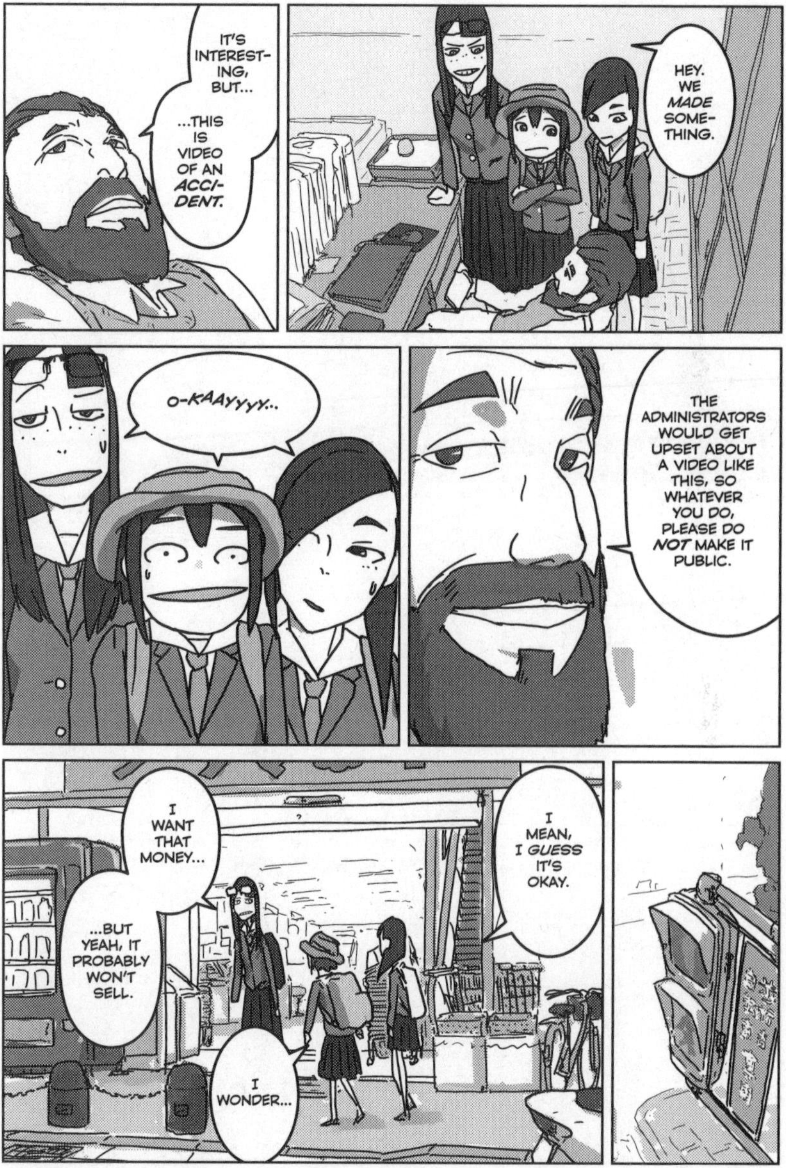
HEY. WE MADE SOMETHING.
IT'S INTERESTING, BUT...
...THIS IS VIDEO OF AN ACCIDENT.
THE ADMINISTRATORS WOULD GET UPSET ABOUT A VIDEO LIKE THIS, SO WHATEVER YOU DO, PLEASE DO NOT MAKE IT PUBLIC.
O-KAAYYYY...
I MEAN, I GUESS IT'S OKAY.
I WANT THAT MONEY...
...BUT YEAH, IT PROBABLY WON'T SELL.
I WONDER...

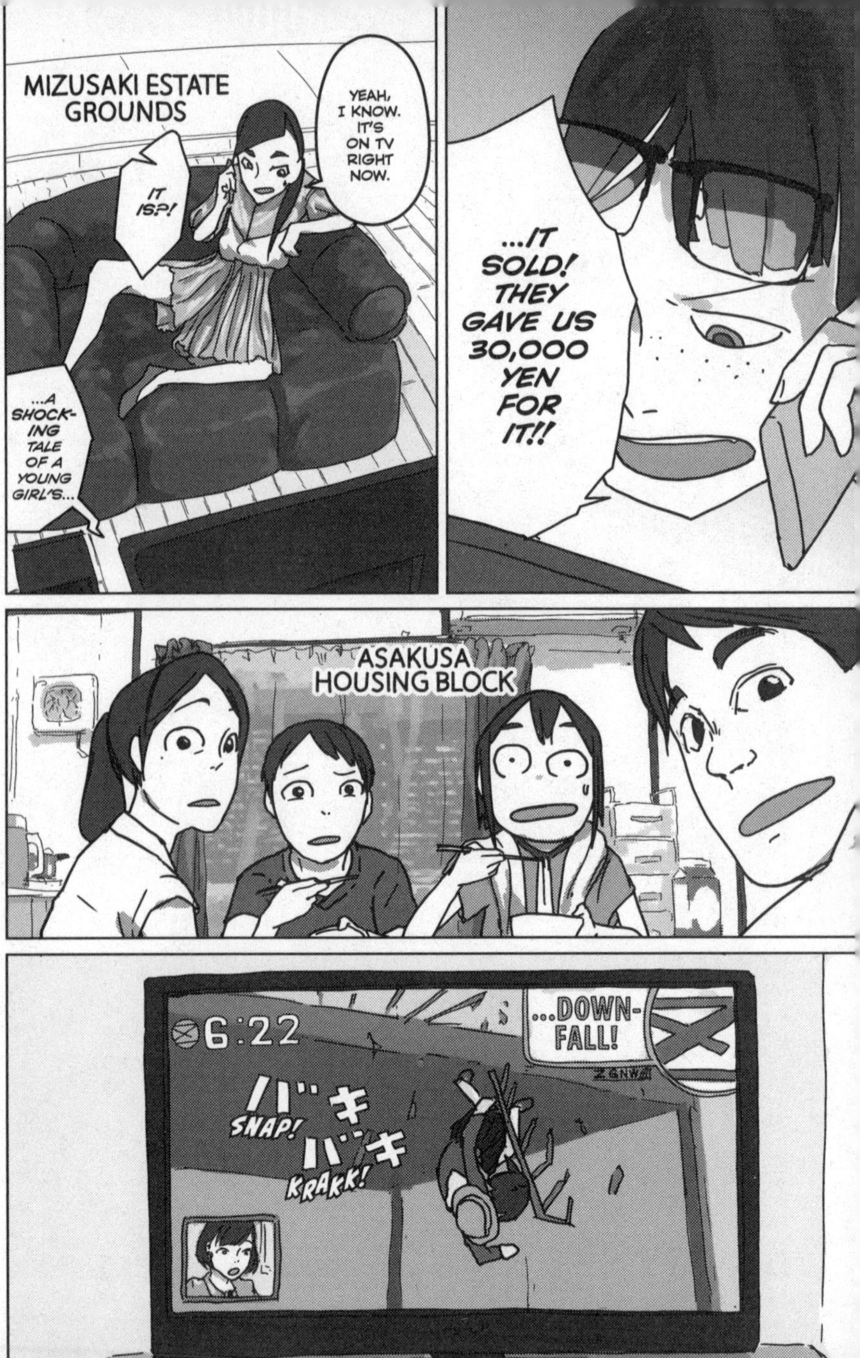
...IT SOLD! THEY GAVE US 30,000 YEN FOR IT!!
YEAH, I KNOW. IT'S ON TV RIGHT NOW.
MIZUSAKI ESTATE GROUNDS
IT IS?!
...A SHOCKING TALE OF A YOUNG GIRL'S...
ASAKUSA HOUSING BLOCK
...DOWN-FALL!
6:22
バキ
SNAP!
バキ
KRAKK!

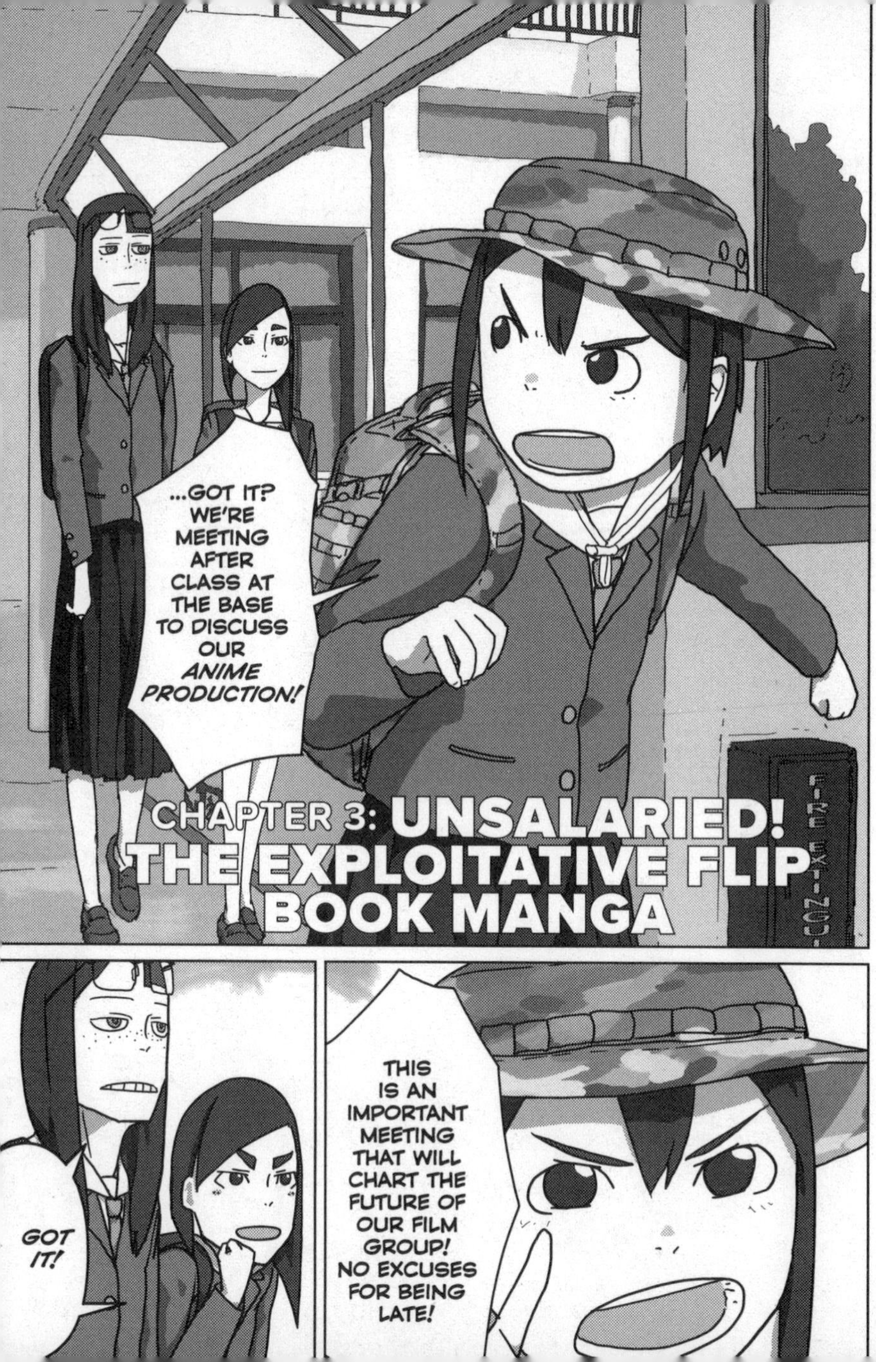
...GOT IT? WE'RE MEETING AFTER CLASS AT THE BASE TO DISCUSS OUR *ANIME PRODUCTION!*
CHAPTER 3: UNSALARIED! THE EXPLOITATIVE FLIP BOOK MANGA
THIS IS AN IMPORTANT MEETING THAT WILL CHART THE FUTURE OF OUR FILM GROUP! NO EXCUSES FOR BEING LATE!
GOT IT!

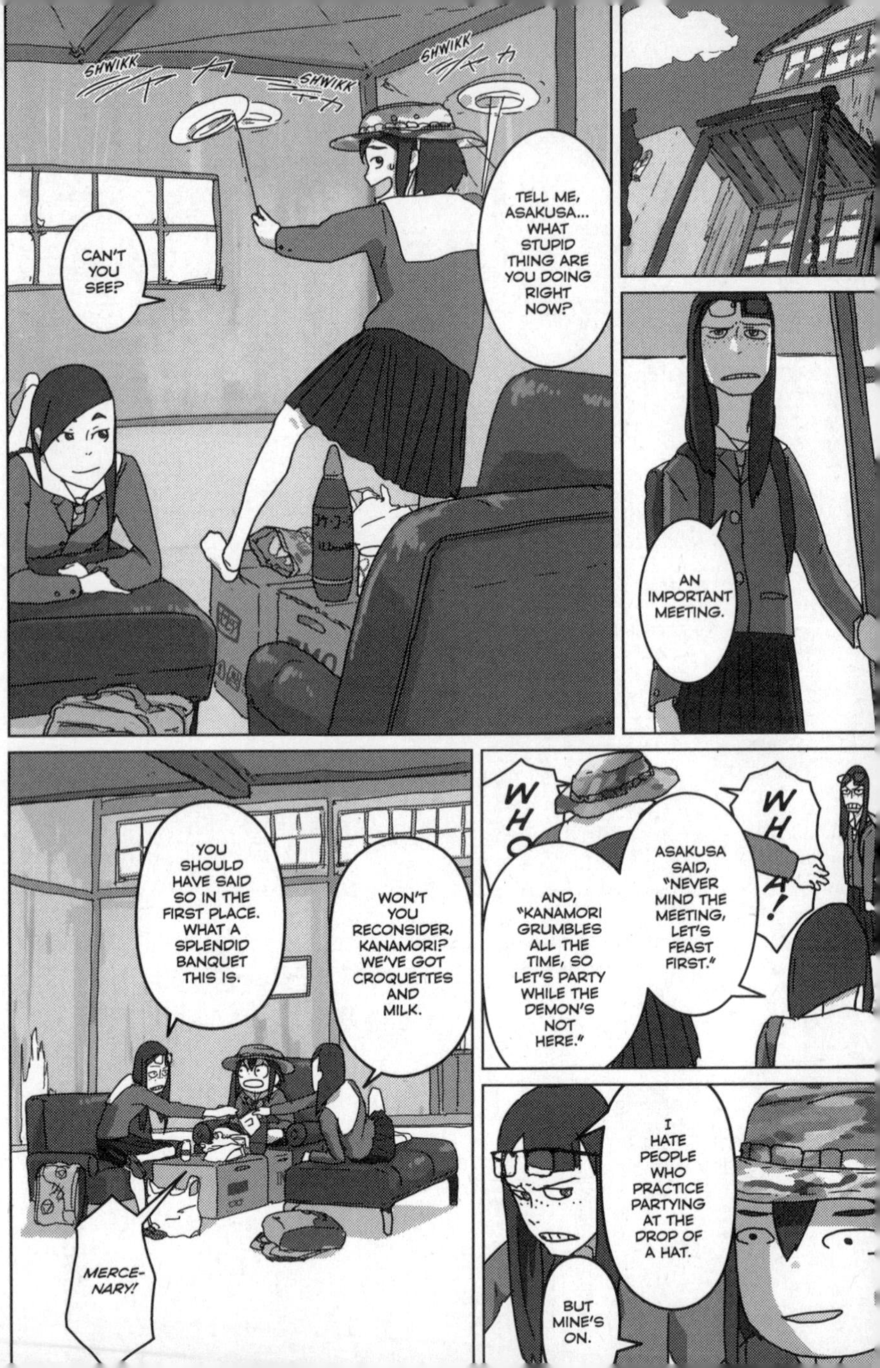
AN IMPORTANT MEETING.
SHWIKK
SHWIKK
TELL ME, ASAKUSA... WHAT STUPID THING ARE YOU DOING RIGHT NOW?
SHWIKK
CAN'T YOU SEE?
WHA!
ASAKUSA SAID, "NEVER MIND THE MEETING, LET'S FEAST FIRST."
WHO
AND, "KANAMORI GRUMBLES ALL THE TIME, SO LET'S PARTY WHILE THE DEMON'S NOT HERE."
I HATE PEOPLE WHO PRACTICE PARTYING AT THE DROP OF A HAT.
BUT MINE'S ON.
WON'T YOU RECONSIDER, KANAMORI? WE'VE GOT CROQUETTES AND MILK.
YOU SHOULD HAVE SAID SO IN THE FIRST PLACE. WHAT A SPLENDID BANQUET THIS IS.
MERCENARY!

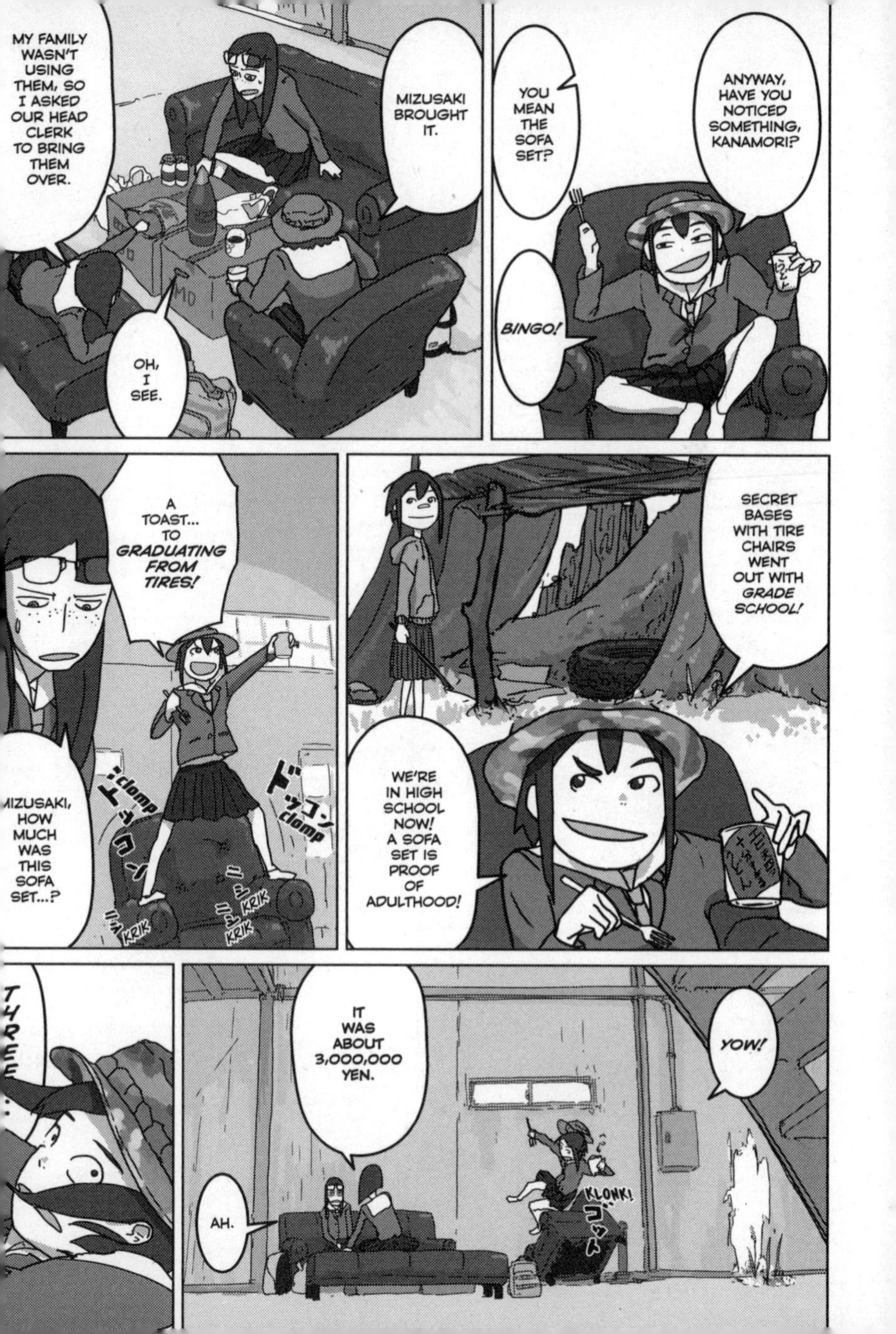
ANYWAY, HAVE YOU NOTICED SOMETHING, KANAMORI?
YOU MEAN THE SOFA SET?
BINGO!
MIZUSAKI BROUGHT IT.
MY FAMILY WASN'T USING THEM, SO I ASKED OUR HEAD CLERK TO BRING THEM OVER.
OH, I SEE.
SECRET BASES WITH TIRE CHAIRS WENT OUT WITH GRADE SCHOOL!
WE'RE IN HIGH SCHOOL NOW! A SOFA SET IS PROOF OF ADULTHOOD!
A TOAST... TO GRADUATING FROM TIRES!
clomp
clomp
KRIK
KRIK
MIZUSAKI, HOW MUCH WAS THIS SOFA SET...?
YOW!
IT WAS ABOUT 3,000,000 YEN.
KLONK!
AH.
THREE...

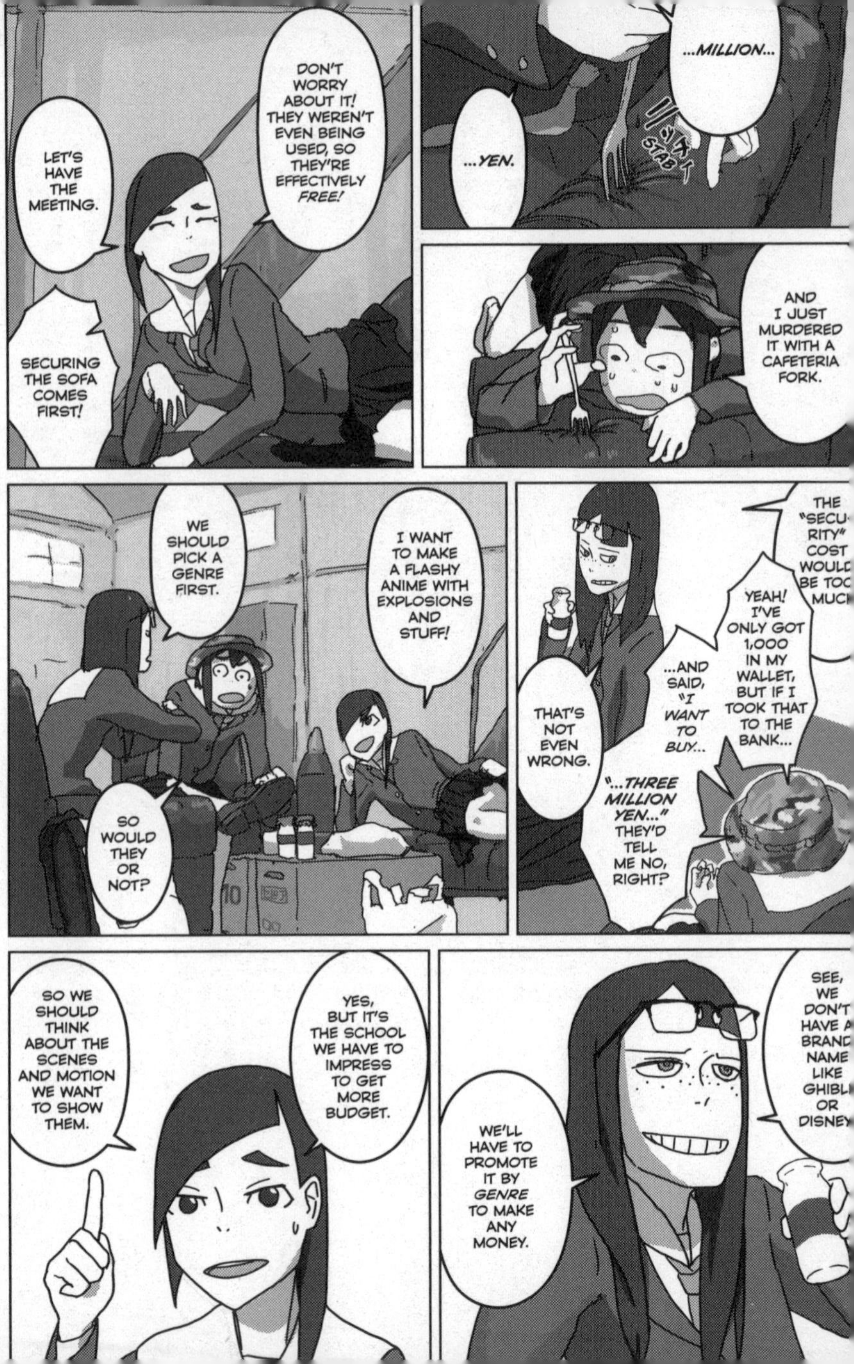
...MILLION...
...YEN.
STAB
AND I JUST MURDERED IT WITH A CAFETERIA FORK.
DON'T WORRY ABOUT IT! THEY WEREN'T EVEN BEING USED, SO THEY'RE EFFECTIVELY *FREE!*
LET'S HAVE THE MEETING.
SECURING THE SOFA COMES FIRST!
THE "SECU-RITY" COST WOULD BE TOO MUCH
YEAH! I'VE ONLY GOT 1,000 IN MY WALLET, BUT IF I TOOK THAT TO THE BANK...
...AND SAID, "*I WANT TO BUY...*
"*...THREE MILLION YEN...*" THEY'D TELL ME NO, RIGHT?
THAT'S NOT EVEN WRONG.
I WANT TO MAKE A FLASHY ANIME WITH EXPLOSIONS AND STUFF!
WE SHOULD PICK A GENRE FIRST.
SO WOULD THEY OR NOT?
SEE, WE DON'T HAVE A BRAND NAME LIKE GHIBLI OR DISNEY
WE'LL HAVE TO PROMOTE IT BY *GENRE* TO MAKE ANY MONEY.
YES, BUT IT'S THE SCHOOL WE HAVE TO IMPRESS TO GET MORE BUDGET.
SO WE SHOULD THINK ABOUT THE SCENES AND MOTION WE WANT TO SHOW THEM.

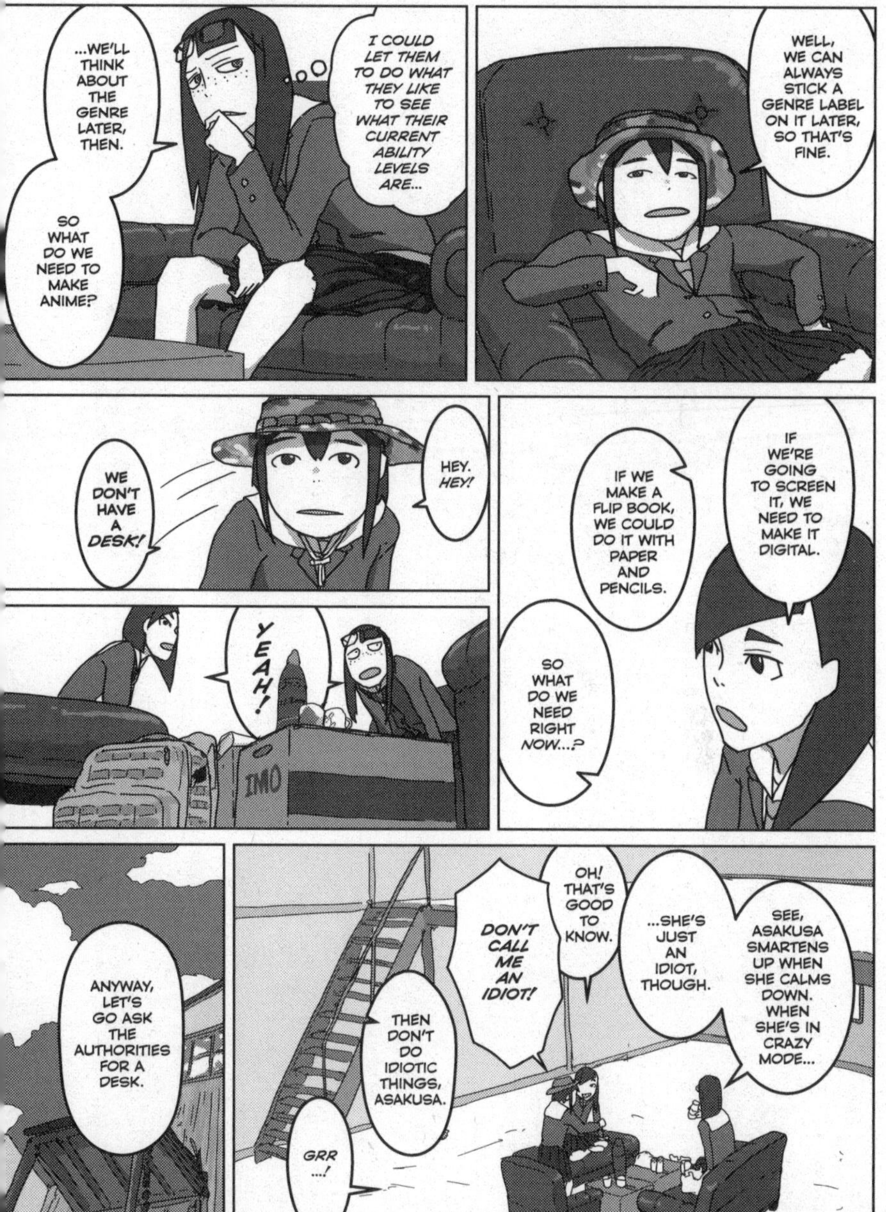
WELL, WE CAN ALWAYS STICK A GENRE LABEL ON IT LATER, SO THAT'S FINE.
I COULD LET THEM TO DO WHAT THEY LIKE TO SEE WHAT THEIR CURRENT ABILITY LEVELS ARE...
...WE'LL THINK ABOUT THE GENRE LATER, THEN.
SO WHAT DO WE NEED TO MAKE ANIME?
IF WE'RE GOING TO SCREEN IT, WE NEED TO MAKE IT DIGITAL.
IF WE MAKE A FLIP BOOK, WE COULD DO IT WITH PAPER AND PENCILS.
SO WHAT DO WE NEED RIGHT NOW...?
HEY. HEY!
WE DON'T HAVE A DESK!
YEAH!
IMO
SEE, ASAKUSA SMARTENS UP WHEN SHE CALMS DOWN. WHEN SHE'S IN CRAZY MODE...
...SHE'S JUST AN IDIOT, THOUGH.
OH! THAT'S GOOD TO KNOW.
DON'T CALL ME AN IDIOT!
THEN DON'T DO IDIOTIC THINGS, ASAKUSA.
GRR...!
ANYWAY, LET'S GO ASK THE AUTHORITIES FOR A DESK.

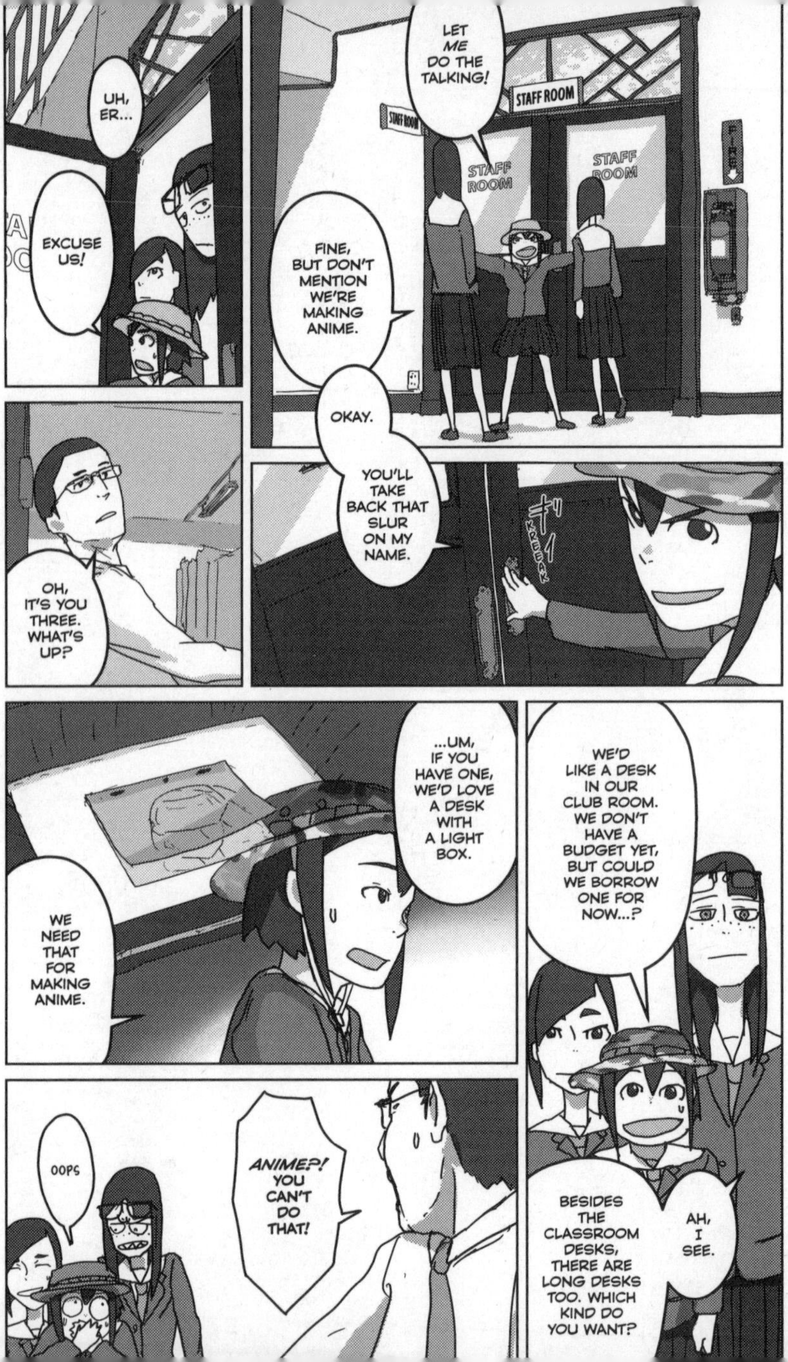
LET ME DO THE TALKING!
STAFF ROOM
FINE, BUT DON'T MENTION WE'RE MAKING ANIME.
OKAY.
UH, ER...
EXCUSE US!
YOU'LL TAKE BACK THAT SLUR ON MY NAME.
KREEAK
OH, IT'S YOU THREE. WHAT'S UP?
WE'D LIKE A DESK IN OUR CLUB ROOM. WE DON'T HAVE A BUDGET YET, BUT COULD WE BORROW ONE FOR NOW...?
...UM, IF YOU HAVE ONE, WE'D LOVE A DESK WITH A LIGHT BOX.
WE NEED THAT FOR MAKING ANIME.
AH, I SEE.
BESIDES THE CLASSROOM DESKS, THERE ARE LONG DESKS TOO. WHICH KIND DO YOU WANT?
ANIME?! YOU CAN'T DO THAT!
OOPS

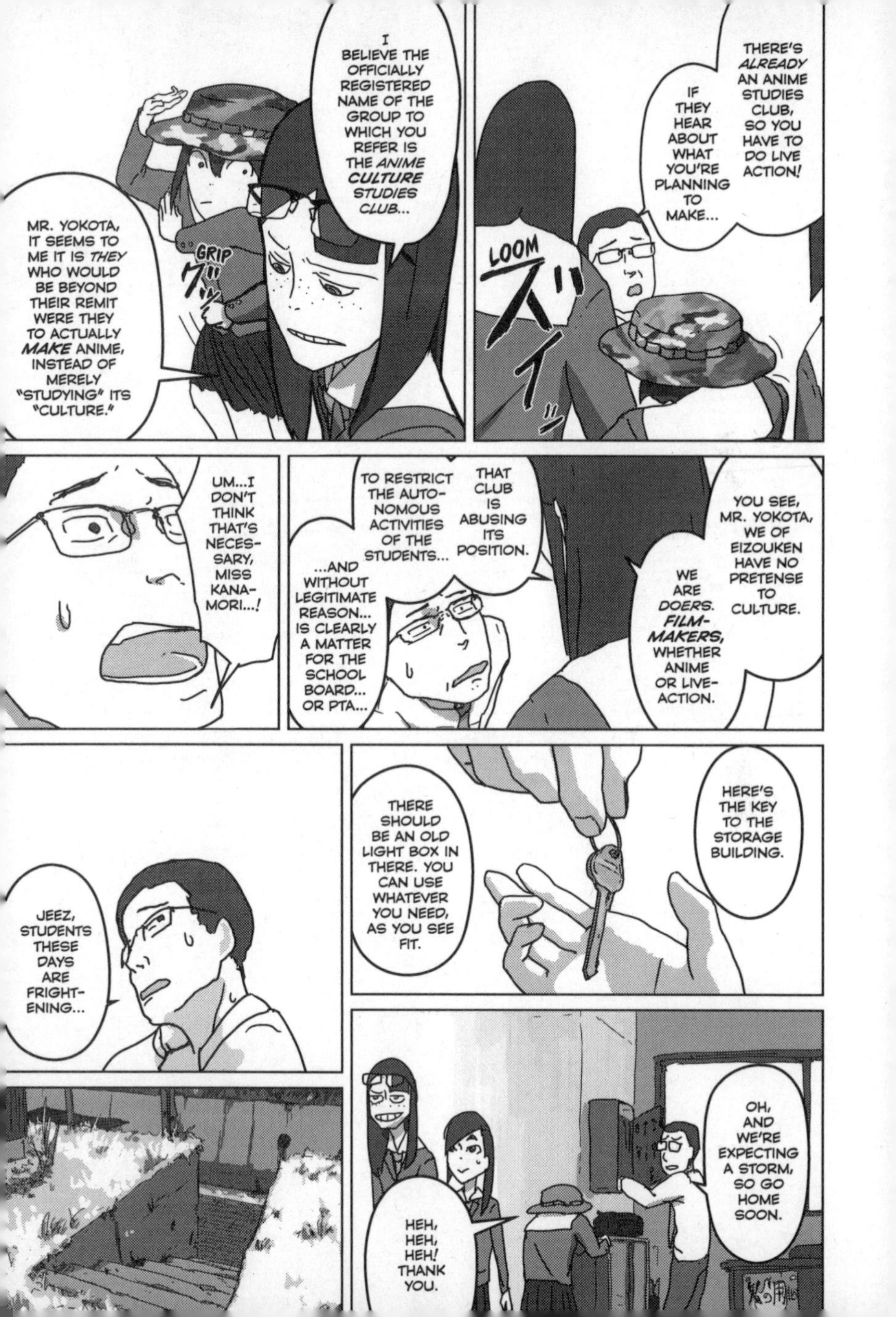
THERE'S *ALREADY* AN ANIME STUDIES CLUB, SO YOU HAVE TO DO LIVE ACTION!
IF THEY HEAR ABOUT WHAT YOU'RE PLANNING TO MAKE...
LOOM
I BELIEVE THE OFFICIALLY REGISTERED NAME OF THE GROUP TO WHICH YOU REFER IS THE *ANIME CULTURE STUDIES CLUB*...
MR. YOKOTA, IT SEEMS TO ME IT IS *THEY* WHO WOULD BE BEYOND THEIR REMIT WERE THEY TO ACTUALLY ***MAKE*** ANIME, INSTEAD OF MERELY "STUDYING" ITS "CULTURE."
GRIP
YOU SEE, MR. YOKOTA, WE OF EIZOUKEN HAVE NO PRETENSE TO CULTURE.
WE ARE *DOERS*. ***FILMMAKERS,*** WHETHER ANIME OR LIVE-ACTION.
THAT CLUB IS ABUSING ITS POSITION.
TO RESTRICT THE AUTONOMOUS ACTIVITIES OF THE STUDENTS...
...AND WITHOUT LEGITIMATE REASON... IS CLEARLY A MATTER FOR THE SCHOOL BOARD... OR PTA...
UM...I DON'T THINK THAT'S NECESSARY, MISS KANAMORI...!
HERE'S THE KEY TO THE STORAGE BUILDING.
THERE SHOULD BE AN OLD LIGHT BOX IN THERE. YOU CAN USE WHATEVER YOU NEED, AS YOU SEE FIT.
JEEZ, STUDENTS THESE DAYS ARE FRIGHTENING...
OH, AND WE'RE EXPECTING A STORM, SO GO HOME SOON.
HEH, HEH, HEH! THANK YOU.

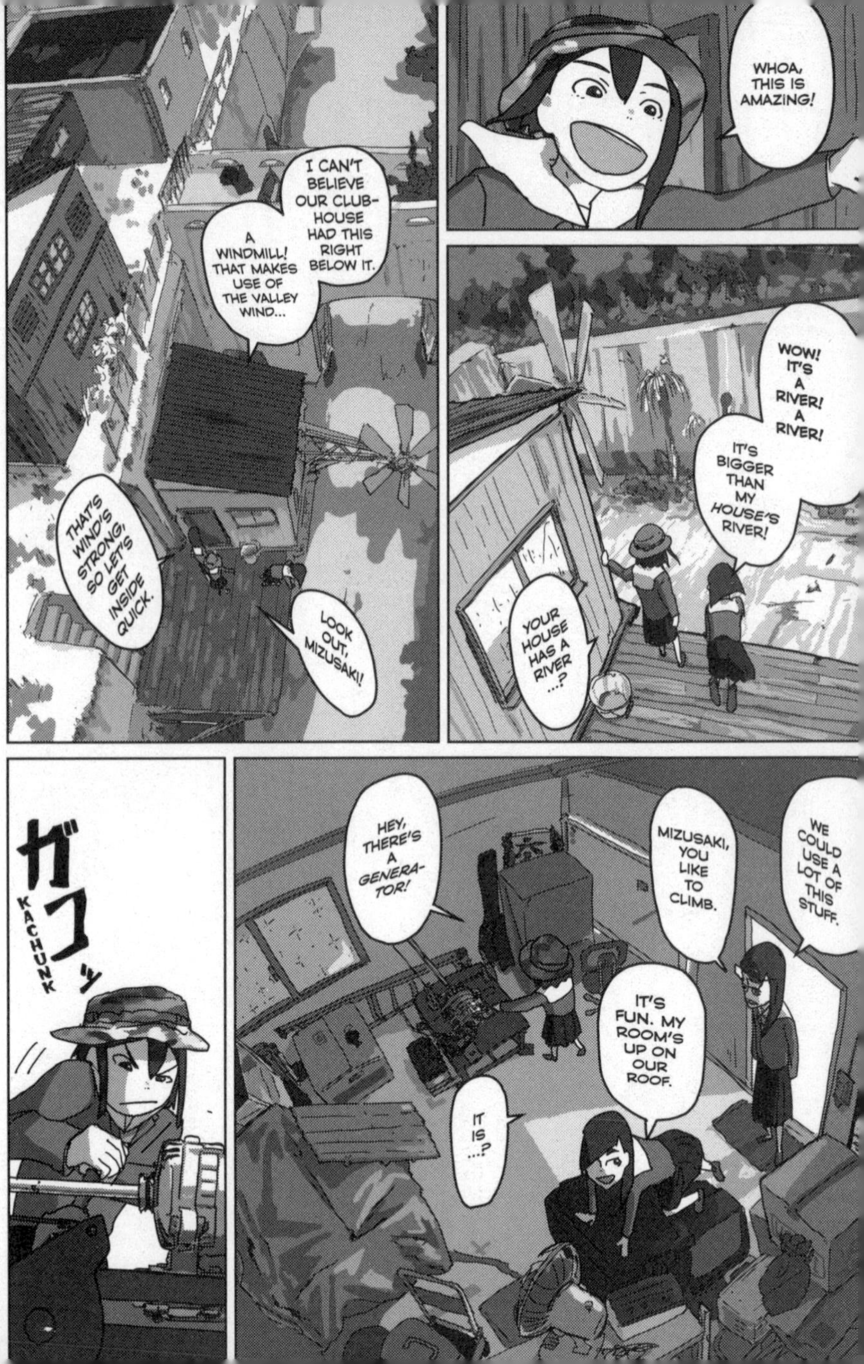
WHOA, THIS IS AMAZING!
WOW! IT'S A RIVER! A RIVER!
IT'S BIGGER THAN MY *HOUSE'S* RIVER!
YOUR HOUSE HAS A RIVER ...?
I CAN'T BELIEVE OUR CLUB-HOUSE HAD THIS RIGHT BELOW IT.
A WINDMILL! THAT MAKES USE OF THE VALLEY WIND...
THAT'S WIND'S STRONG, SO LET'S GET INSIDE QUICK.
LOOK OUT, MIZUSAKI!
WE COULD USE A LOT OF THIS STUFF.
MIZUSAKI, YOU LIKE TO CLIMB.
HEY, THERE'S A *GENERA-TOR!*
IT'S FUN. MY ROOM'S UP ON OUR ROOF.
IT IS ...?
ガコッ
KACHUNK

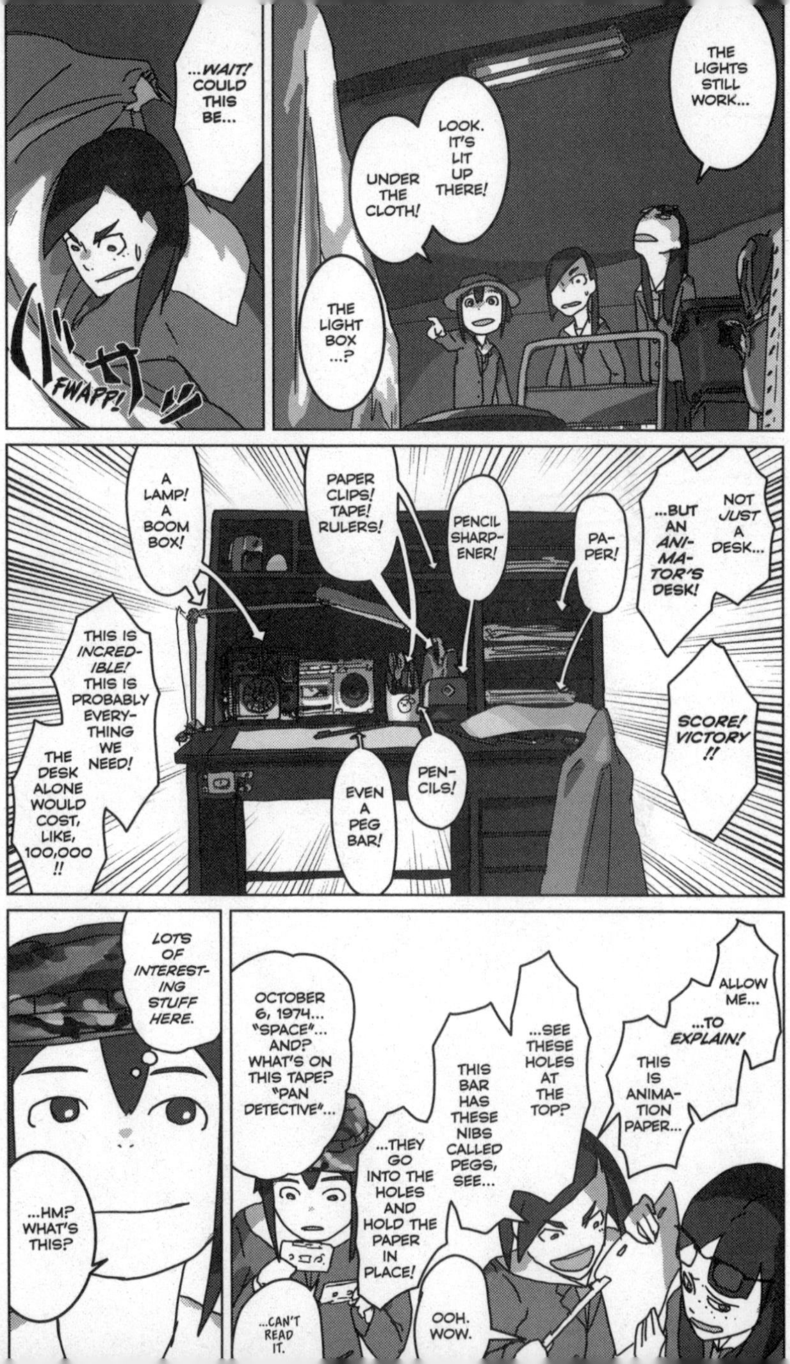
THE LIGHTS STILL WORK...
LOOK. IT'S LIT UP THERE!
UNDER THE CLOTH!
THE LIGHT BOX ...?
...WAIT! COULD THIS BE...
FWAPP!
NOT JUST A DESK...
...BUT AN ANIMATOR'S DESK!
PAPER!
PENCIL SHARPENER!
PAPER CLIPS! TAPE! RULERS!
A LAMP! A BOOM BOX!
SCORE! VICTORY!!
PENCILS!
EVEN A PEG BAR!
THIS IS INCREDIBLE! THIS IS PROBABLY EVERYTHING WE NEED!
THE DESK ALONE WOULD COST, LIKE, 100,000!!
ALLOW ME...
...TO EXPLAIN!
THIS IS ANIMATION PAPER...
...SEE THESE HOLES AT THE TOP?
THIS BAR HAS THESE NIBS CALLED PEGS, SEE...
...THEY GO INTO THE HOLES AND HOLD THE PAPER IN PLACE!
OCTOBER 6, 1974... "SPACE"... AND? WHAT'S ON THIS TAPE? "PAN DETECTIVE"...
OOH. WOW.
...CAN'T READ IT.
LOTS OF INTERESTING STUFF HERE.
...HM? WHAT'S THIS?

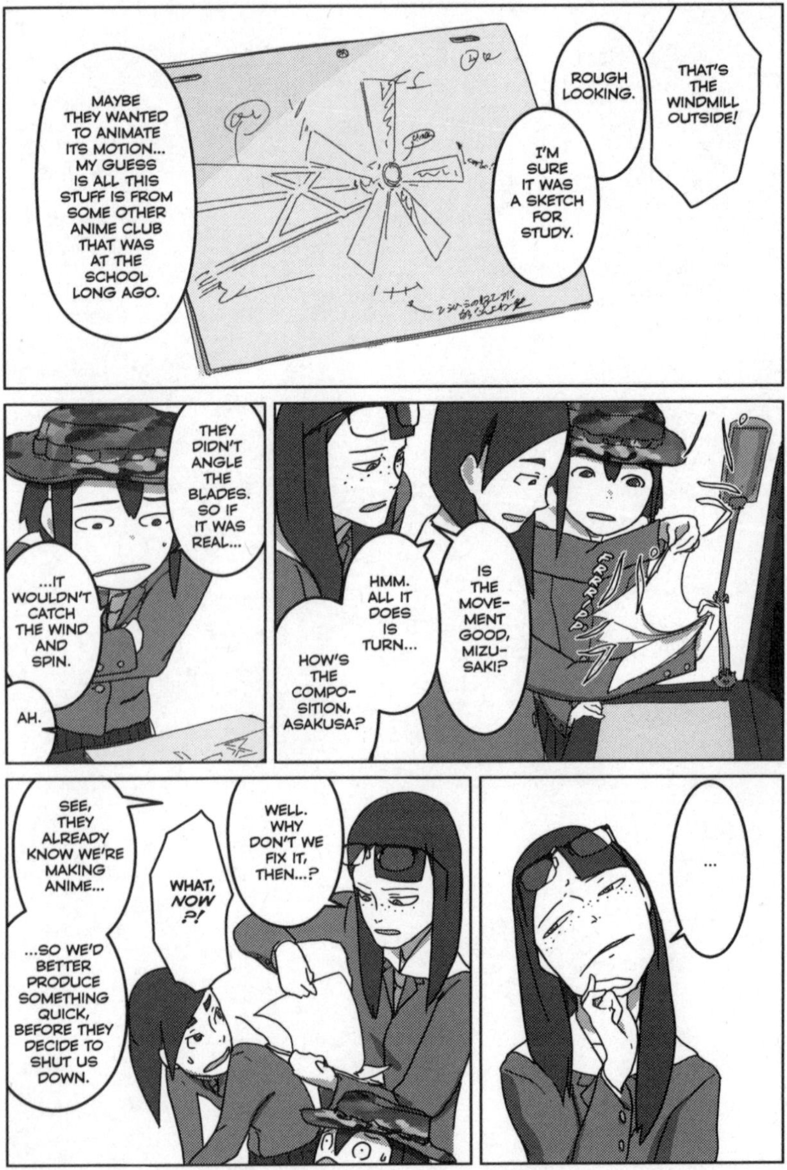
THAT'S THE WINDMILL OUTSIDE!
ROUGH LOOKING.
I'M SURE IT WAS A SKETCH FOR STUDY.
MAYBE THEY WANTED TO ANIMATE ITS MOTION... MY GUESS IS ALL THIS STUFF IS FROM SOME OTHER ANIME CLUB THAT WAS AT THE SCHOOL LONG AGO.
IS THE MOVEMENT GOOD, MIZUSAKI?
FRRR-PP
HMM. ALL IT DOES IS TURN...
HOW'S THE COMPOSITION, ASAKUSA?
THEY DIDN'T ANGLE THE BLADES. SO IF IT WAS REAL...
...IT WOULDN'T CATCH THE WIND AND SPIN.
AH.
...
WELL. WHY DON'T WE FIX IT, THEN...?
WHAT, *NOW*?!
SEE, THEY ALREADY KNOW WE'RE MAKING ANIME...
...SO WE'D BETTER PRODUCE SOMETHING QUICK, BEFORE THEY DECIDE TO SHUT US DOWN.

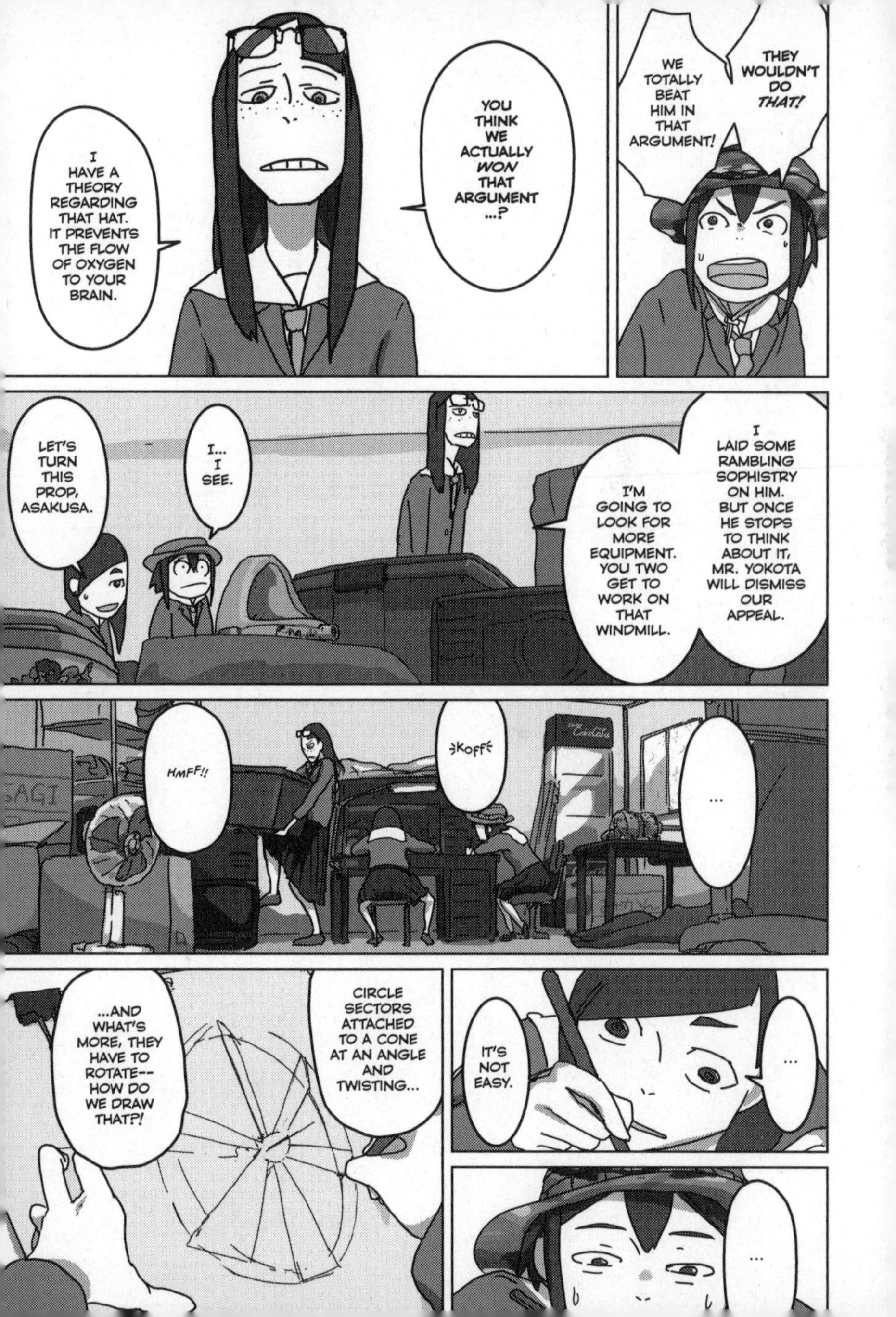
THEY WOULDN'T DO *THAT!*
WE TOTALLY BEAT HIM IN THAT ARGUMENT!
YOU THINK WE ACTUALLY *WON* THAT ARGUMENT ...?
I HAVE A THEORY REGARDING THAT HAT. IT PREVENTS THE FLOW OF OXYGEN TO YOUR BRAIN.
I LAID SOME RAMBLING SOPHISTRY ON HIM. BUT ONCE HE STOPS TO THINK ABOUT IT, MR. YOKOTA WILL DISMISS OUR APPEAL.
I'M GOING TO LOOK FOR MORE EQUIPMENT. YOU TWO GET TO WORK ON THAT WINDMILL.
I... I SEE.
LET'S TURN THIS PROP, ASAKUSA.
...
KOFF
HMFF!!
...
IT'S NOT EASY.
...
CIRCLE SECTORS ATTACHED TO A CONE AT AN ANGLE AND TWISTING...
...AND WHAT'S MORE, THEY HAVE TO ROTATE-- HOW DO WE DRAW THAT?!

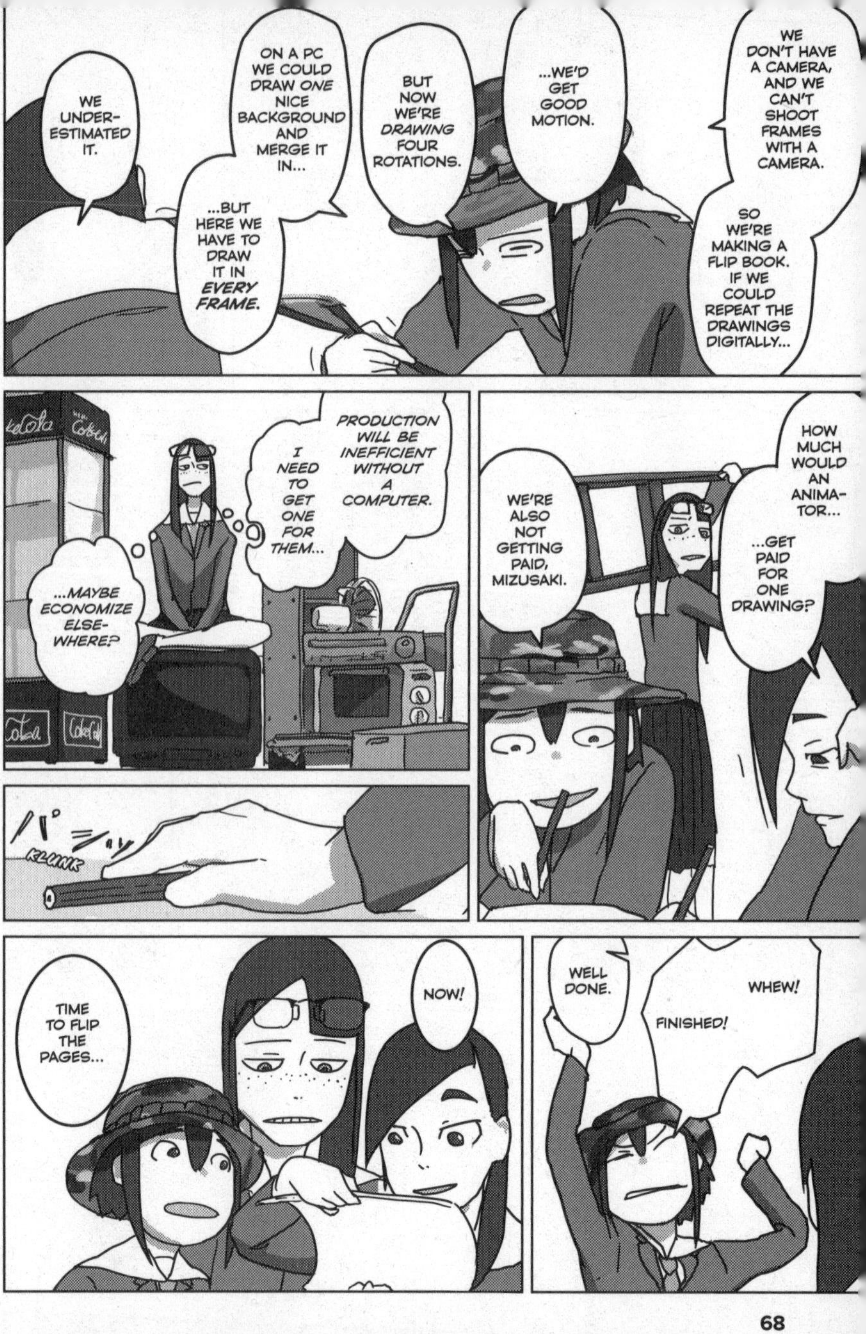
WE DON'T HAVE A CAMERA, AND WE CAN'T SHOOT FRAMES WITH A CAMERA.
SO WE'RE MAKING A FLIP BOOK. IF WE COULD REPEAT THE DRAWINGS DIGITALLY...
...WE'D GET GOOD MOTION.
BUT NOW WE'RE *DRAWING* FOUR ROTATIONS.
ON A PC WE COULD DRAW *ONE* NICE BACKGROUND AND MERGE IT IN...
...BUT HERE WE HAVE TO DRAW IT IN *EVERY FRAME*.
WE UNDER-ESTIMATED IT.
HOW MUCH WOULD AN ANIMATOR...
...GET PAID FOR ONE DRAWING?
WE'RE ALSO NOT GETTING PAID, MIZUSAKI.
PRODUCTION WILL BE INEFFICIENT WITHOUT A COMPUTER.
I NEED TO GET ONE FOR THEM...
...MAYBE ECONOMIZE ELSE-WHERE?
KLUNK
WELL DONE.
WHEW!
FINISHED!
NOW!
TIME TO FLIP THE PAGES...

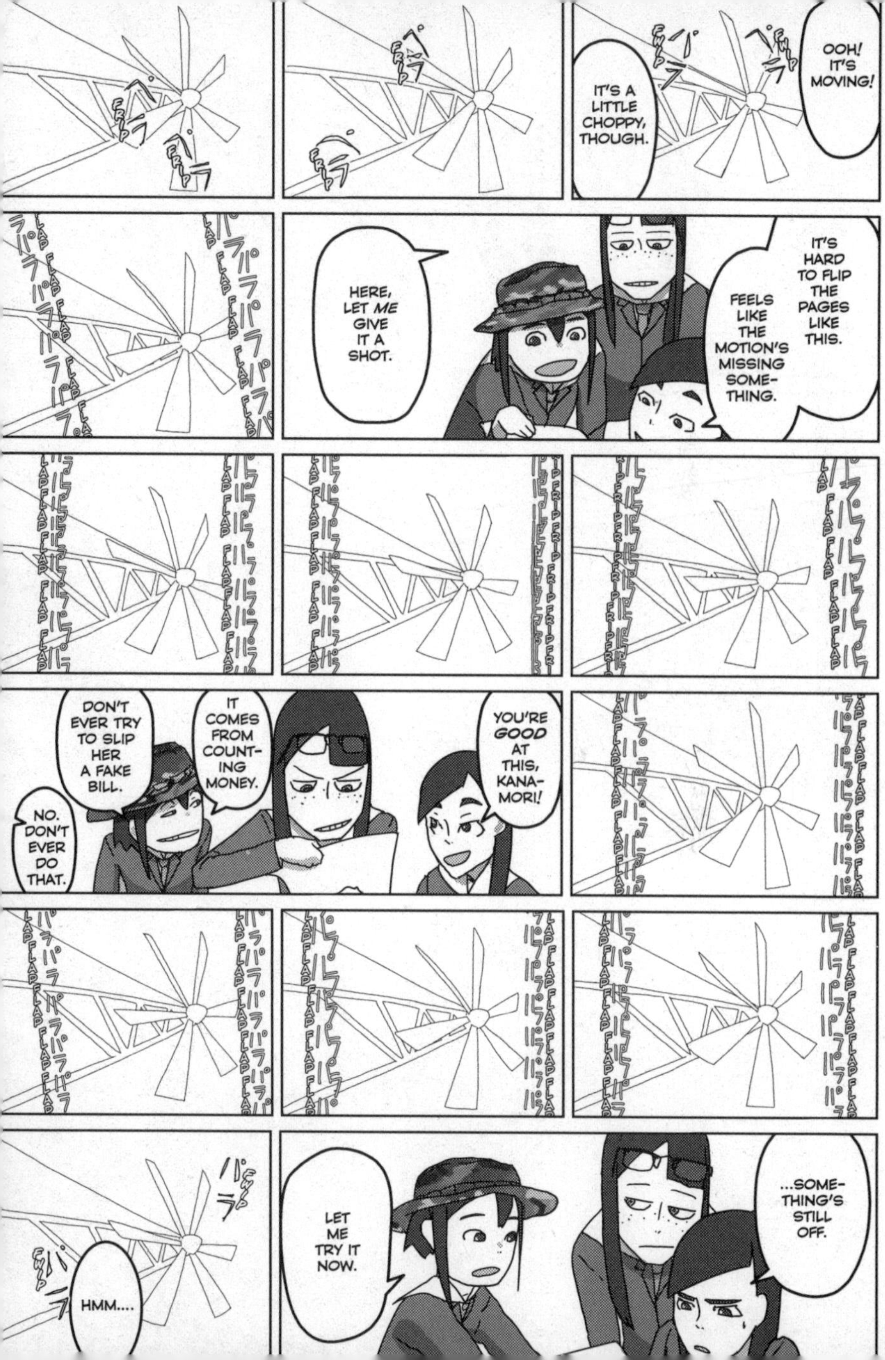
OOH! IT'S MOVING!
FWIP
IT'S A LITTLE CHOPPY, THOUGH.
FWIP
FRIP
FRIP
FRIP
FRIP
IT'S HARD TO FLIP THE PAGES LIKE THIS.
FEELS LIKE THE MOTION'S MISSING SOME-THING.
HERE, LET ME GIVE IT A SHOT.
FLAP FLAP FLAP
FLAP FLAP FLAP
FLAP FLAP FLAP
FRIP FRIP FRIP
FLAP FLAP FLAP
FLAP FLAP FLAP
FLAP FLAP FLAP
YOU'RE *GOOD* AT THIS, KANAMORI!
IT COMES FROM COUNTING MONEY.
DON'T EVER TRY TO SLIP HER A FAKE BILL.
NO. DON'T EVER DO THAT.
FLAP FLAP FLAP
FLAP FLAP FLAP
FLAP FLAP FLAP
...SOME-THING'S STILL OFF.
LET ME TRY IT NOW.
FWIP
FWIP
HMM....

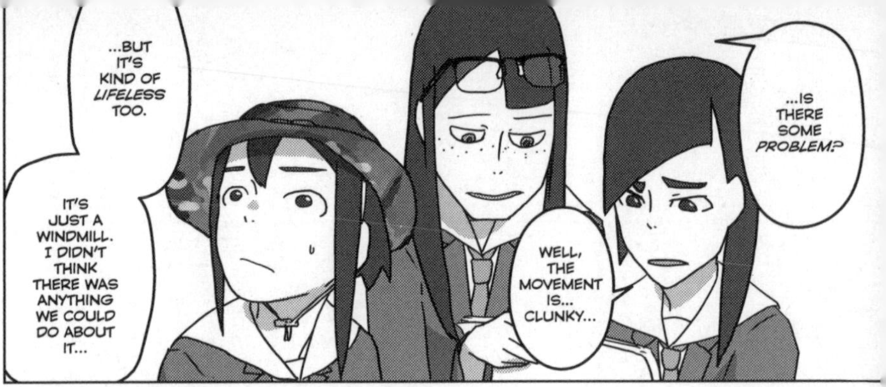
...IS THERE SOME *PROBLEM?*
WELL, THE MOVEMENT IS... CLUNKY...
...BUT IT'S KIND OF *LIFELESS* TOO.
IT'S JUST A WINDMILL. I DIDN'T THINK THERE WAS ANYTHING WE COULD DO ABOUT IT...
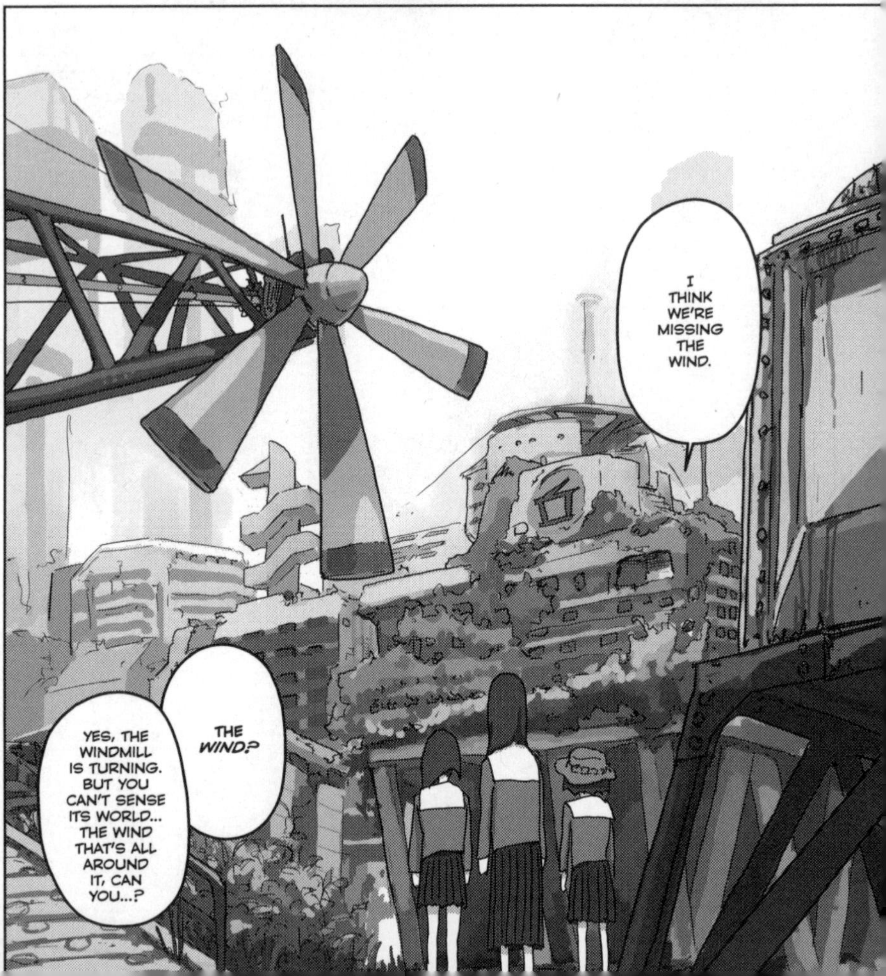
I THINK WE'RE MISSING THE WIND.
THE *WIND?*
YES, THE WINDMILL IS TURNING. BUT YOU CAN'T SENSE ITS WORLD... THE WIND THAT'S ALL AROUND IT, CAN YOU...?

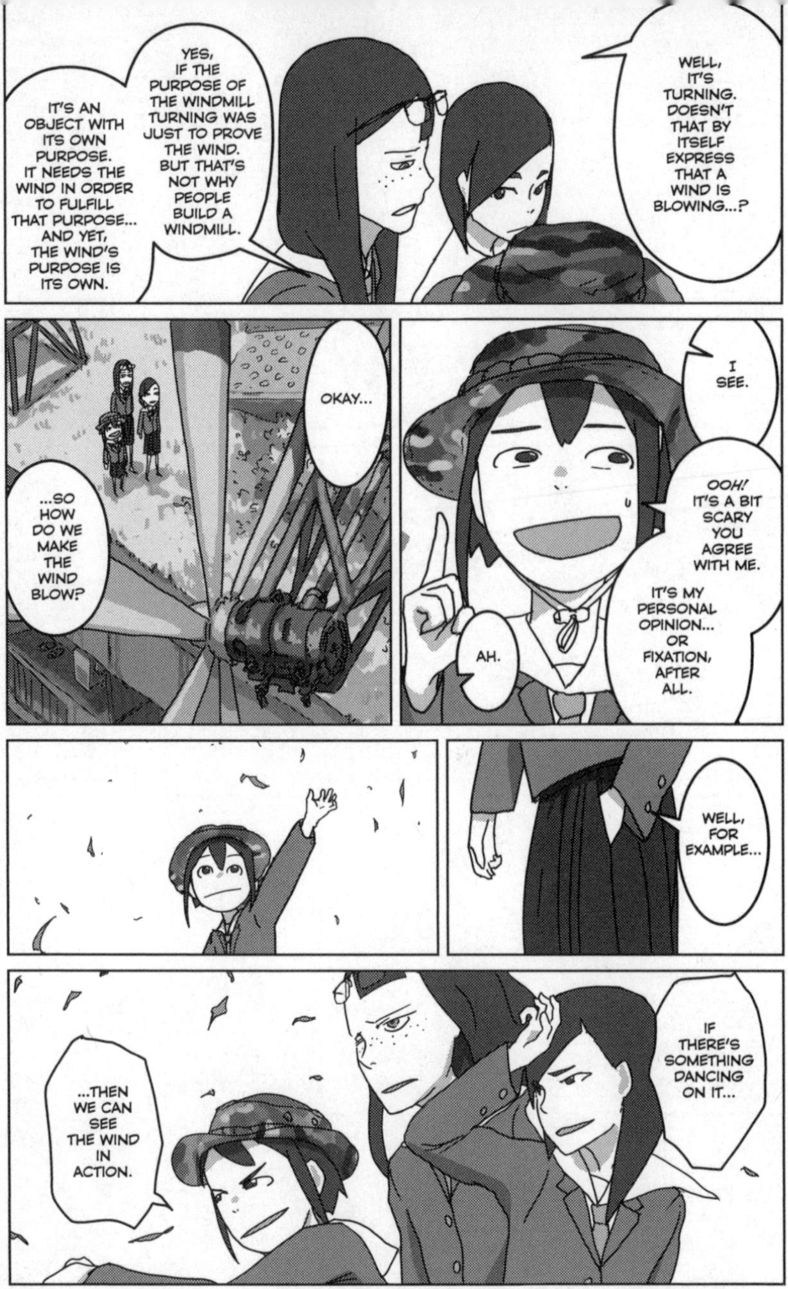
WELL, IT'S TURNING. DOESN'T THAT BY ITSELF EXPRESS THAT A WIND IS BLOWING...?
YES, IF THE PURPOSE OF THE WINDMILL TURNING WAS JUST TO PROVE THE WIND. BUT THAT'S NOT WHY PEOPLE BUILD A WINDMILL.
IT'S AN OBJECT WITH ITS OWN PURPOSE. IT NEEDS THE WIND IN ORDER TO FULFILL THAT PURPOSE... AND YET, THE WIND'S PURPOSE IS ITS OWN.
I SEE.
OOH! IT'S A BIT SCARY YOU AGREE WITH ME.
IT'S MY PERSONAL OPINION... OR FIXATION, AFTER ALL.
AH.
OKAY...
...SO HOW DO WE MAKE THE WIND BLOW?
WELL, FOR EXAMPLE...
IF THERE'S SOMETHING DANCING ON IT...
...THEN WE CAN SEE THE WIND IN ACTION.

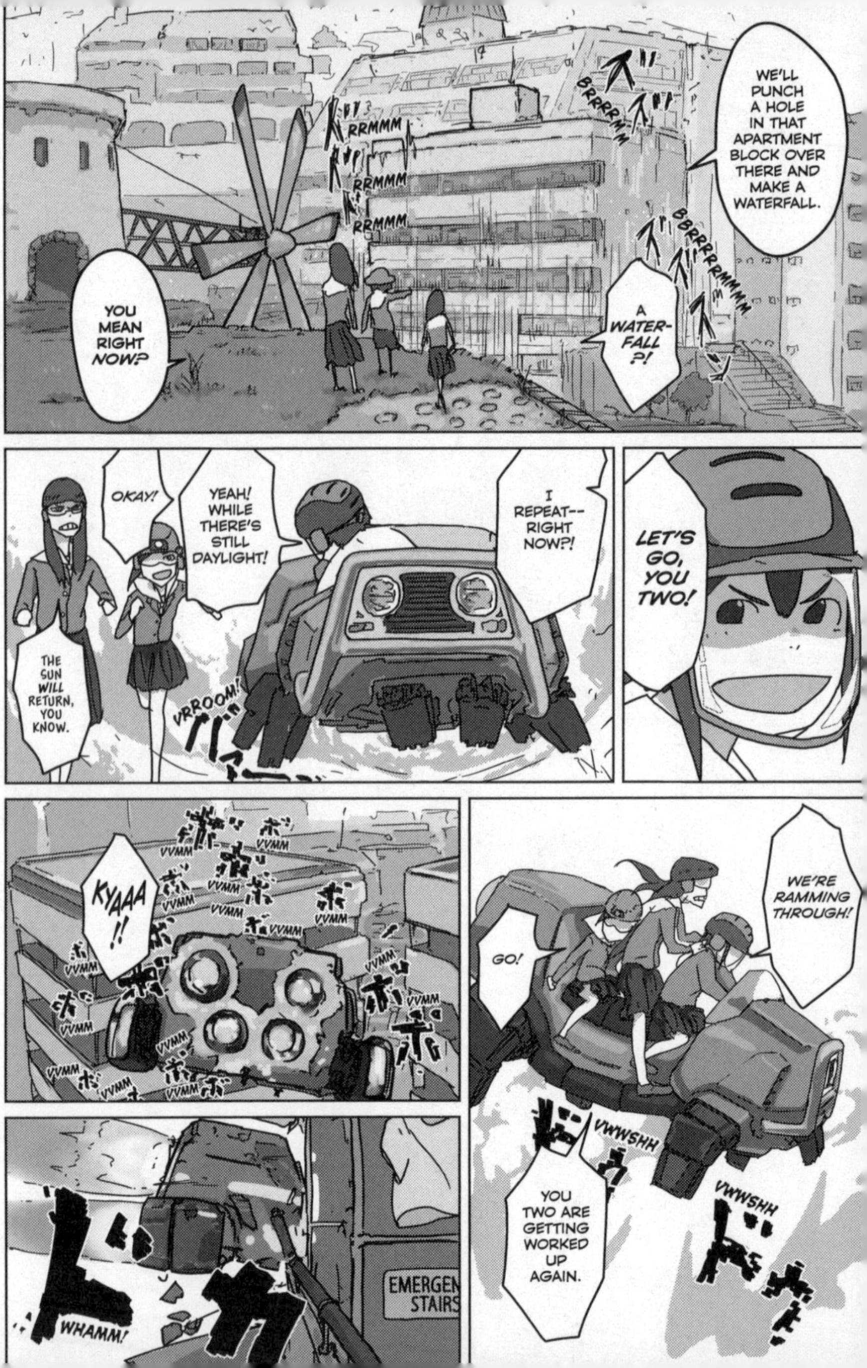
WE'LL PUNCH A HOLE IN THAT APARTMENT BLOCK OVER THERE AND MAKE A WATERFALL.
BRRRRMM
BBRRRRRMMMM
A WATERFALL?!
RRMMM
RRMMM
RRMMM
YOU MEAN RIGHT NOW?
LET'S GO, YOU TWO!
I REPEAT-- RIGHT NOW?!
YEAH! WHILE THERE'S STILL DAYLIGHT!
OKAY!
VRROOM!
THE SUN WILL RETURN, YOU KNOW.
WE'RE RAMMING THROUGH!
GO!
VWWSHH
VWWSHH
YOU TWO ARE GETTING WORKED UP AGAIN.
KYAAA!!
VVMM
WHAMM!
EMERGEN
STAIRS

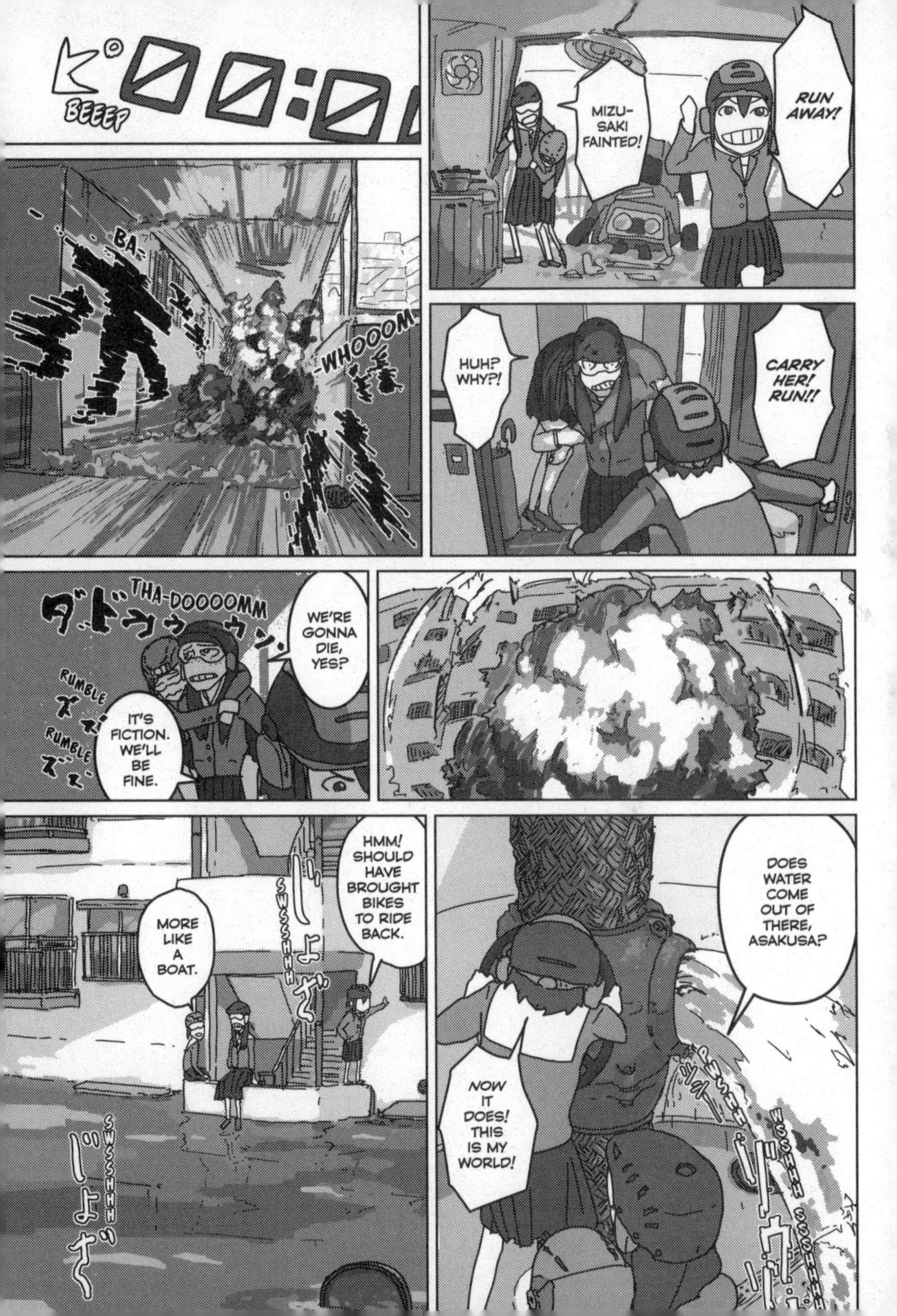
RUN AWAY!
MIZU-SAKI FAINTED!
BEEEP
00:0
CARRY HER! RUN!!
HUH? WHY?!
BA-
WHOOOM
THA-DOOOOMM
WE'RE GONNA DIE, YES?
IT'S FICTION. WE'LL BE FINE.
RUMBLE
RUMBLE
DOES WATER COME OUT OF THERE, ASAKUSA?
NOW IT DOES! THIS IS MY WORLD!
WSSHHH
SSSHHHH
HMM! SHOULD HAVE BROUGHT BIKES TO RIDE BACK.
MORE LIKE A BOAT.
SWSSHHH
SWSSHHH

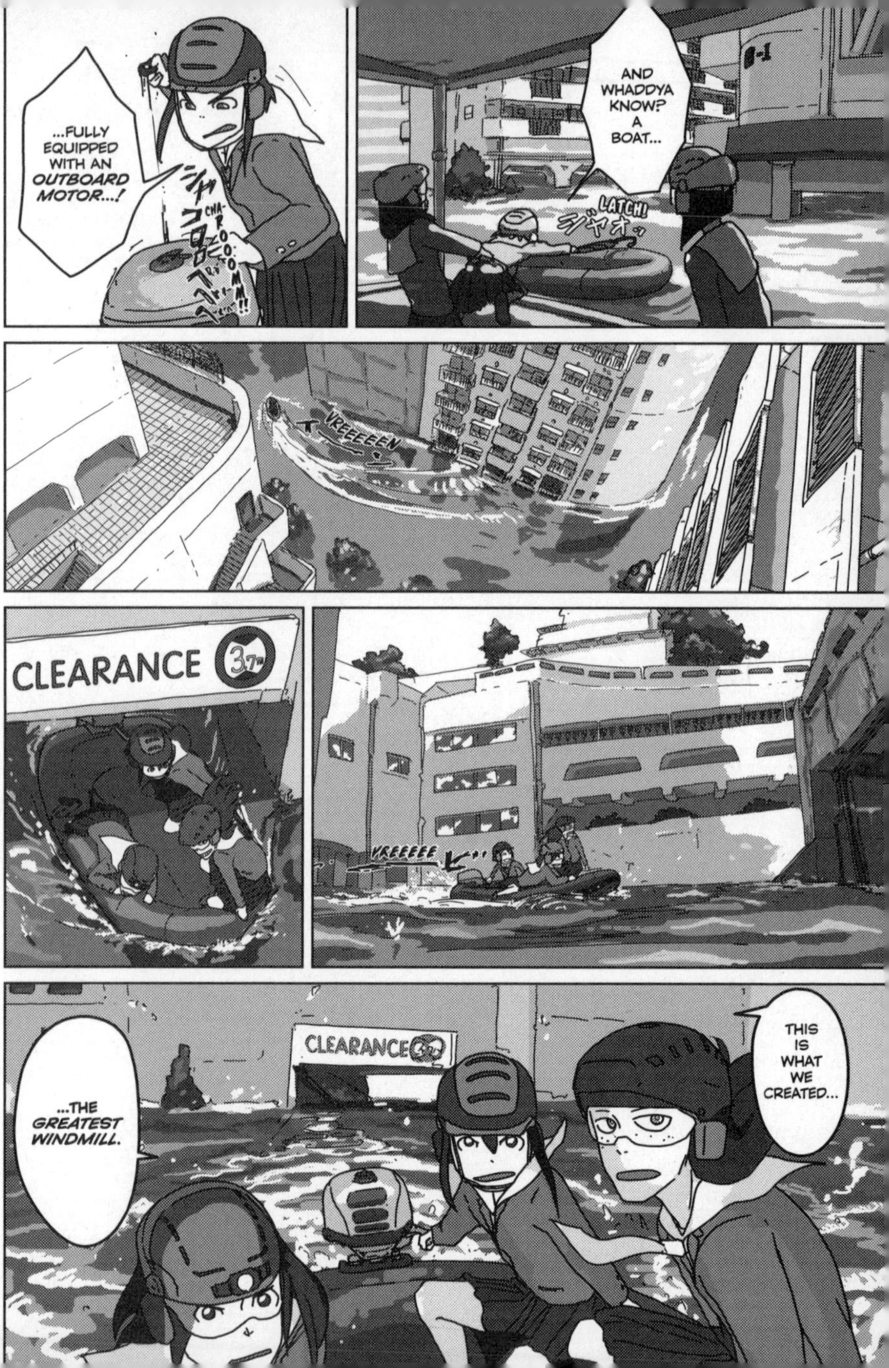
AND WHADDYA KNOW? A BOAT...
LATCH!
...FULLY EQUIPPED WITH AN OUTBOARD MOTOR...!
CHA-ROOOOOMM!!
VREEEEEN
VREEEEEE
CLEARANCE 3.7m
THIS IS WHAT WE CREATED...
...THE GREATEST WINDMILL.
CLEARANCE

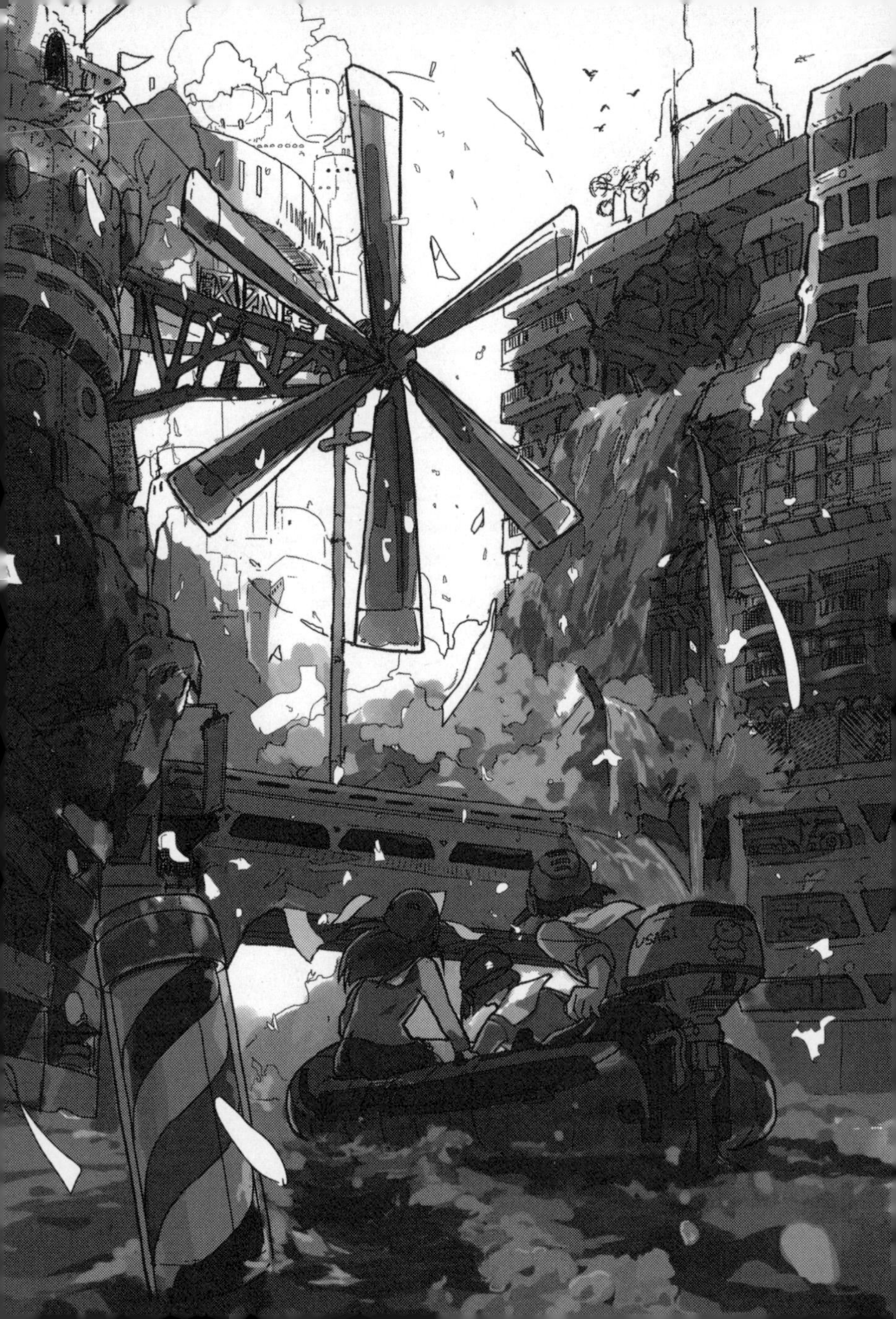

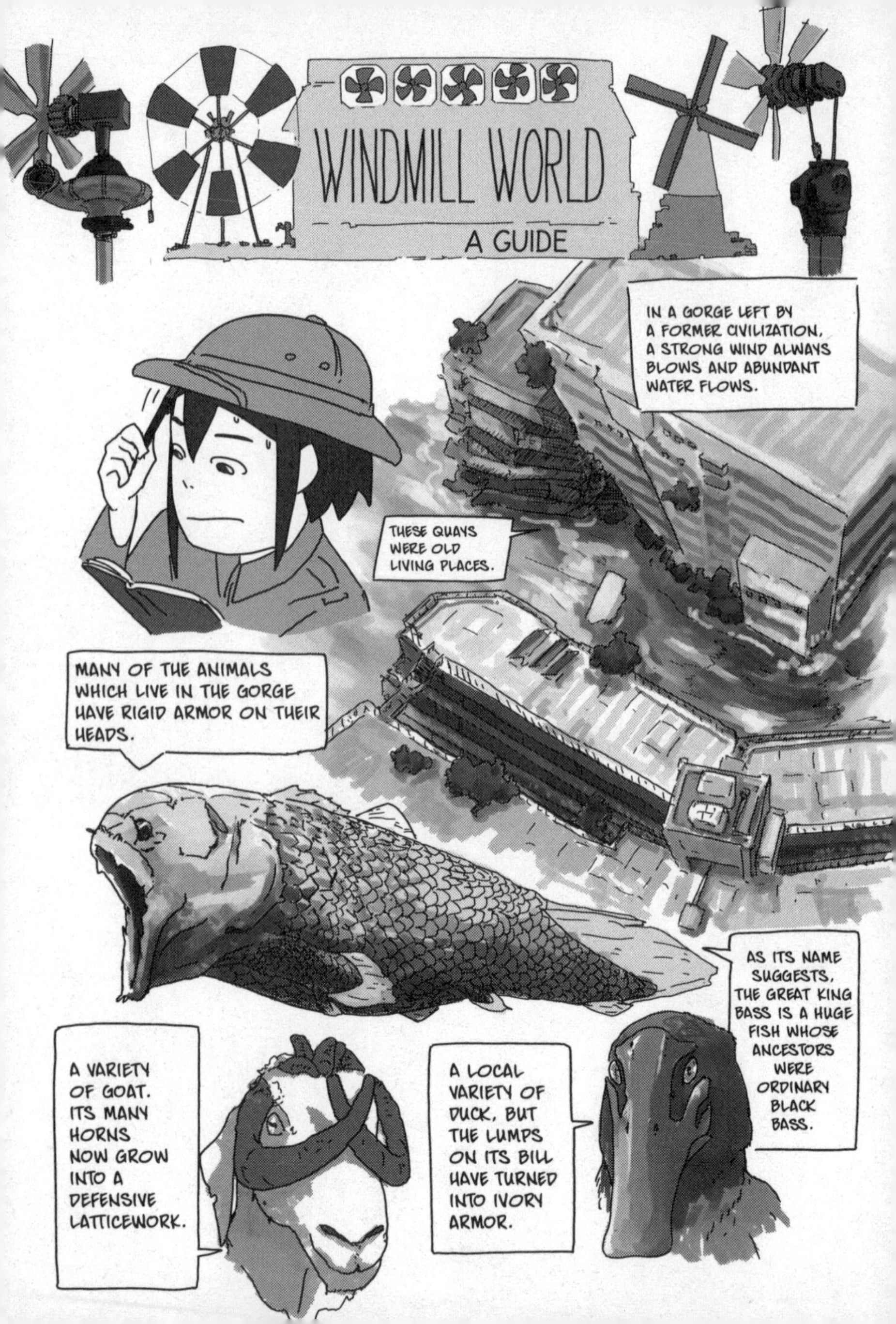
WINDMILL WORLD
A GUIDE
IN A GORGE LEFT BY A FORMER CIVILIZATION, A STRONG WIND ALWAYS BLOWS AND ABUNDANT WATER FLOWS.
THESE QUAYS WERE OLD LIVING PLACES.
MANY OF THE ANIMALS WHICH LIVE IN THE GORGE HAVE RIGID ARMOR ON THEIR HEADS.
AS ITS NAME SUGGESTS, THE GREAT KING BASS IS A HUGE FISH WHOSE ANCESTORS WERE ORDINARY BLACK BASS.
A LOCAL VARIETY OF DUCK, BUT THE LUMPS ON ITS BILL HAVE TURNED INTO IVORY ARMOR.
A VARIETY OF GOAT. ITS MANY HORNS NOW GROW INTO A DEFENSIVE LATTICEWORK.

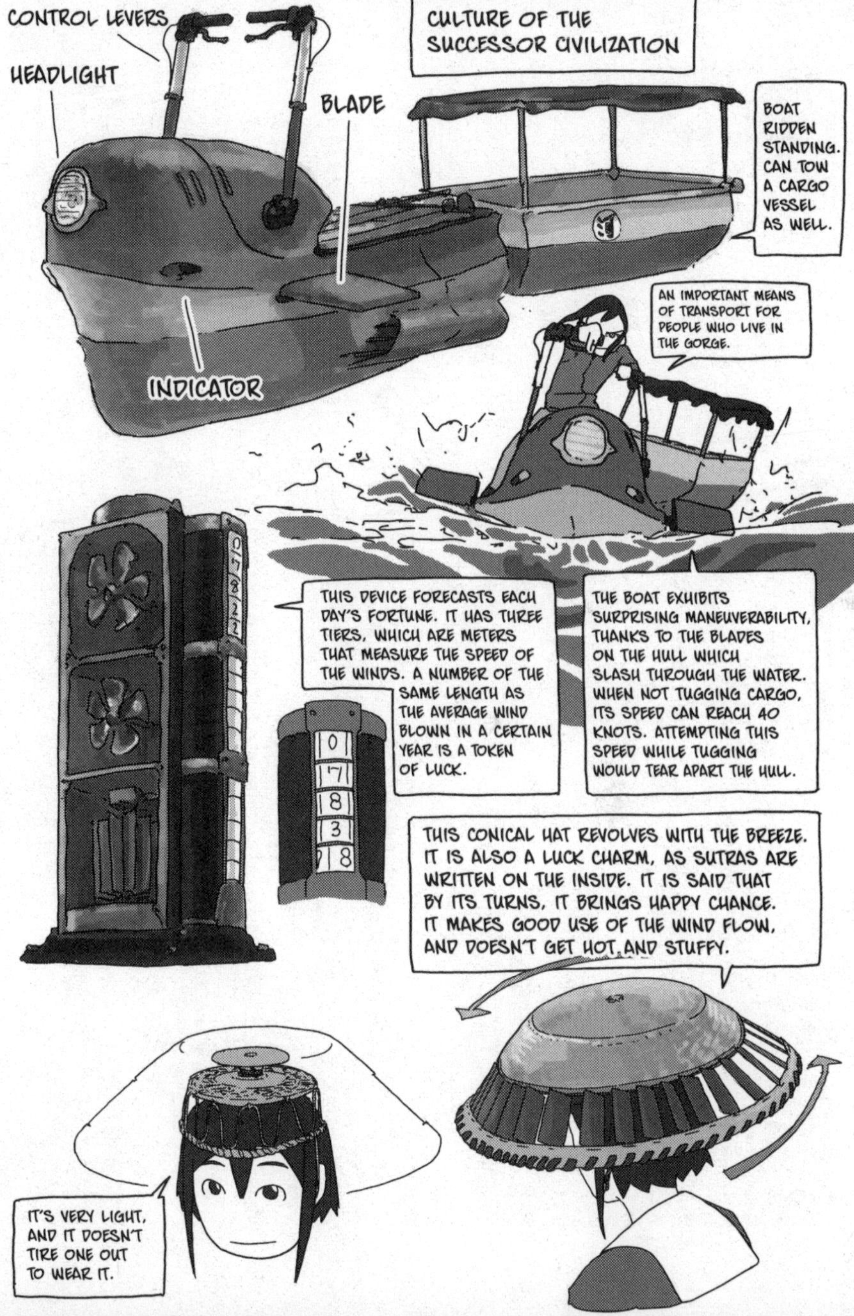
CULTURE OF THE SUCCESSOR CIVILIZATION
BOAT RIDDEN STANDING. CAN TOW A CARGO VESSEL AS WELL.
CONTROL LEVERS
HEADLIGHT
BLADE
INDICATOR
AN IMPORTANT MEANS OF TRANSPORT FOR PEOPLE WHO LIVE IN THE GORGE.
THE BOAT EXHIBITS SURPRISING MANEUVERABILITY, THANKS TO THE BLADES ON THE HULL WHICH SLASH THROUGH THE WATER. WHEN NOT TUGGING CARGO, ITS SPEED CAN REACH 40 KNOTS. ATTEMPTING THIS SPEED WHILE TUGGING WOULD TEAR APART THE HULL.
THIS DEVICE FORECASTS EACH DAY'S FORTUNE. IT HAS THREE TIERS, WHICH ARE METERS THAT MEASURE THE SPEED OF THE WINDS. A NUMBER OF THE SAME LENGTH AS THE AVERAGE WIND BLOWN IN A CERTAIN YEAR IS A TOKEN OF LUCK.
THIS CONICAL HAT REVOLVES WITH THE BREEZE. IT IS ALSO A LUCK CHARM, AS SUTRAS ARE WRITTEN ON THE INSIDE. IT IS SAID THAT BY ITS TURNS, IT BRINGS HAPPY CHANCE. IT MAKES GOOD USE OF THE WIND FLOW, AND DOESN'T GET HOT AND STUFFY.
IT'S VERY LIGHT, AND IT DOESN'T TIRE ONE OUT TO WEAR IT.

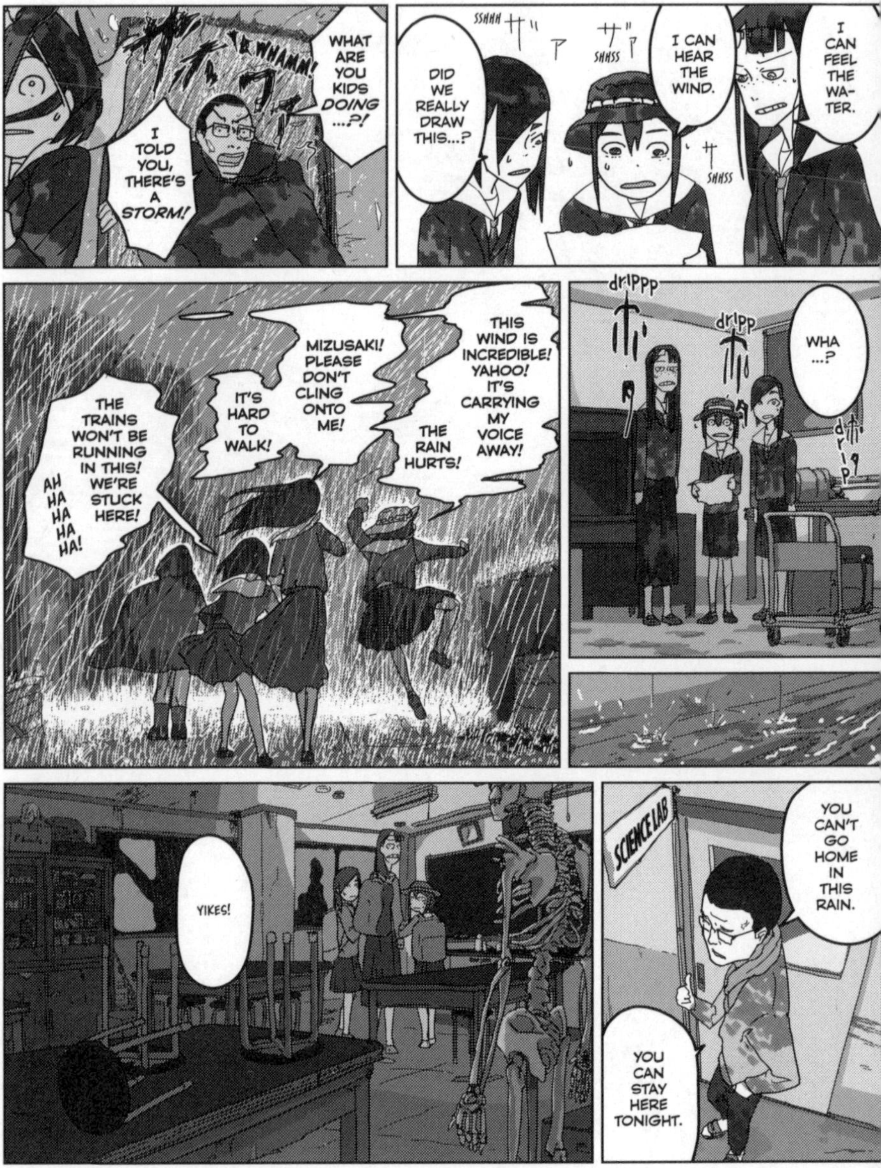
SSHHH ザァ
ザァ SHHSS
I CAN FEEL THE WATER.
I CAN HEAR THE WIND.
DID WE REALLY DRAW THIS...?
サ SHHSS
WHAT ARE YOU KIDS DOING ...?!
WHAMM!
I TOLD YOU, THERE'S A STORM!
drippp
dripp
WHA ...?
drip
THIS WIND IS INCREDIBLE! YAHOO! IT'S CARRYING MY VOICE AWAY!
THE RAIN HURTS!
MIZUSAKI! PLEASE DON'T CLING ONTO ME!
IT'S HARD TO WALK!
THE TRAINS WON'T BE RUNNING IN THIS! WE'RE STUCK HERE!
AH HA HA HA HA!
SCIENCE LAB
YOU CAN'T GO HOME IN THIS RAIN.
YOU CAN STAY HERE TONIGHT.
YIKES!

CHAPTER 4: EIZOUKEN'S DISASTER DAY

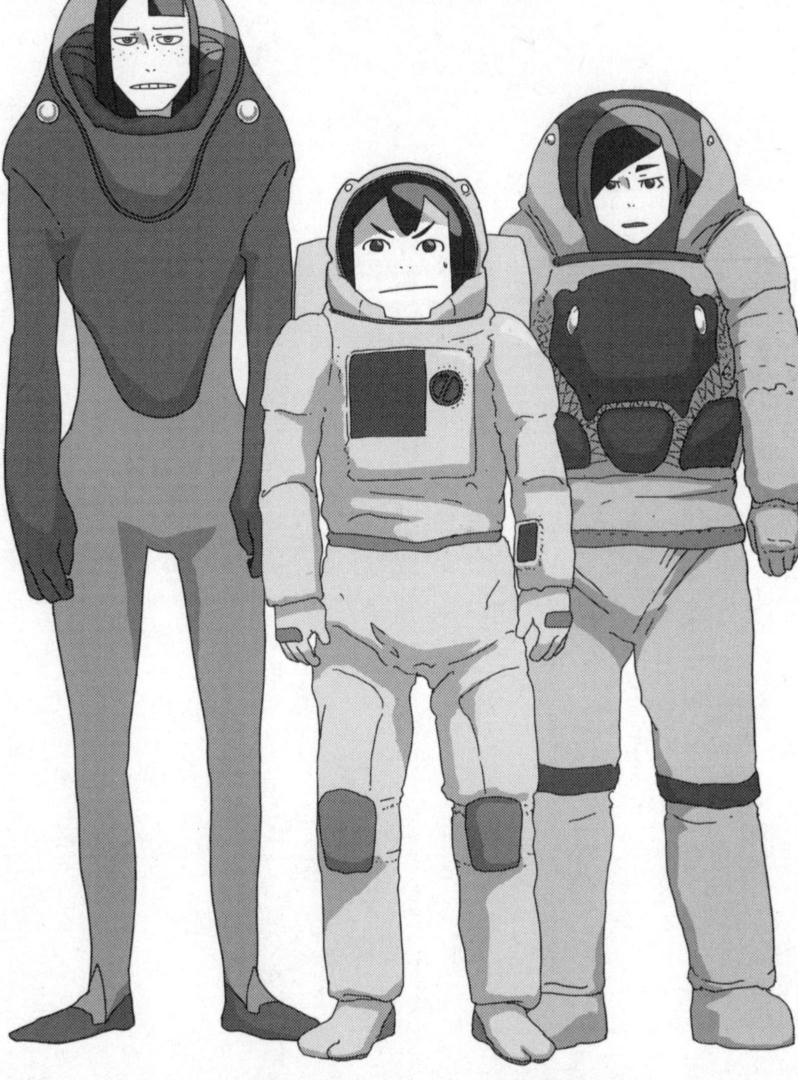

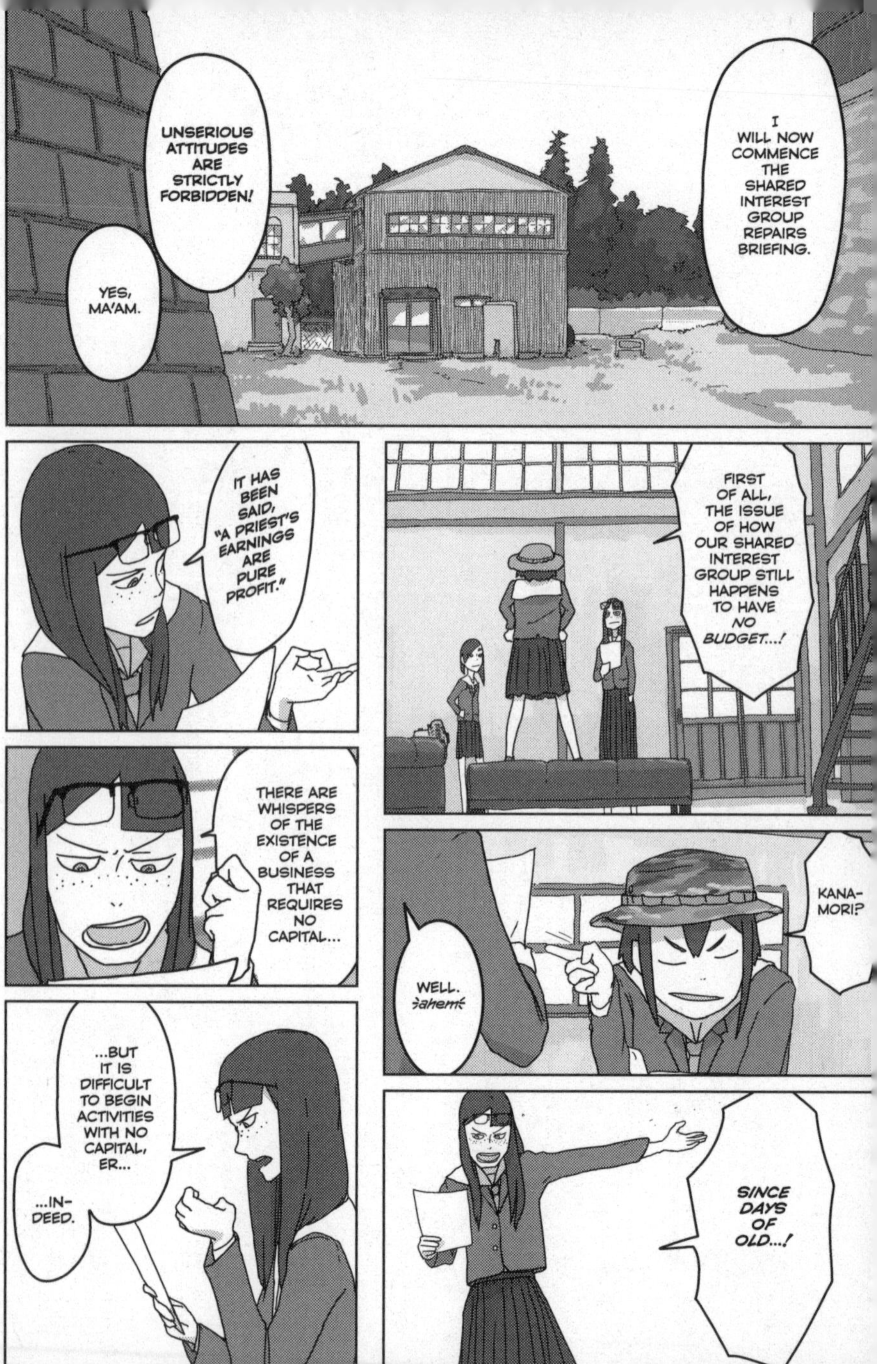
I WILL NOW COMMENCE THE SHARED INTEREST GROUP REPAIRS BRIEFING.
UNSERIOUS ATTITUDES ARE STRICTLY FORBIDDEN!
YES, MA'AM.
FIRST OF ALL, THE ISSUE OF HOW OUR SHARED INTEREST GROUP STILL HAPPENS TO HAVE *NO BUDGET*...!
IT HAS BEEN SAID, "A PRIEST'S EARNINGS ARE PURE PROFIT."
THERE ARE WHISPERS OF THE EXISTENCE OF A BUSINESS THAT REQUIRES NO CAPITAL...
KANAMORI?
WELL. *ahem*
SINCE DAYS OF OLD...!
...BUT IT IS DIFFICULT TO BEGIN ACTIVITIES WITH NO CAPITAL, ER...
...IN-DEED.

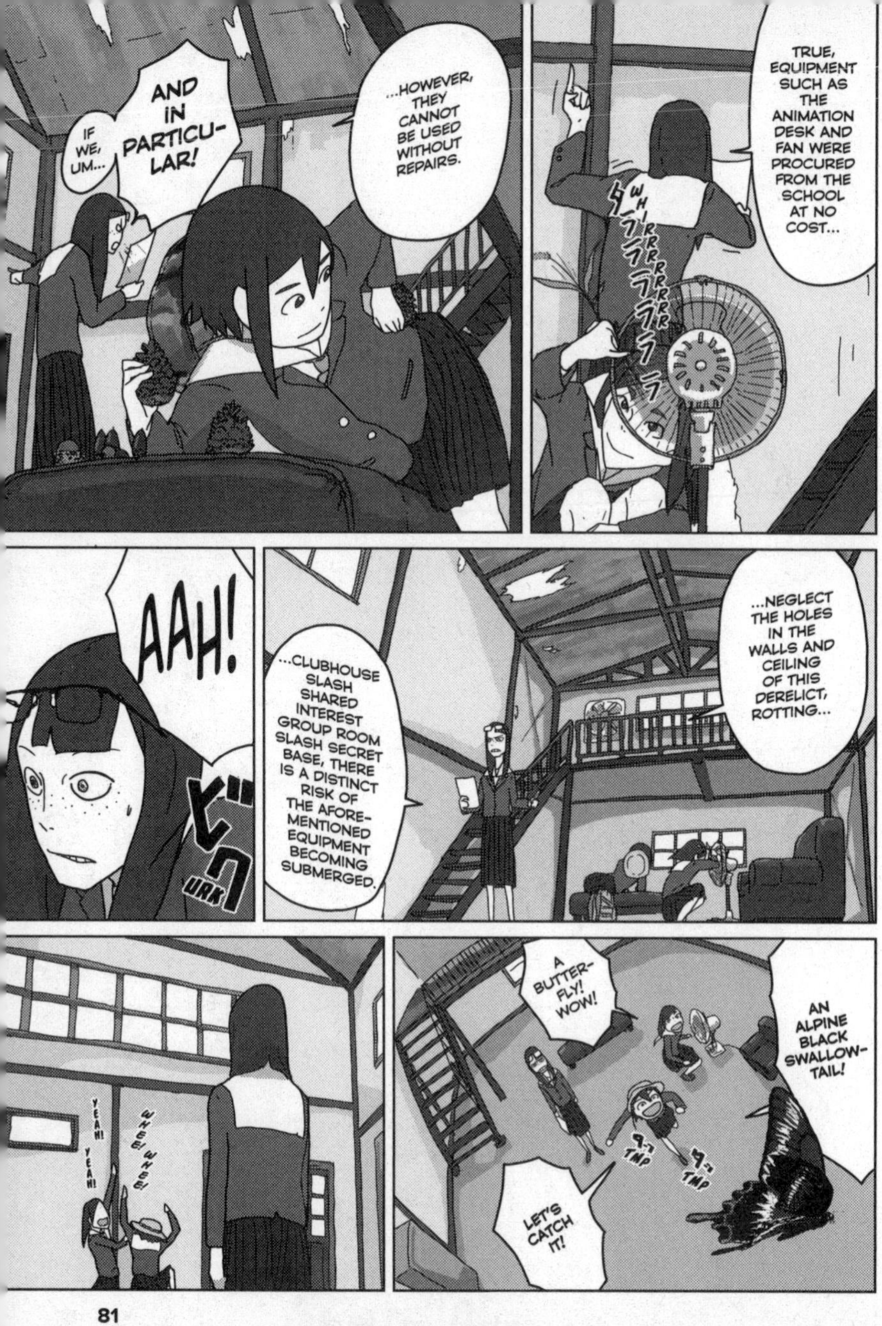
TRUE, EQUIPMENT SUCH AS THE ANIMATION DESK AND FAN WERE PROCURED FROM THE SCHOOL AT NO COST...
WHIRRRRRRR
...HOWEVER, THEY CANNOT BE USED WITHOUT REPAIRS.
AND IN PARTICU-LAR!
IF WE, UM...
...NEGLECT THE HOLES IN THE WALLS AND CEILING OF THIS DERELICT, ROTTING...
...CLUBHOUSE SLASH SHARED INTEREST GROUP ROOM SLASH SECRET BASE, THERE IS A DISTINCT RISK OF THE AFORE-MENTIONED EQUIPMENT BECOMING SUBMERGED.
AAH!
URK
A BUTTER-FLY! WOW!
AN ALPINE BLACK SWALLOW-TAIL!
TMP
TMP
LET'S CATCH IT!
WHEE! WHEE!
YEAH! YEAH!

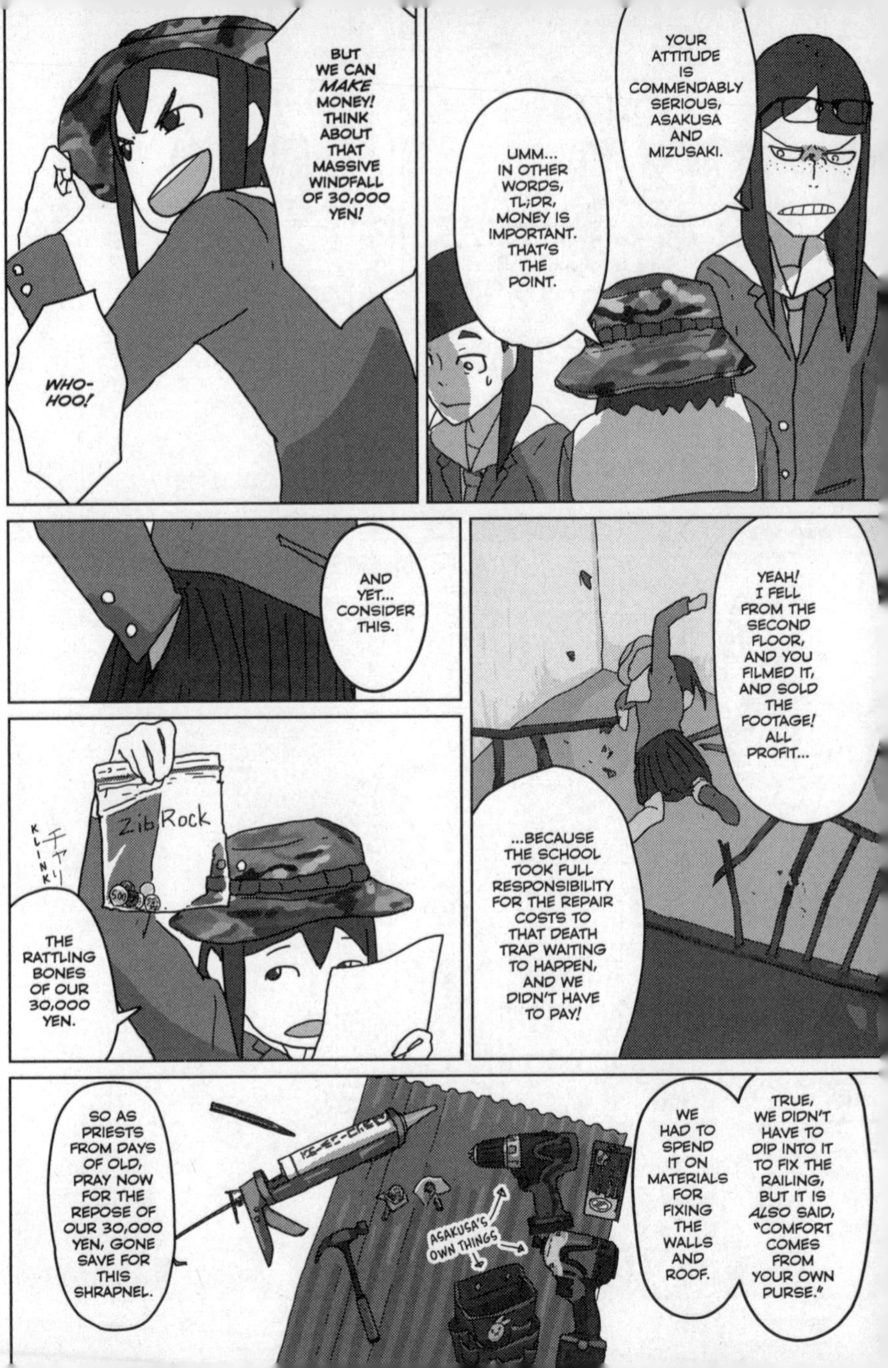
YOUR ATTITUDE IS COMMENDABLY SERIOUS, ASAKUSA AND MIZUSAKI.
UMM... IN OTHER WORDS, TL;DR, MONEY IS IMPORTANT. THAT'S THE POINT.
BUT WE CAN *MAKE* MONEY! THINK ABOUT THAT MASSIVE WINDFALL OF 30,000 YEN!
WHO-HOO!
YEAH! I FELL FROM THE SECOND FLOOR, AND YOU FILMED IT, AND SOLD THE FOOTAGE! ALL PROFIT...
...BECAUSE THE SCHOOL TOOK FULL RESPONSIBILITY FOR THE REPAIR COSTS TO THAT DEATH TRAP WAITING TO HAPPEN, AND WE DIDN'T HAVE TO PAY!
AND YET... CONSIDER THIS.
チャリ
KLINK
Zib Rock
THE RATTLING BONES OF OUR 30,000 YEN.
TRUE, WE DIDN'T HAVE TO DIP INTO IT TO FIX THE RAILING, BUT IT IS *ALSO* SAID, "COMFORT COMES FROM YOUR OWN PURSE."
WE HAD TO SPEND IT ON MATERIALS FOR FIXING THE WALLS AND ROOF.
ASAKUSA'S OWN THINGS
SO AS PRIESTS FROM DAYS OF OLD, PRAY NOW FOR THE REPOSE OF OUR 30,000 YEN, GONE SAVE FOR THIS SHRAPNEL.

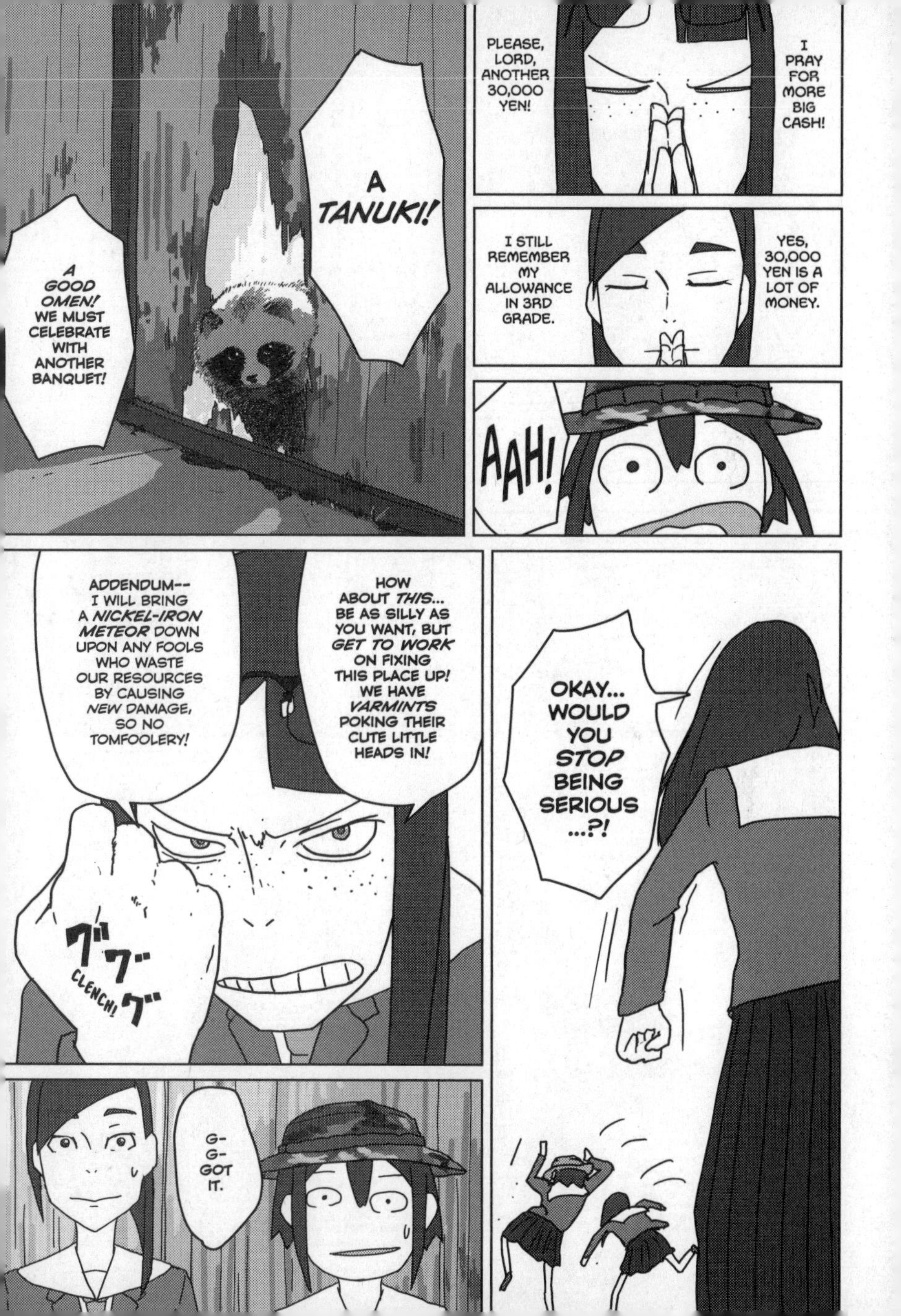
I PRAY FOR MORE BIG CASH!
PLEASE, LORD, ANOTHER 30,000 YEN!
YES, 30,000 YEN IS A LOT OF MONEY.
I STILL REMEMBER MY ALLOWANCE IN 3RD GRADE.
AAH!
A *TANUKI!*
A *GOOD OMEN!* WE MUST CELEBRATE WITH ANOTHER BANQUET!
OKAY... WOULD YOU *STOP* BEING SERIOUS ...?!
HOW ABOUT *THIS*... BE AS SILLY AS YOU WANT, BUT *GET TO WORK* ON FIXING THIS PLACE UP! WE HAVE *VARMINTS* POKING THEIR CUTE LITTLE HEADS IN!
ADDENDUM-- I WILL BRING A *NICKEL-IRON METEOR* DOWN UPON ANY FOOLS WHO WASTE OUR RESOURCES BY CAUSING *NEW* DAMAGE, SO NO TOMFOOLERY!
CLENCH!
G-G-GOT IT.

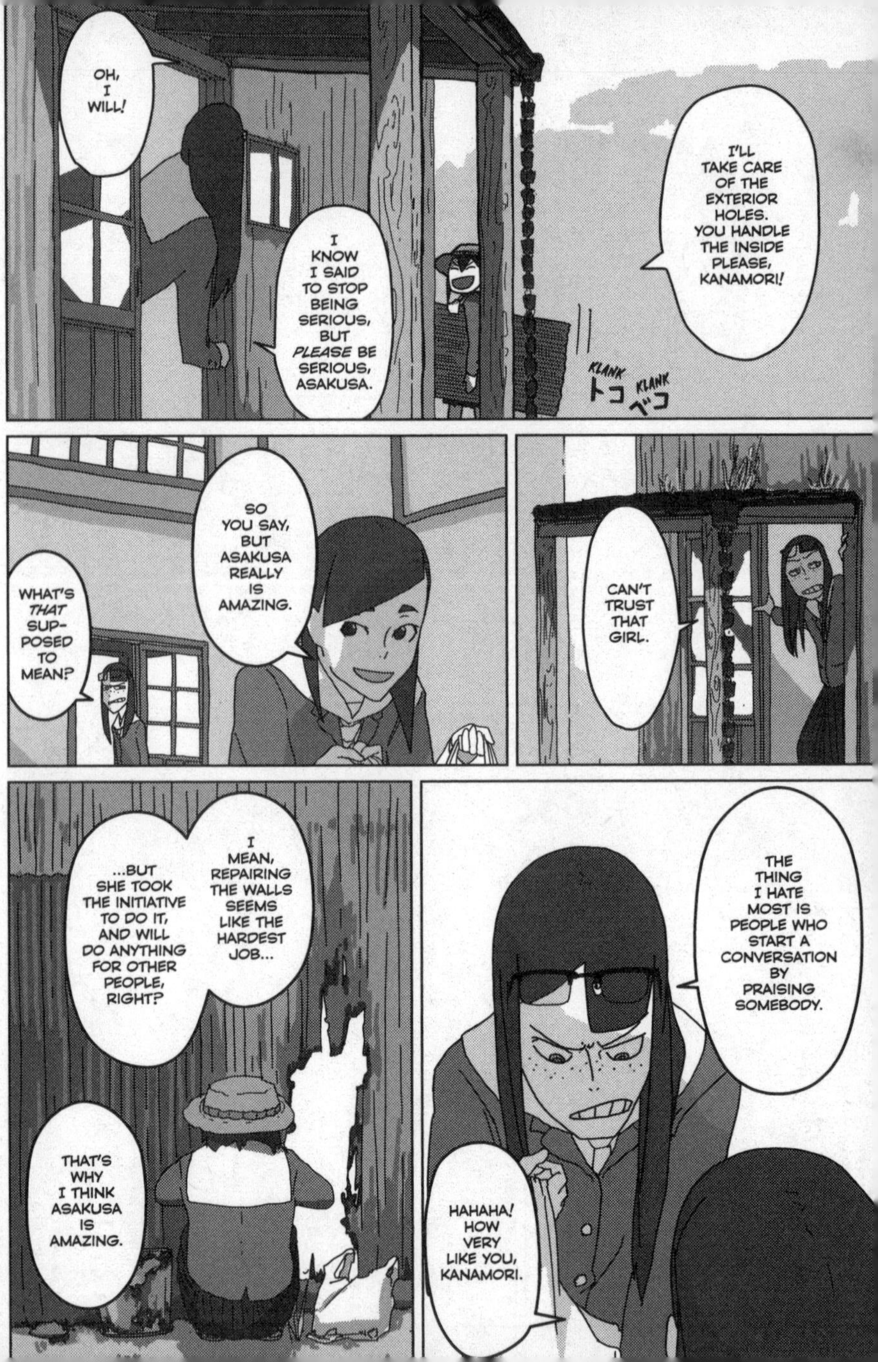
I'LL TAKE CARE OF THE EXTERIOR HOLES. YOU HANDLE THE INSIDE PLEASE, KANAMORI!
KLANK トコ KLANK べコ
I KNOW I SAID TO STOP BEING SERIOUS, BUT *PLEASE* BE SERIOUS, ASAKUSA.
OH, I WILL!
CAN'T TRUST THAT GIRL.
SO YOU SAY, BUT ASAKUSA REALLY IS AMAZING.
WHAT'S *THAT* SUP-POSED TO MEAN?
THE THING I HATE MOST IS PEOPLE WHO START A CONVERSATION BY PRAISING SOMEBODY.
HAHAHA! HOW VERY LIKE YOU, KANAMORI.
I MEAN, REPAIRING THE WALLS SEEMS LIKE THE HARDEST JOB...
...BUT SHE TOOK THE INITIATIVE TO DO IT, AND WILL DO ANYTHING FOR OTHER PEOPLE, RIGHT?
THAT'S WHY I THINK ASAKUSA IS AMAZING.

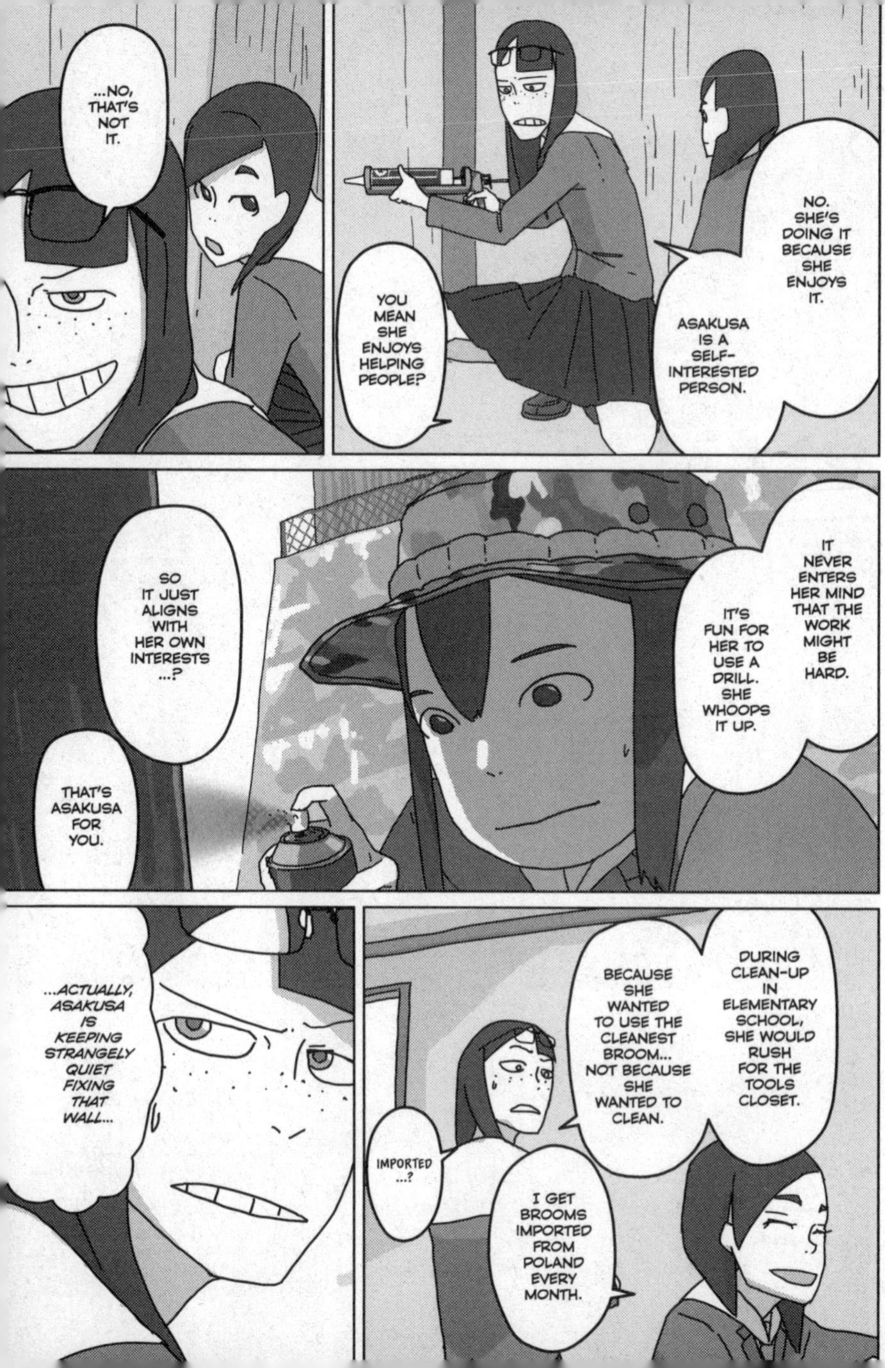

NO. SHE'S DOING IT BECAUSE SHE ENJOYS IT.
ASAKUSA IS A SELF-INTERESTED PERSON.
YOU MEAN SHE ENJOYS HELPING PEOPLE?
...NO, THAT'S NOT IT.
IT NEVER ENTERS HER MIND THAT THE WORK MIGHT BE HARD.
IT'S FUN FOR HER TO USE A DRILL. SHE WHOOPS IT UP.
SO IT JUST ALIGNS WITH HER OWN INTERESTS ...?
THAT'S ASAKUSA FOR YOU.
DURING CLEAN-UP IN ELEMENTARY SCHOOL, SHE WOULD RUSH FOR THE TOOLS CLOSET.
BECAUSE SHE WANTED TO USE THE CLEANEST BROOM... NOT BECAUSE SHE WANTED TO CLEAN.
IMPORTED ...?
I GET BROOMS IMPORTED FROM POLAND EVERY MONTH.
...ACTUALLY, ASAKUSA IS KEEPING STRANGELY QUIET FIXING THAT WALL...

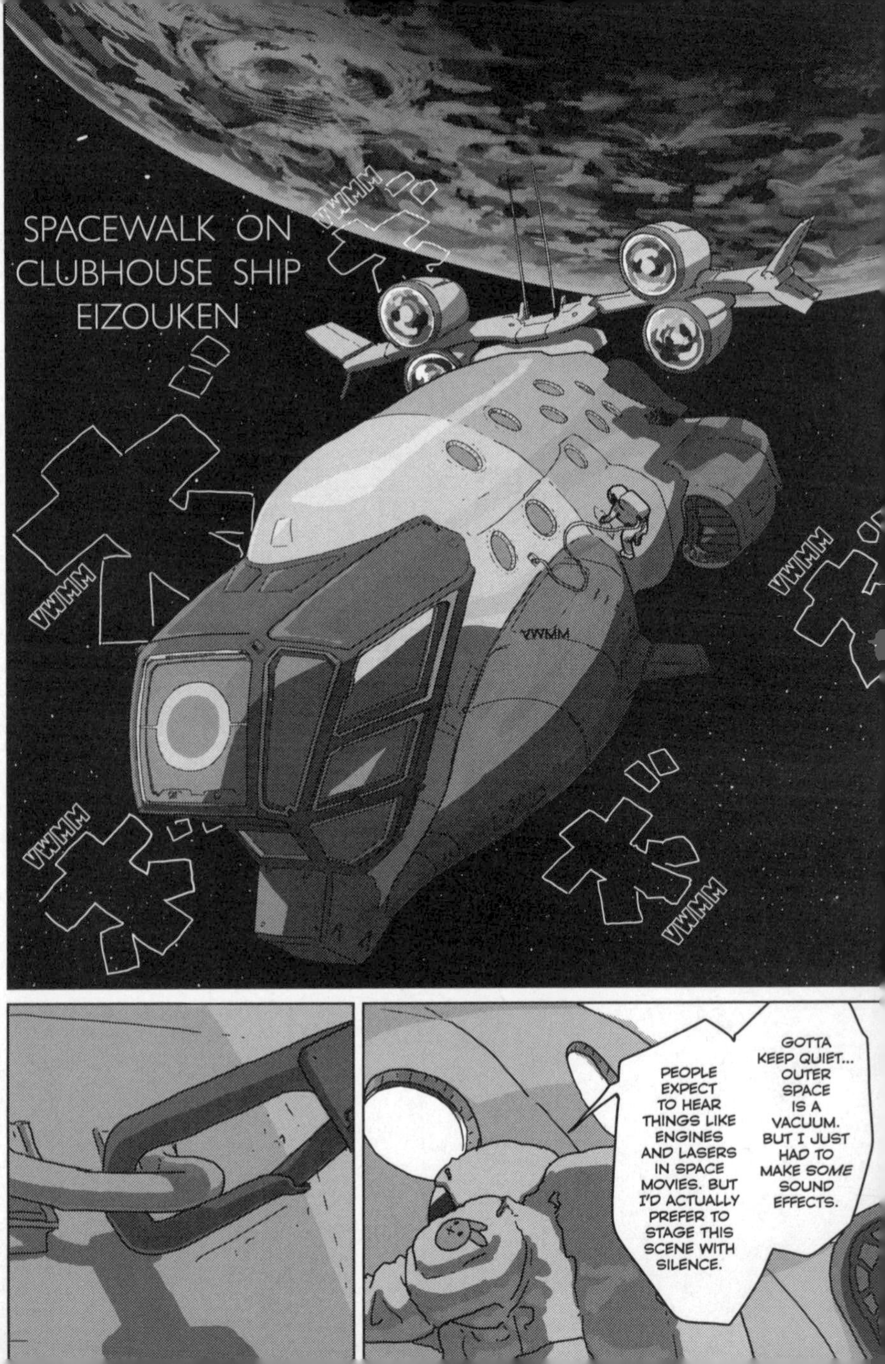
SPACEWALK ON CLUBHOUSE SHIP EIZOUKEN
VWMM
VWMM
VWMM
VWMM
VWMM
VWMM
GOTTA KEEP QUIET... OUTER SPACE IS A VACUUM. BUT I JUST HAD TO MAKE *SOME* SOUND EFFECTS.
PEOPLE EXPECT TO HEAR THINGS LIKE ENGINES AND LASERS IN SPACE MOVIES. BUT I'D ACTUALLY PREFER TO STAGE THIS SCENE WITH SILENCE.

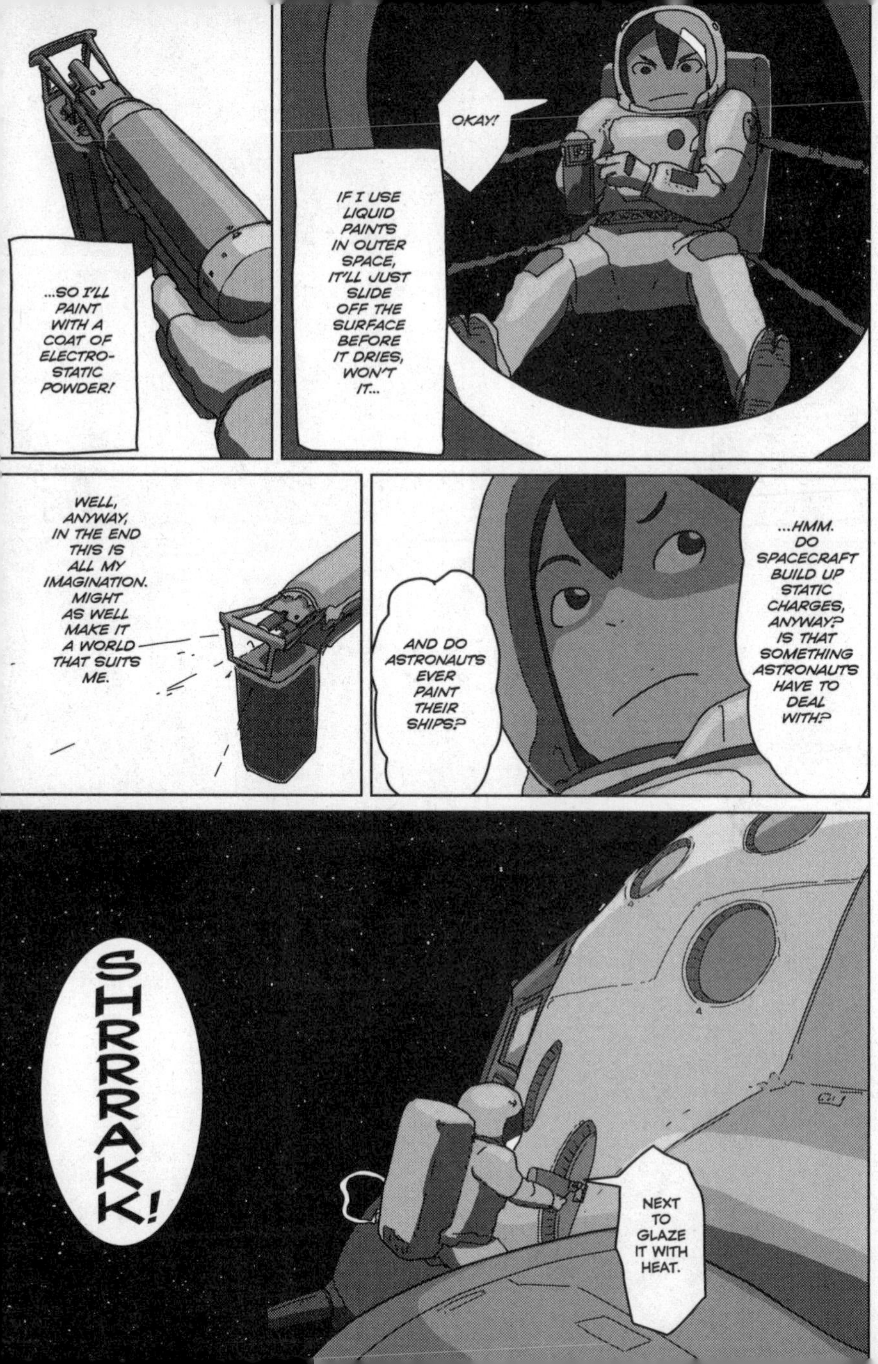
OKAY!
IF I USE LIQUID PAINTS IN OUTER SPACE, IT'LL JUST SLIDE OFF THE SURFACE BEFORE IT DRIES, WON'T IT...
...SO I'LL PAINT WITH A COAT OF ELECTRO-STATIC POWDER!
...HMM. DO SPACECRAFT BUILD UP STATIC CHARGES, ANYWAY? IS THAT SOMETHING ASTRONAUTS HAVE TO DEAL WITH?
AND DO ASTRONAUTS EVER PAINT THEIR SHIPS?
WELL, ANYWAY, IN THE END THIS IS ALL MY IMAGINATION. MIGHT AS WELL MAKE IT A WORLD THAT SUITS ME.
SHRRAKK!
NEXT TO GLAZE IT WITH HEAT.

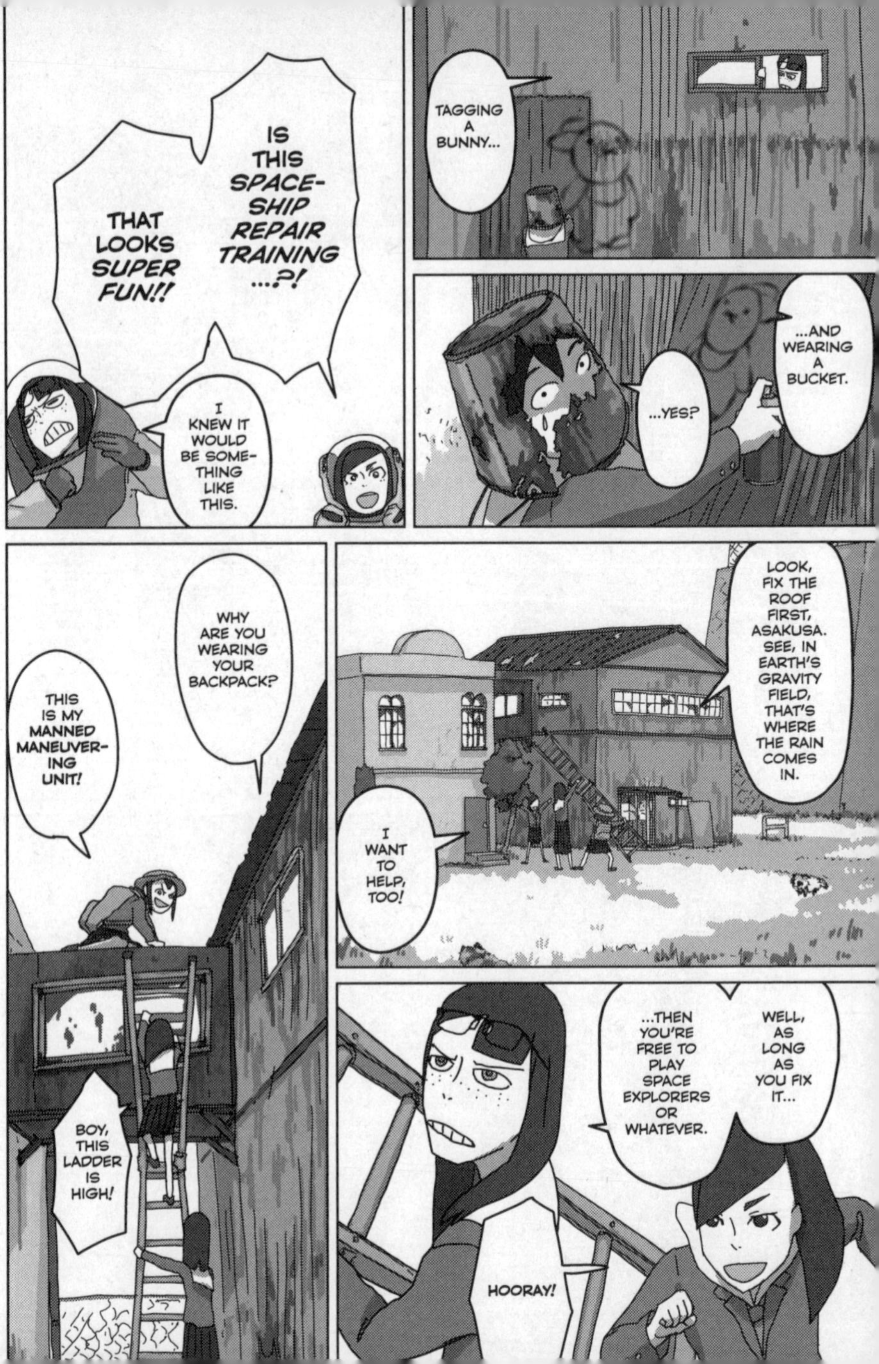
TAGGING A BUNNY...
...AND WEARING A BUCKET.
...YES?
IS THIS SPACESHIP REPAIR TRAINING ...?!
THAT LOOKS SUPER FUN!!
I KNEW IT WOULD BE SOMETHING LIKE THIS.
LOOK, FIX THE ROOF FIRST, ASAKUSA. SEE, IN EARTH'S GRAVITY FIELD, THAT'S WHERE THE RAIN COMES IN.
I WANT TO HELP, TOO!
WELL, AS LONG AS YOU FIX IT...
...THEN YOU'RE FREE TO PLAY SPACE EXPLORERS OR WHATEVER.
HOORAY!
WHY ARE YOU WEARING YOUR BACKPACK?
THIS IS MY MANNED MANEUVERING UNIT!
BOY, THIS LADDER IS HIGH!

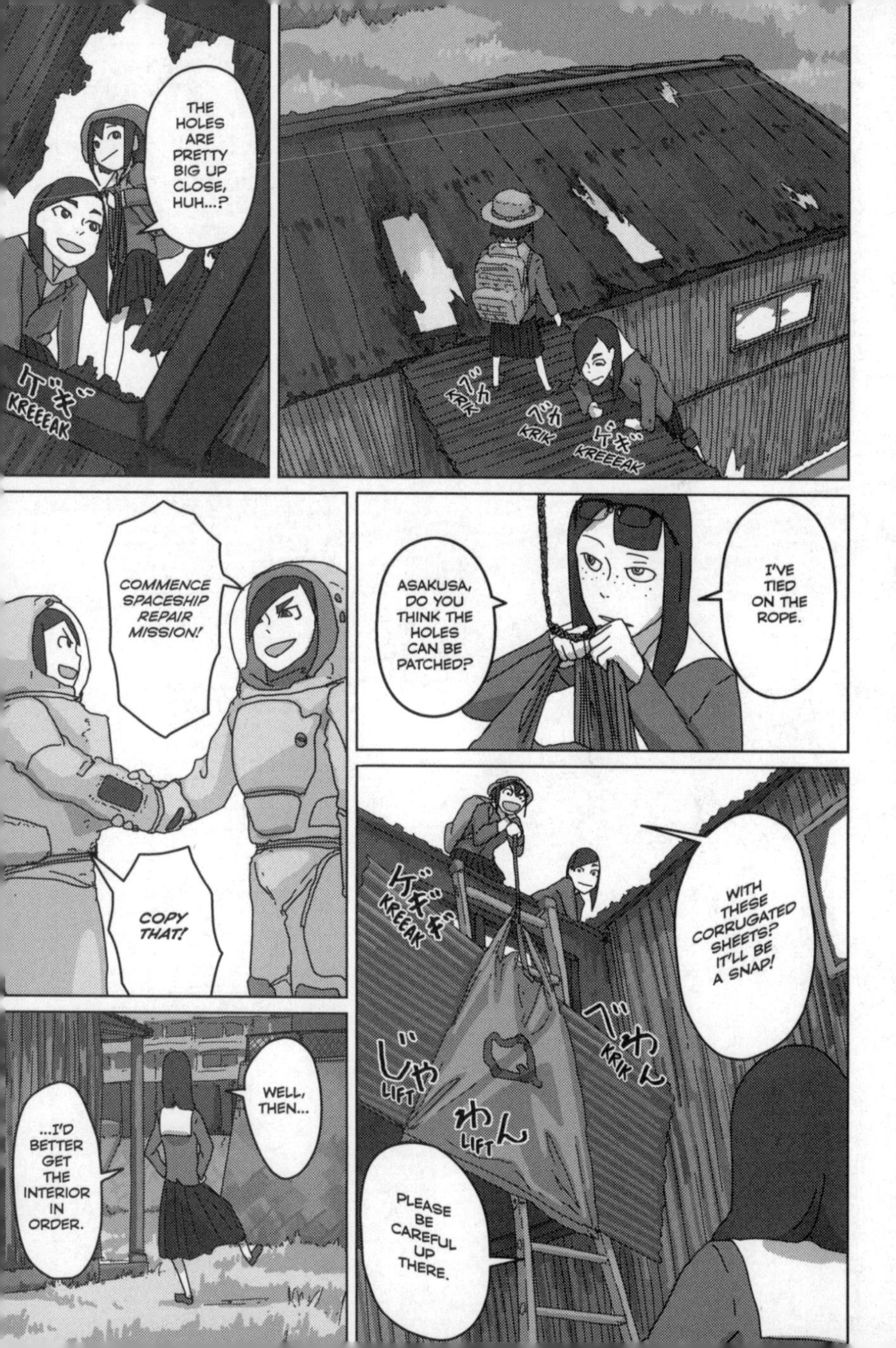
べカ
KRIK
べカ
KRIK
ゲギ
KREEEAK
THE HOLES ARE PRETTY BIG UP CLOSE, HUH...?
ゲギ
KREEEAK
I'VE TIED ON THE ROPE.
ASAKUSA, DO YOU THINK THE HOLES CAN BE PATCHED?
COMMENCE SPACESHIP REPAIR MISSION!
COPY THAT!
WITH THESE CORRUGATED SHEETS? IT'LL BE A SNAP!
ゲギギ
KREEAK
べわん
KRIK
じゃ
LIFT
わん
LIFT
PLEASE BE CAREFUL UP THERE.
WELL, THEN...
...I'D BETTER GET THE INTERIOR IN ORDER.

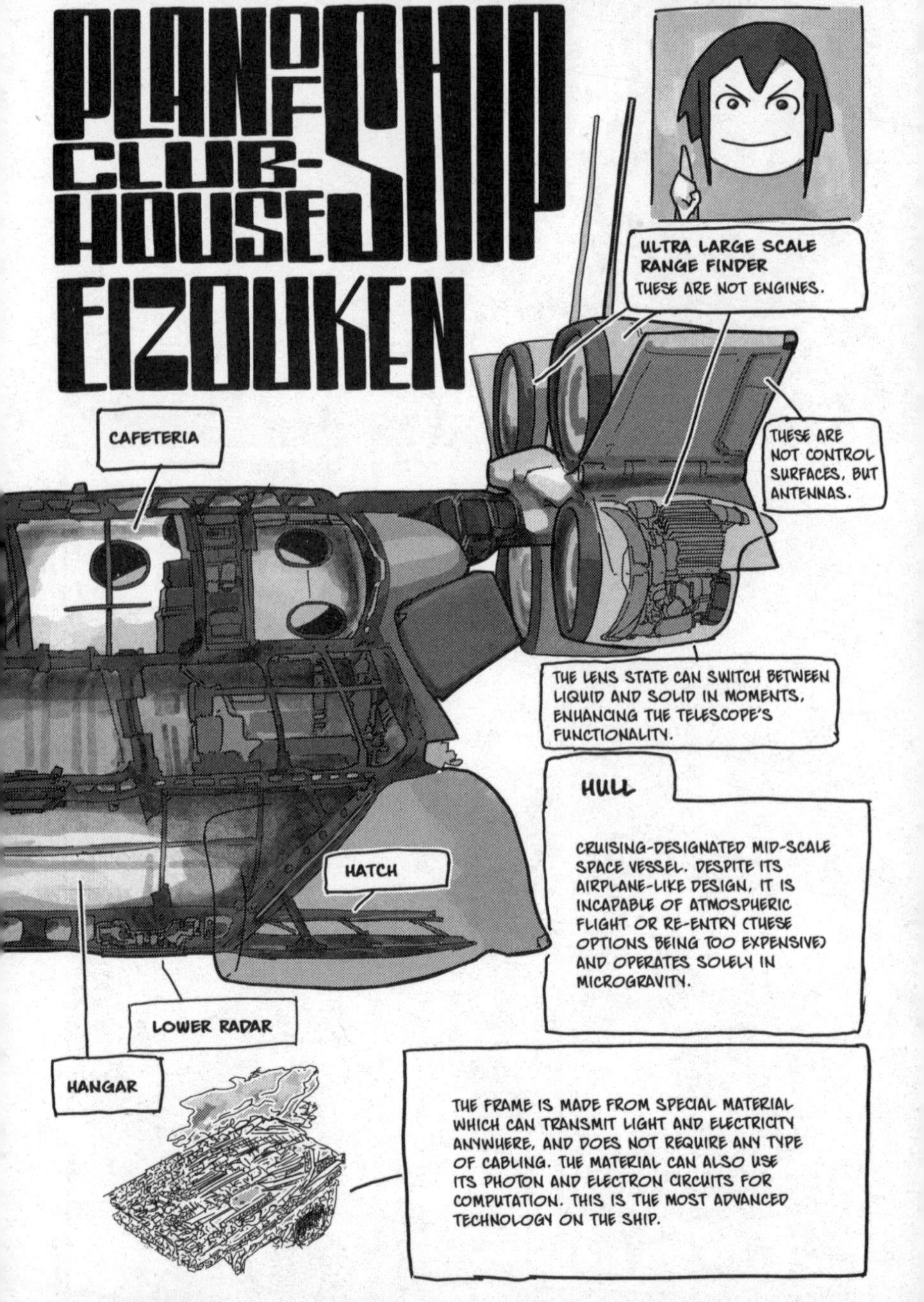
PLAN OF CLUB-HOUSE SHIP
EIZOUKEN
ULTRA LARGE SCALE RANGE FINDER
THESE ARE NOT ENGINES.
THESE ARE NOT CONTROL SURFACES, BUT ANTENNAS.
CAFETERIA
THE LENS STATE CAN SWITCH BETWEEN LIQUID AND SOLID IN MOMENTS, ENHANCING THE TELESCOPE'S FUNCTIONALITY.
HULL
CRUISING-DESIGNATED MID-SCALE SPACE VESSEL. DESPITE ITS AIRPLANE-LIKE DESIGN, IT IS INCAPABLE OF ATMOSPHERIC FLIGHT OR RE-ENTRY (THESE OPTIONS BEING TOO EXPENSIVE) AND OPERATES SOLELY IN MICROGRAVITY.
HATCH
LOWER RADAR
HANGAR
THE FRAME IS MADE FROM SPECIAL MATERIAL WHICH CAN TRANSMIT LIGHT AND ELECTRICITY ANYWHERE, AND DOES NOT REQUIRE ANY TYPE OF CABLING. THE MATERIAL CAN ALSO USE ITS PHOTON AND ELECTRON CIRCUITS FOR COMPUTATION. THIS IS THE MOST ADVANCED TECHNOLOGY ON THE SHIP.

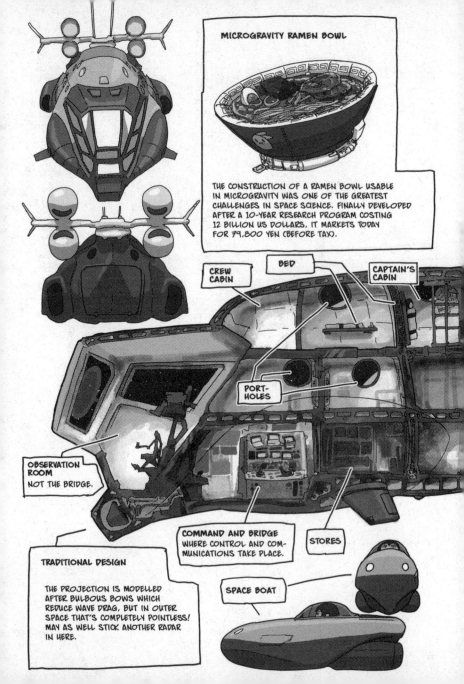

MICROGRAVITY RAMEN BOWL

THE CONSTRUCTION OF A RAMEN BOWL USABLE IN MICROGRAVITY WAS ONE OF THE GREATEST CHALLENGES IN SPACE SCIENCE. FINALLY DEVELOPED AFTER A 10-YEAR RESEARCH PROGRAM COSTING 12 BILLION US DOLLARS, IT MARKETS TODAY FOR 79,800 YEN (BEFORE TAX).

CREW CABIN

BED

CAPTAIN'S CABIN

PORT-HOLES

OBSERVATION ROOM
NOT THE BRIDGE.

COMMAND AND BRIDGE
WHERE CONTROL AND COMMUNICATIONS TAKE PLACE.

STORES

TRADITIONAL DESIGN

THE PROJECTION IS MODELLED AFTER BULBOUS BOWS WHICH REDUCE WAVE DRAG, BUT IN OUTER SPACE THAT'S COMPLETELY POINTLESS! MAY AS WELL STICK ANOTHER RADAR IN HERE.

SPACE BOAT

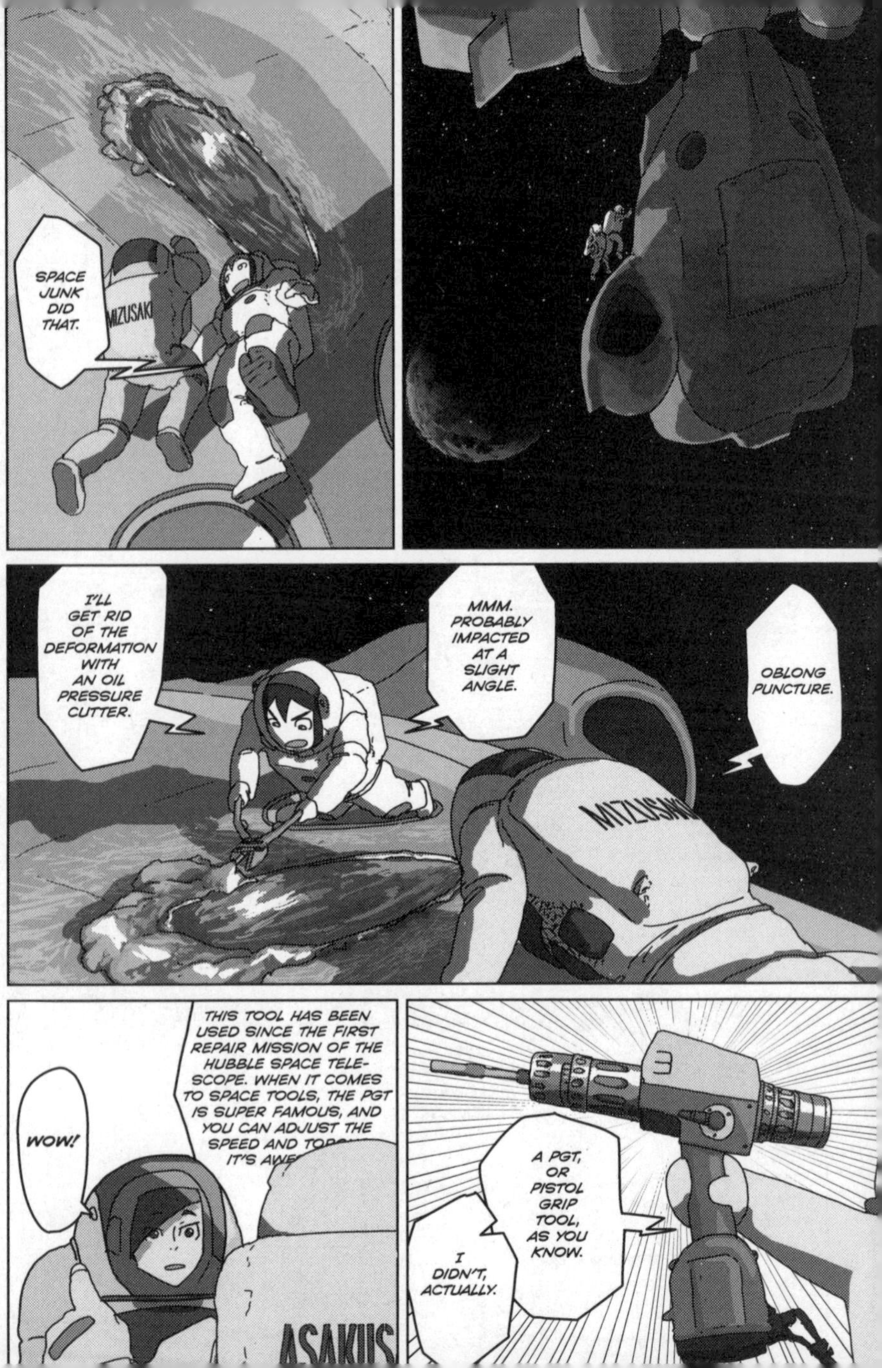
SPACE JUNK DID THAT.
MIZUSAKI
OBLONG PUNCTURE.
MMM. PROBABLY IMPACTED AT A SLIGHT ANGLE.
I'LL GET RID OF THE DEFORMATION WITH AN OIL PRESSURE CUTTER.
MIZUSAKI
A PGT, OR PISTOL GRIP TOOL, AS YOU KNOW.
I DIDN'T, ACTUALLY.
THIS TOOL HAS BEEN USED SINCE THE FIRST REPAIR MISSION OF THE HUBBLE SPACE TELE-SCOPE. WHEN IT COMES TO SPACE TOOLS, THE PGT IS SUPER FAMOUS, AND YOU CAN ADJUST THE SPEED AND TO
WOW!
ASAKUS

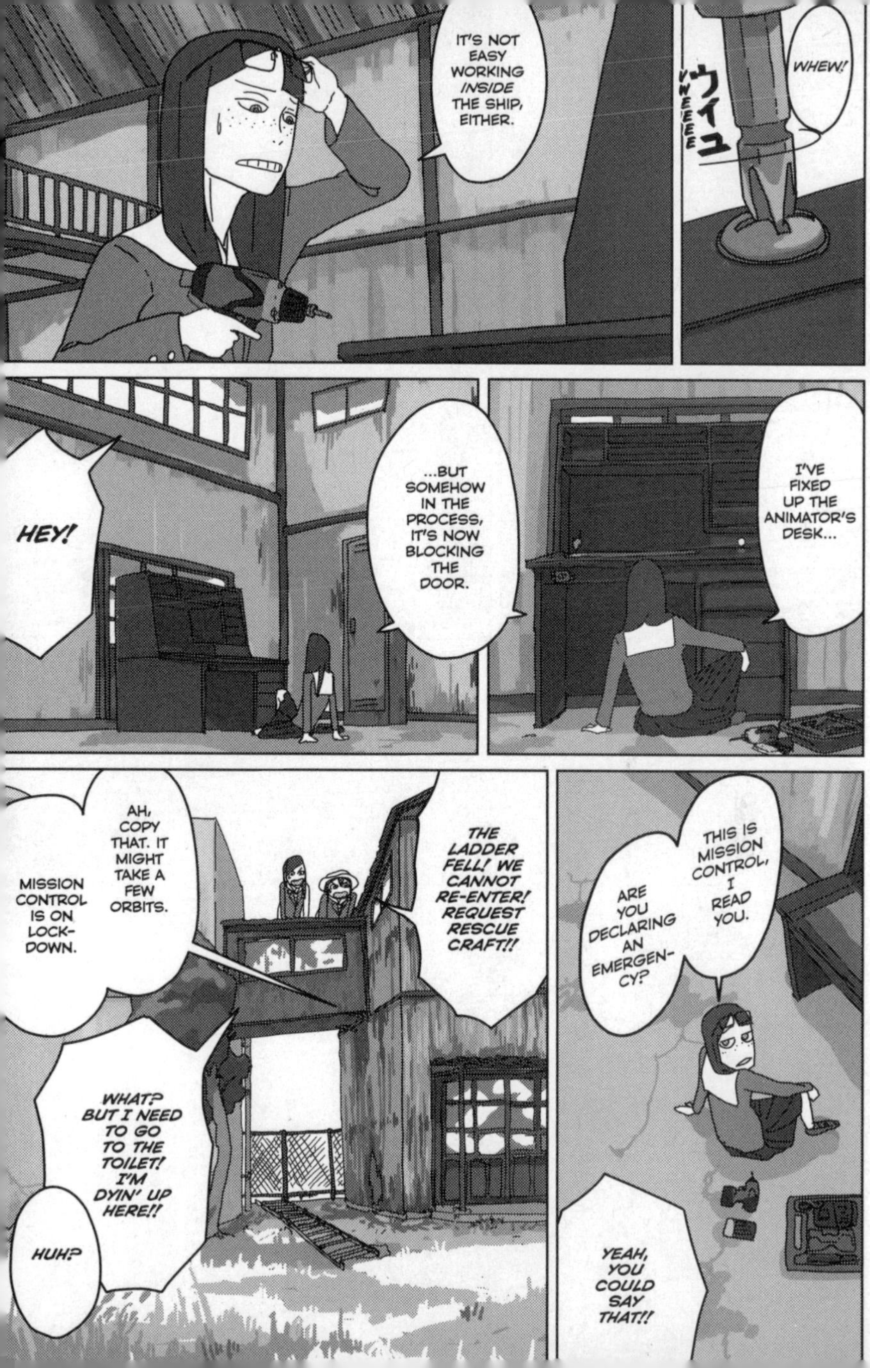
WHEW!
ウイユ
WHEEEE
IT'S NOT EASY WORKING *INSIDE* THE SHIP, EITHER.
I'VE FIXED UP THE ANIMATOR'S DESK...
...BUT SOMEHOW IN THE PROCESS, IT'S NOW BLOCKING THE DOOR.
HEY!
THIS IS MISSION CONTROL, I READ YOU.
ARE YOU DECLARING AN EMERGEN-CY?
YEAH, YOU COULD SAY THAT!!
THE LADDER FELL! WE CANNOT RE-ENTER! REQUEST RESCUE CRAFT!!
AH, COPY THAT. IT MIGHT TAKE A FEW ORBITS.
MISSION CONTROL IS ON LOCK-DOWN.
WHAT? BUT I NEED TO GO TO THE TOILET! I'M DYIN' UP HERE!!
HUH?

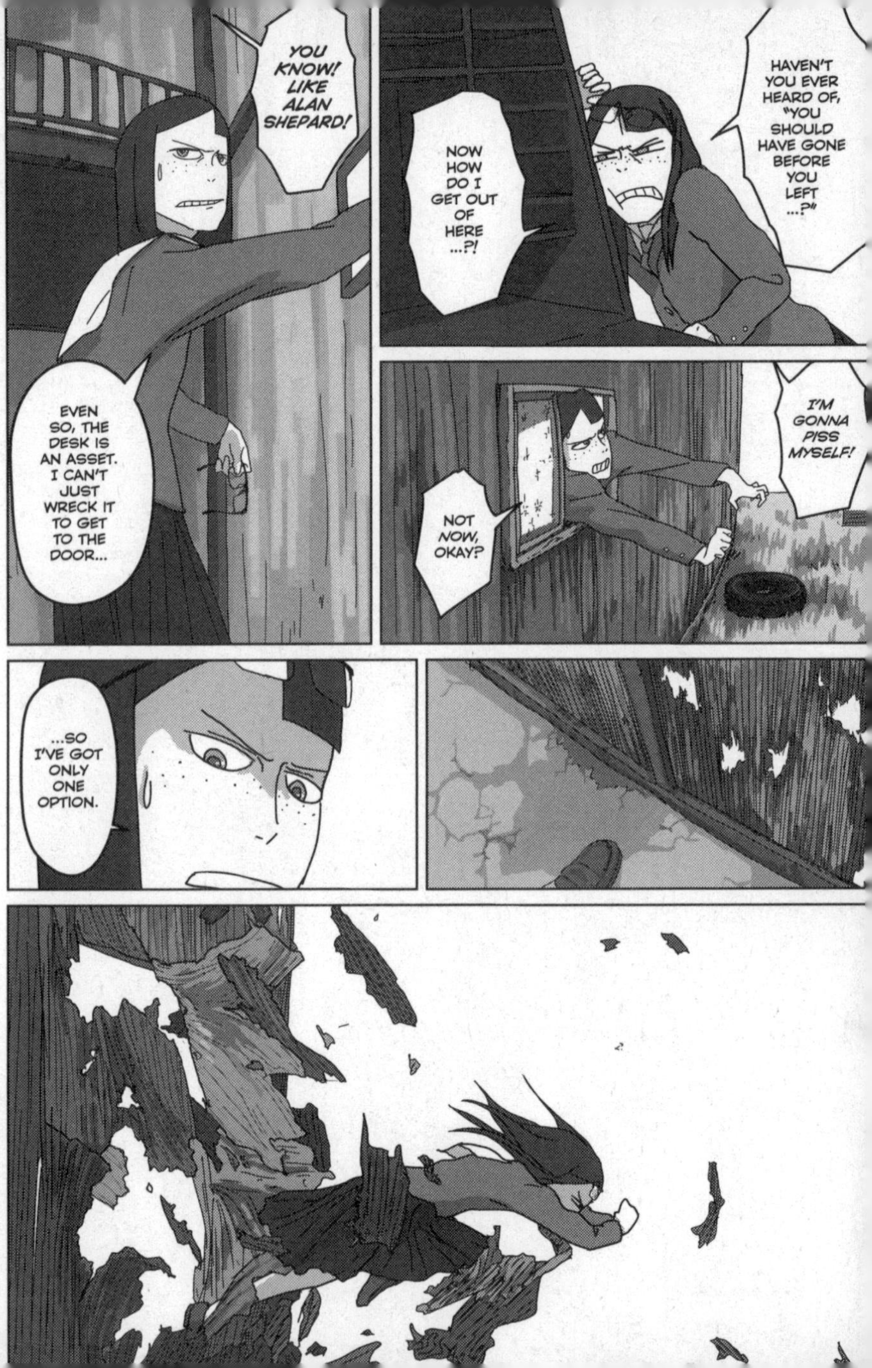
HAVEN'T YOU EVER HEARD OF, "YOU SHOULD HAVE GONE BEFORE YOU LEFT ...?"
NOW HOW DO I GET OUT OF HERE ...?!
I'M GONNA *PISS* MYSELF!
NOT *NOW*, OKAY?
YOU KNOW! LIKE ALAN SHEPARD!
EVEN SO, THE DESK IS AN ASSET. I CAN'T JUST WRECK IT TO GET TO THE DOOR...
...SO I'VE GOT ONLY ONE OPTION.

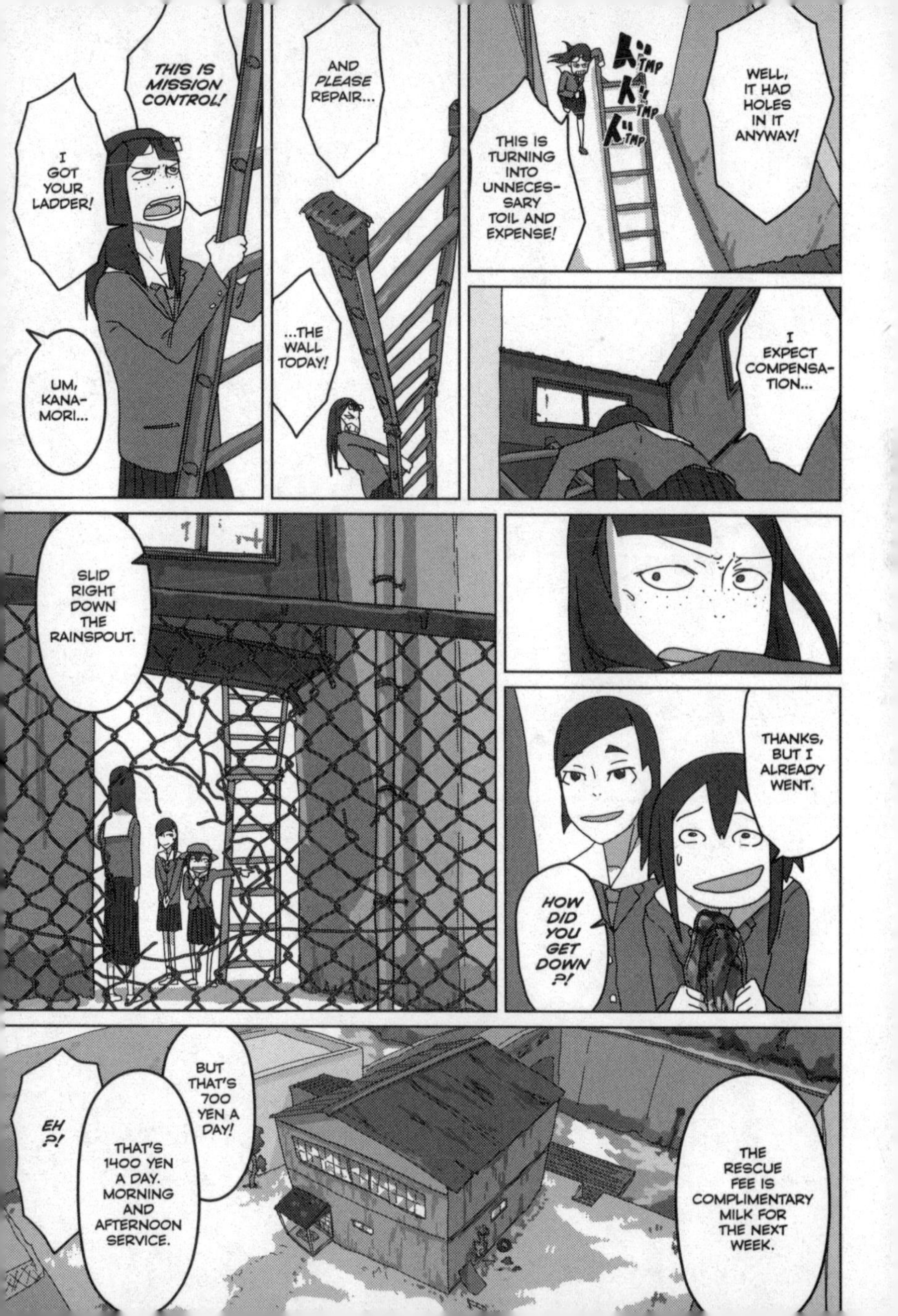
WELL, IT HAD HOLES IN IT ANYWAY!
TMP TMP TMP
THIS IS TURNING INTO UNNECES-SARY TOIL AND EXPENSE!
I EXPECT COMPENSA-TION...
AND PLEASE REPAIR...
...THE WALL TODAY!
THIS IS MISSION CONTROL!
I GOT YOUR LADDER!
UM, KANAMORI...
THANKS, BUT I ALREADY WENT.
HOW DID YOU GET DOWN?!
SLID RIGHT DOWN THE RAINSPOUT.
THE RESCUE FEE IS COMPLIMENTARY MILK FOR THE NEXT WEEK.
BUT THAT'S 700 YEN A DAY!
THAT'S 1400 YEN A DAY. MORNING AND AFTERNOON SERVICE.
EH?!

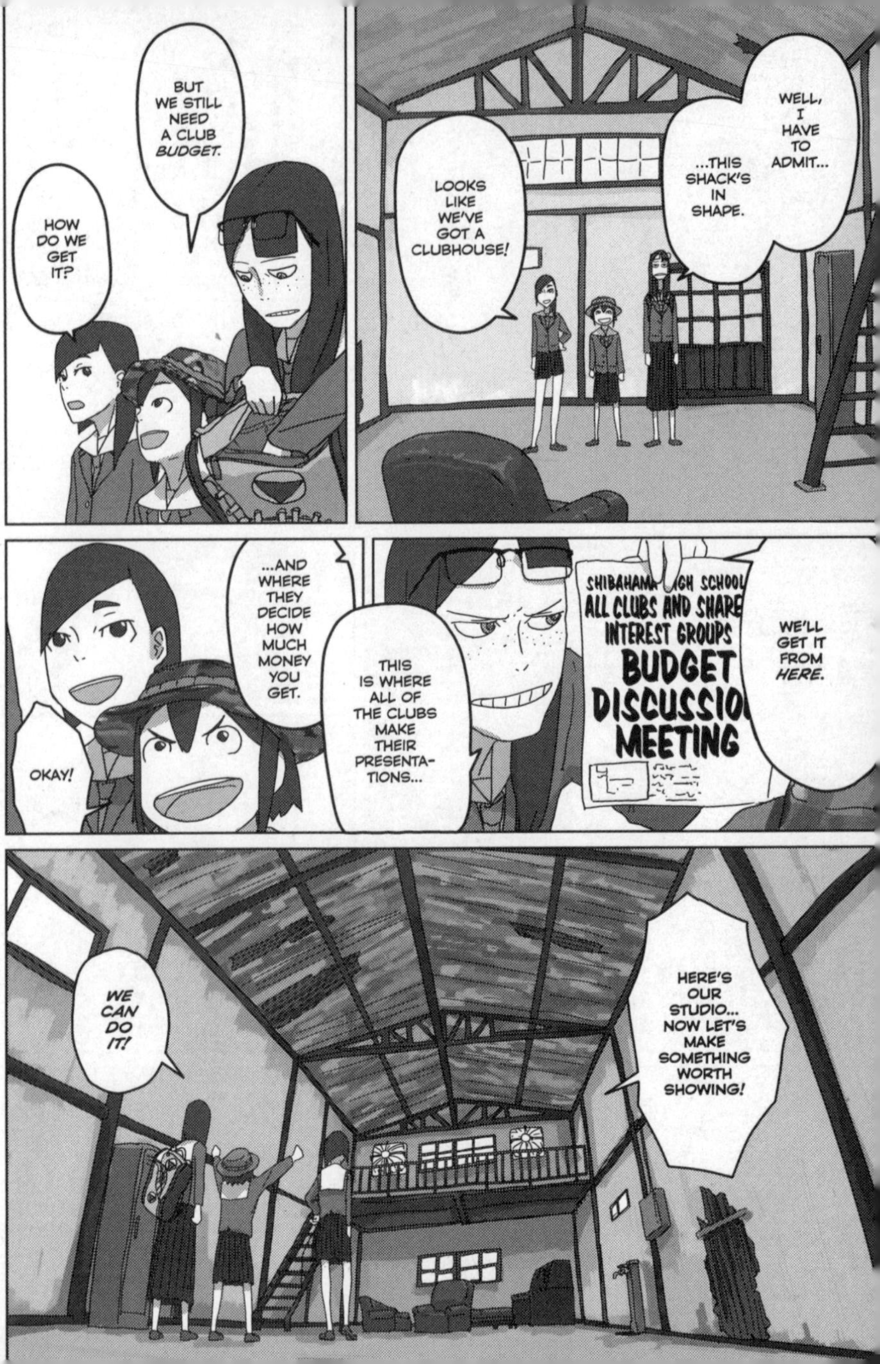
WELL, I HAVE TO ADMIT...
...THIS SHACK'S IN SHAPE.
LOOKS LIKE WE'VE GOT A CLUBHOUSE!
BUT WE STILL NEED A CLUB *BUDGET*.
HOW DO WE GET IT?
WE'LL GET IT FROM *HERE*.
SHIBAHAMA GH SCHOOL
ALL CLUBS AND SHARE
INTEREST GROUPS
BUDGET
DISCUSSIO
MEETING
THIS IS WHERE ALL OF THE CLUBS MAKE THEIR PRESENTATIONS...
...AND WHERE THEY DECIDE HOW MUCH MONEY YOU GET.
OKAY!
HERE'S OUR STUDIO... NOW LET'S MAKE SOMETHING WORTH SHOWING!
WE CAN DO IT!

CHAPTER 5: LESS WORK AND MORE FLASH!!

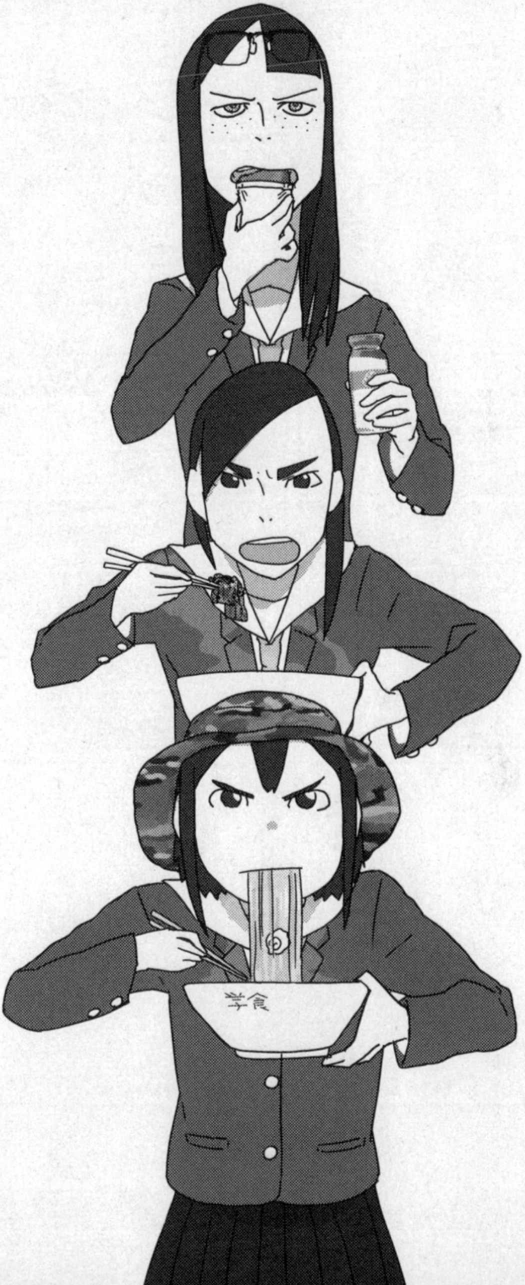
学食

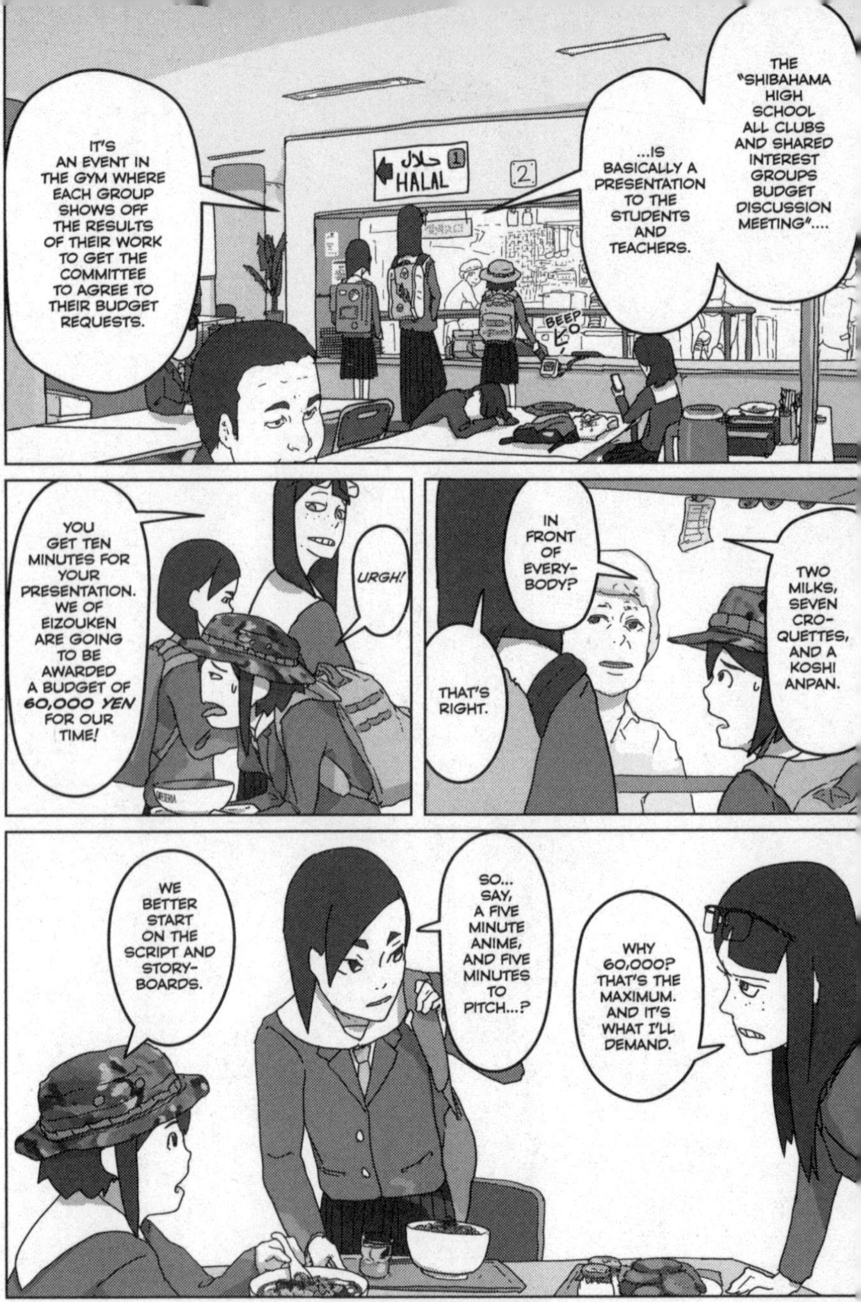
THE "SHIBAHAMA HIGH SCHOOL ALL CLUBS AND SHARED INTEREST GROUPS BUDGET DISCUSSION MEETING"....
...IS BASICALLY A PRESENTATION TO THE STUDENTS AND TEACHERS.
HALAL
BEEP
IT'S AN EVENT IN THE GYM WHERE EACH GROUP SHOWS OFF THE RESULTS OF THEIR WORK TO GET THE COMMITTEE TO AGREE TO THEIR BUDGET REQUESTS.
TWO MILKS, SEVEN CRO-QUETTES, AND A KOSHI ANPAN.
IN FRONT OF EVERY-BODY?
THAT'S RIGHT.
URGH!
YOU GET TEN MINUTES FOR YOUR PRESENTATION. WE OF EIZOUKEN ARE GOING TO BE AWARDED A BUDGET OF *60,000 YEN* FOR OUR TIME!
WHY 60,000? THAT'S THE MAXIMUM. AND IT'S WHAT I'LL DEMAND.
SO... SAY, A FIVE MINUTE ANIME, AND FIVE MINUTES TO PITCH...?
WE BETTER START ON THE SCRIPT AND STORY-BOARDS.

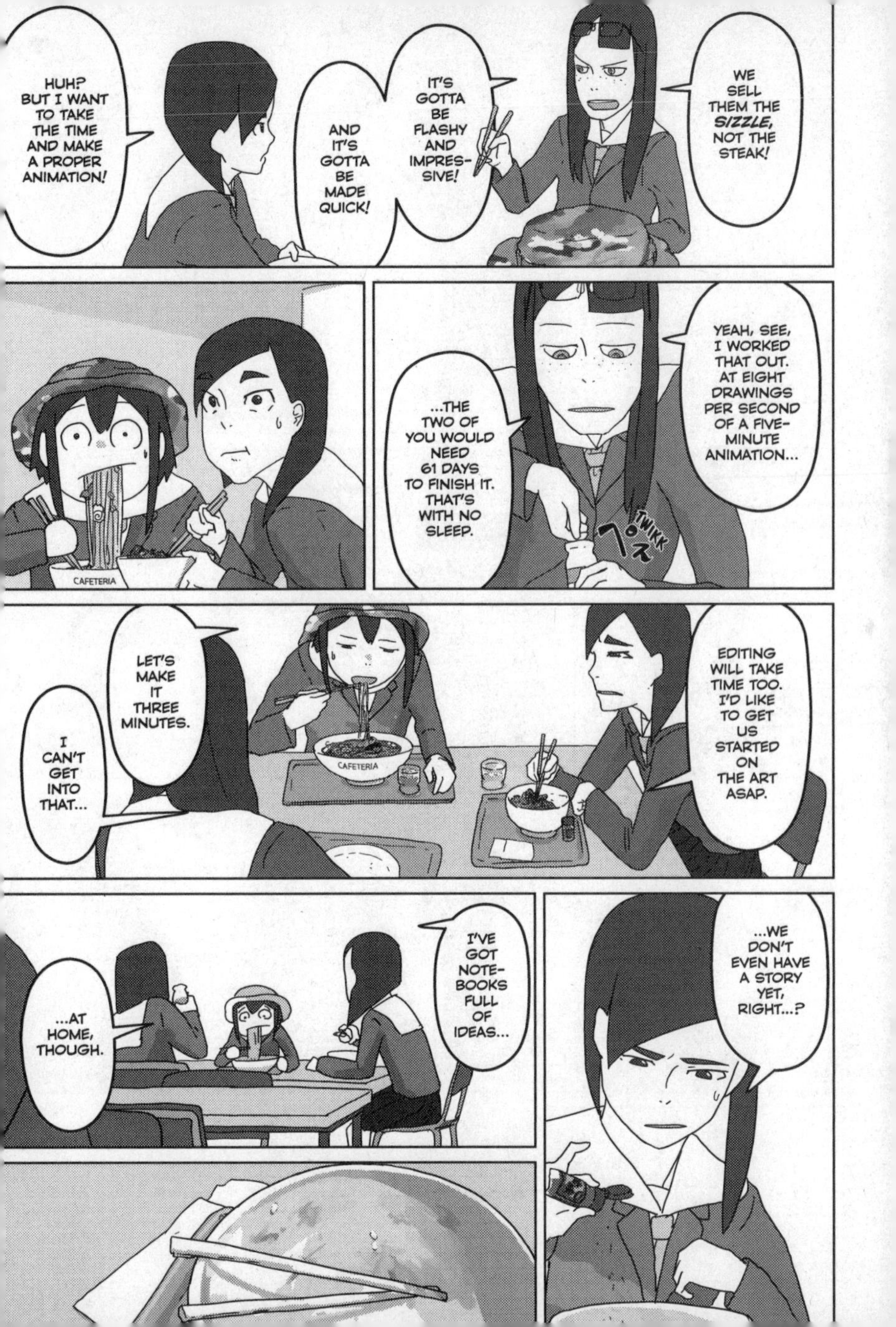
WE SELL THEM THE *SIZZLE*, NOT THE STEAK!
IT'S GOTTA BE FLASHY AND IMPRESSIVE!
AND IT'S GOTTA BE MADE QUICK!
HUH? BUT I WANT TO TAKE THE TIME AND MAKE A PROPER ANIMATION!
YEAH, SEE, I WORKED THAT OUT. AT EIGHT DRAWINGS PER SECOND OF A FIVE-MINUTE ANIMATION...
...THE TWO OF YOU WOULD NEED 61 DAYS TO FINISH IT. THAT'S WITH NO SLEEP.
TWIKK
CAFETERIA
EDITING WILL TAKE TIME TOO. I'D LIKE TO GET US STARTED ON THE ART ASAP.
CAFETERIA
LET'S MAKE IT THREE MINUTES.
I CAN'T GET INTO THAT...
...WE DON'T EVEN HAVE A STORY YET, RIGHT...?
I'VE GOT NOTEBOOKS FULL OF IDEAS...
...AT HOME, THOUGH.

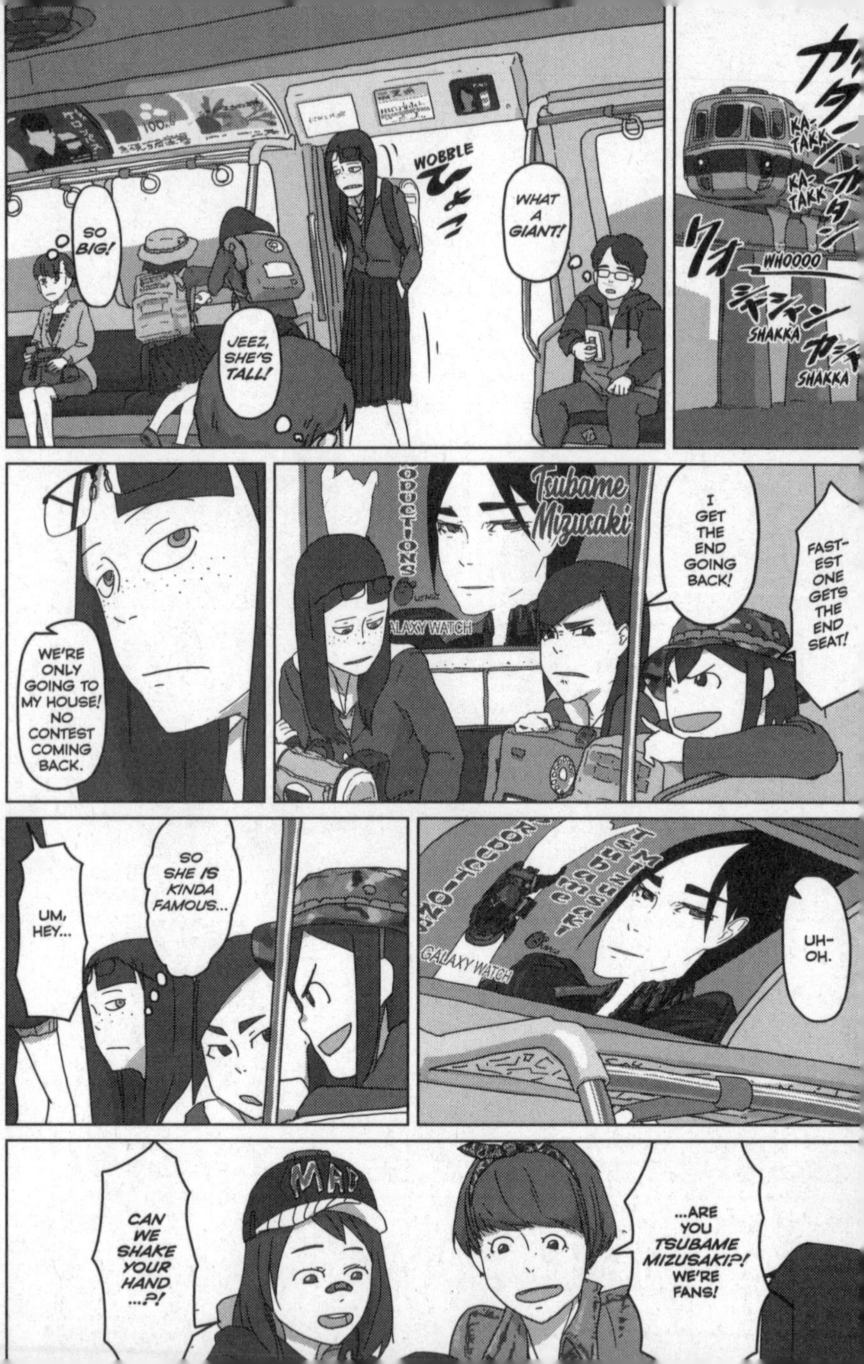
KA-TAKK
KA-TAKK
WHOOOO
SHAKKA
SHAKKA
WHAT A GIANT!
WOBBLE
SO BIG!
JEEZ, SHE'S TALL!
FAST-EST ONE GETS THE END SEAT!
I GET THE END GOING BACK!
Tsubame Mizusaki
GALAXY WATCH
WE'RE ONLY GOING TO MY HOUSE! NO CONTEST COMING BACK.
UH-OH.
GALAXY WATCH
SO SHE IS KINDA FAMOUS...
UM, HEY...
...ARE YOU TSUBAME MIZUSAKI!?! WE'RE FANS!
CAN WE SHAKE YOUR HAND ...?!

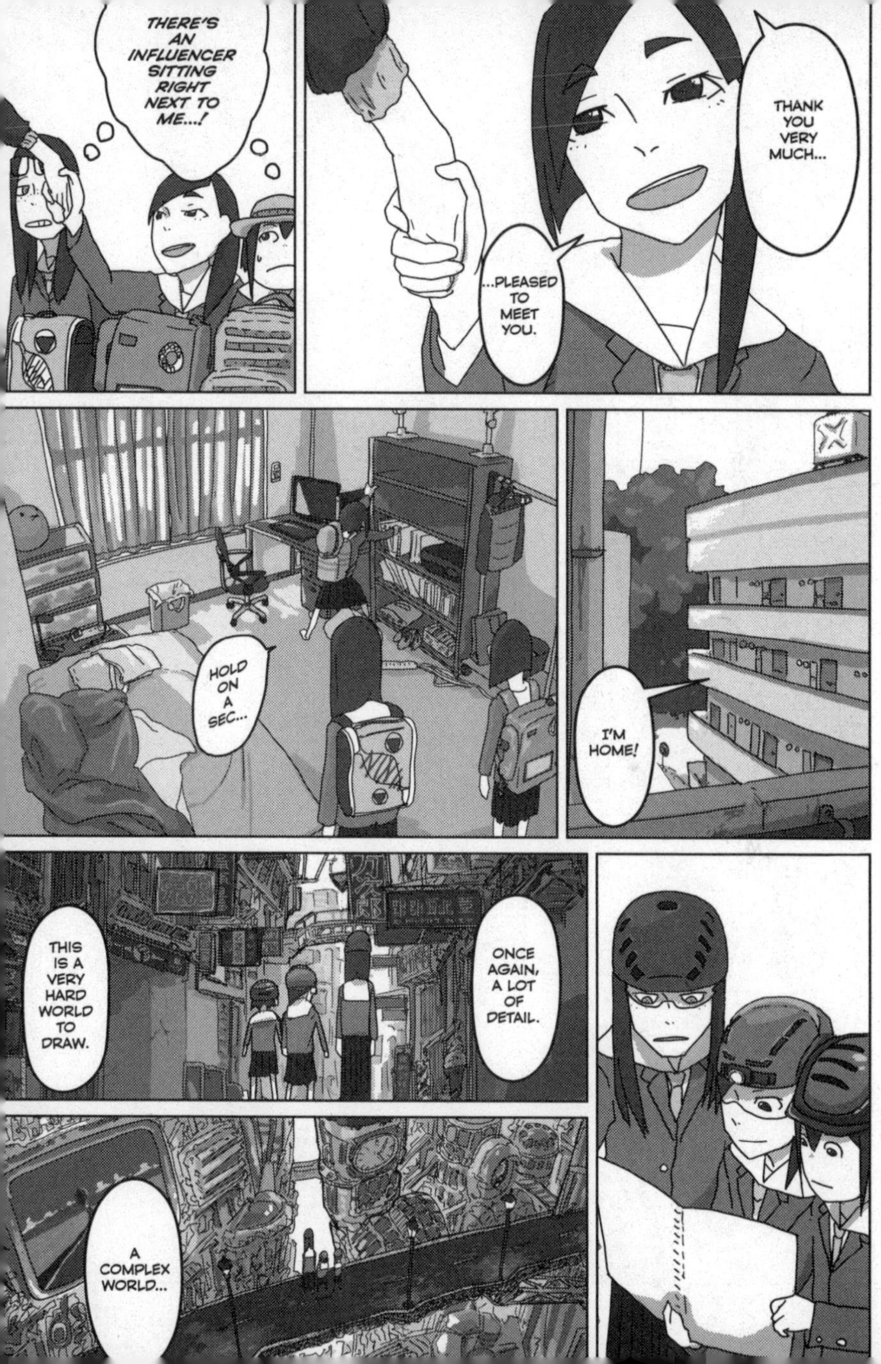
THANK YOU VERY MUCH...
...PLEASED TO MEET YOU.
THERE'S AN INFLUENCER SITTING RIGHT NEXT TO ME...!
I'M HOME!
HOLD ON A SEC...
ONCE AGAIN, A LOT OF DETAIL.
THIS IS A VERY HARD WORLD TO DRAW.
A COMPLEX WORLD...

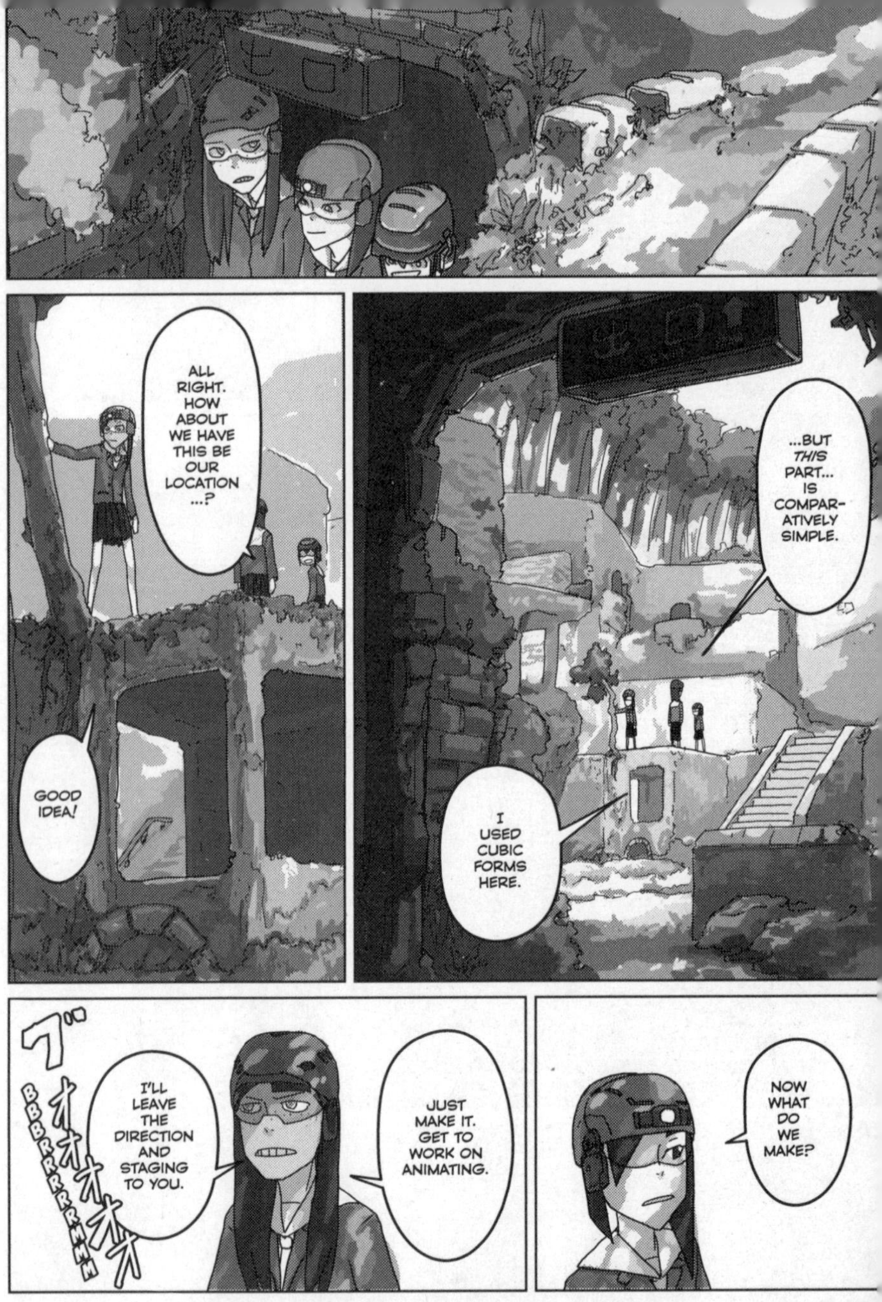
...BUT *THIS* PART... IS COMPARATIVELY SIMPLE.
I USED CUBIC FORMS HERE.
ALL RIGHT. HOW ABOUT WE HAVE THIS BE OUR LOCATION ...?
GOOD IDEA!
NOW WHAT DO WE MAKE?
JUST MAKE IT. GET TO WORK ON ANIMATING.
I'LL LEAVE THE DIRECTION AND STAGING TO YOU.
BBBRRRRRMMM

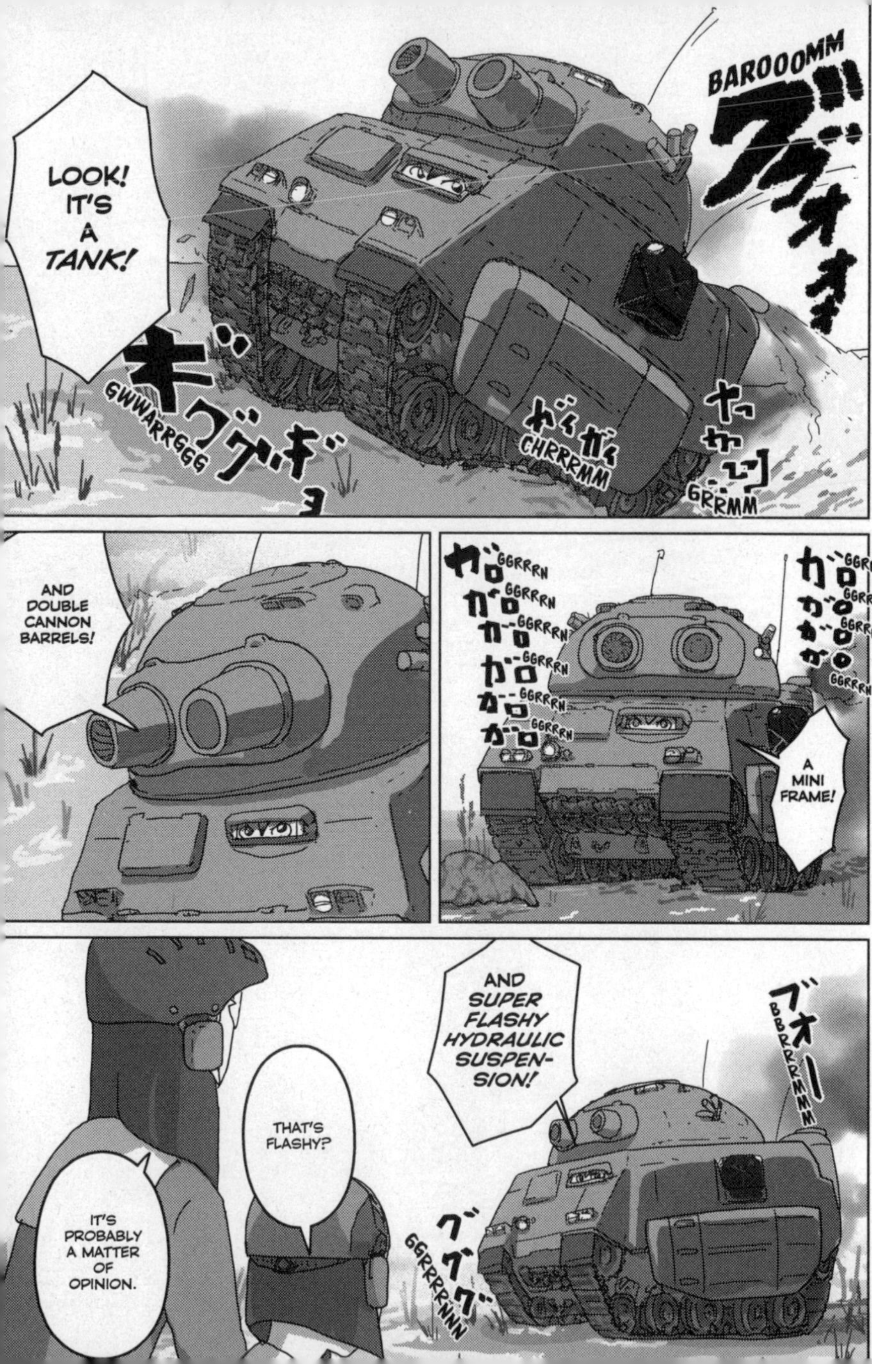
BAROOOMM
LOOK! IT'S A TANK!
GRRMM
CHRRRMM
GWWARRGGG
GGRRRN GGRRRN GGRRRN GGRRRN GGRRRN
A MINI FRAME!
GGRRRN GGRRRN GGRRRN GGRRRN GGRRRN GGRRRN
AND DOUBLE CANNON BARRELS!
BBBRRRRMMM
AND SUPER FLASHY HYDRAULIC SUSPENSION!
GGRRRRNNN
THAT'S FLASHY?
IT'S PROBABLY A MATTER OF OPINION.

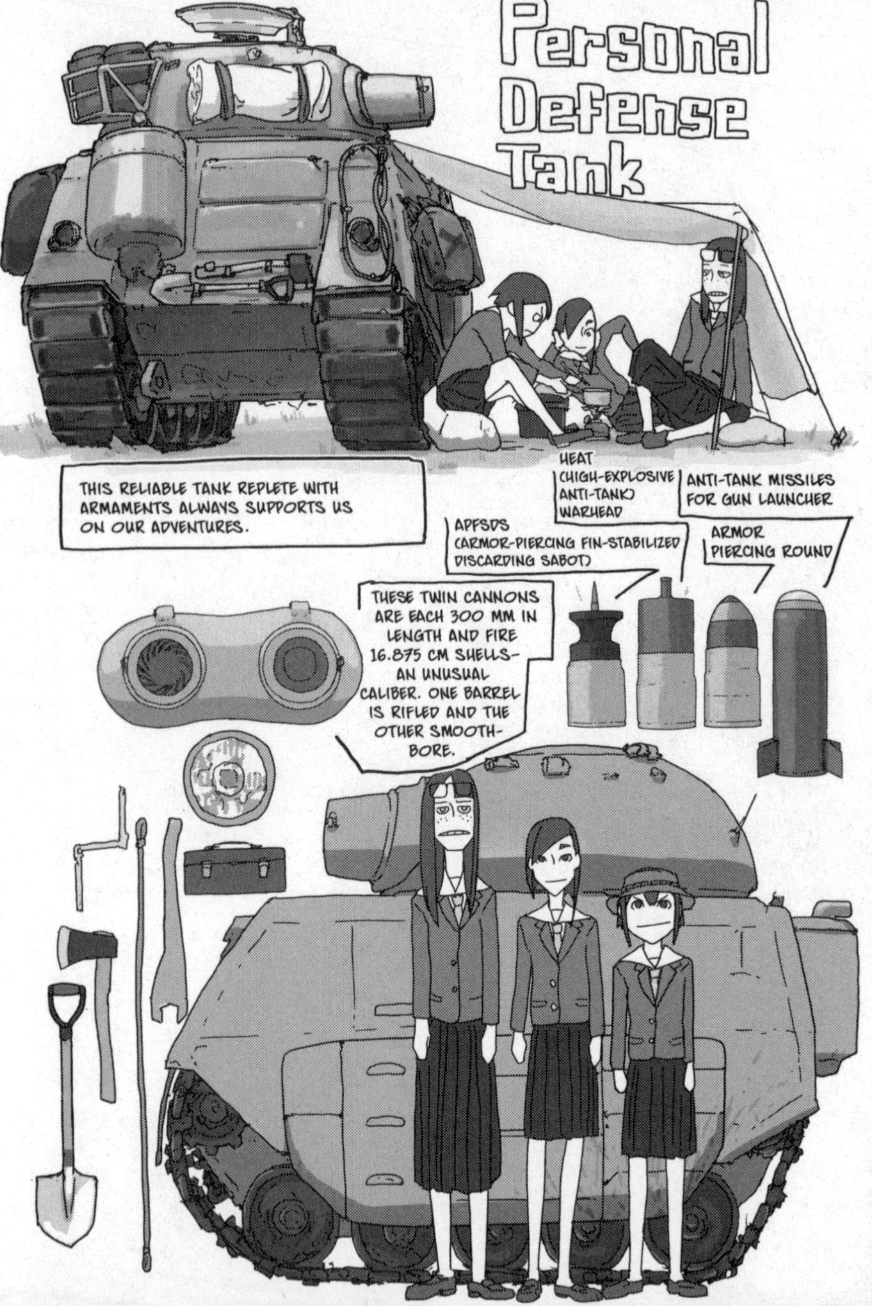
Personal Defense Tank
THIS RELIABLE TANK REPLETE WITH ARMAMENTS ALWAYS SUPPORTS US ON OUR ADVENTURES.
ANTI-TANK MISSILES FOR GUN LAUNCHER
HEAT (HIGH-EXPLOSIVE ANTI-TANK) WARHEAD
ARMOR PIERCING ROUND
APFSDS (ARMOR-PIERCING FIN-STABILIZED DISCARDING SABOT)
THESE TWIN CANNONS ARE EACH 300 MM IN LENGTH AND FIRE 16.875 CM SHELLS- AN UNUSUAL CALIBER. ONE BARREL IS RIFLED AND THE OTHER SMOOTH-BORE.

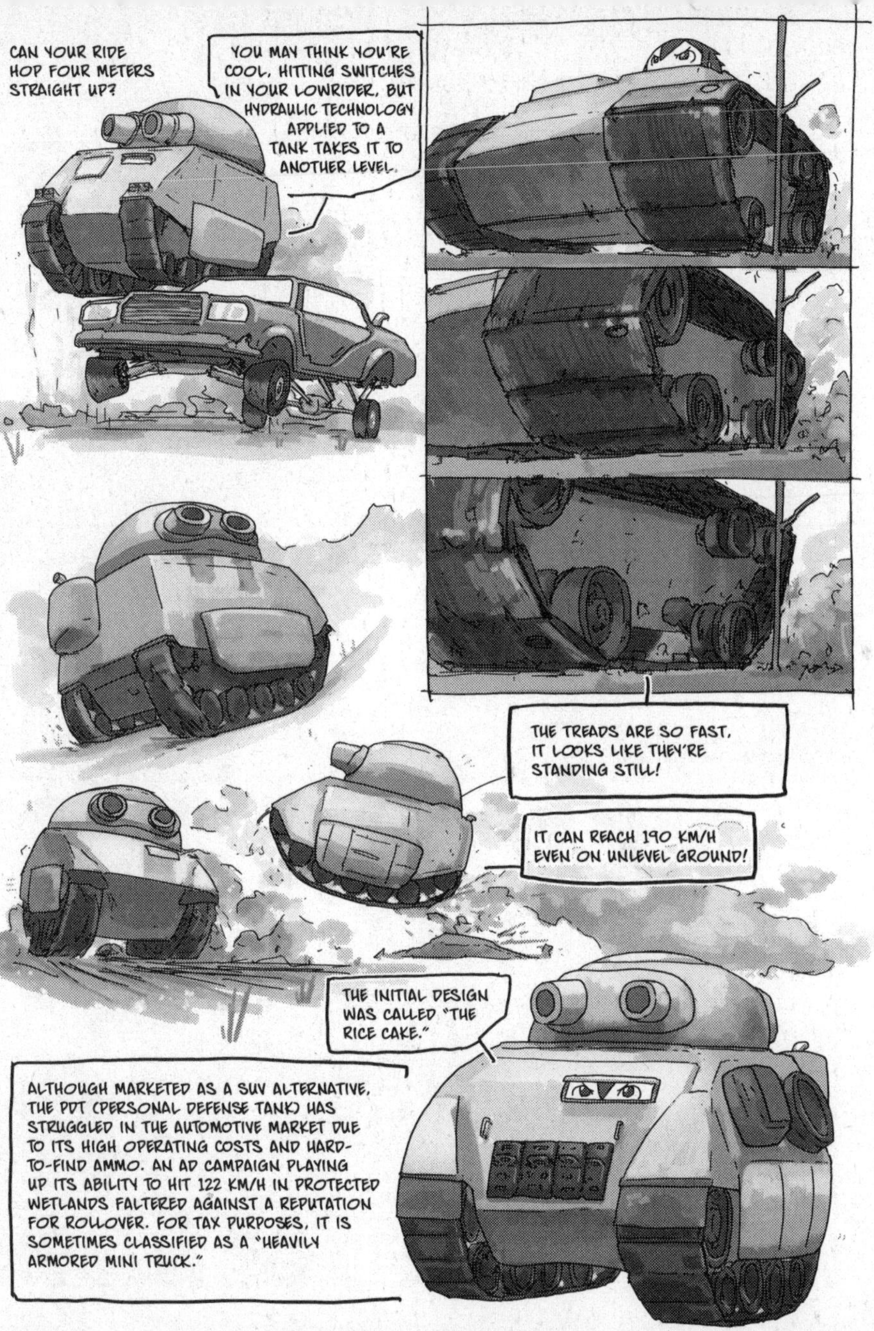
THE TREADS ARE SO FAST, IT LOOKS LIKE THEY'RE STANDING STILL!
YOU MAY THINK YOU'RE COOL, HITTING SWITCHES IN YOUR LOWRIDER, BUT HYDRAULIC TECHNOLOGY APPLIED TO A TANK TAKES IT TO ANOTHER LEVEL.
CAN YOUR RIDE HOP FOUR METERS STRAIGHT UP?
IT CAN REACH 190 KM/H EVEN ON UNLEVEL GROUND!
THE INITIAL DESIGN WAS CALLED "THE RICE CAKE."
ALTHOUGH MARKETED AS A SUV ALTERNATIVE, THE PDT (PERSONAL DEFENSE TANK) HAS STRUGGLED IN THE AUTOMOTIVE MARKET DUE TO ITS HIGH OPERATING COSTS AND HARD-TO-FIND AMMO. AN AD CAMPAIGN PLAYING UP ITS ABILITY TO HIT 122 KM/H IN PROTECTED WETLANDS FALTERED AGAINST A REPUTATION FOR ROLLOVER. FOR TAX PURPOSES, IT IS SOMETIMES CLASSIFIED AS A "HEAVILY ARMORED MINI TRUCK."

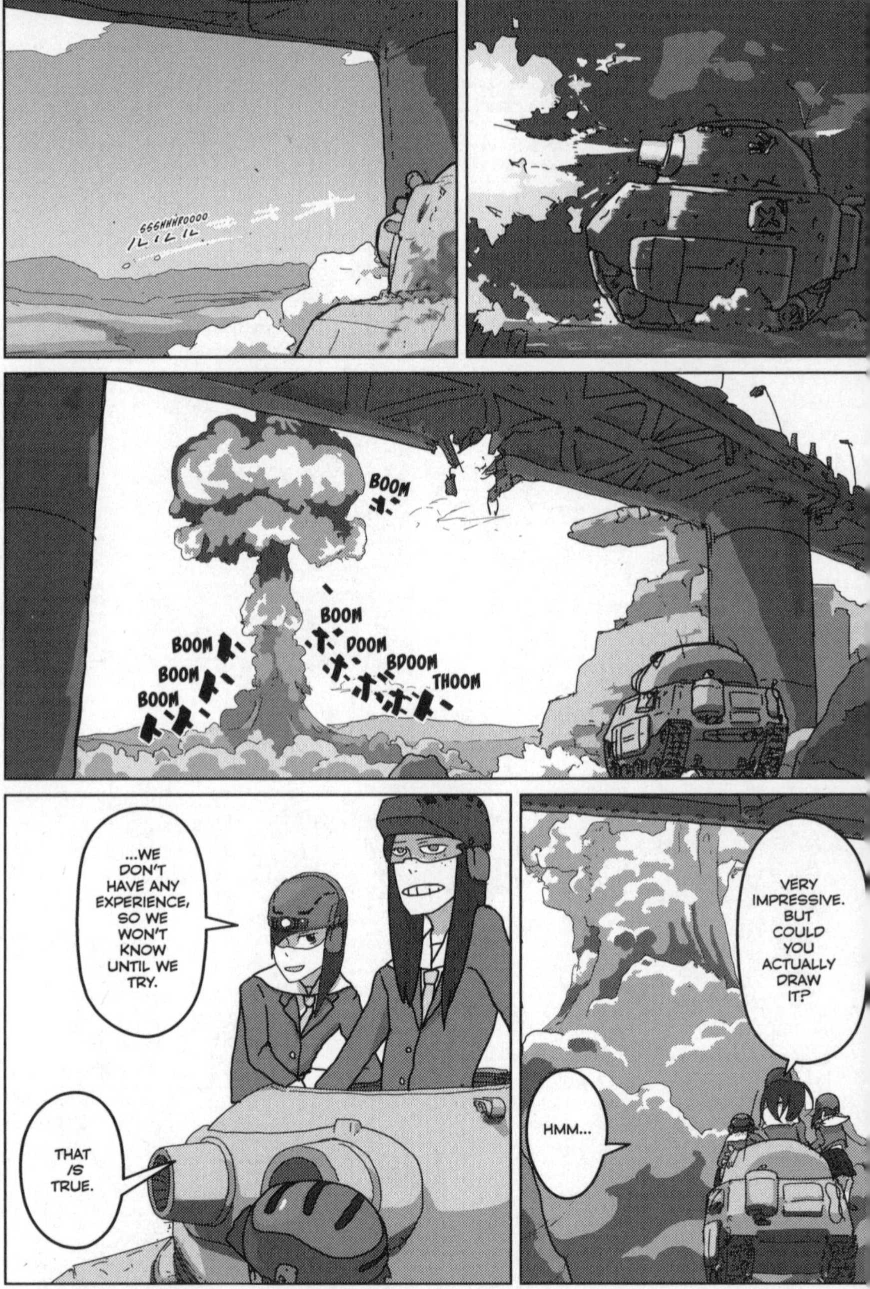
SSSHHHROOOO
BOOM
BOOM
DOOM
BDOOM
THOOM
BOOM
BOOM
BOOM
VERY IMPRESSIVE. BUT COULD YOU ACTUALLY DRAW IT?
HMM...
...WE DON'T HAVE ANY EXPERIENCE, SO WE WON'T KNOW UNTIL WE TRY.
THAT IS TRUE.

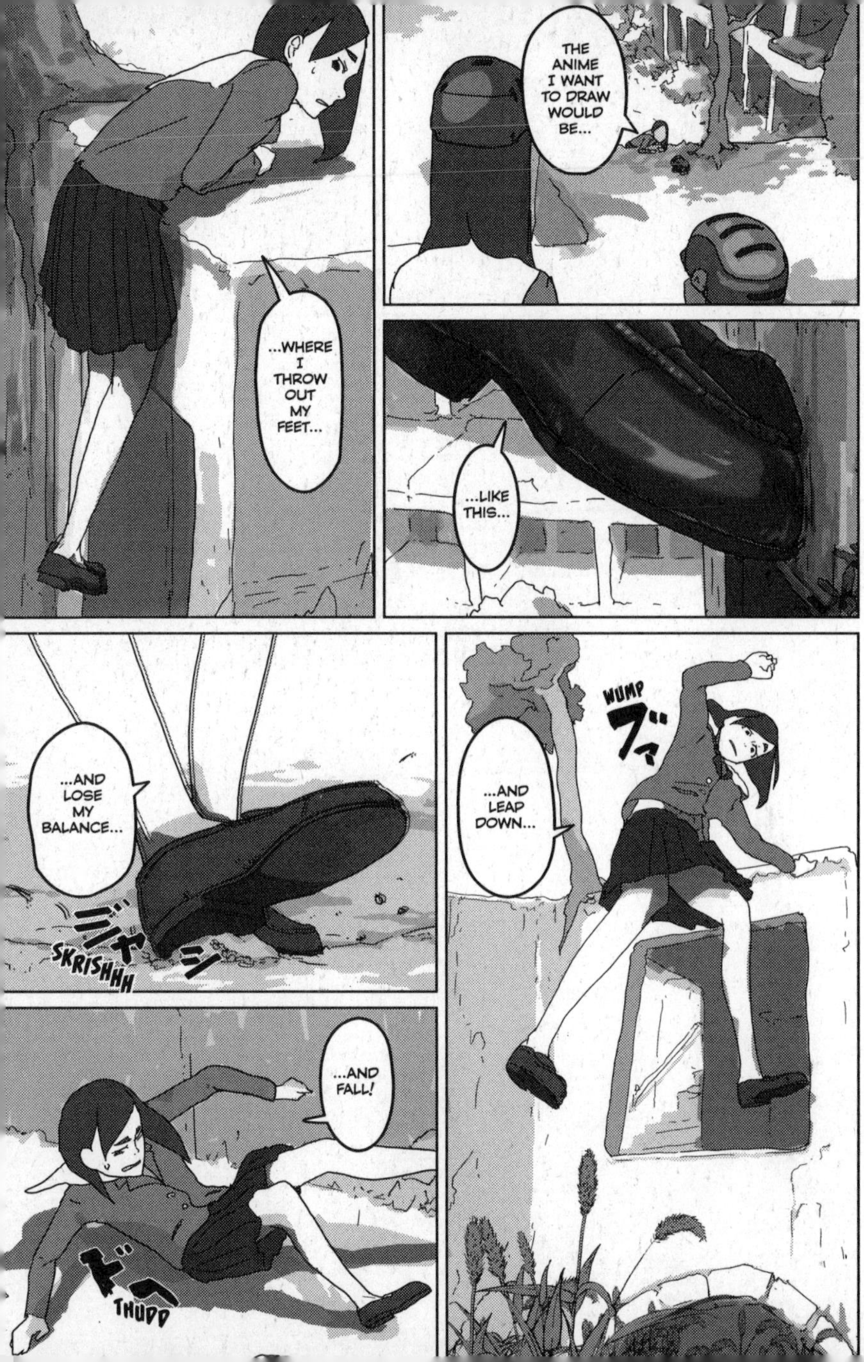
THE ANIME I WANT TO DRAW WOULD BE...
...LIKE THIS...
...WHERE I THROW OUT MY FEET...
WUMP
...AND LEAP DOWN...
...AND LOSE MY BALANCE...
SKRISHHH
...AND FALL!
THUDD

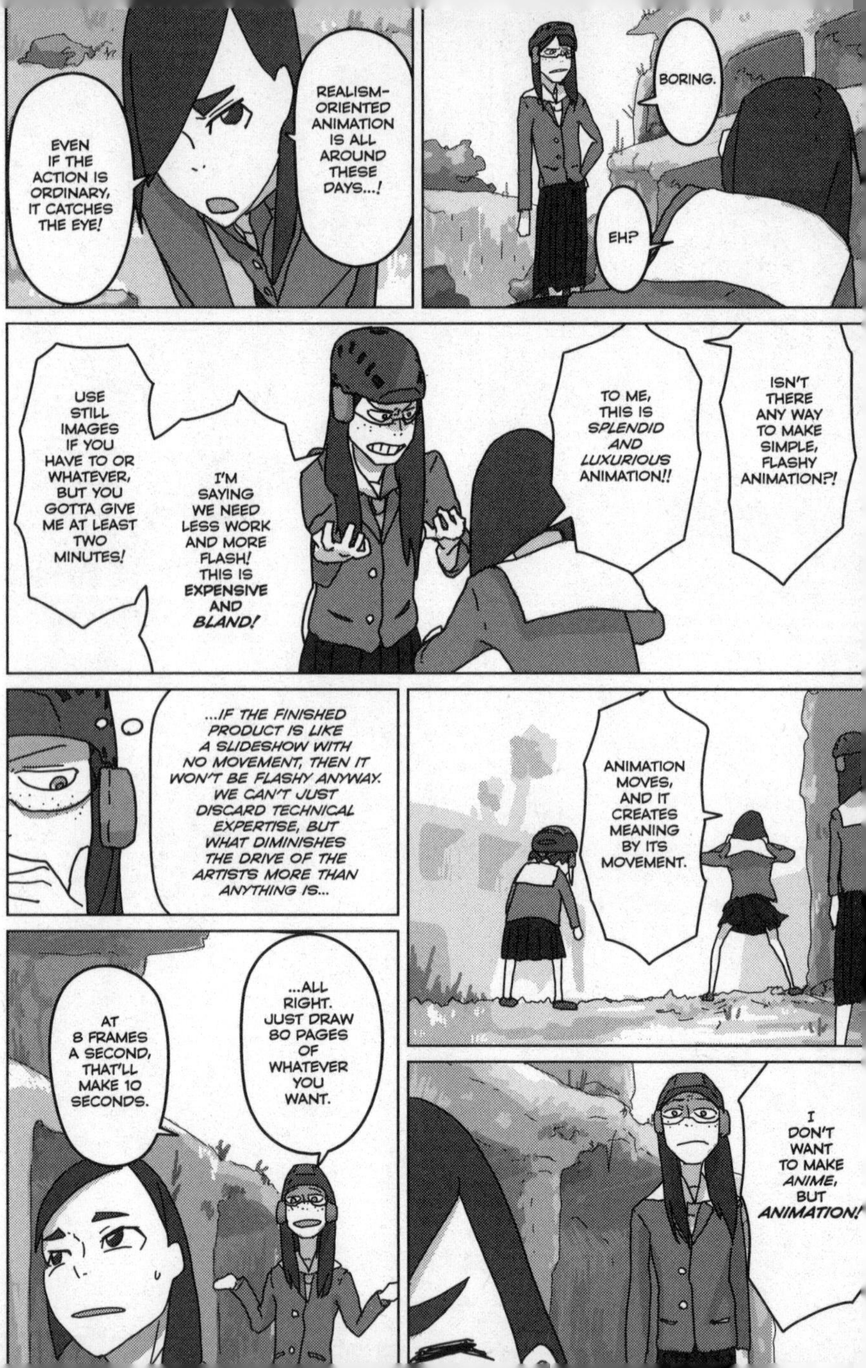
BORING.
EH?
REALISM-ORIENTED ANIMATION IS ALL AROUND THESE DAYS...!
EVEN IF THE ACTION IS ORDINARY, IT CATCHES THE EYE!
ISN'T THERE ANY WAY TO MAKE SIMPLE, FLASHY ANIMATION?!
TO ME, THIS IS *SPLENDID AND LUXURIOUS* ANIMATION!!
I'M SAYING WE NEED LESS WORK AND MORE FLASH! THIS IS EXPENSIVE AND *BLAND!*
USE STILL IMAGES IF YOU HAVE TO OR WHATEVER, BUT YOU GOTTA GIVE ME AT LEAST TWO MINUTES!
ANIMATION MOVES, AND IT CREATES MEANING BY ITS MOVEMENT.
...IF THE FINISHED PRODUCT IS LIKE A SLIDESHOW WITH NO MOVEMENT, THEN IT WON'T BE FLASHY ANYWAY. WE CAN'T JUST DISCARD TECHNICAL EXPERTISE, BUT WHAT DIMINISHES THE DRIVE OF THE ARTISTS MORE THAN ANYTHING IS...
I DON'T WANT TO MAKE *ANIME,* BUT ***ANIMATION!***
...ALL RIGHT. JUST DRAW 80 PAGES OF WHATEVER YOU WANT.
AT 8 FRAMES A SECOND, THAT'LL MAKE 10 SECONDS.

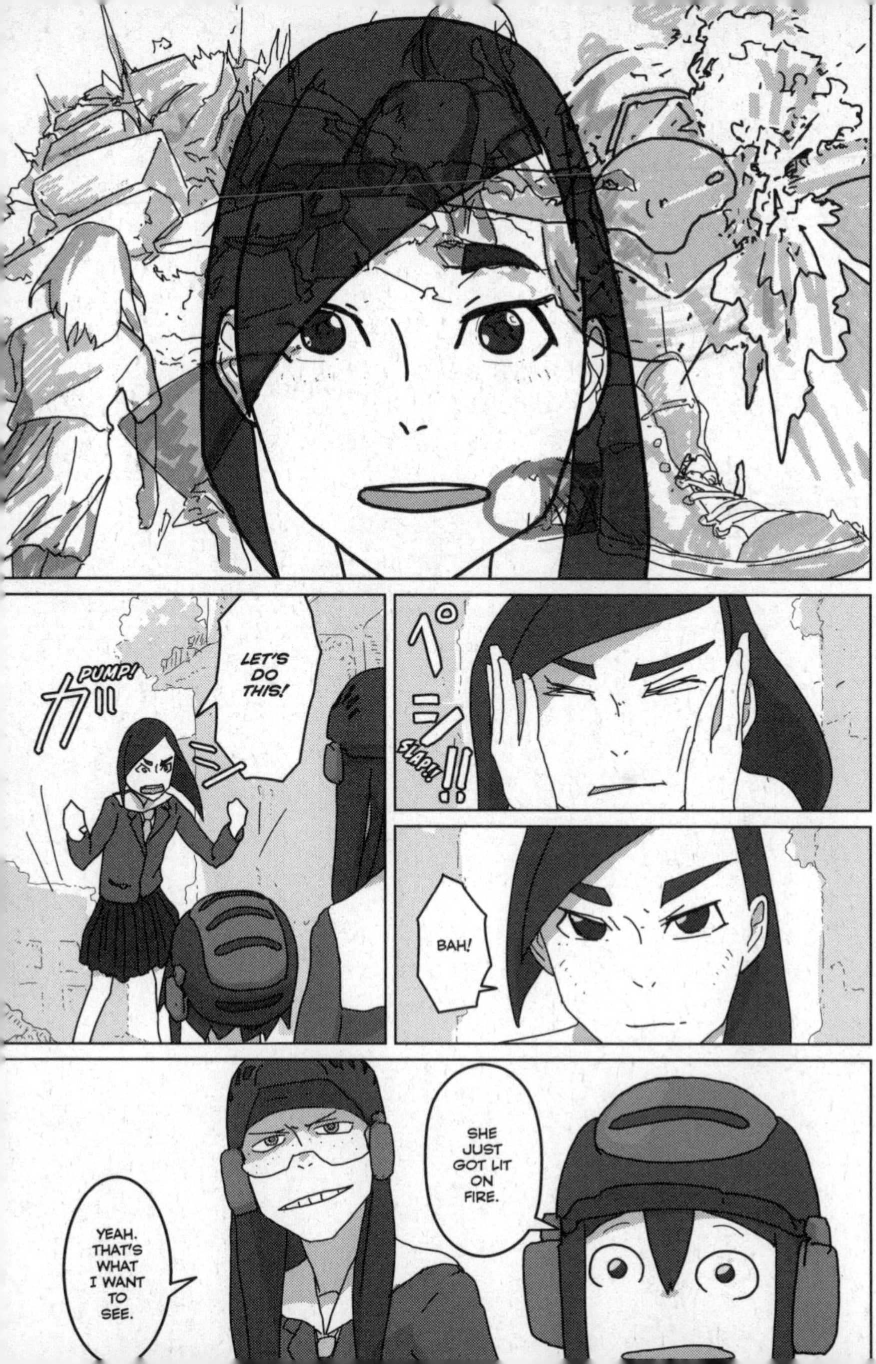
SLAP!!
BAH!
PUMP!
LET'S DO THIS!
SHE JUST GOT LIT ON FIRE.
YEAH. THAT'S WHAT I WANT TO SEE.

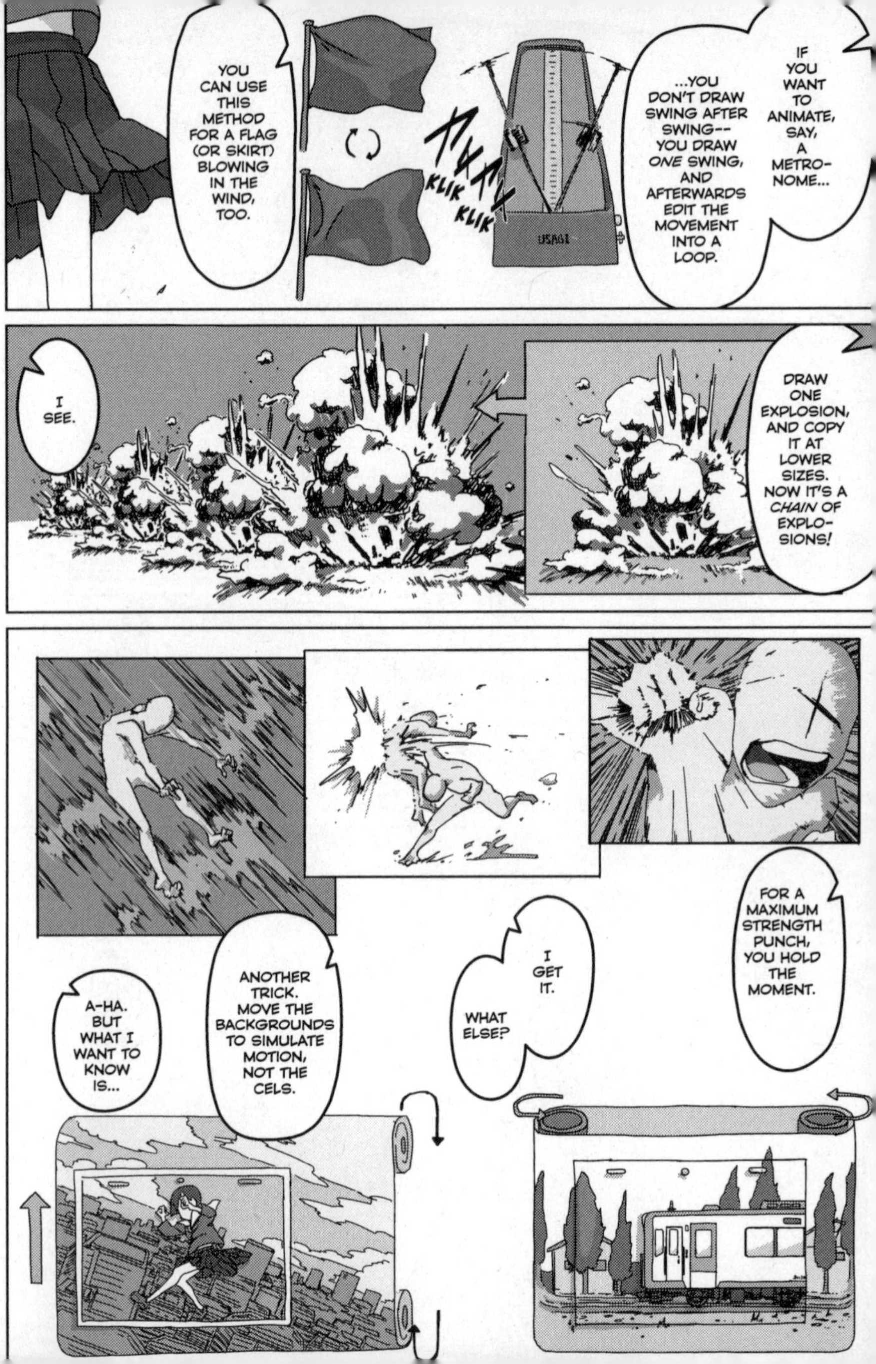
IF YOU WANT TO ANIMATE, SAY, A METRONOME...
...YOU DON'T DRAW SWING AFTER SWING-- YOU DRAW *ONE* SWING, AND AFTERWARDS EDIT THE MOVEMENT INTO A LOOP.
KLIK KLIK
USAGI
YOU CAN USE THIS METHOD FOR A FLAG (OR SKIRT) BLOWING IN THE WIND, TOO.
DRAW ONE EXPLOSION, AND COPY IT AT LOWER SIZES. NOW IT'S A *CHAIN* OF EXPLOSIONS!
I SEE.
FOR A MAXIMUM STRENGTH PUNCH, YOU HOLD THE MOMENT.
I GET IT.
WHAT ELSE?
ANOTHER TRICK. MOVE THE BACKGROUNDS TO SIMULATE MOTION, NOT THE CELS.
A-HA. BUT WHAT I WANT TO KNOW IS...

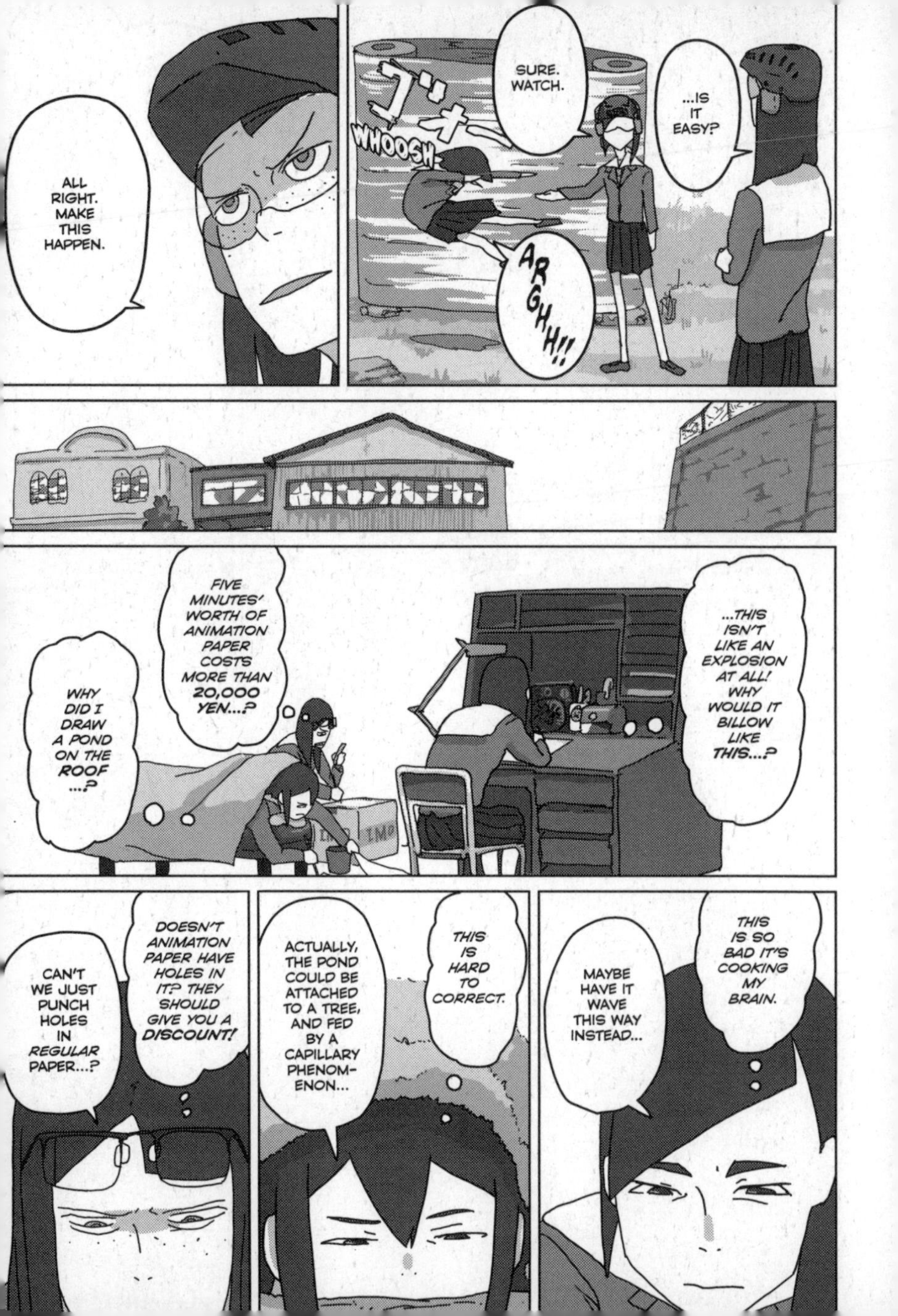
...IS IT EASY?
SURE. WATCH.
WHOOSH
ARGHH!!
ALL RIGHT. MAKE THIS HAPPEN.
...THIS ISN'T LIKE AN EXPLOSION AT ALL! WHY WOULD IT BILLOW LIKE THIS...?
FIVE MINUTES' WORTH OF ANIMATION PAPER COSTS MORE THAN 20,000 YEN...?
WHY DID I DRAW A POND ON THE ROOF...?
THIS IS SO BAD IT'S COOKING MY BRAIN.
MAYBE HAVE IT WAVE THIS WAY INSTEAD...
THIS IS HARD TO CORRECT.
ACTUALLY, THE POND COULD BE ATTACHED TO A TREE, AND FED BY A CAPILLARY PHENOM-ENON...
DOESN'T ANIMATION PAPER HAVE HOLES IN IT? THEY SHOULD GIVE YOU A DISCOUNT!
CAN'T WE JUST PUNCH HOLES IN REGULAR PAPER...?

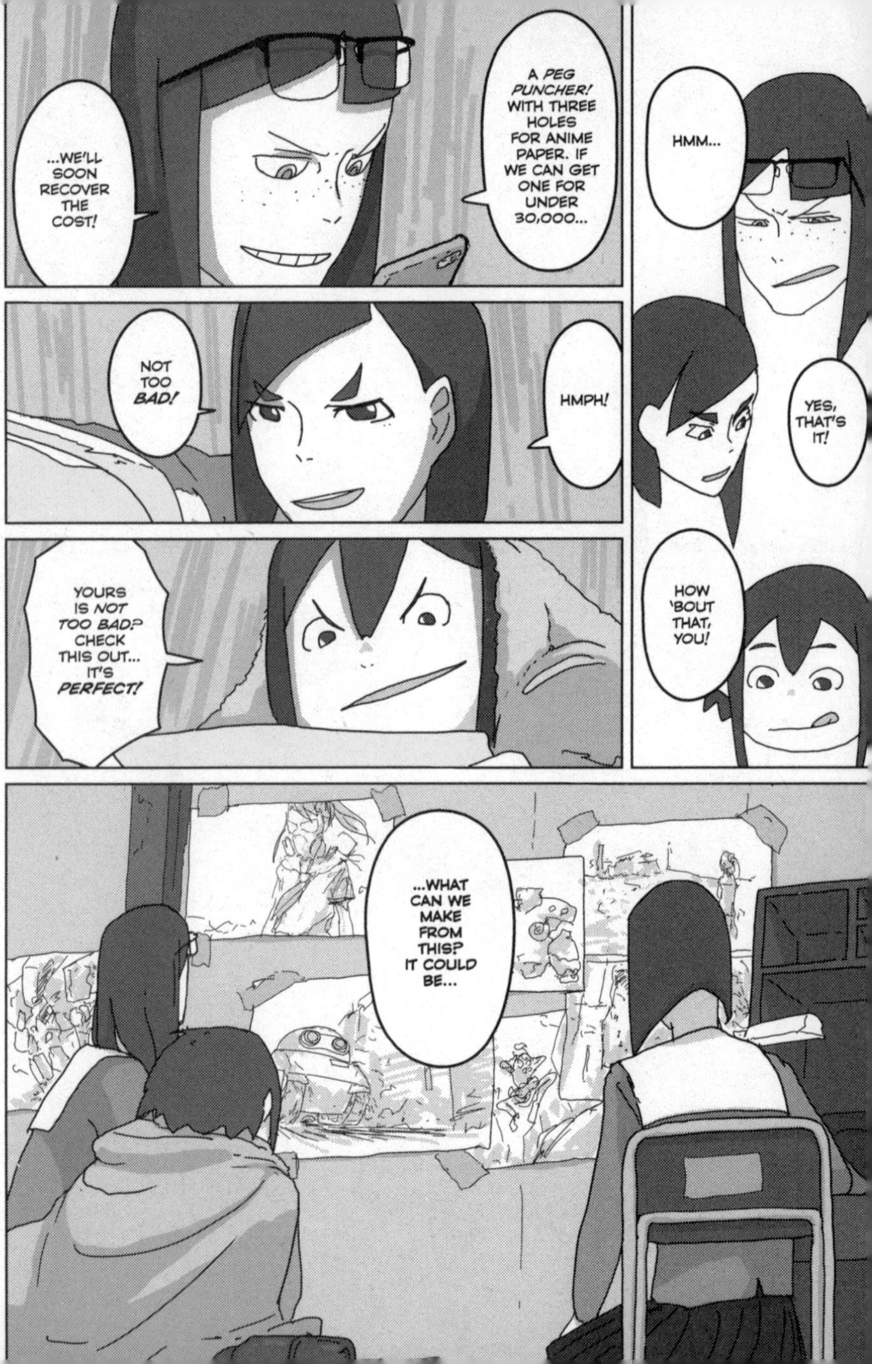
HMM...
YES, THAT'S IT!
A *PEG PUNCHER!* WITH THREE HOLES FOR ANIME PAPER. IF WE CAN GET ONE FOR UNDER 30,000...
...WE'LL SOON RECOVER THE COST!
HMPH!
NOT TOO *BAD!*
HOW 'BOUT THAT, YOU!
YOURS IS *NOT TOO BAD?* CHECK THIS OUT... IT'S *PERFECT!*
...WHAT CAN WE MAKE FROM THIS? IT COULD BE...

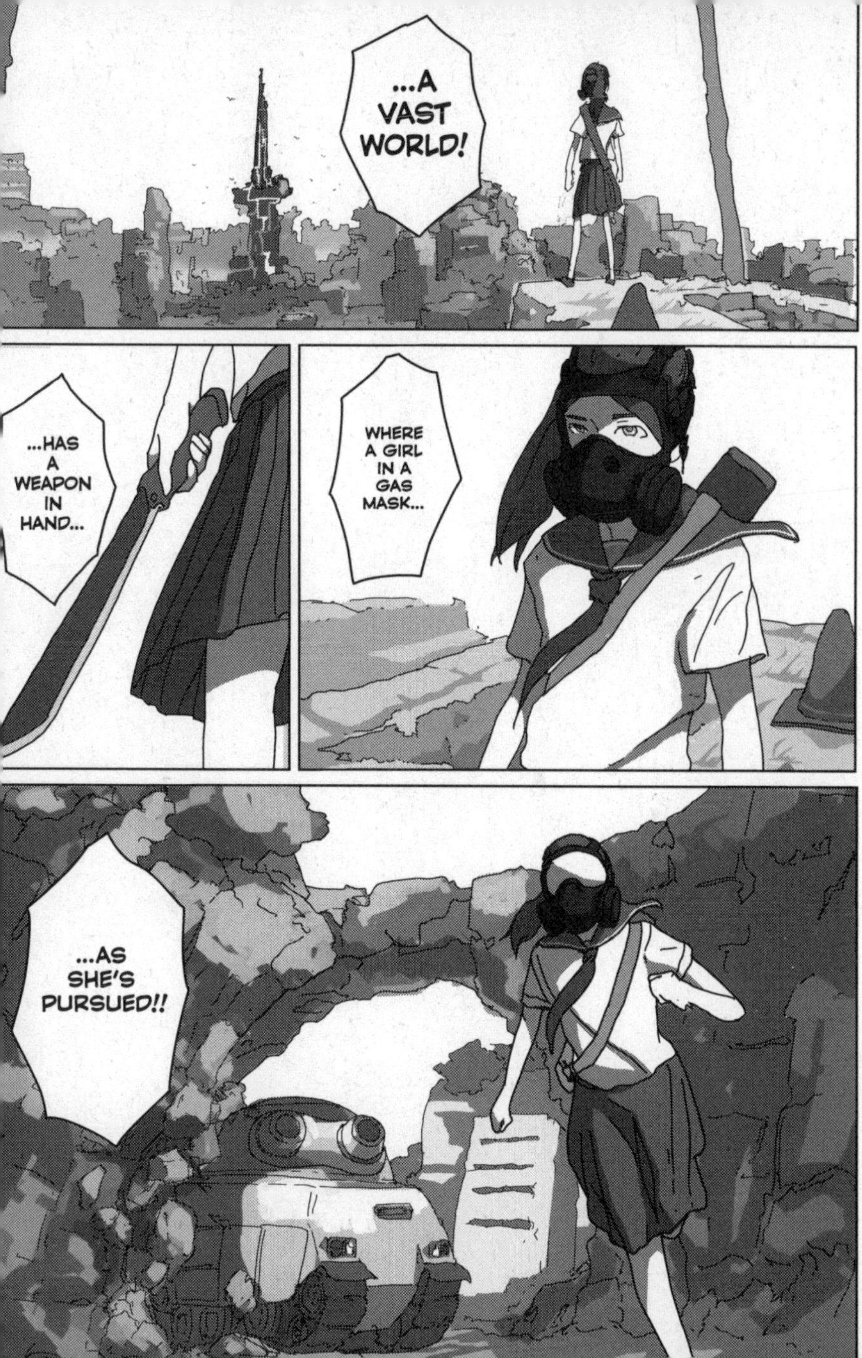
...A VAST WORLD!
WHERE A GIRL IN A GAS MASK...
...HAS A WEAPON IN HAND...
...AS SHE'S PURSUED!!

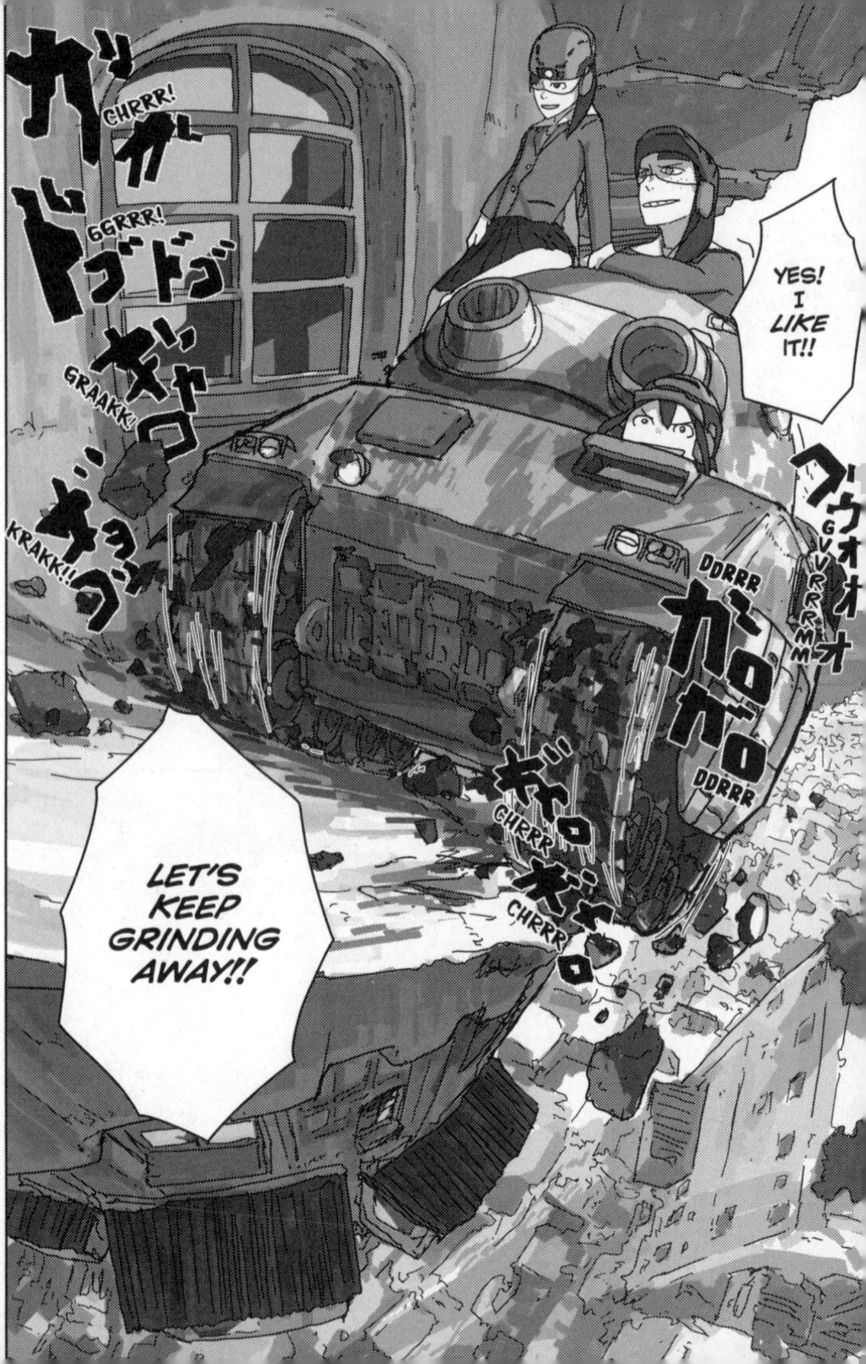
YES! I LIKE IT!!
GVVRRRMM
DDRRR
DDRRR
CHRRR
CHRRR
CHRRR!
GGRRR!
GRAAKK!
KRAKK!!
LET'S KEEP GRINDING AWAY!!

CHAPTER 6:
THE 48-HOURS-A-DAY OF TOIL CRISIS

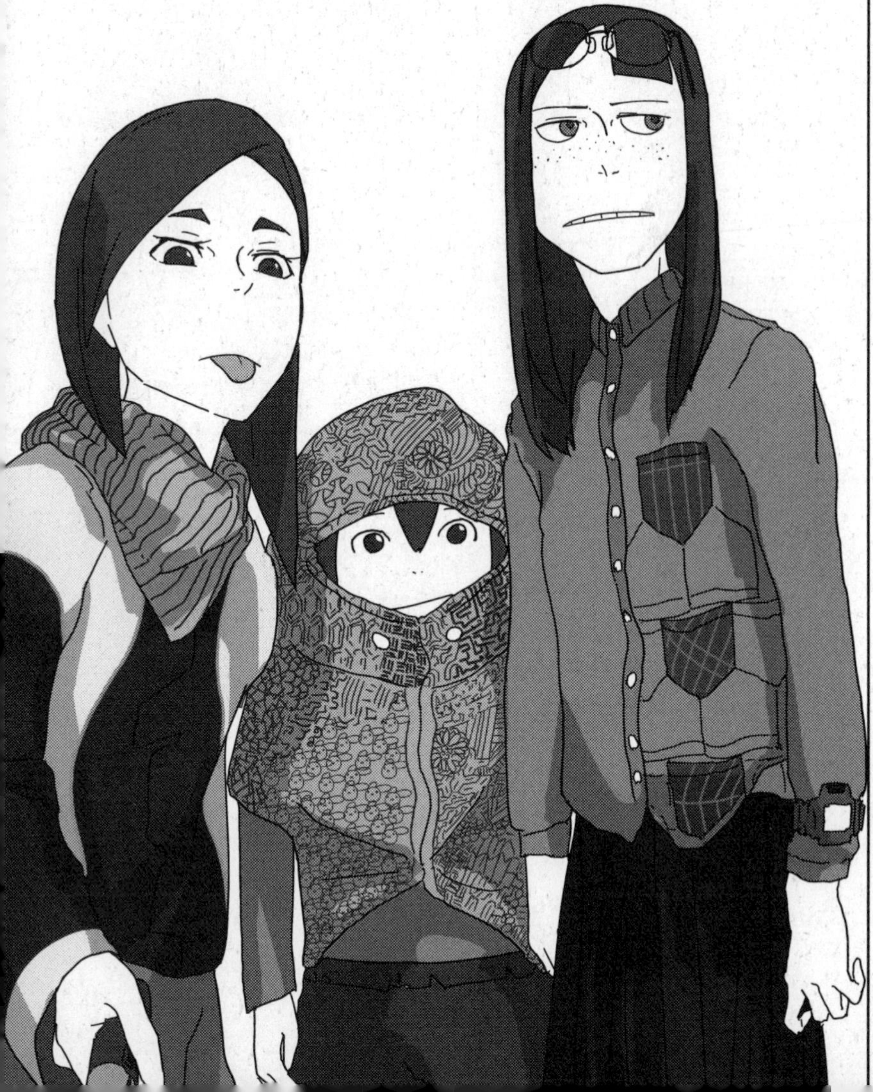

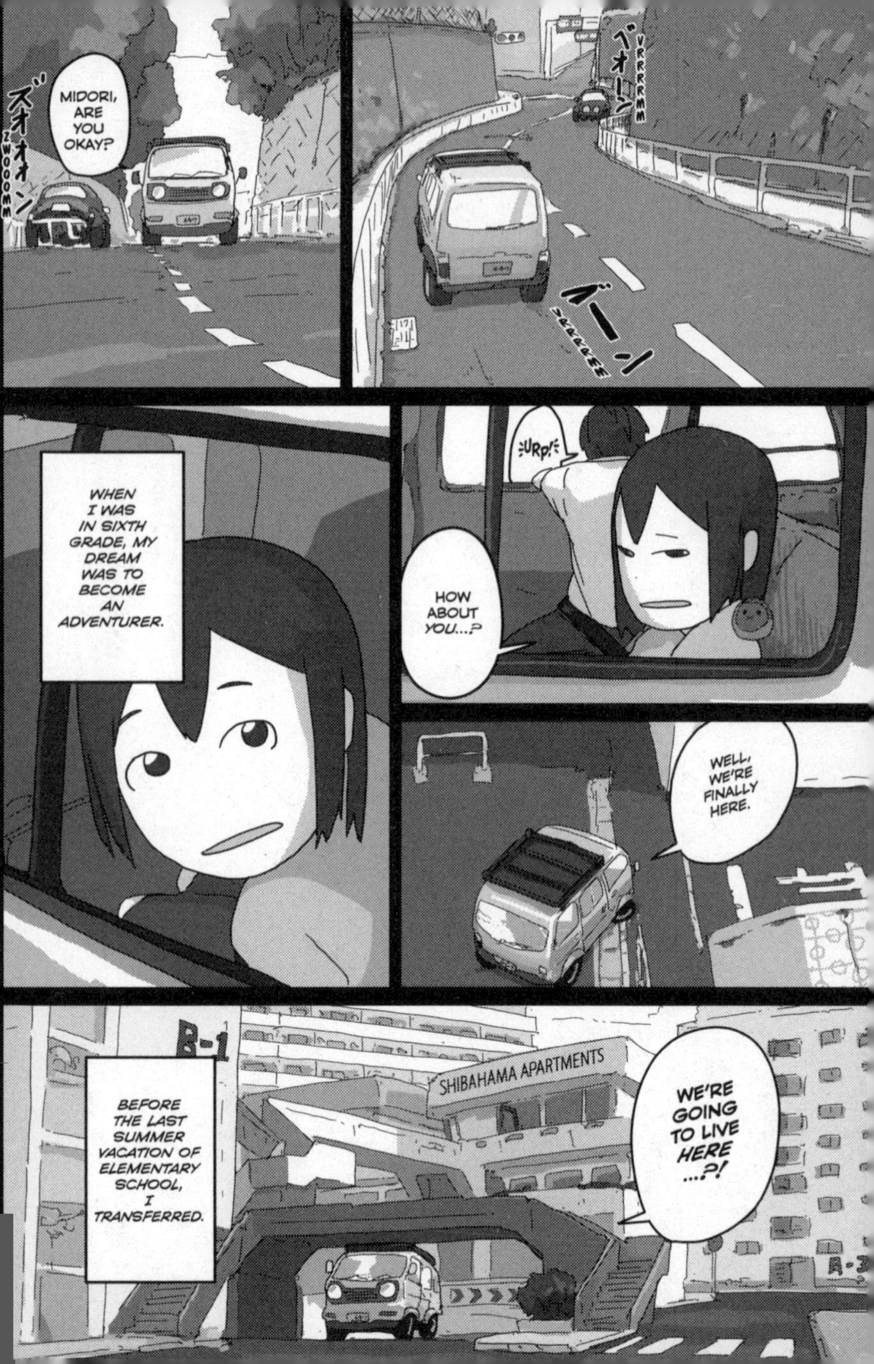
ベオーン
VRRRRMM
ブーン
VRRRRRMM
MIDORI, ARE YOU OKAY?
ズオオオン
ZWOOOMM
URP!
HOW ABOUT YOU...?
WELL, WE'RE FINALLY HERE.
WHEN I WAS IN SIXTH GRADE, MY DREAM WAS TO BECOME AN ADVENTURER.
A-3
SHIBAHAMA APARTMENTS
WE'RE GOING TO LIVE HERE...?!
B-1
BEFORE THE LAST SUMMER VACATION OF ELEMENTARY SCHOOL, I TRANSFERRED.

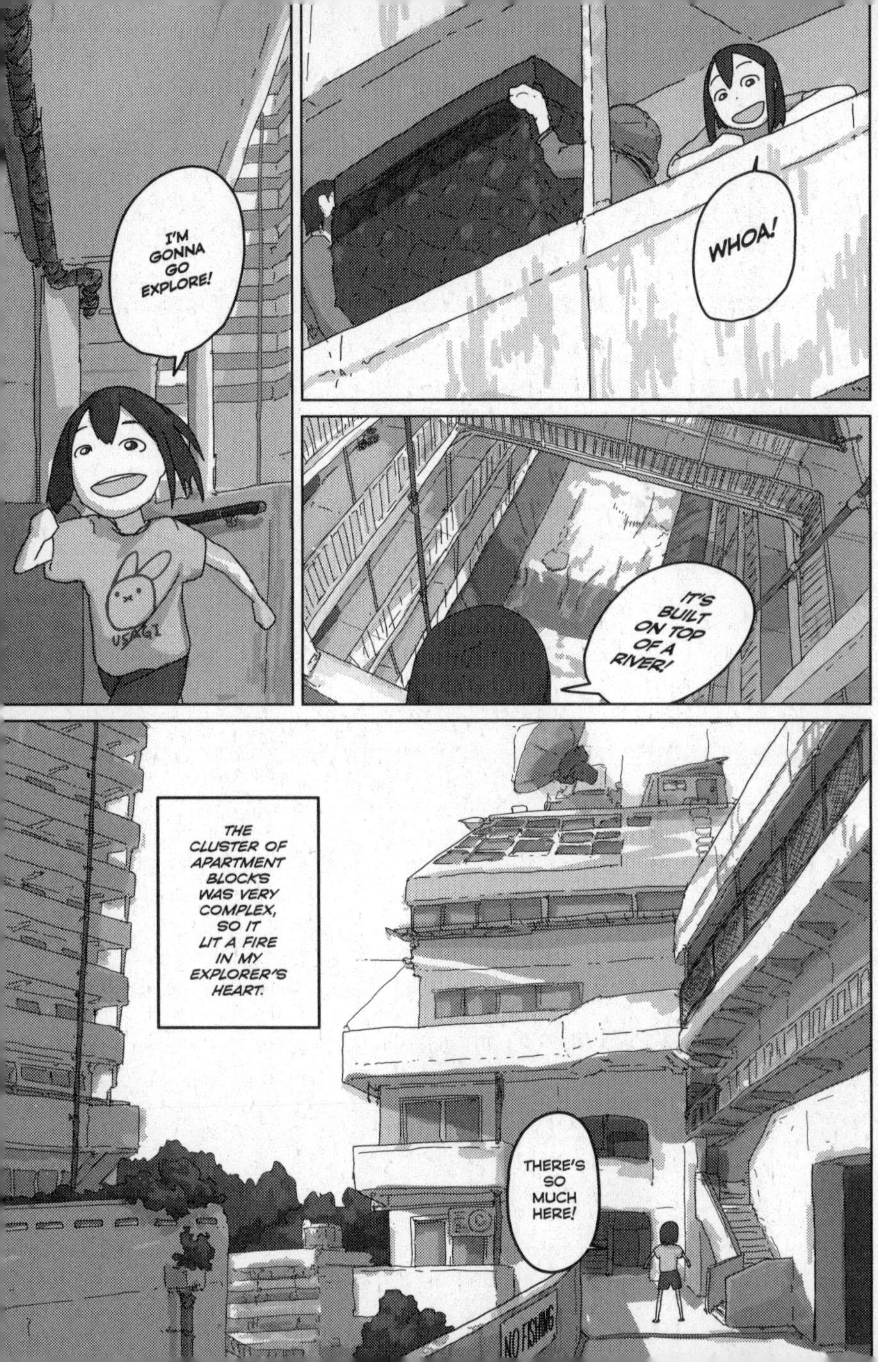
WHOA!
IT'S BUILT ON TOP OF A RIVER!
I'M GONNA GO EXPLORE!
THE CLUSTER OF APARTMENT BLOCKS WAS VERY COMPLEX, SO IT LIT A FIRE IN MY EXPLORER'S HEART.
THERE'S SO MUCH HERE!
NO FISHING

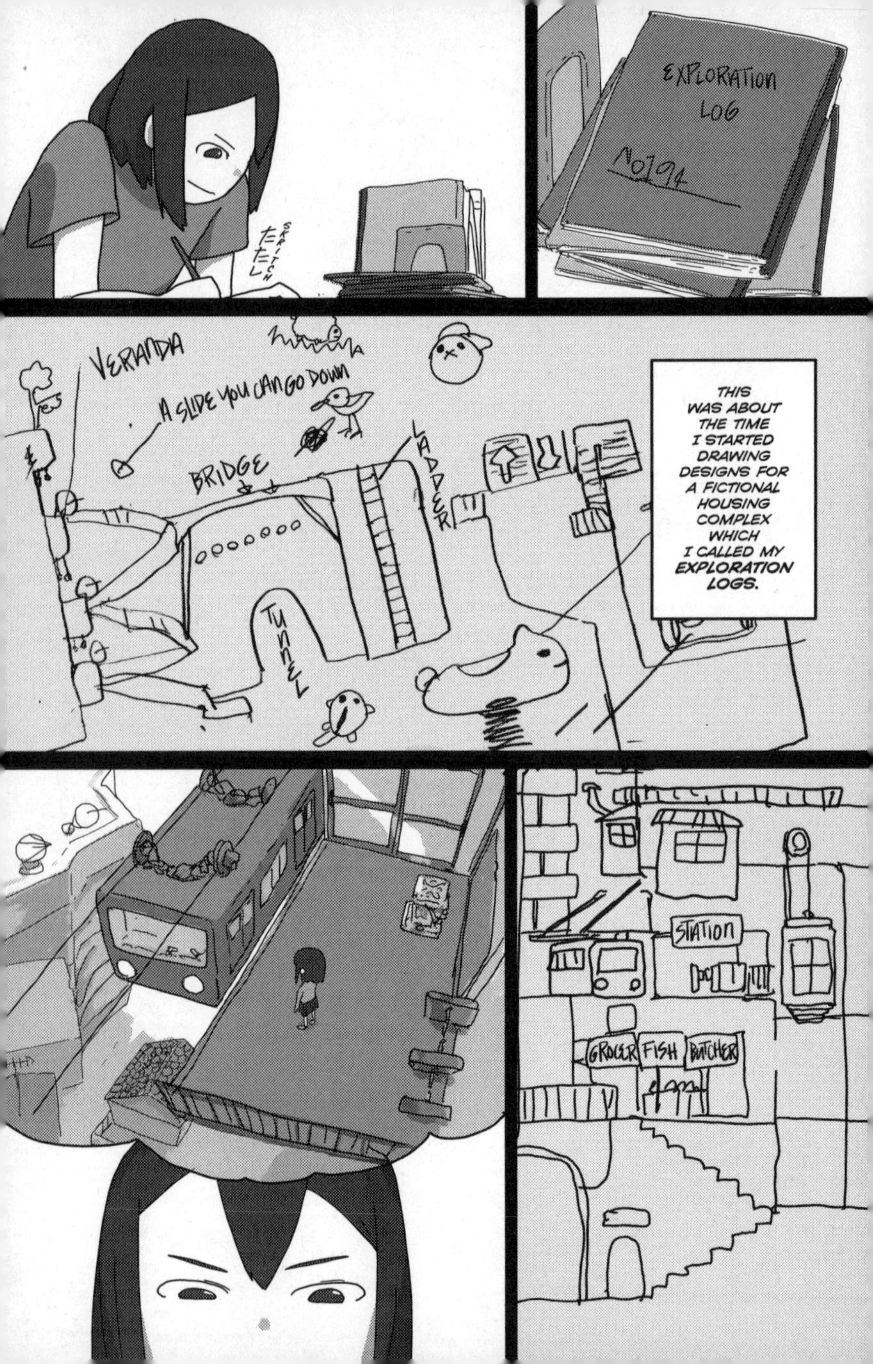
EXPLORATION LOG
No194
SKRITCH
THIS WAS ABOUT THE TIME I STARTED DRAWING DESIGNS FOR A FICTIONAL HOUSING COMPLEX WHICH I CALLED MY **EXPLORATION LOGS.**
LADDER
A SLIDE YOU CAN GO DOWN
VERANDA
BRIDGE
TUNNEL
STATION
BUTCHER
FISH
GROCER

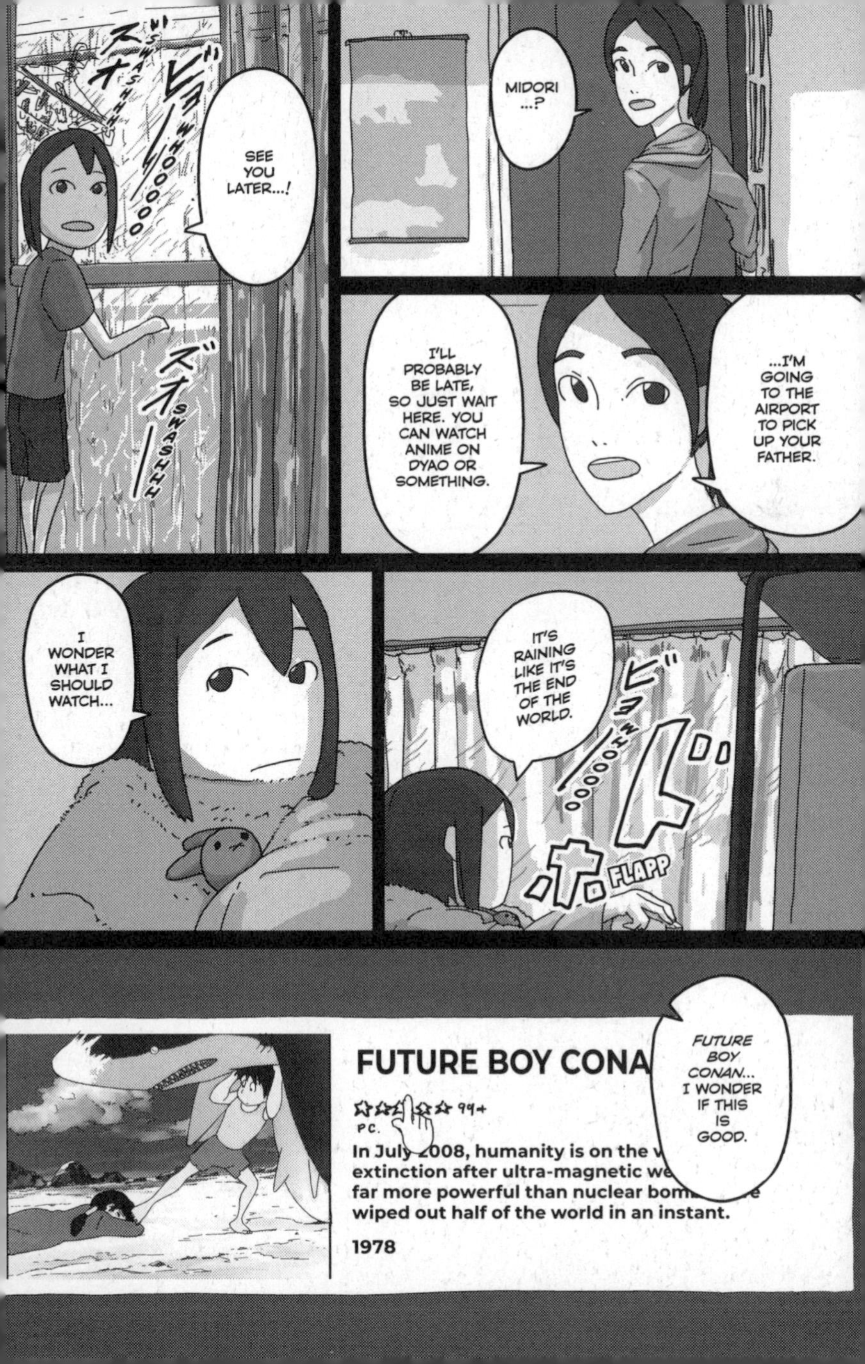
MIDORI ...?
...I'M GOING TO THE AIRPORT TO PICK UP YOUR FATHER.
I'LL PROBABLY BE LATE, SO JUST WAIT HERE. YOU CAN WATCH ANIME ON DYAO OR SOMETHING.
SWASHHH
WHOOOOOO
SEE YOU LATER...!
SWASHHH
IT'S RAINING LIKE IT'S THE END OF THE WORLD.
WHOOOOO
FLAPP
I WONDER WHAT I SHOULD WATCH...
FUTURE BOY CONA
99+
P.C.
In July 2008, humanity is on the v
extinction after ultra-magnetic we
far more powerful than nuclear bomb
wiped out half of the world in an instant.
1978
FUTURE BOY CONAN... I WONDER IF THIS IS GOOD.

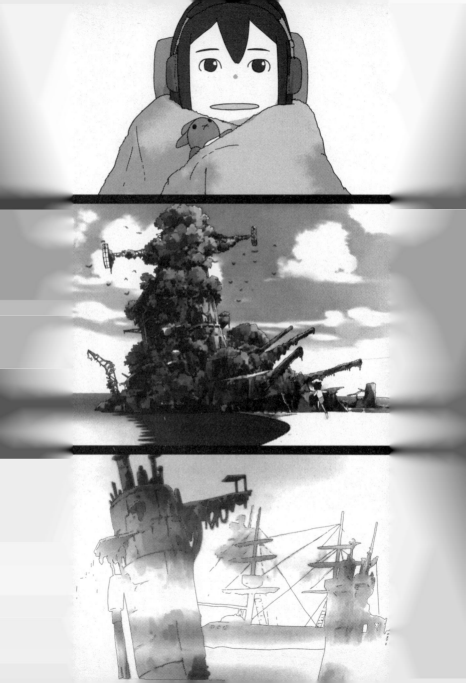

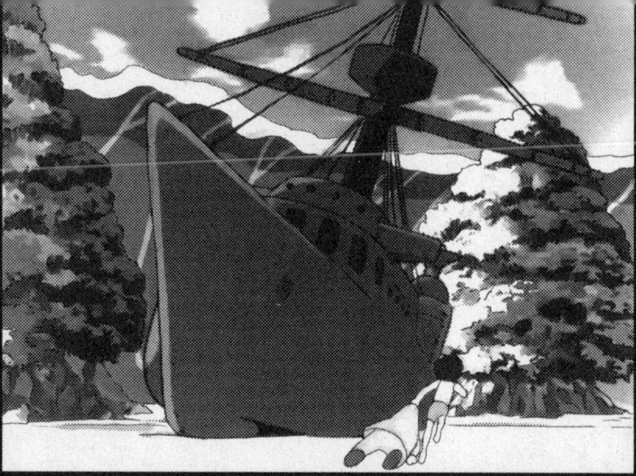

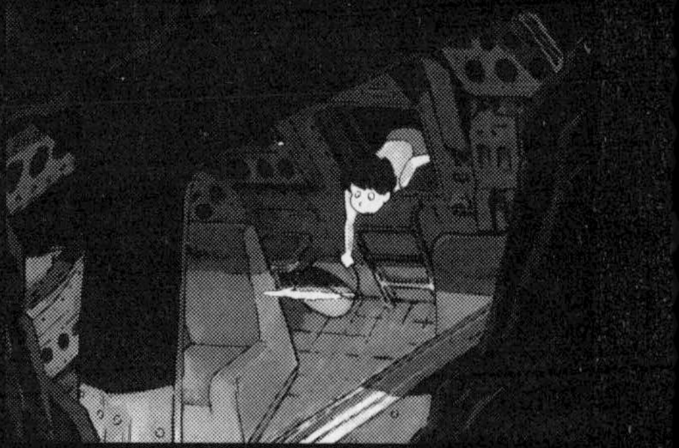

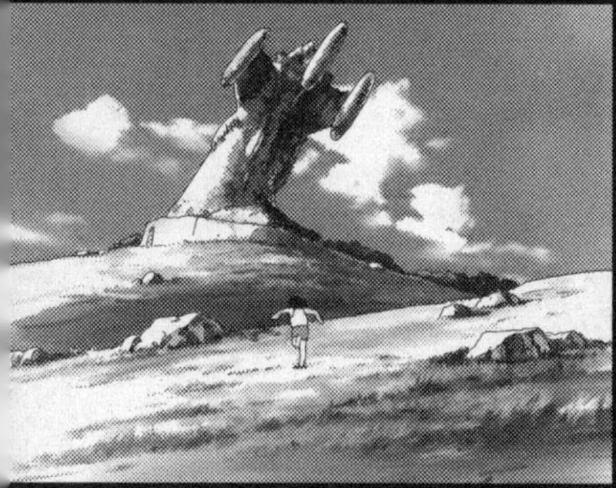

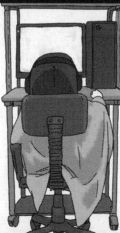

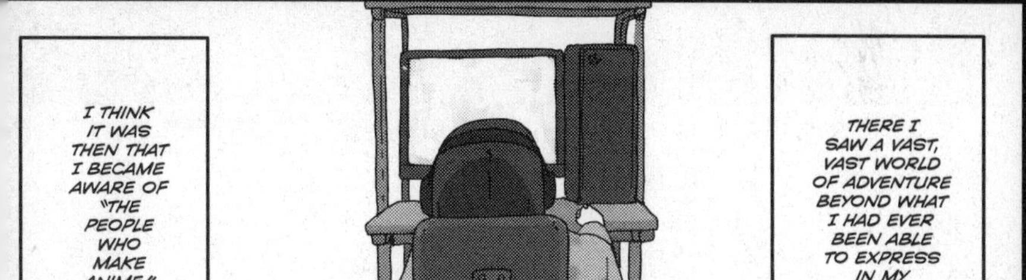
THERE I SAW A VAST, VAST WORLD OF ADVENTURE BEYOND WHAT I HAD EVER BEEN ABLE TO EXPRESS IN MY NOTEBOOKS.
I THINK IT WAS THEN THAT I BECAME AWARE OF "THE PEOPLE WHO MAKE ANIME."

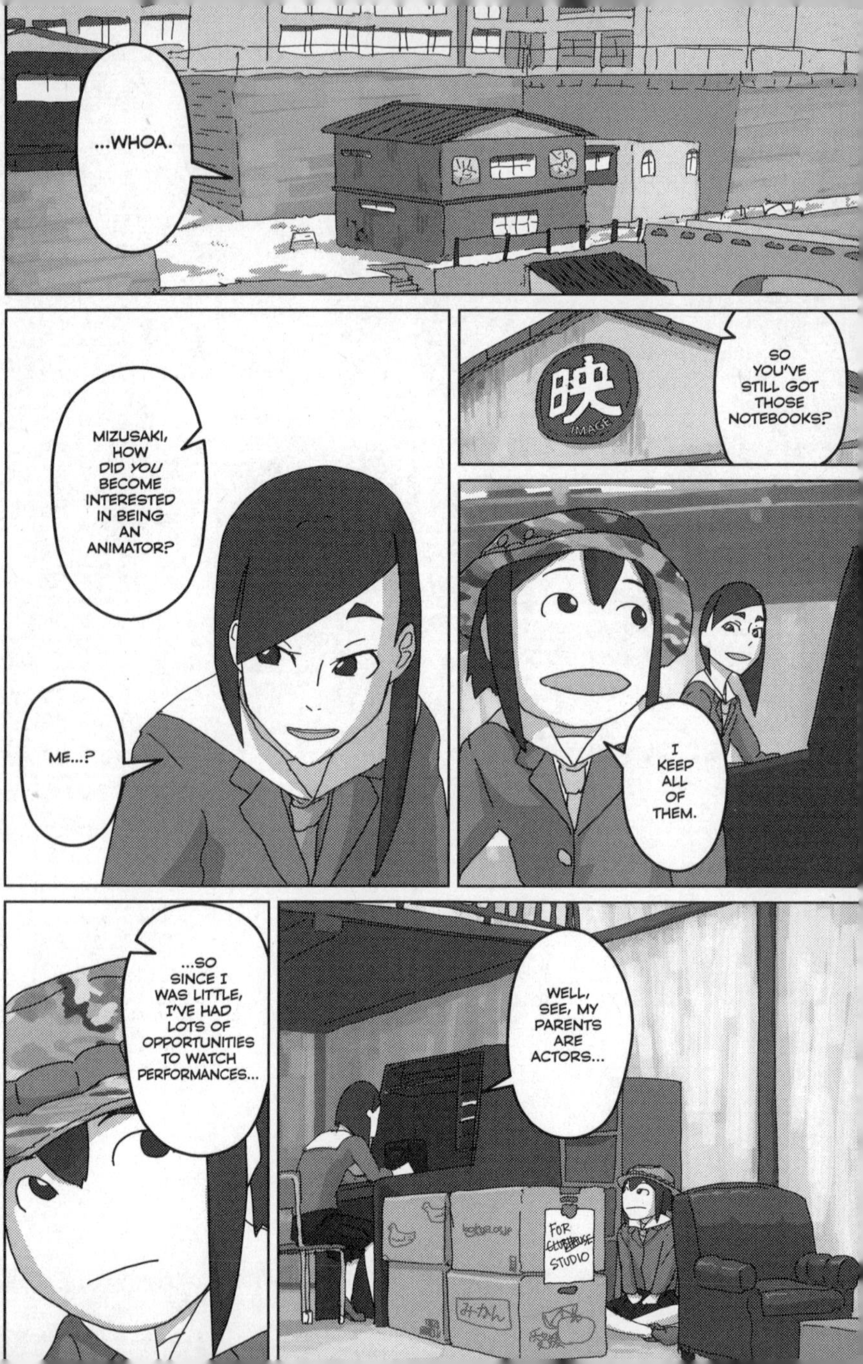
...WHOA.
映 IMAGE
SO YOU'VE STILL GOT THOSE NOTEBOOKS?
I KEEP ALL OF THEM.
MIZUSAKI, HOW DID *YOU* BECOME INTERESTED IN BEING AN ANIMATOR?
ME...?
WELL, SEE, MY PARENTS ARE ACTORS...
FOR ~~CLUBHOUSE~~ STUDIO
みかん
...SO SINCE I WAS LITTLE, I'VE HAD LOTS OF OPPORTUNITIES TO WATCH PERFORMANCES...

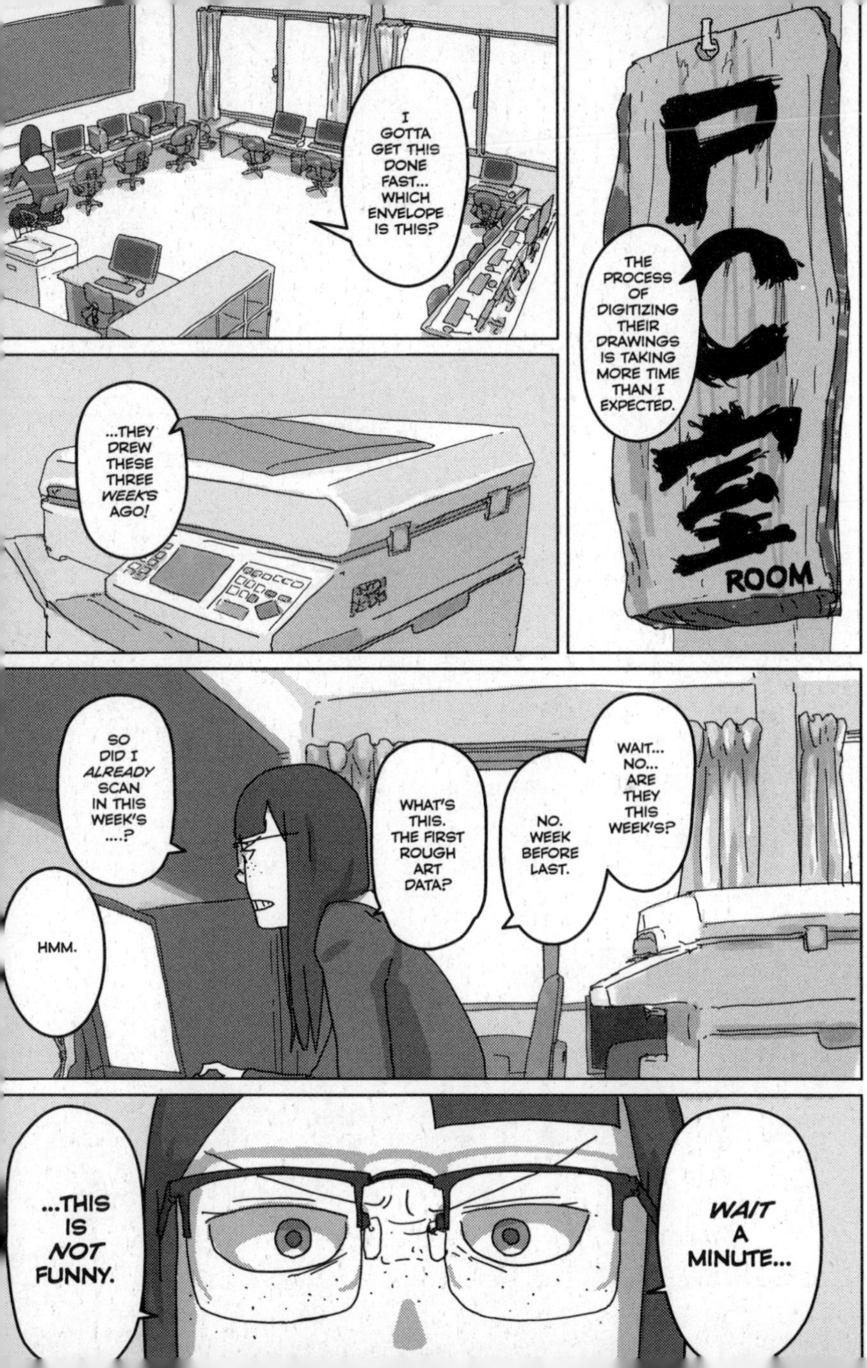
ROOM
THE PROCESS OF DIGITIZING THEIR DRAWINGS IS TAKING MORE TIME THAN I EXPECTED.
I GOTTA GET THIS DONE FAST... WHICH ENVELOPE IS THIS?
...THEY DREW THESE THREE *WEEKS* AGO!
WAIT... NO... ARE THEY THIS WEEK'S?
NO. WEEK BEFORE LAST.
WHAT'S THIS. THE FIRST ROUGH ART DATA?
SO DID I *ALREADY* SCAN IN THIS WEEK'S ....?
HMM.
WAIT A MINUTE...
...THIS IS *NOT* FUNNY.

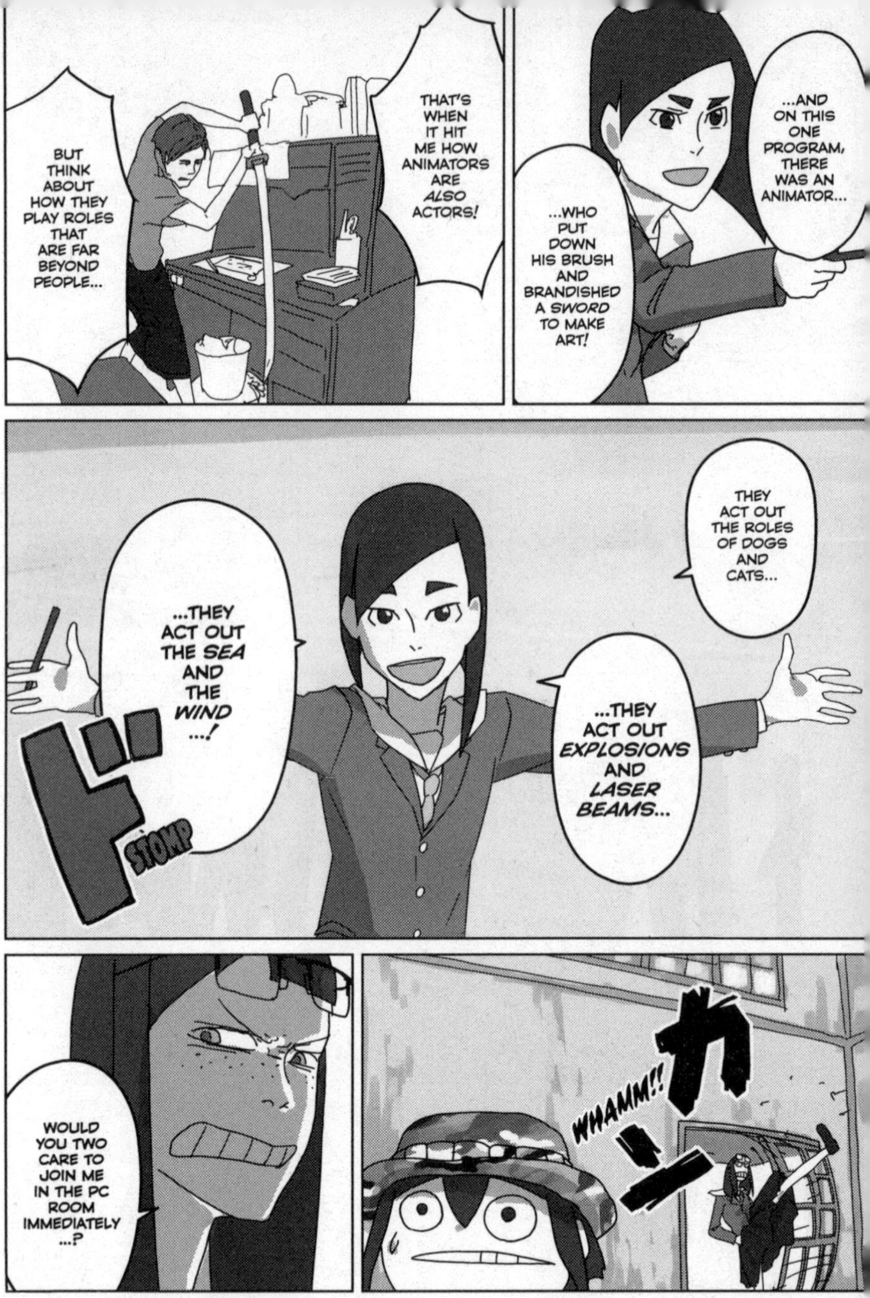
...AND ON THIS ONE PROGRAM, THERE WAS AN ANIMATOR...
...WHO PUT DOWN HIS BRUSH AND BRANDISHED A *SWORD* TO MAKE ART!
THAT'S WHEN IT HIT ME HOW ANIMATORS ARE *ALSO* ACTORS!
BUT THINK ABOUT HOW THEY PLAY ROLES THAT ARE FAR BEYOND PEOPLE...
THEY ACT OUT THE ROLES OF DOGS AND CATS...
...THEY ACT OUT *EXPLOSIONS* AND *LASER BEAMS*...
...THEY ACT OUT THE *SEA* AND THE *WIND* ...!
STOMP
WHAMM!!
WOULD YOU TWO CARE TO JOIN ME IN THE PC ROOM IMMEDIATELY ...?

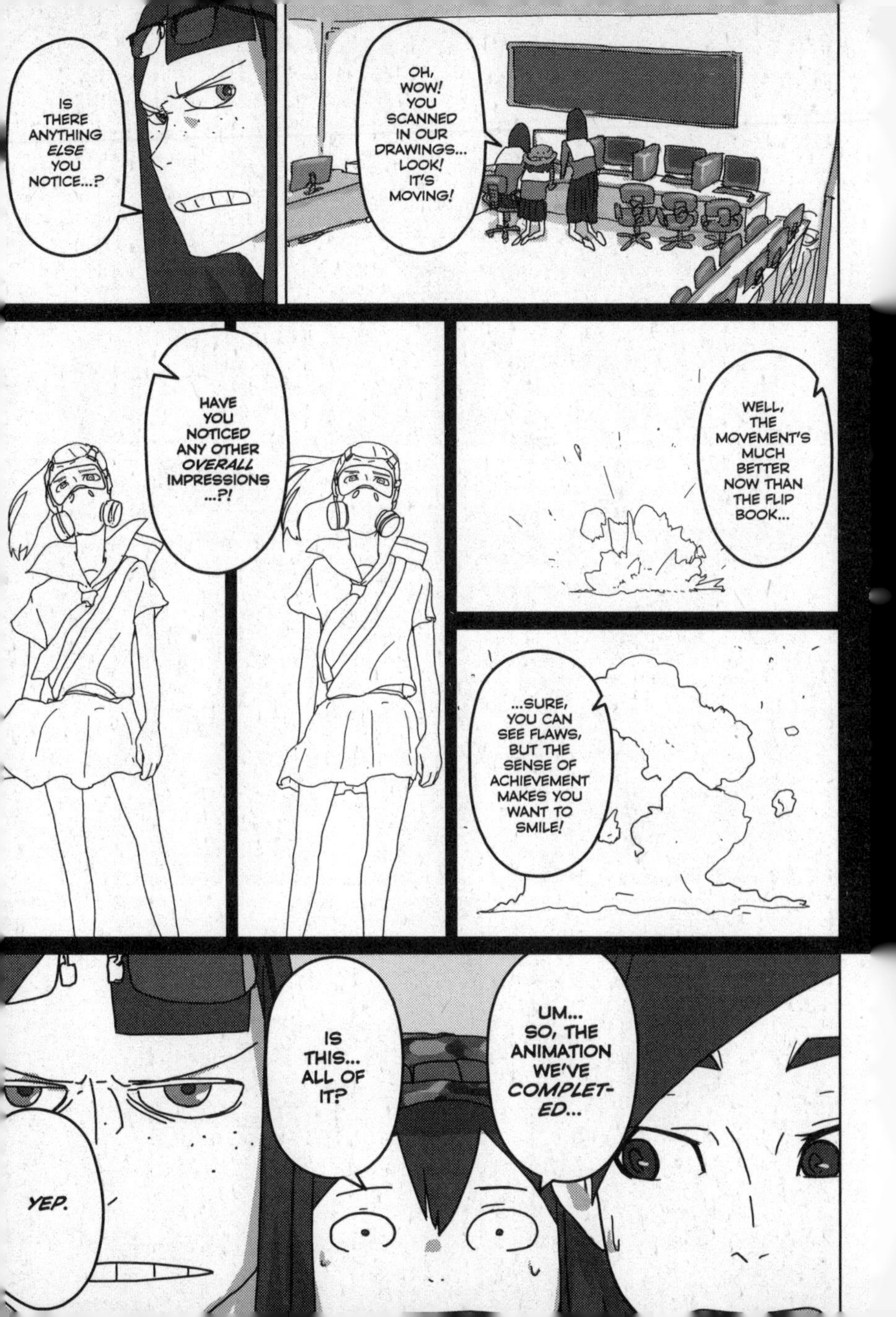

OH, WOW! YOU SCANNED IN OUR DRAWINGS... LOOK! IT'S MOVING!
IS THERE ANYTHING *ELSE* YOU NOTICE...?
WELL, THE MOVEMENT'S MUCH BETTER NOW THAN THE FLIP BOOK...
...SURE, YOU CAN SEE FLAWS, BUT THE SENSE OF ACHIEVEMENT MAKES YOU WANT TO SMILE!
HAVE YOU NOTICED ANY OTHER *OVERALL* IMPRESSIONS ...?!
UM... SO, THE ANIMATION WE'VE *COMPLETED*...
IS THIS... ALL OF IT?
YEP.

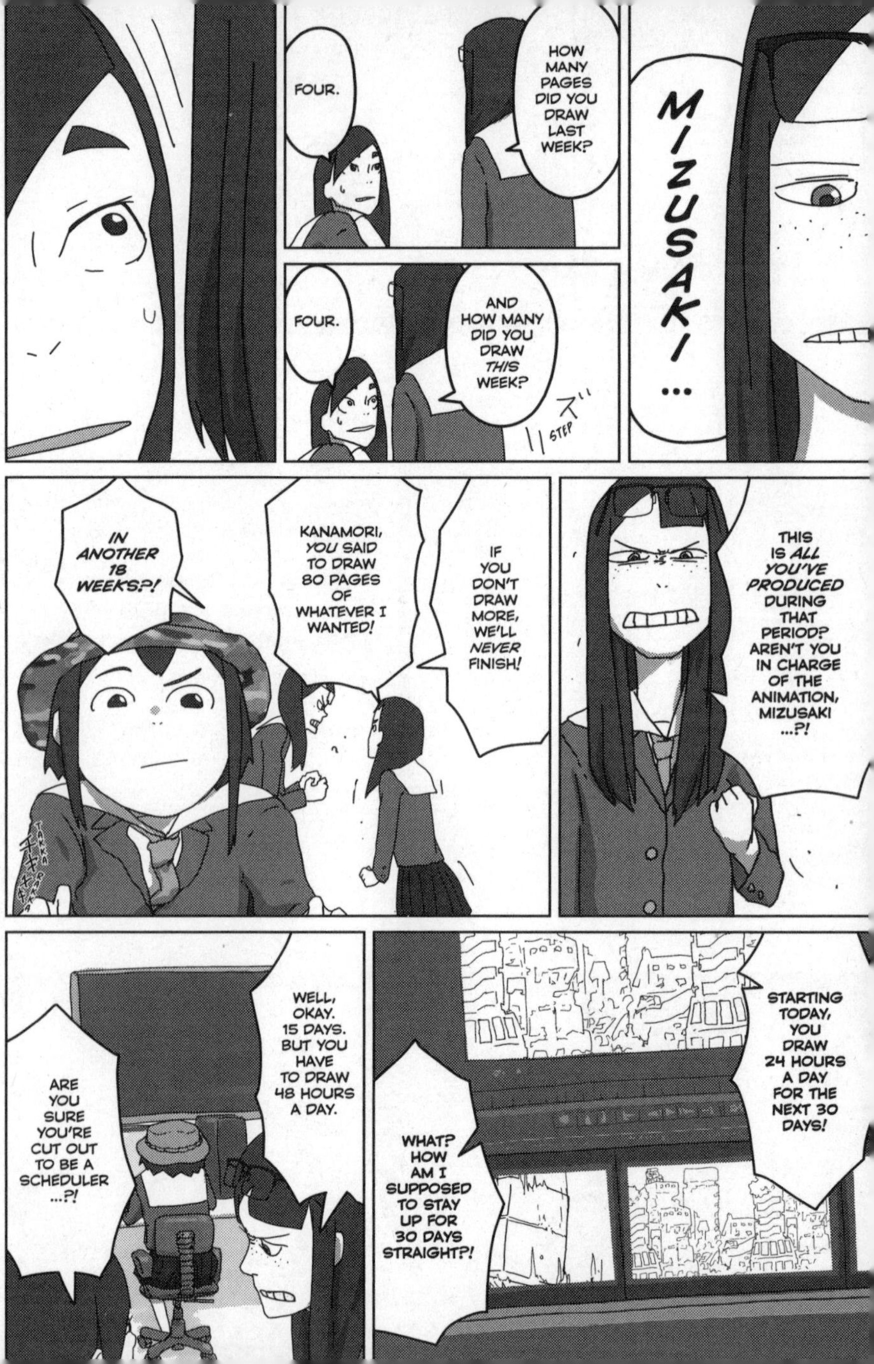
MIZUSAKI...
HOW MANY PAGES DID YOU DRAW LAST WEEK?
FOUR.
AND HOW MANY DID YOU DRAW *THIS* WEEK?
STEP
FOUR.
THIS IS *ALL YOU'VE PRODUCED* DURING THAT PERIOD? AREN'T YOU IN CHARGE OF THE ANIMATION, MIZUSAKI ...?!
IF YOU DON'T DRAW MORE, WE'LL *NEVER* FINISH!
KANAMORI, *YOU* SAID TO DRAW 80 PAGES OF WHATEVER I WANTED!
IN ANOTHER 18 WEEKS?!
TAKKA RAKKA
STARTING TODAY, YOU DRAW 24 HOURS A DAY FOR THE NEXT 30 DAYS!
WHAT? HOW AM I SUPPOSED TO STAY UP FOR 30 DAYS STRAIGHT?!
WELL, OKAY. 15 DAYS. BUT YOU HAVE TO DRAW 48 HOURS A DAY.
ARE YOU SURE YOU'RE CUT OUT TO BE A SCHEDULER ...?!

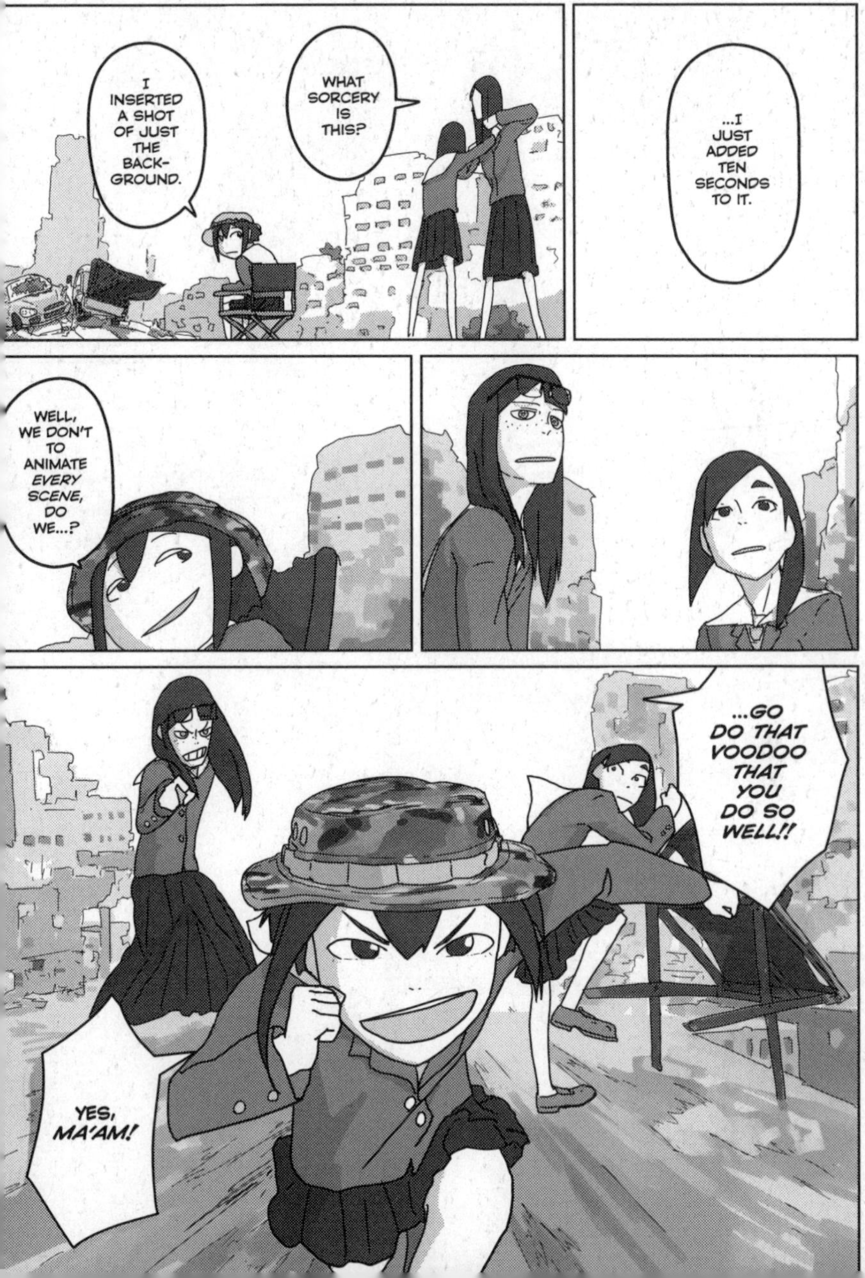
...I JUST ADDED TEN SECONDS TO IT.
WHAT SORCERY IS THIS?
I INSERTED A SHOT OF JUST THE BACK-GROUND.
WELL, WE DON'T TO ANIMATE *EVERY* SCENE, DO WE...?
...GO DO THAT VOODOO THAT YOU DO SO WELL!!
YES, *MA'AM!*

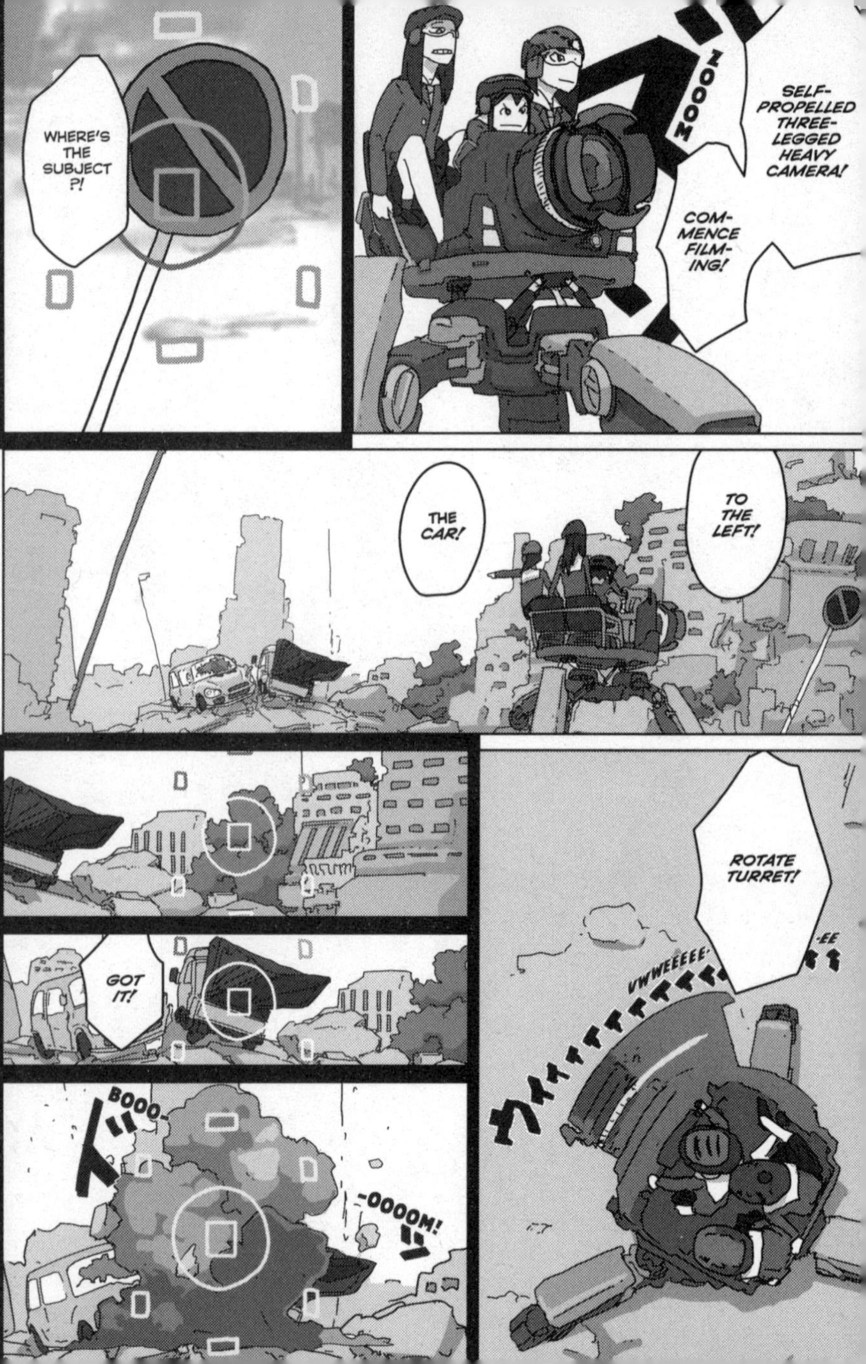
ZOOOM
SELF-PROPELLED THREE-LEGGED HEAVY CAMERA!
COMMENCE FILMING!
WHERE'S THE SUBJECT?!
TO THE LEFT!
THE CAR!
ROTATE TURRET!
VWWEEEEE- -EE
GOT IT!
BOOO-
-OOOOM!

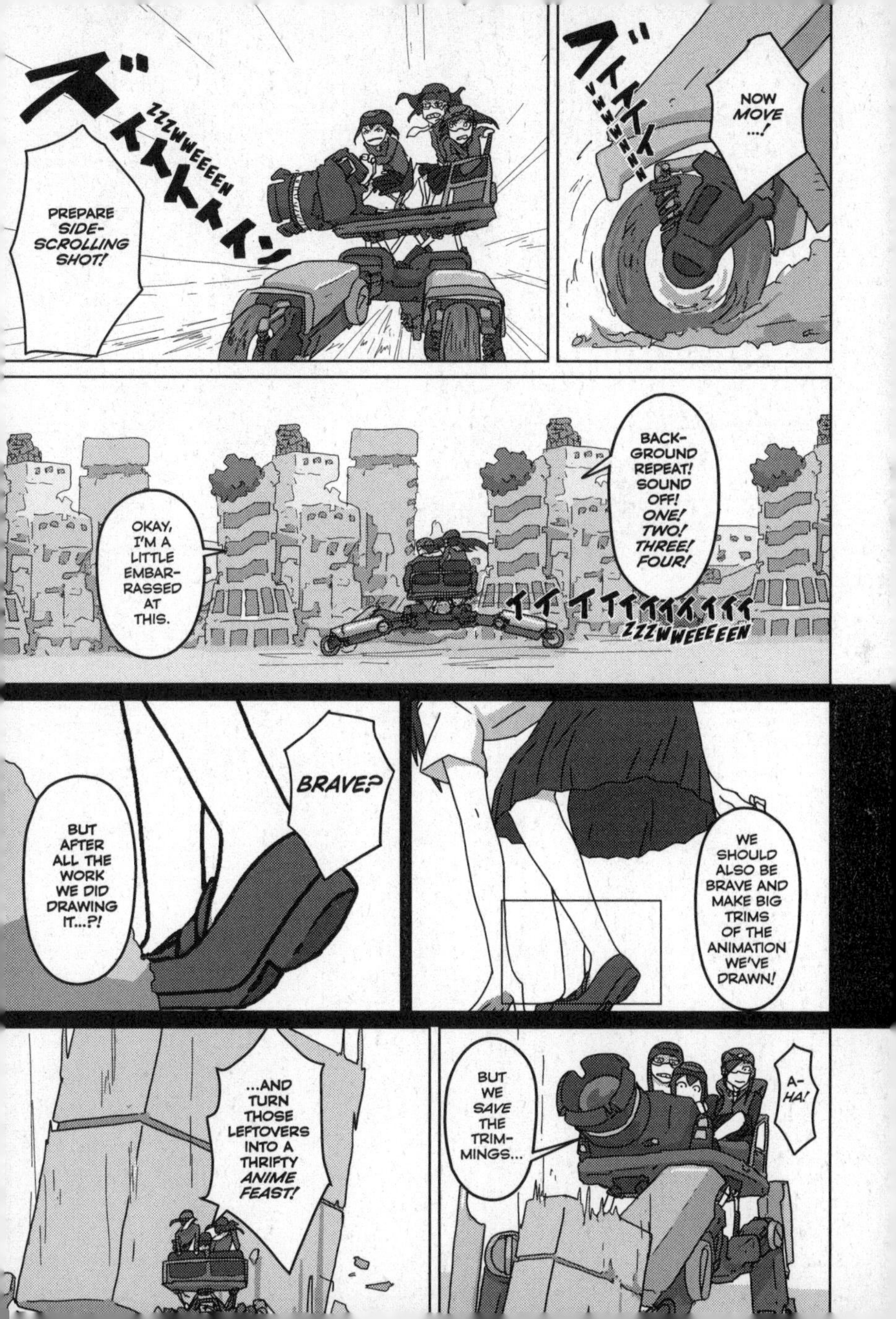
NOW MOVE ...!
VWWWWNNN
ZZZWWEEEEEN
PREPARE SIDE-SCROLLING SHOT!
BACK-GROUND REPEAT! SOUND OFF! ONE! TWO! THREE! FOUR!
OKAY, I'M A LITTLE EMBAR-RASSED AT THIS.
ZZZWWEEEEEN
WE SHOULD ALSO BE BRAVE AND MAKE BIG TRIMS OF THE ANIMATION WE'VE DRAWN!
BRAVE?
BUT AFTER ALL THE WORK WE DID DRAWING IT...?!
A-HA!
BUT WE SAVE THE TRIM-MINGS...
...AND TURN THOSE LEFTOVERS INTO A THRIFTY ANIME FEAST!

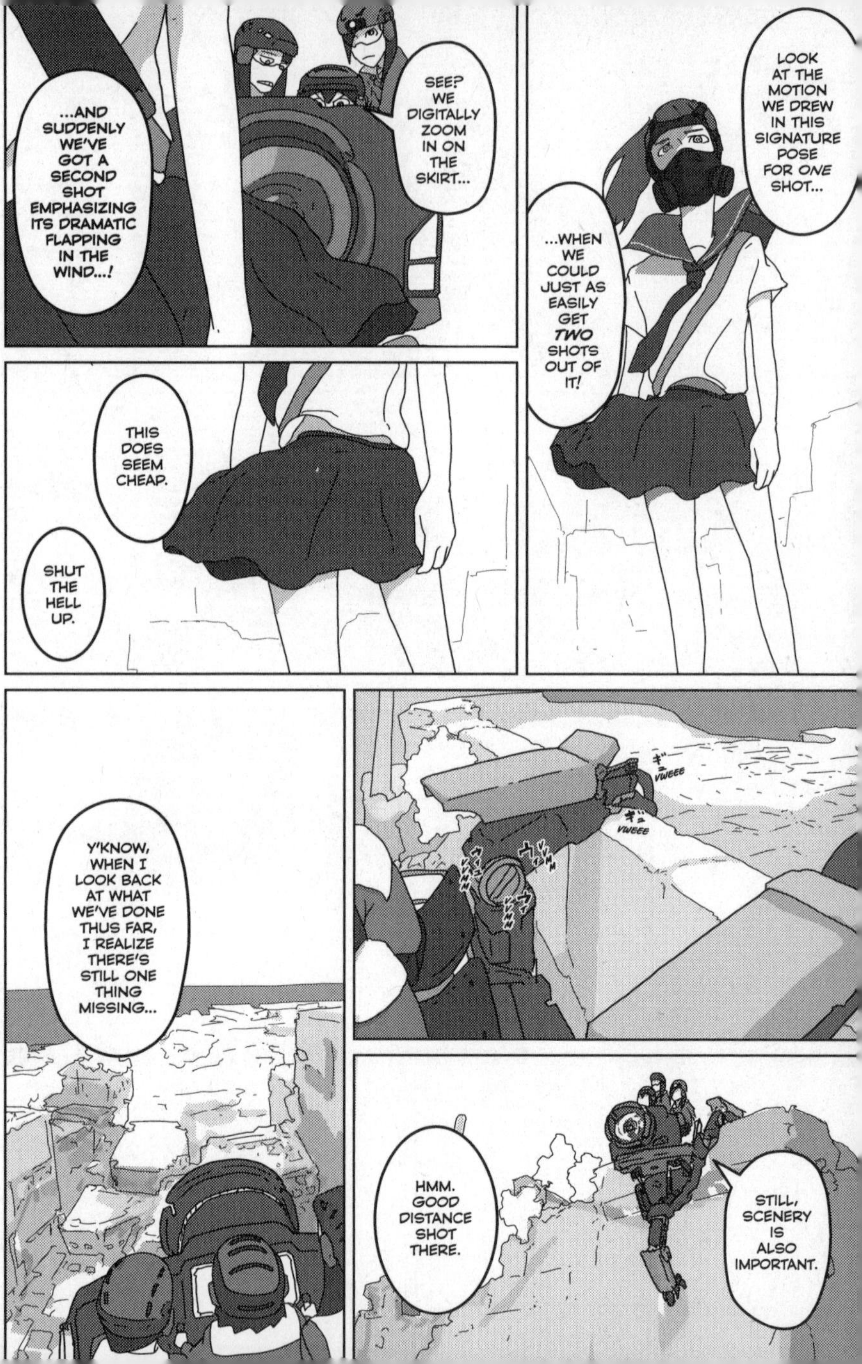
LOOK AT THE MOTION WE DREW IN THIS SIGNATURE POSE FOR *ONE* SHOT...
...WHEN WE COULD JUST AS EASILY GET ***TWO*** SHOTS OUT OF IT!
SEE? WE DIGITALLY ZOOM IN ON THE SKIRT...
...AND SUDDENLY WE'VE GOT A SECOND SHOT EMPHASIZING ITS DRAMATIC FLAPPING IN THE WIND...!
THIS DOES SEEM CHEAP.
SHUT THE HELL UP.
ギ VWEEE
ギ VWEEE
VVMM
VVMM
VVMM
VVMM
STILL, SCENERY IS ALSO IMPORTANT.
HMM. GOOD DISTANCE SHOT THERE.
Y'KNOW, WHEN I LOOK BACK AT WHAT WE'VE DONE THUS FAR, I REALIZE THERE'S STILL ONE THING MISSING...

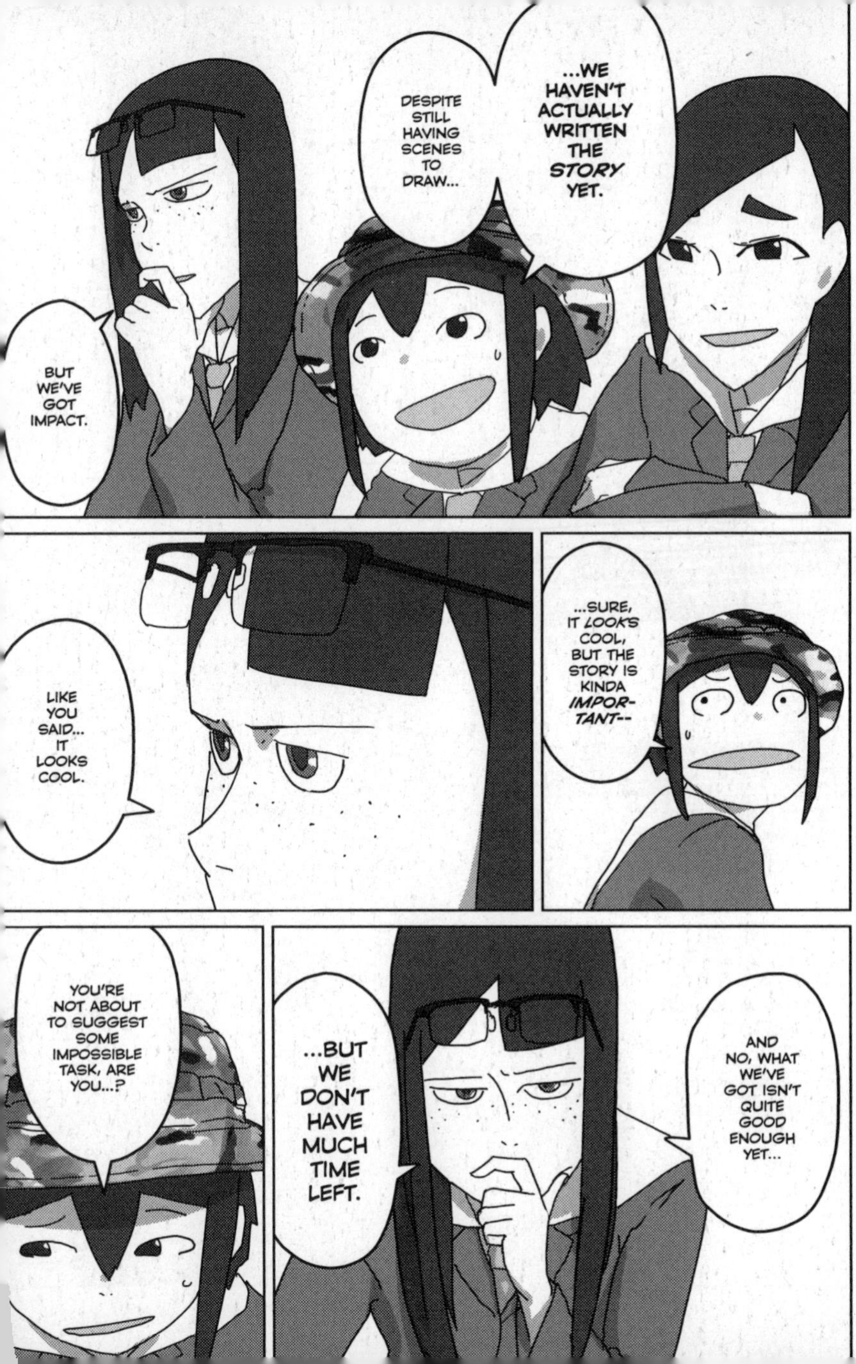
DESPITE STILL HAVING SCENES TO DRAW...
...WE HAVEN'T ACTUALLY WRITTEN THE *STORY* YET.
BUT WE'VE GOT IMPACT.
...SURE, IT *LOOKS* COOL, BUT THE STORY IS KINDA *IMPORTANT*--
LIKE YOU SAID... IT LOOKS COOL.
AND NO, WHAT WE'VE GOT ISN'T QUITE GOOD ENOUGH YET...
...BUT WE DON'T HAVE MUCH TIME LEFT.
YOU'RE NOT ABOUT TO SUGGEST SOME IMPOSSIBLE TASK, ARE YOU...?

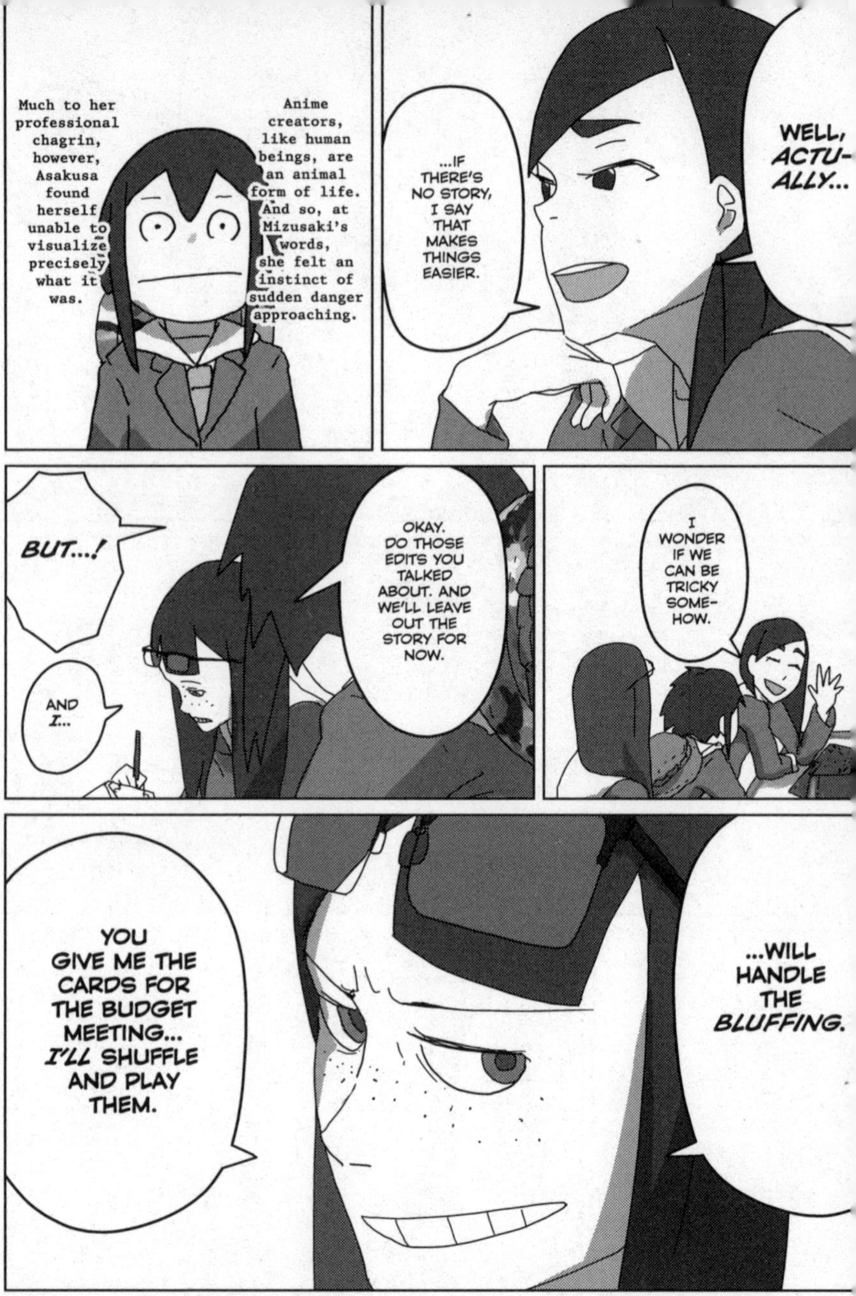
WELL, *ACTU-ALLY...*
...IF THERE'S NO STORY, I SAY THAT MAKES THINGS EASIER.
Anime creators, like human beings, are an animal form of life. And so, at Mizusaki's words, she felt an instinct of sudden danger approaching.
Much to her professional chagrin, however, Asakusa found herself unable to visualize precisely what it was.
I WONDER IF WE CAN BE TRICKY SOME-HOW.
OKAY. DO THOSE EDITS YOU TALKED ABOUT. AND WE'LL LEAVE OUT THE STORY FOR NOW.
BUT...!
AND *I...*
...WILL HANDLE THE *BLUFFING.*
YOU GIVE ME THE CARDS FOR THE BUDGET MEETING... *I'LL* SHUFFLE AND PLAY THEM.

CHAPTER 7: CLUTCH THAT PENCIL WITH STRENGTH!

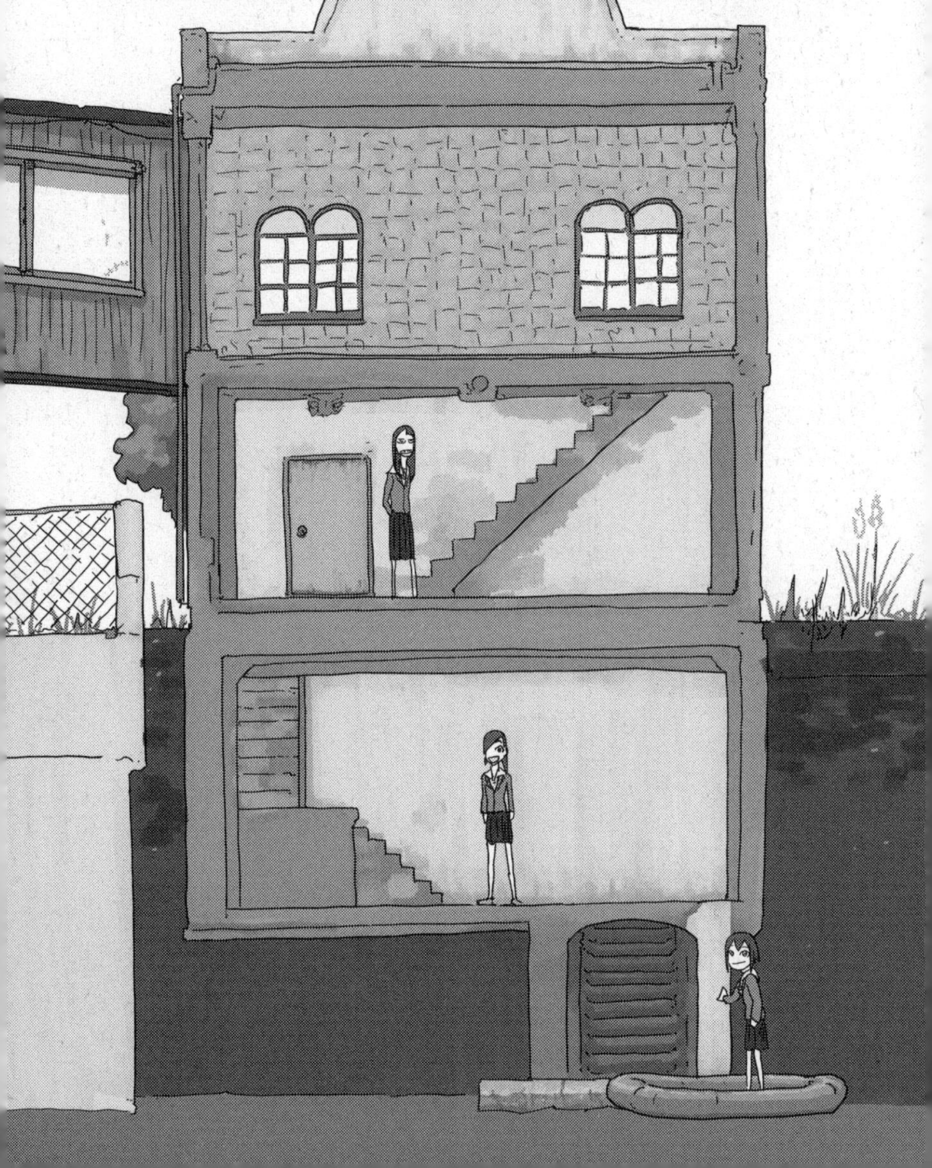

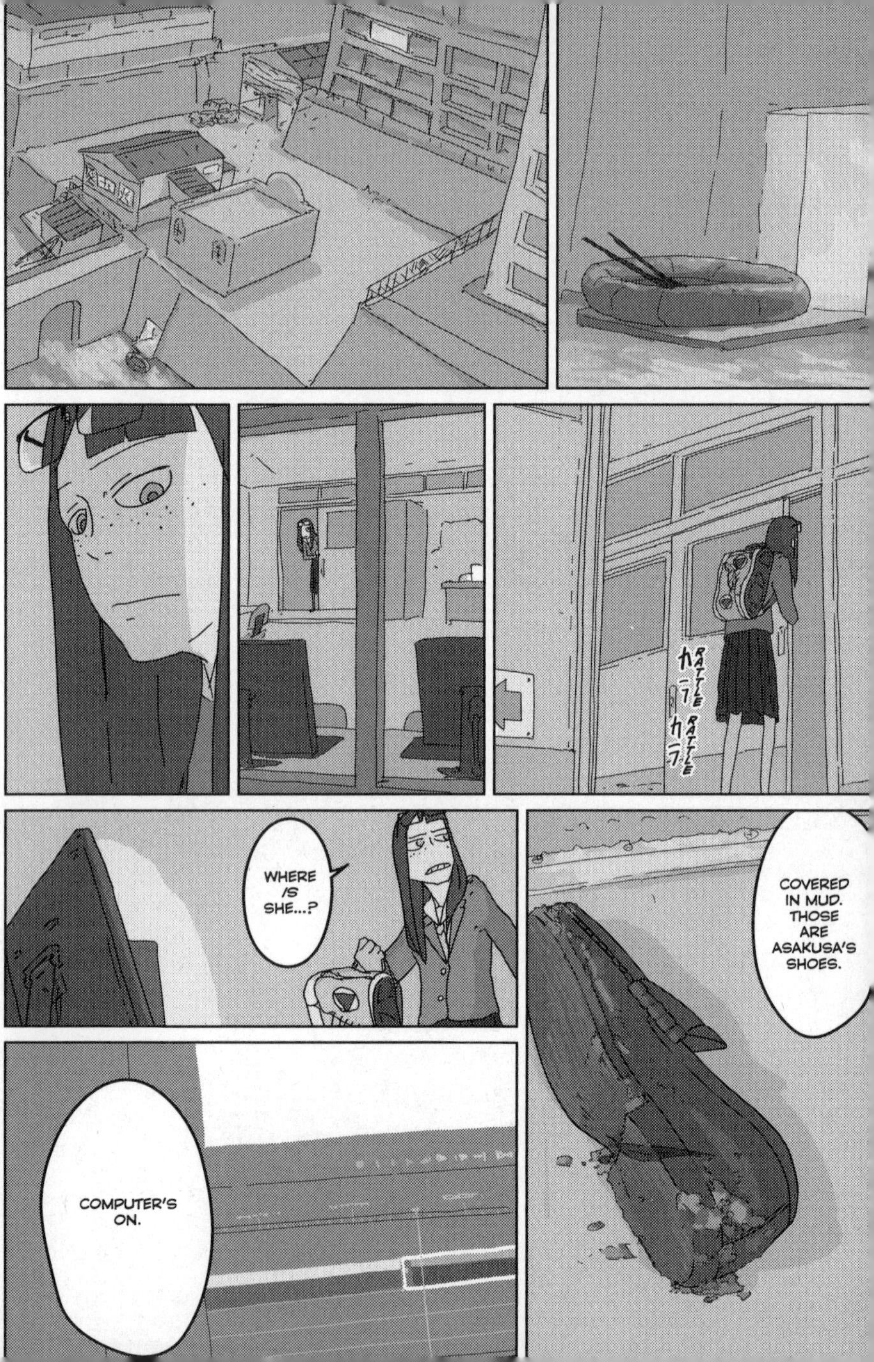
カーラ
RATTLE
カーラ
RATTLE
COVERED IN MUD. THOSE ARE ASAKUSA'S SHOES.
WHERE IS SHE...?
COMPUTER'S ON.

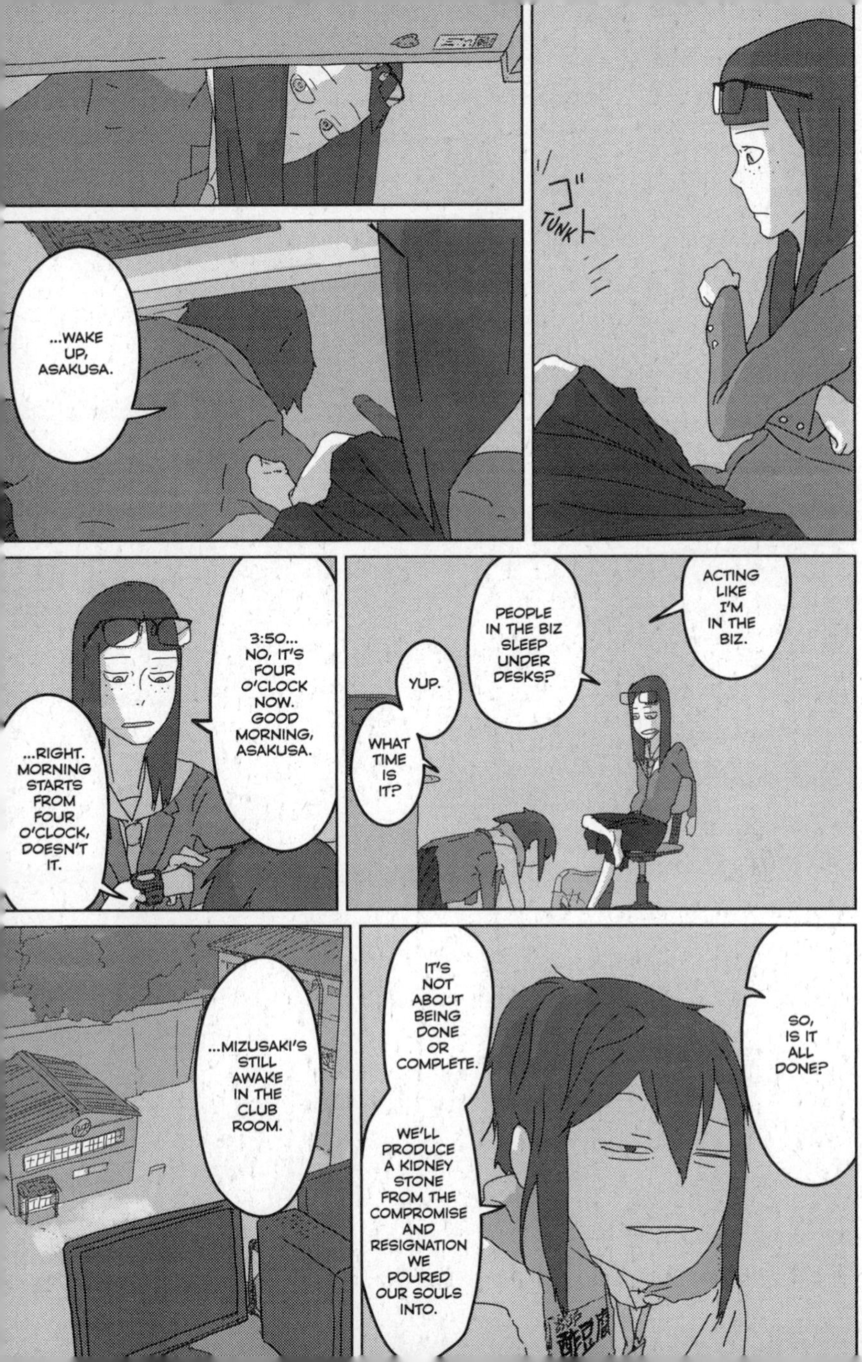
ゴト
TUNK
...WAKE UP, ASAKUSA.
ACTING LIKE I'M IN THE BIZ.
PEOPLE IN THE BIZ SLEEP UNDER DESKS?
YUP.
WHAT TIME IS IT?
3:50... NO, IT'S FOUR O'CLOCK NOW. GOOD MORNING, ASAKUSA.
...RIGHT. MORNING STARTS FROM FOUR O'CLOCK, DOESN'T IT.
SO, IS IT ALL DONE?
IT'S NOT ABOUT BEING DONE OR COMPLETE.
WE'LL PRODUCE A KIDNEY STONE FROM THE COMPROMISE AND RESIGNATION WE POURED OUR SOULS INTO.
...MIZUSAKI'S STILL AWAKE IN THE CLUB ROOM.

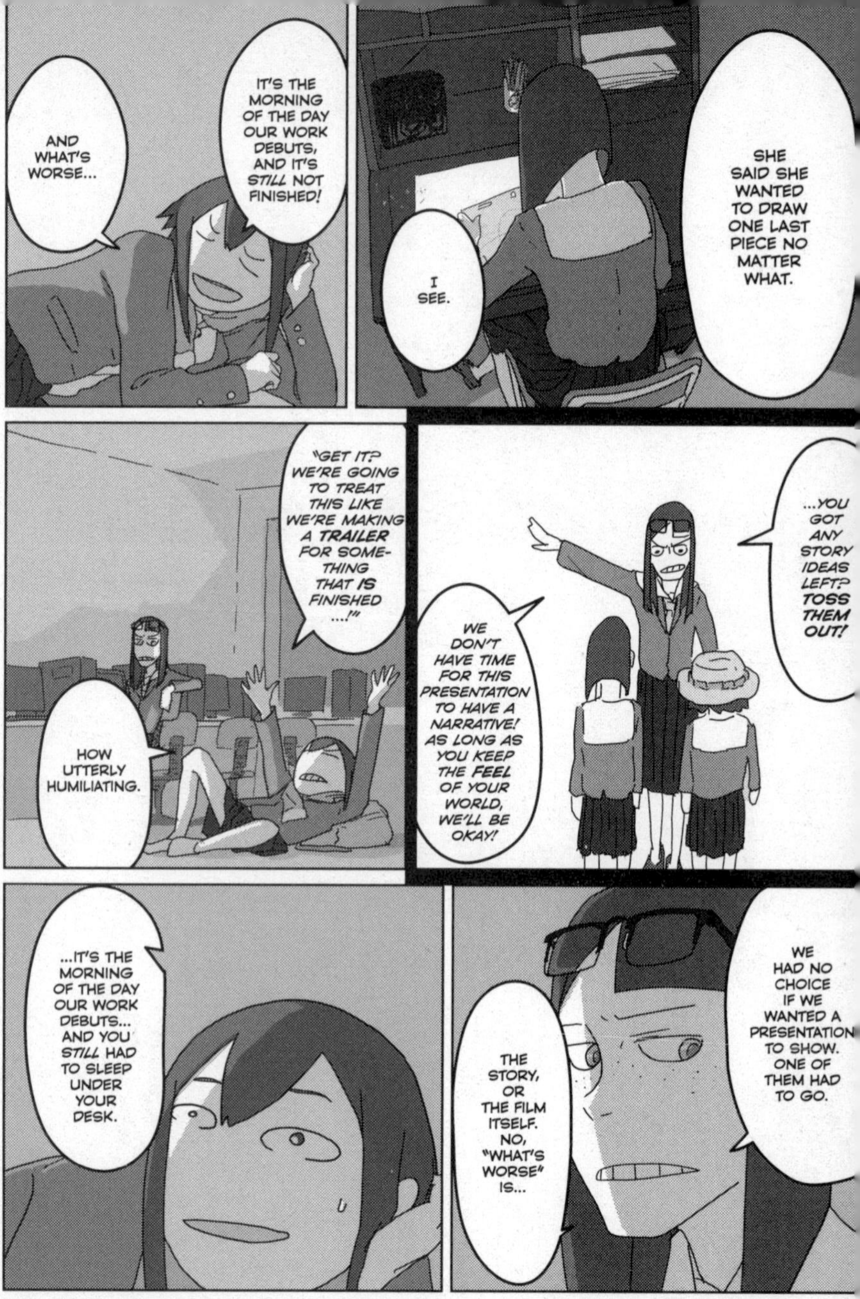
SHE SAID SHE WANTED TO DRAW ONE LAST PIECE NO MATTER WHAT.
I SEE.
IT'S THE MORNING OF THE DAY OUR WORK DEBUTS, AND IT'S STILL NOT FINISHED!
AND WHAT'S WORSE...
...YOU GOT ANY STORY IDEAS LEFT? TOSS THEM OUT!
WE DON'T HAVE TIME FOR THIS PRESENTATION TO HAVE A NARRATIVE! AS LONG AS YOU KEEP THE FEEL OF YOUR WORLD, WE'LL BE OKAY!
"GET IT? WE'RE GOING TO TREAT THIS LIKE WE'RE MAKING A TRAILER FOR SOME-THING THAT IS FINISHED ...!"
HOW UTTERLY HUMILIATING.
WE HAD NO CHOICE IF WE WANTED A PRESENTATION TO SHOW. ONE OF THEM HAD TO GO.
THE STORY, OR THE FILM ITSELF. NO, "WHAT'S WORSE" IS...
...IT'S THE MORNING OF THE DAY OUR WORK DEBUTS... AND YOU STILL HAD TO SLEEP UNDER YOUR DESK.

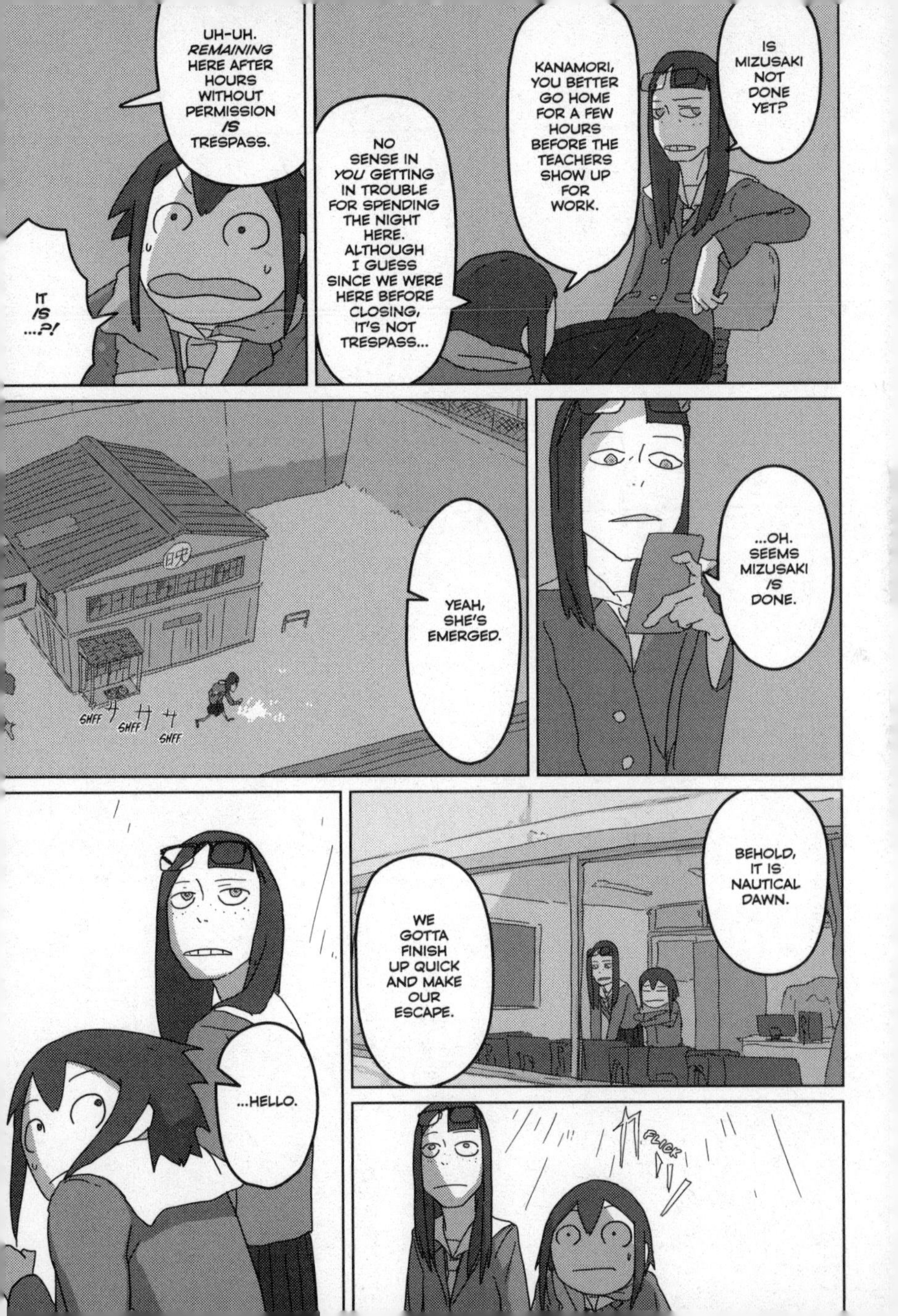
IS MIZUSAKI NOT DONE YET?
KANAMORI, YOU BETTER GO HOME FOR A FEW HOURS BEFORE THE TEACHERS SHOW UP FOR WORK.
NO SENSE IN *YOU* GETTING IN TROUBLE FOR SPENDING THE NIGHT HERE. ALTHOUGH I GUESS SINCE WE WERE HERE BEFORE CLOSING, IT'S NOT TRESPASS...
UH-UH. *REMAINING* HERE AFTER HOURS WITHOUT PERMISSION *IS* TRESPASS.
IT *IS* ...?!
...OH. SEEMS MIZUSAKI *IS* DONE.
YEAH, SHE'S EMERGED.
SHFF
SHFF
SHFF
BEHOLD, IT IS NAUTICAL DAWN.
WE GOTTA FINISH UP QUICK AND MAKE OUR ESCAPE.
FLICK
...HELLO.

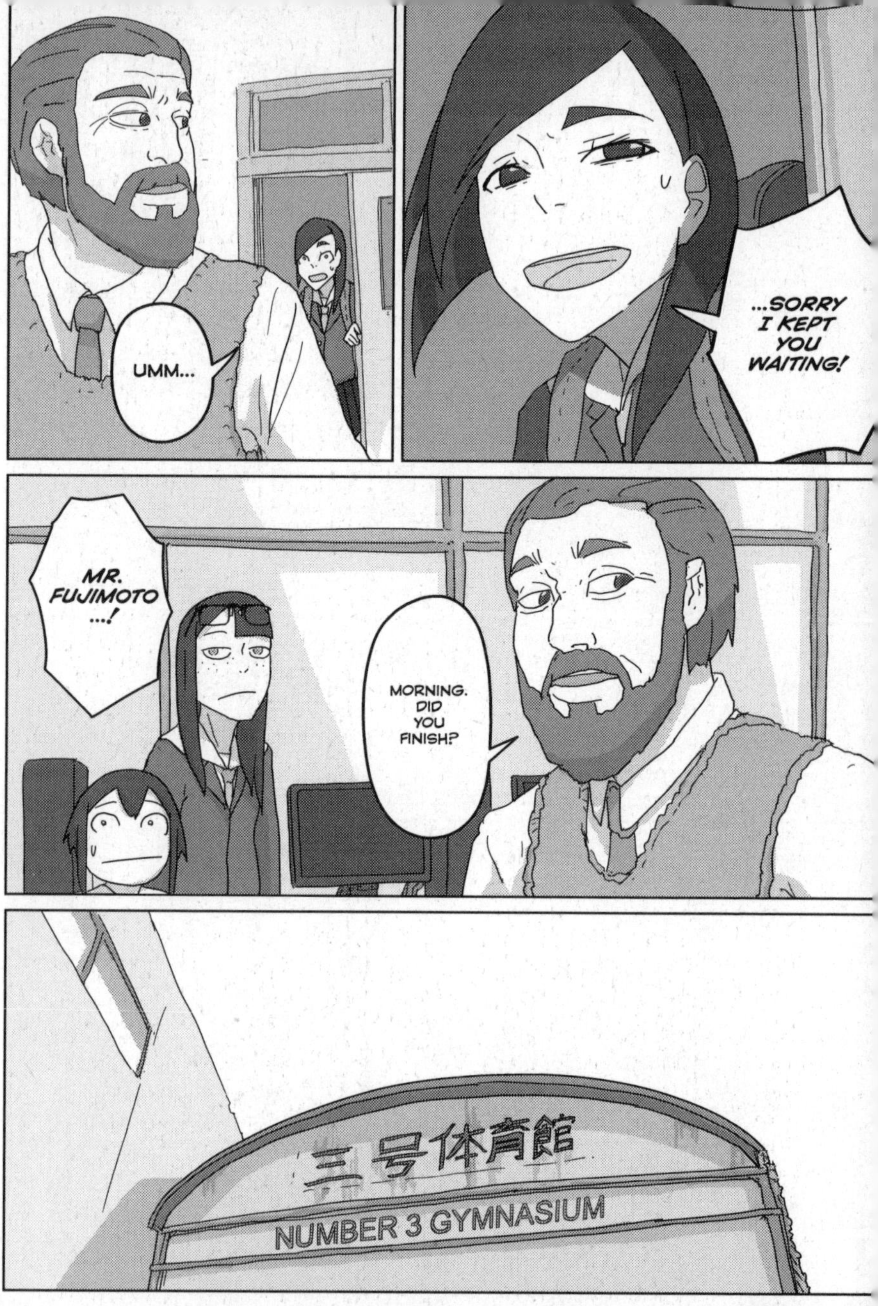
...SORRY I KEPT YOU WAITING!
UMM...
MORNING. DID YOU FINISH?
MR. FUJIMOTO ...!
三号体育館
NUMBER 3 GYMNASIUM

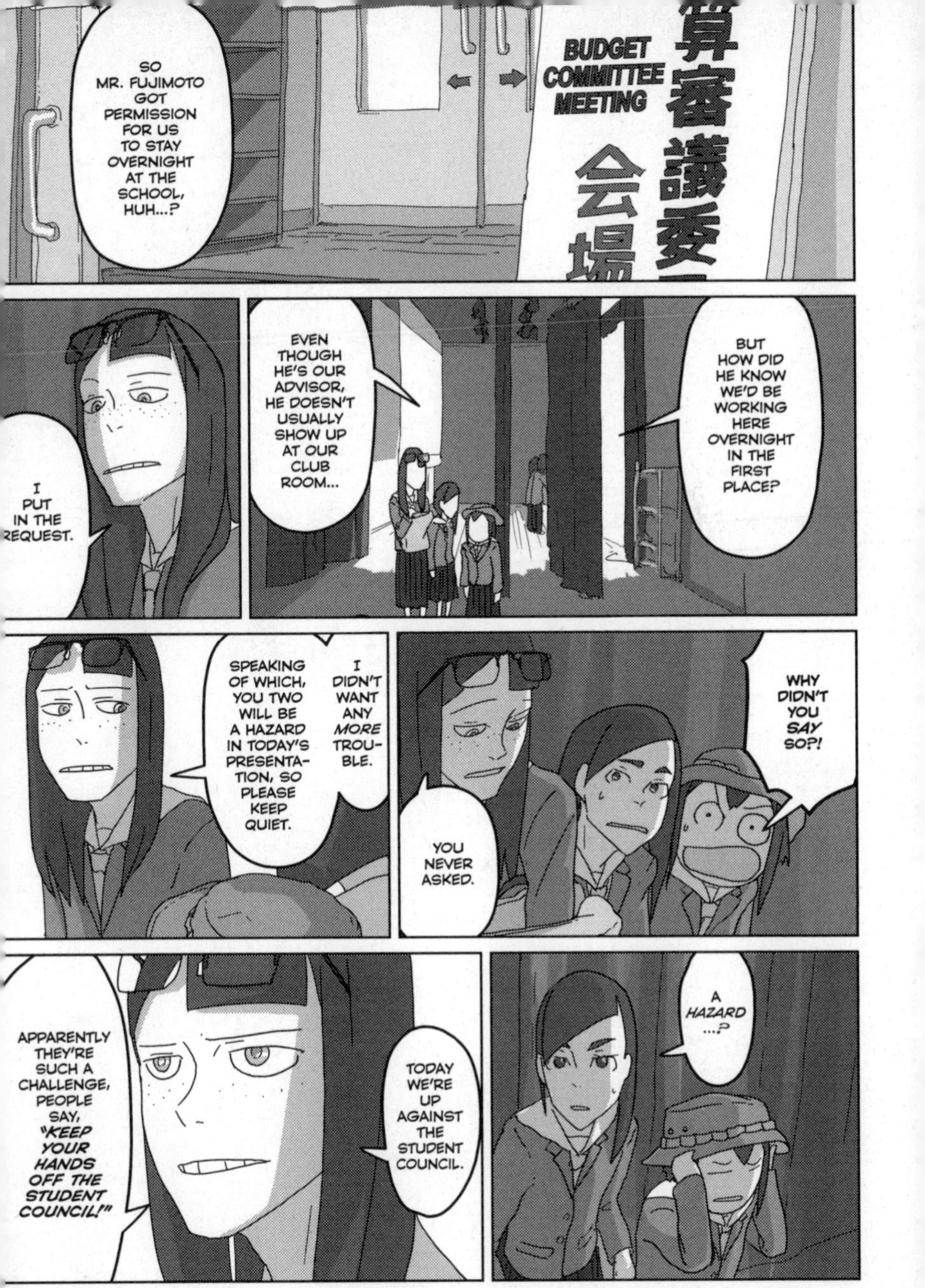

BUDGET COMMITTEE MEETING
算審議委
会場
SO MR. FUJIMOTO GOT PERMISSION FOR US TO STAY OVERNIGHT AT THE SCHOOL, HUH...?
BUT HOW DID HE KNOW WE'D BE WORKING HERE OVERNIGHT IN THE FIRST PLACE?
EVEN THOUGH HE'S OUR ADVISOR, HE DOESN'T USUALLY SHOW UP AT OUR CLUB ROOM...
I PUT IN THE REQUEST.
WHY DIDN'T YOU *SAY* SO?!
YOU NEVER ASKED.
I DIDN'T WANT ANY *MORE* TROUBLE.
SPEAKING OF WHICH, YOU TWO WILL BE A HAZARD IN TODAY'S PRESENTATION, SO PLEASE KEEP QUIET.
A *HAZARD*...?
TODAY WE'RE UP AGAINST THE STUDENT COUNCIL.
APPARENTLY THEY'RE SUCH A CHALLENGE, PEOPLE SAY, ***"KEEP YOUR HANDS OFF THE STUDENT COUNCIL!"***

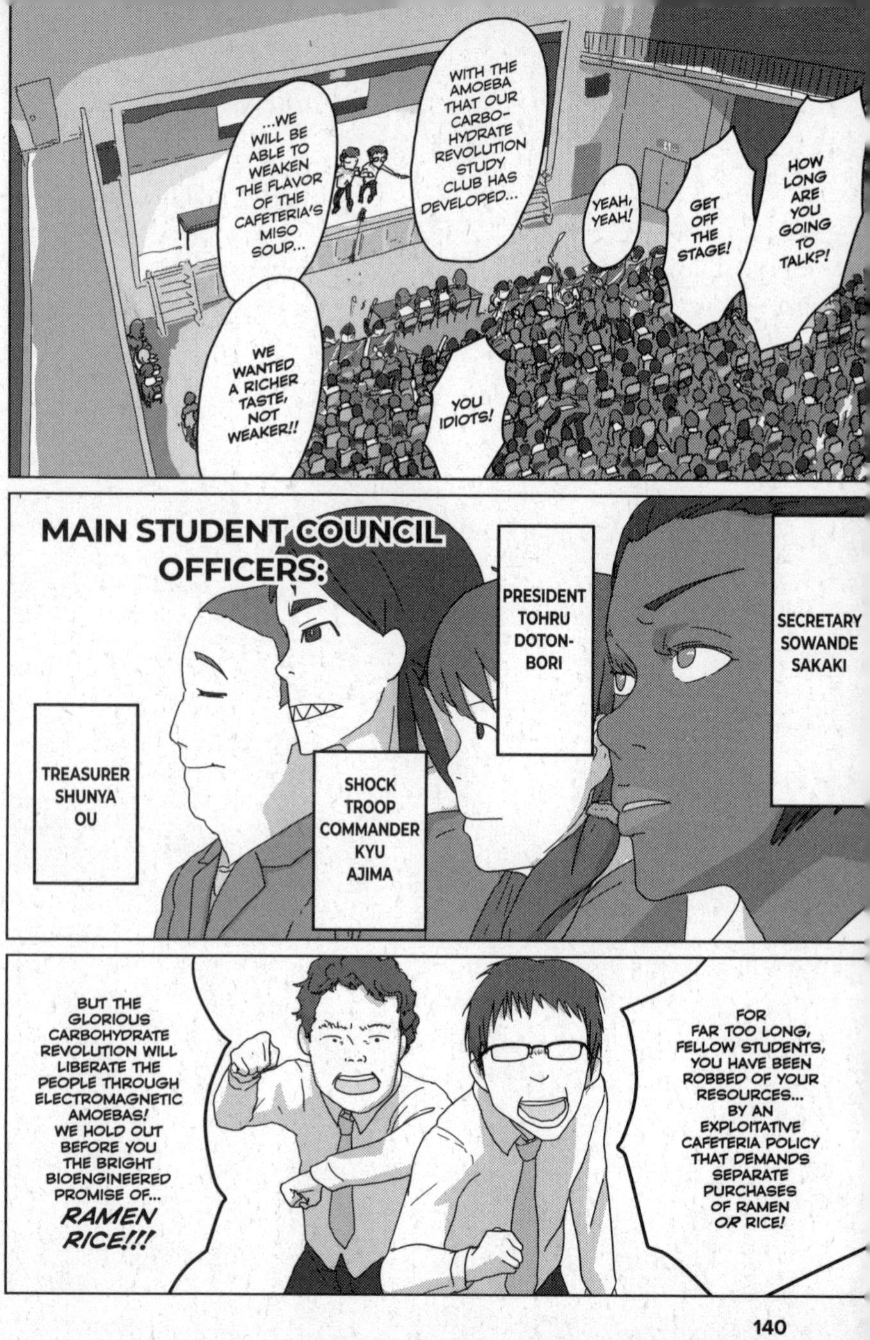
HOW LONG ARE YOU GOING TO TALK?!
GET OFF THE STAGE!
YEAH, YEAH!
WITH THE AMOEBA THAT OUR CARBO-HYDRATE REVOLUTION STUDY CLUB HAS DEVELOPED...
...WE WILL BE ABLE TO WEAKEN THE FLAVOR OF THE CAFETERIA'S MISO SOUP...
YOU IDIOTS!
WE WANTED A RICHER TASTE, NOT WEAKER!!
MAIN STUDENT COUNCIL OFFICERS:
SECRETARY SOWANDE SAKAKI
PRESIDENT TOHRU DOTON-BORI
SHOCK TROOP COMMANDER KYU AJIMA
TREASURER SHUNYA OU
FOR FAR TOO LONG, FELLOW STUDENTS, YOU HAVE BEEN ROBBED OF YOUR RESOURCES... BY AN EXPLOITATIVE CAFETERIA POLICY THAT DEMANDS SEPARATE PURCHASES OF RAMEN *OR* RICE!
BUT THE GLORIOUS CARBOHYDRATE REVOLUTION WILL LIBERATE THE PEOPLE THROUGH ELECTROMAGNETIC AMOEBAS! WE HOLD OUT BEFORE YOU THE BRIGHT BIOENGINEERED PROMISE OF... *RAMEN RICE!!!*

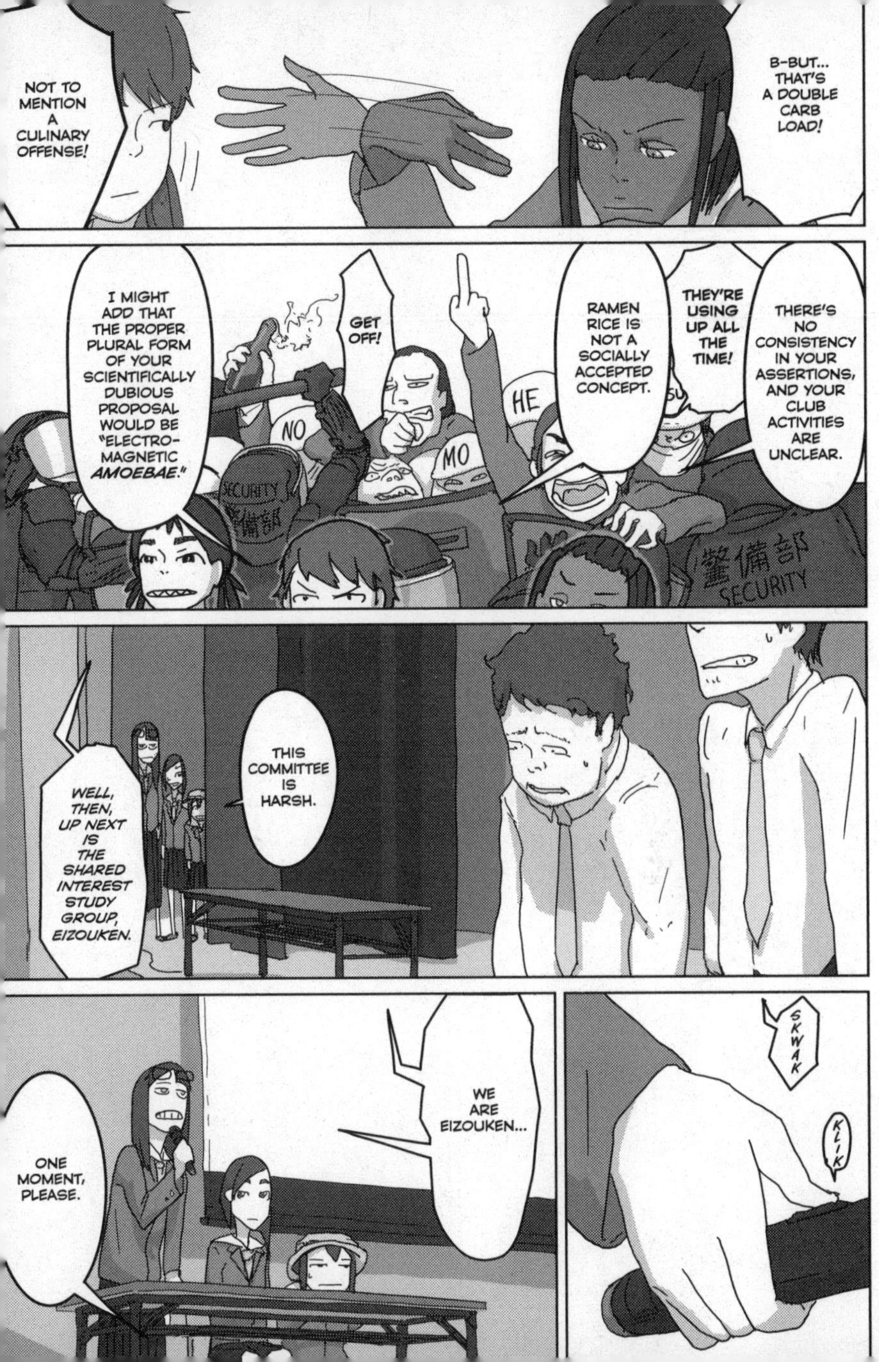
B-BUT... THAT'S A DOUBLE CARB LOAD!
NOT TO MENTION A CULINARY OFFENSE!
THERE'S NO CONSISTENCY IN YOUR ASSERTIONS, AND YOUR CLUB ACTIVITIES ARE UNCLEAR.
THEY'RE USING UP ALL THE TIME!
RAMEN RICE IS NOT A SOCIALLY ACCEPTED CONCEPT.
警備部 SECURITY
HE
MO
NO
GET OFF!
SECURITY 警備部
I MIGHT ADD THAT THE PROPER PLURAL FORM OF YOUR SCIENTIFICALLY DUBIOUS PROPOSAL WOULD BE "ELECTRO-MAGNETIC *AMOEBAE*."
THIS COMMITTEE IS HARSH.
WELL, THEN, UP NEXT IS THE SHARED INTEREST STUDY GROUP, EIZOUKEN.
SKWAK
KLIK
WE ARE EIZOUKEN...
ONE MOMENT, PLEASE.

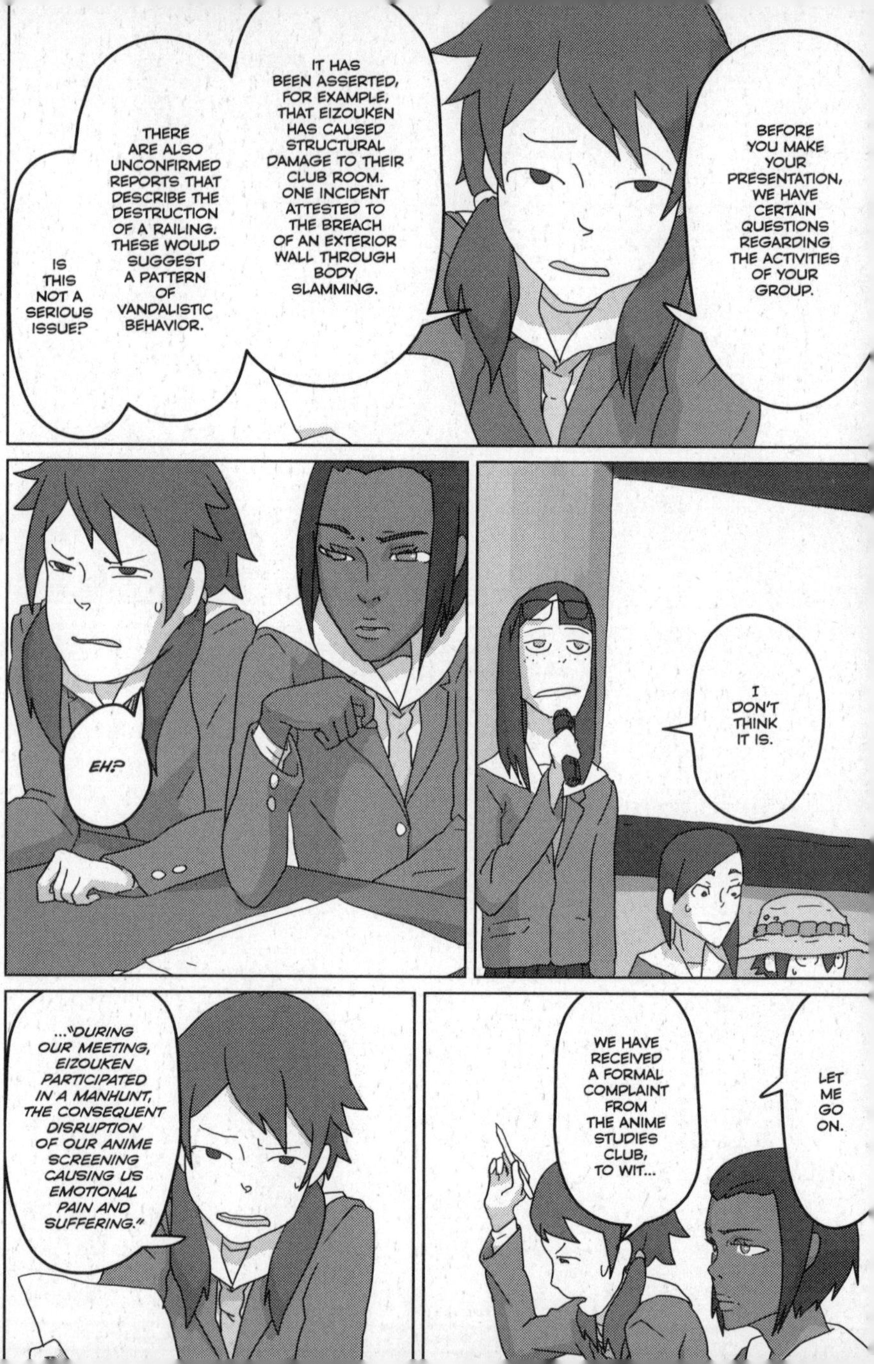
BEFORE YOU MAKE YOUR PRESENTATION, WE HAVE CERTAIN QUESTIONS REGARDING THE ACTIVITIES OF YOUR GROUP.
IT HAS BEEN ASSERTED, FOR EXAMPLE, THAT EIZOUKEN HAS CAUSED STRUCTURAL DAMAGE TO THEIR CLUB ROOM. ONE INCIDENT ATTESTED TO THE BREACH OF AN EXTERIOR WALL THROUGH BODY SLAMMING.
THERE ARE ALSO UNCONFIRMED REPORTS THAT DESCRIBE THE DESTRUCTION OF A RAILING. THESE WOULD SUGGEST A PATTERN OF VANDALISTIC BEHAVIOR.
IS THIS NOT A SERIOUS ISSUE?
I DON'T THINK IT IS.
EH?
LET ME GO ON.
WE HAVE RECEIVED A FORMAL COMPLAINT FROM THE ANIME STUDIES CLUB, TO WIT...
..."DURING OUR MEETING, EIZOUKEN PARTICIPATED IN A MANHUNT, THE CONSEQUENT DISRUPTION OF OUR ANIME SCREENING CAUSING US EMOTIONAL PAIN AND SUFFERING."

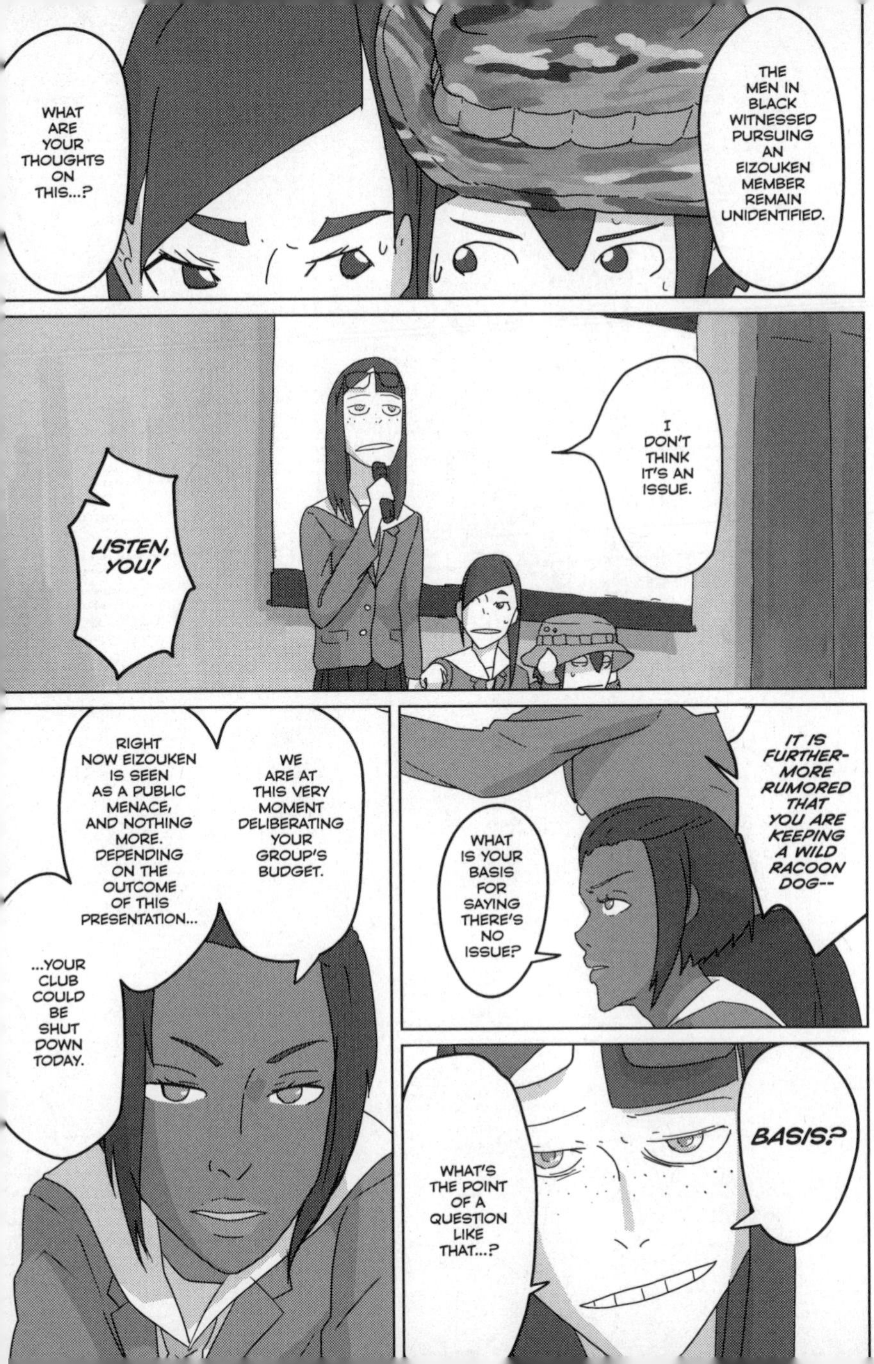
THE MEN IN BLACK WITNESSED PURSUING AN EIZOUKEN MEMBER REMAIN UNIDENTIFIED.
WHAT ARE YOUR THOUGHTS ON THIS...?
I DON'T THINK IT'S AN ISSUE.
LISTEN, YOU!
IT IS FURTHER-MORE RUMORED THAT YOU ARE KEEPING A WILD RACOON DOG--
WHAT IS YOUR BASIS FOR SAYING THERE'S NO ISSUE?
BASIS?
WHAT'S THE POINT OF A QUESTION LIKE THAT...?
WE ARE AT THIS VERY MOMENT DELIBERATING YOUR GROUP'S BUDGET.
RIGHT NOW EIZOUKEN IS SEEN AS A PUBLIC MENACE, AND NOTHING MORE. DEPENDING ON THE OUTCOME OF THIS PRESENTATION...
...YOUR CLUB COULD BE SHUT DOWN TODAY.

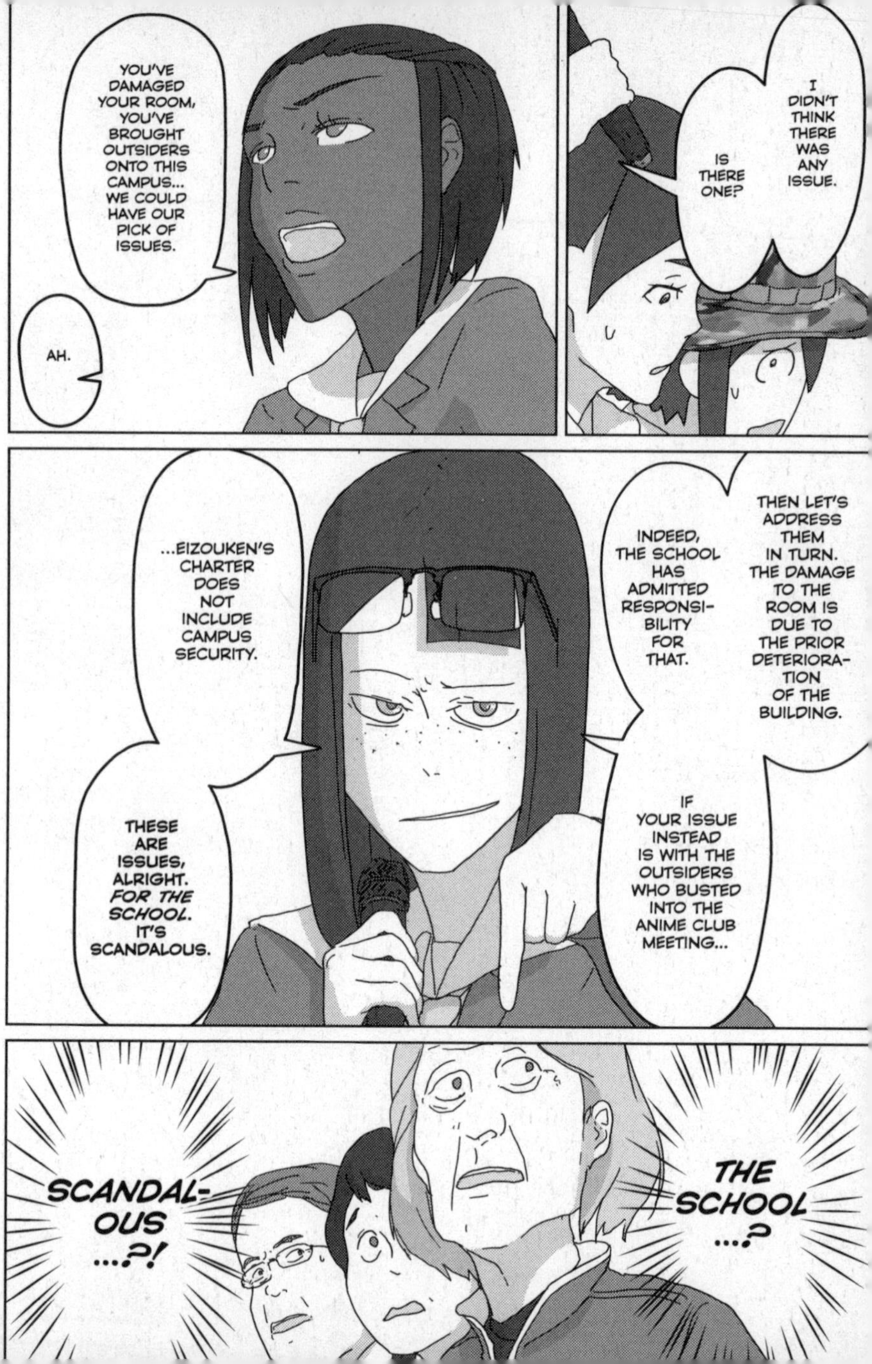
I DIDN'T THINK THERE WAS ANY ISSUE.
IS THERE ONE?
YOU'VE DAMAGED YOUR ROOM, YOU'VE BROUGHT OUTSIDERS ONTO THIS CAMPUS... WE COULD HAVE OUR PICK OF ISSUES.
AH.
THEN LET'S ADDRESS THEM IN TURN. THE DAMAGE TO THE ROOM IS DUE TO THE PRIOR DETERIORA-TION OF THE BUILDING.
INDEED, THE SCHOOL HAS ADMITTED RESPONSI-BILITY FOR THAT.
IF YOUR ISSUE INSTEAD IS WITH THE OUTSIDERS WHO BUSTED INTO THE ANIME CLUB MEETING...
...EIZOUKEN'S CHARTER DOES NOT INCLUDE CAMPUS SECURITY.
THESE ARE ISSUES, ALRIGHT. *FOR THE SCHOOL*. IT'S SCANDALOUS.
THE SCHOOL ...?
SCANDAL-OUS ...?!

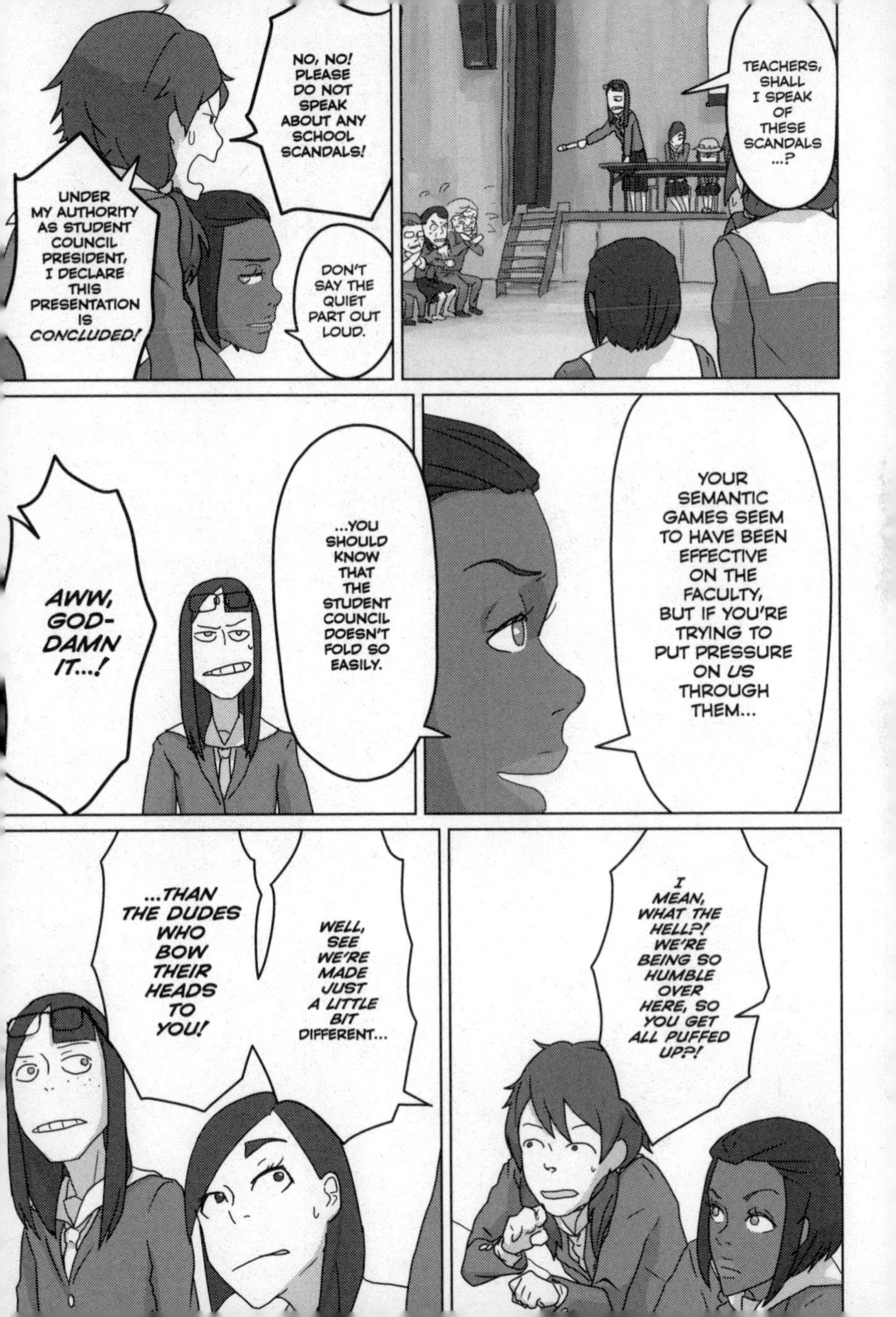
TEACHERS, SHALL I SPEAK OF THESE SCANDALS ...?
NO, NO! PLEASE DO NOT SPEAK ABOUT ANY SCHOOL SCANDALS!
UNDER MY AUTHORITY AS STUDENT COUNCIL PRESIDENT, I DECLARE THIS PRESENTATION IS *CONCLUDED!*
DON'T SAY THE QUIET PART OUT LOUD.
YOUR SEMANTIC GAMES SEEM TO HAVE BEEN EFFECTIVE ON THE FACULTY, BUT IF YOU'RE TRYING TO PUT PRESSURE ON *US* THROUGH THEM...
...YOU SHOULD KNOW THAT THE STUDENT COUNCIL DOESN'T FOLD SO EASILY.
AWW, GOD-DAMN IT...!
I MEAN, WHAT THE HELL?! WE'RE BEING SO HUMBLE OVER HERE, SO YOU GET ALL PUFFED UP?!
WELL, SEE WE'RE MADE JUST A LITTLE BIT DIFFERENT...
...THAN THE DUDES WHO BOW THEIR HEADS TO YOU!

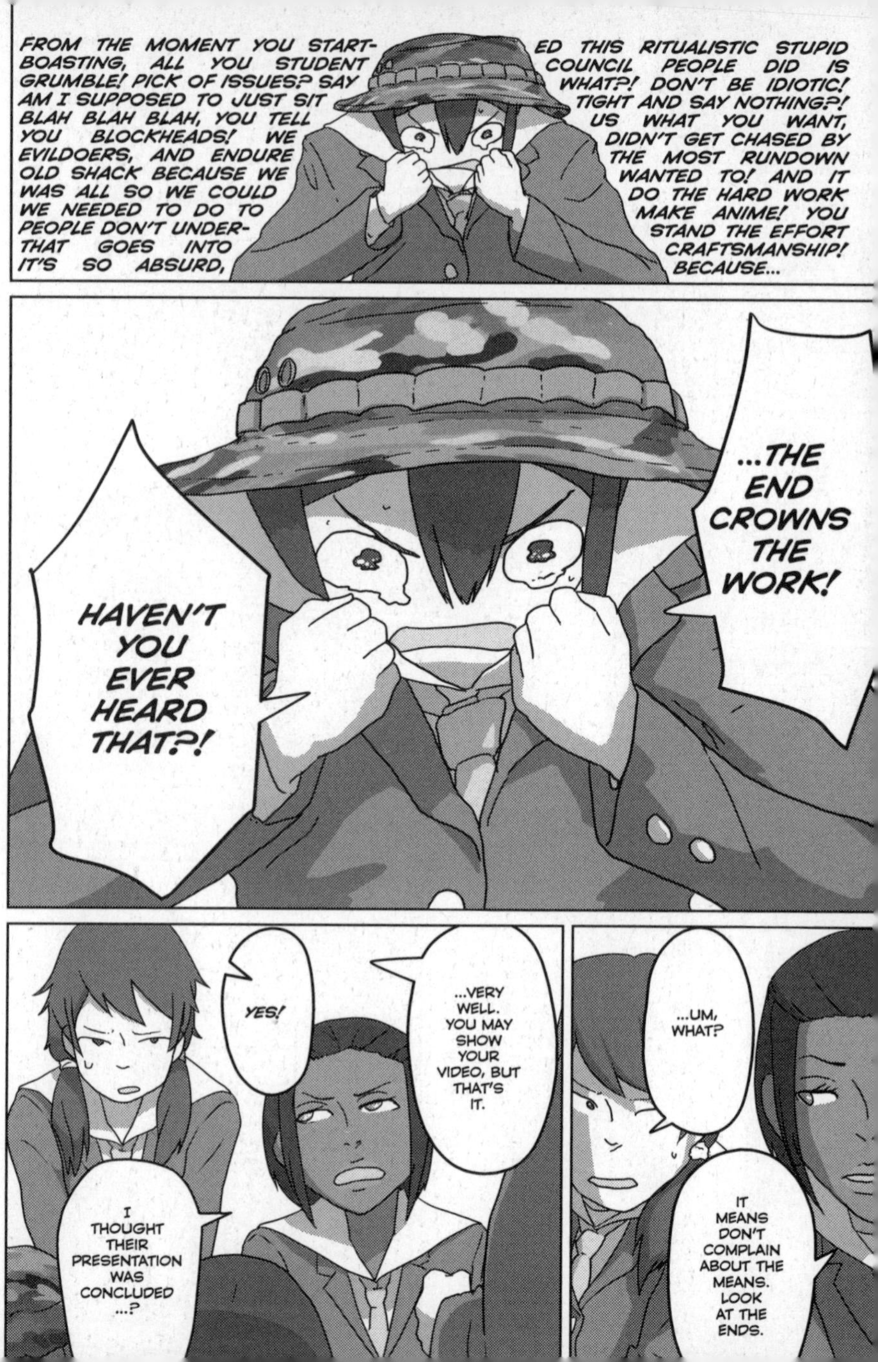
FROM THE MOMENT YOU START-ED THIS RITUALISTIC STUPID BOASTING, ALL YOU STUDENT COUNCIL PEOPLE DID IS GRUMBLE! PICK OF ISSUES? SAY WHAT?! DON'T BE IDIOTIC! AM I SUPPOSED TO JUST SIT TIGHT AND SAY NOTHING?! BLAH BLAH BLAH, YOU TELL US WHAT YOU WANT, YOU BLOCKHEADS! WE DIDN'T GET CHASED BY EVILDOERS, AND ENDURE THE MOST RUNDOWN OLD SHACK BECAUSE WE WANTED TO! AND IT WAS ALL SO WE COULD DO THE HARD WORK WE NEEDED TO DO TO MAKE ANIME! YOU PEOPLE DON'T UNDER-STAND THE EFFORT THAT GOES INTO CRAFTSMANSHIP! IT'S SO ABSURD, BECAUSE...
...THE END CROWNS THE WORK!
HAVEN'T YOU EVER HEARD THAT?!
...UM, WHAT?
IT MEANS DON'T COMPLAIN ABOUT THE MEANS. LOOK AT THE ENDS.
...VERY WELL. YOU MAY SHOW YOUR VIDEO, BUT THAT'S IT.
YES!
I THOUGHT THEIR PRESENTATION WAS CONCLUDED ...?

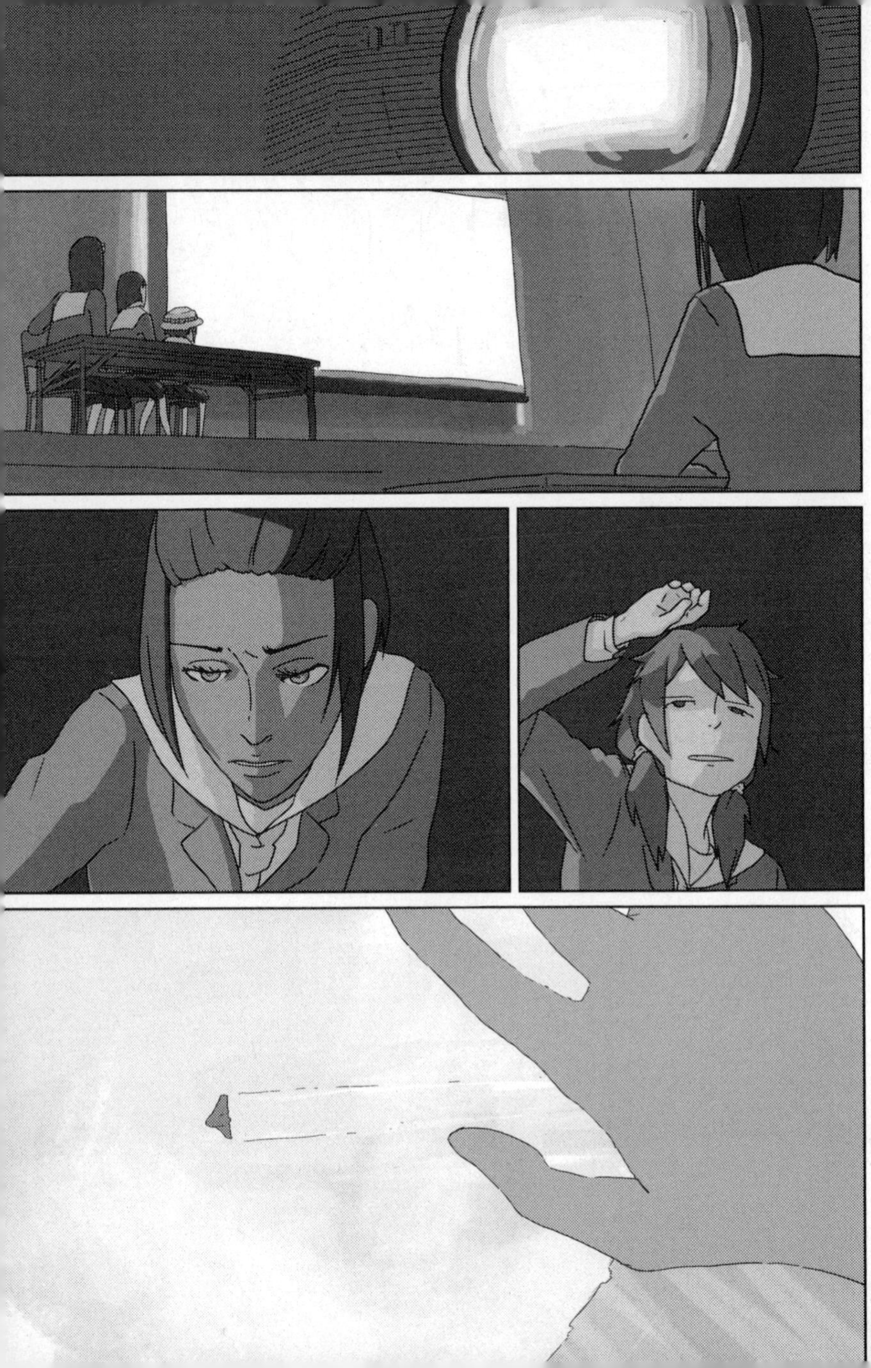

CLUTCH THAT MACHETE WITH STRENGTH!

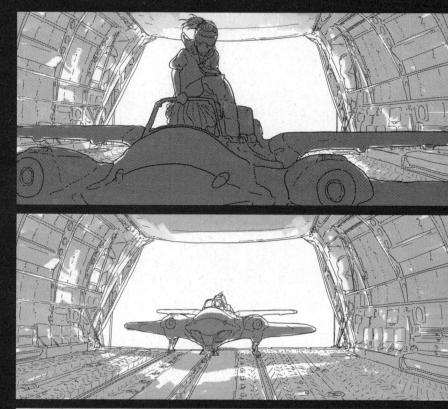

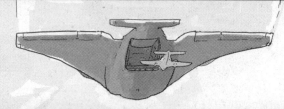

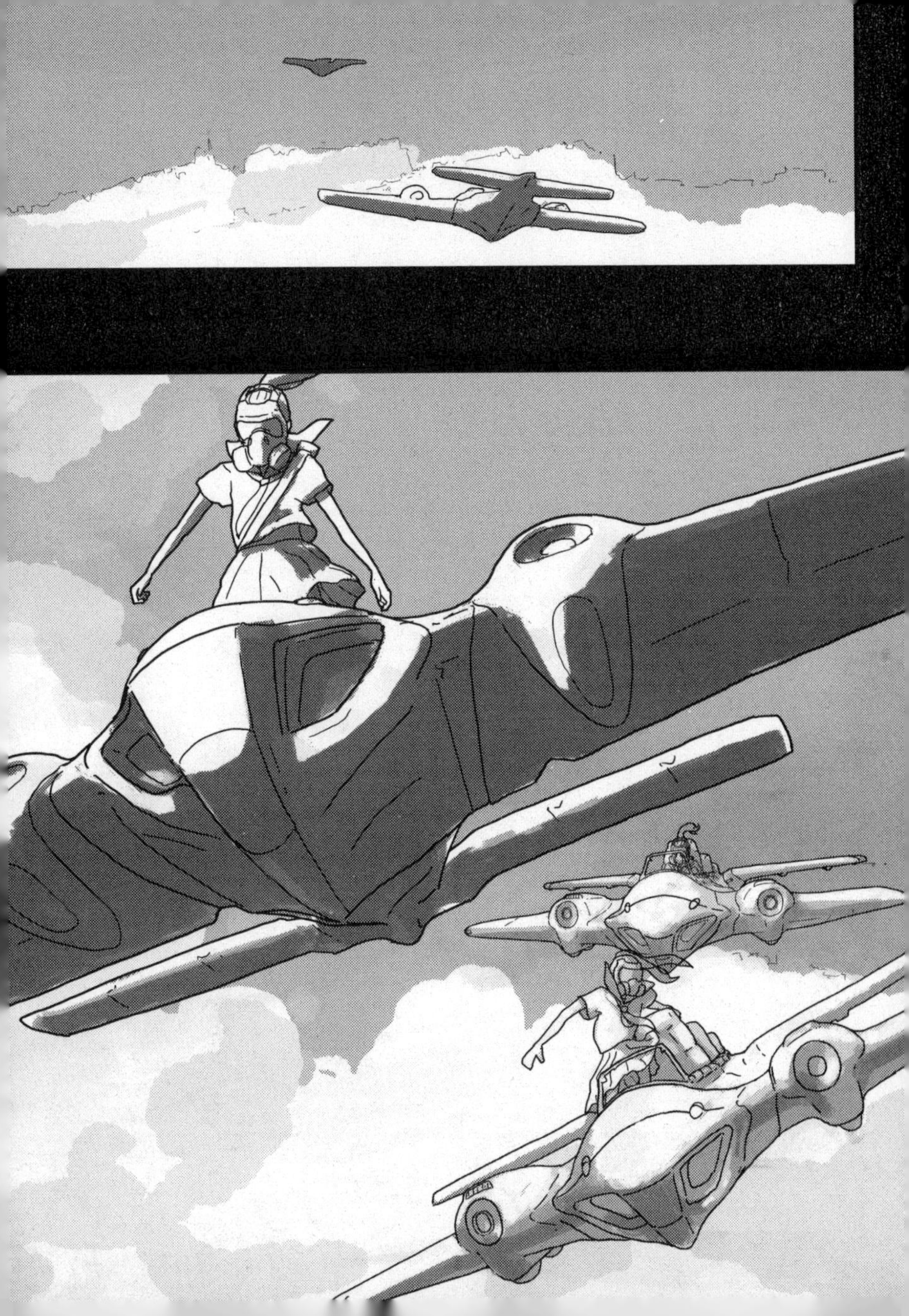

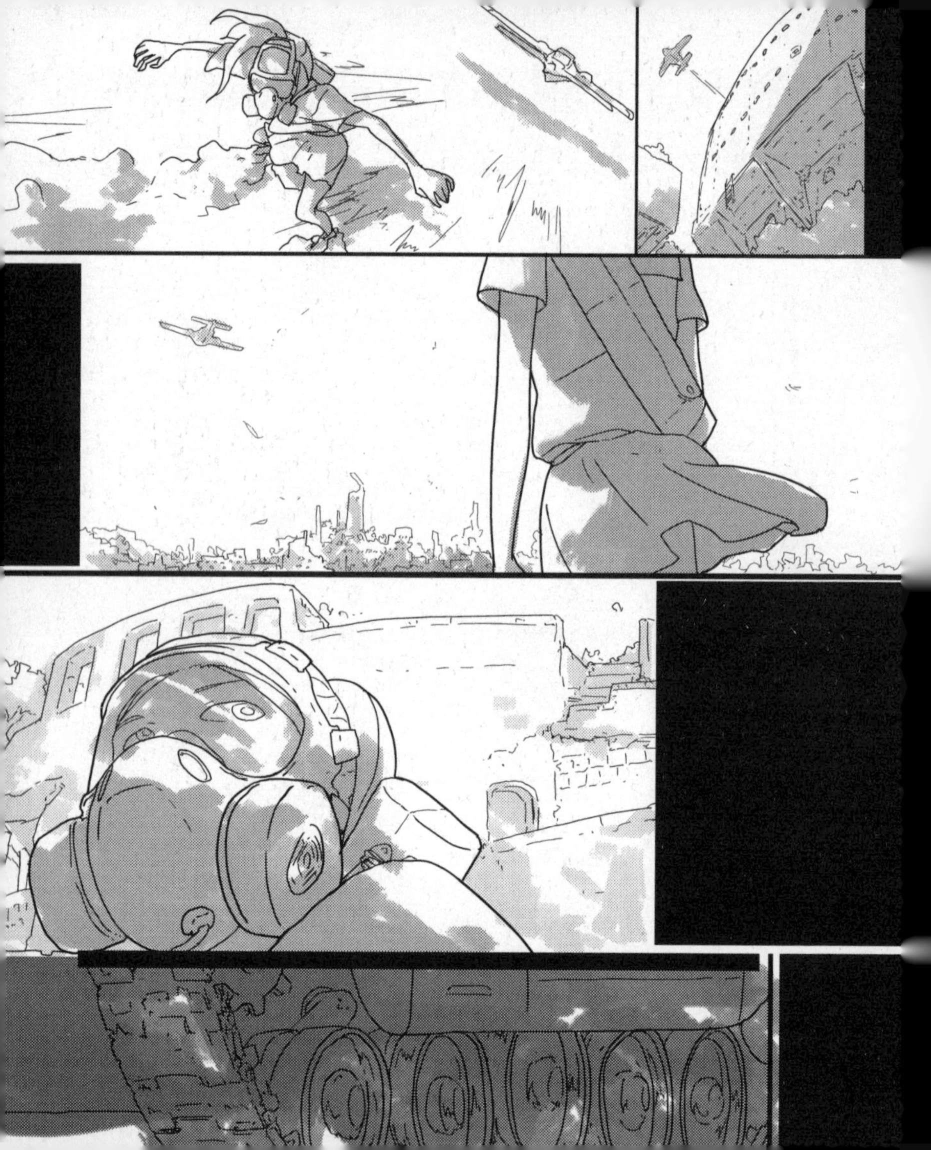

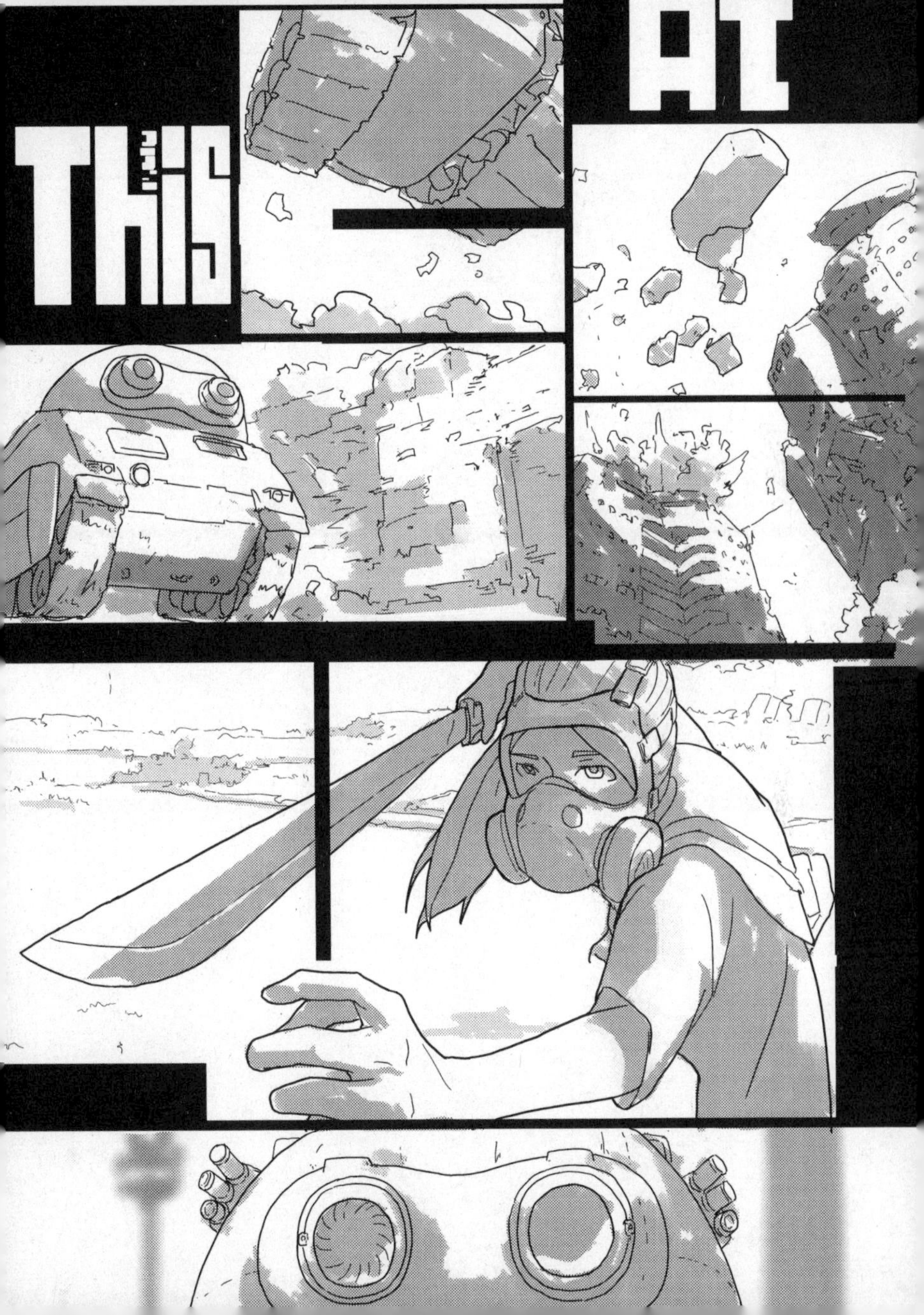
AI
ThiS

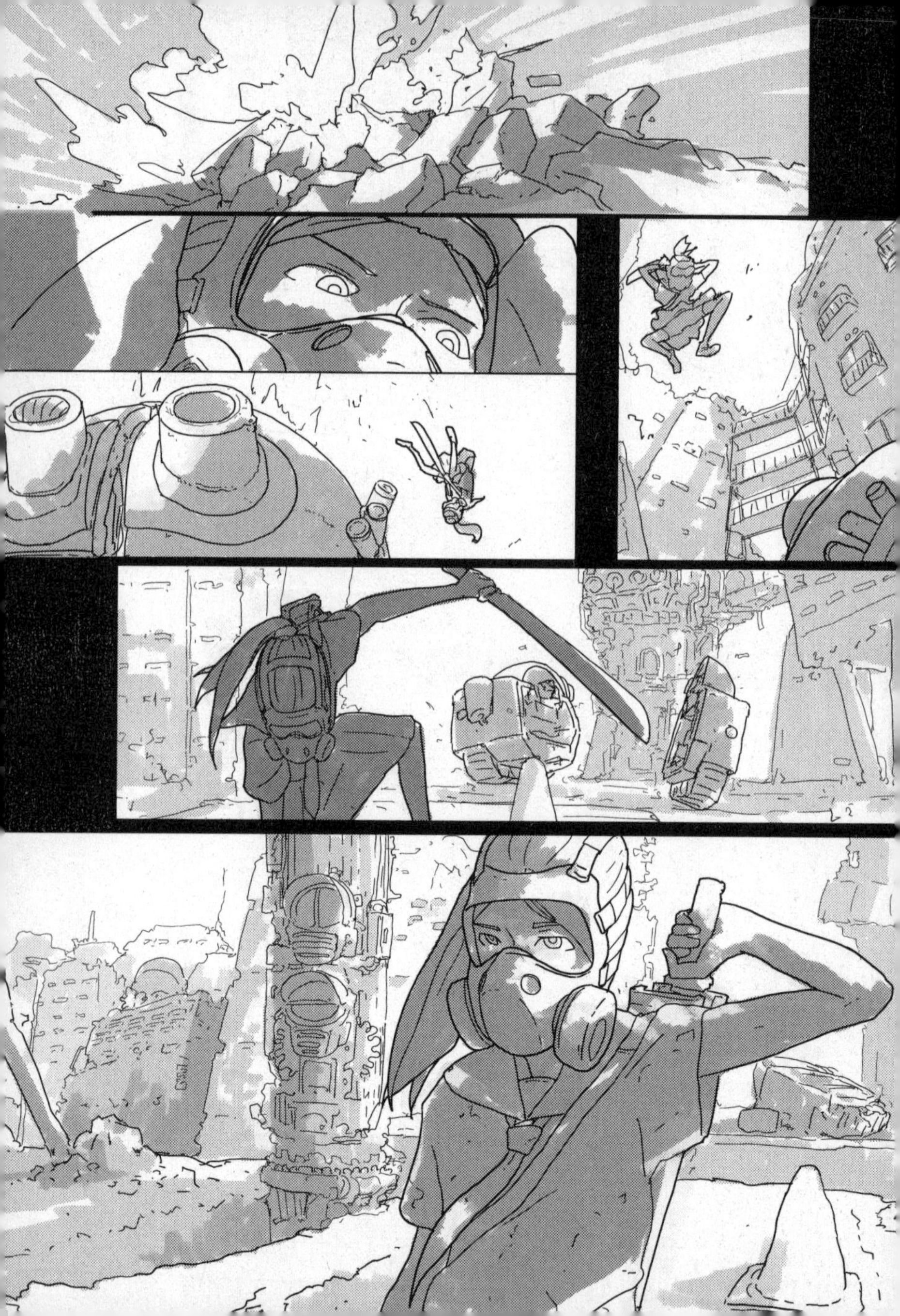

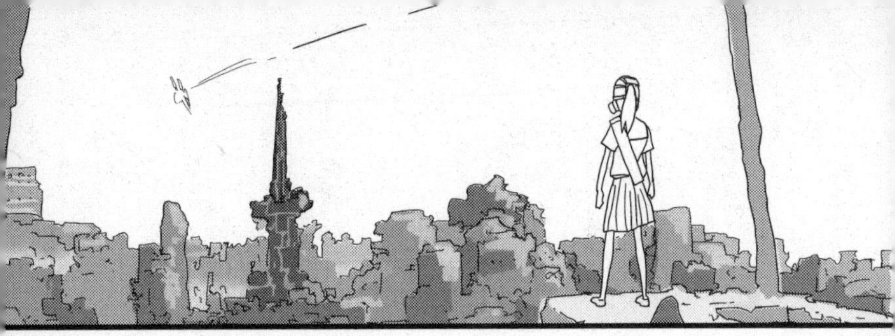
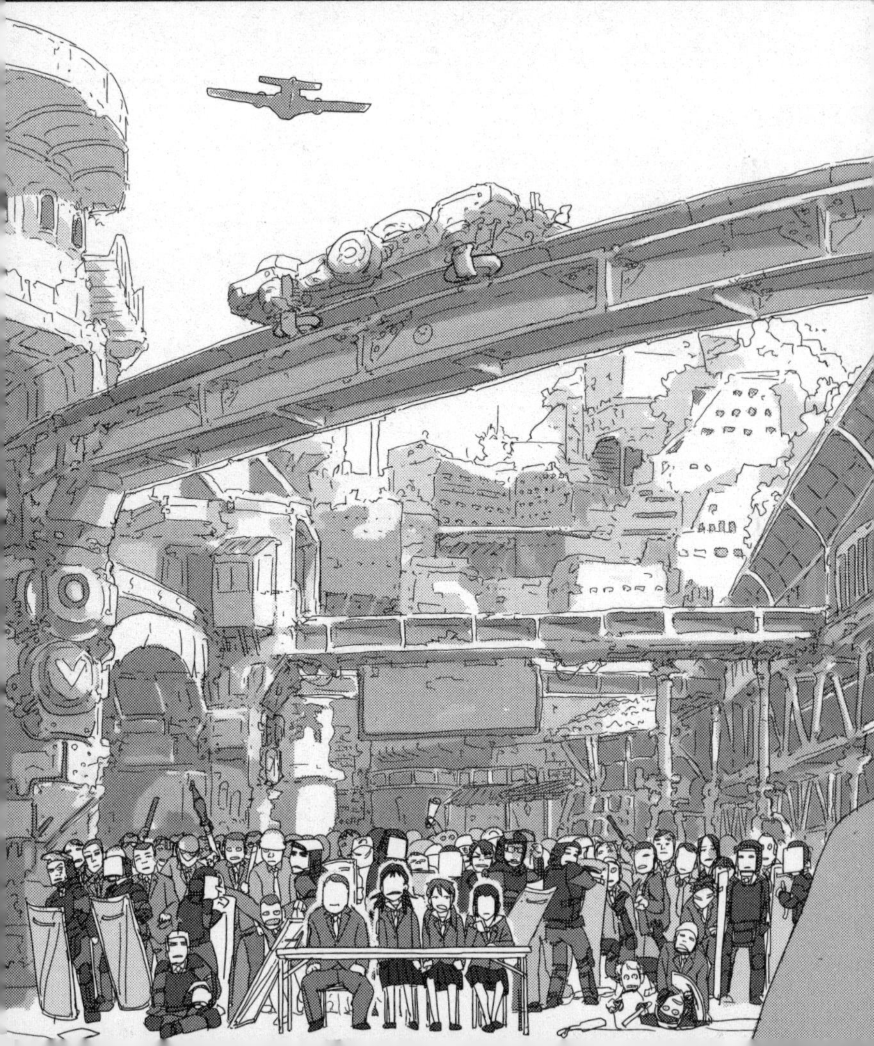

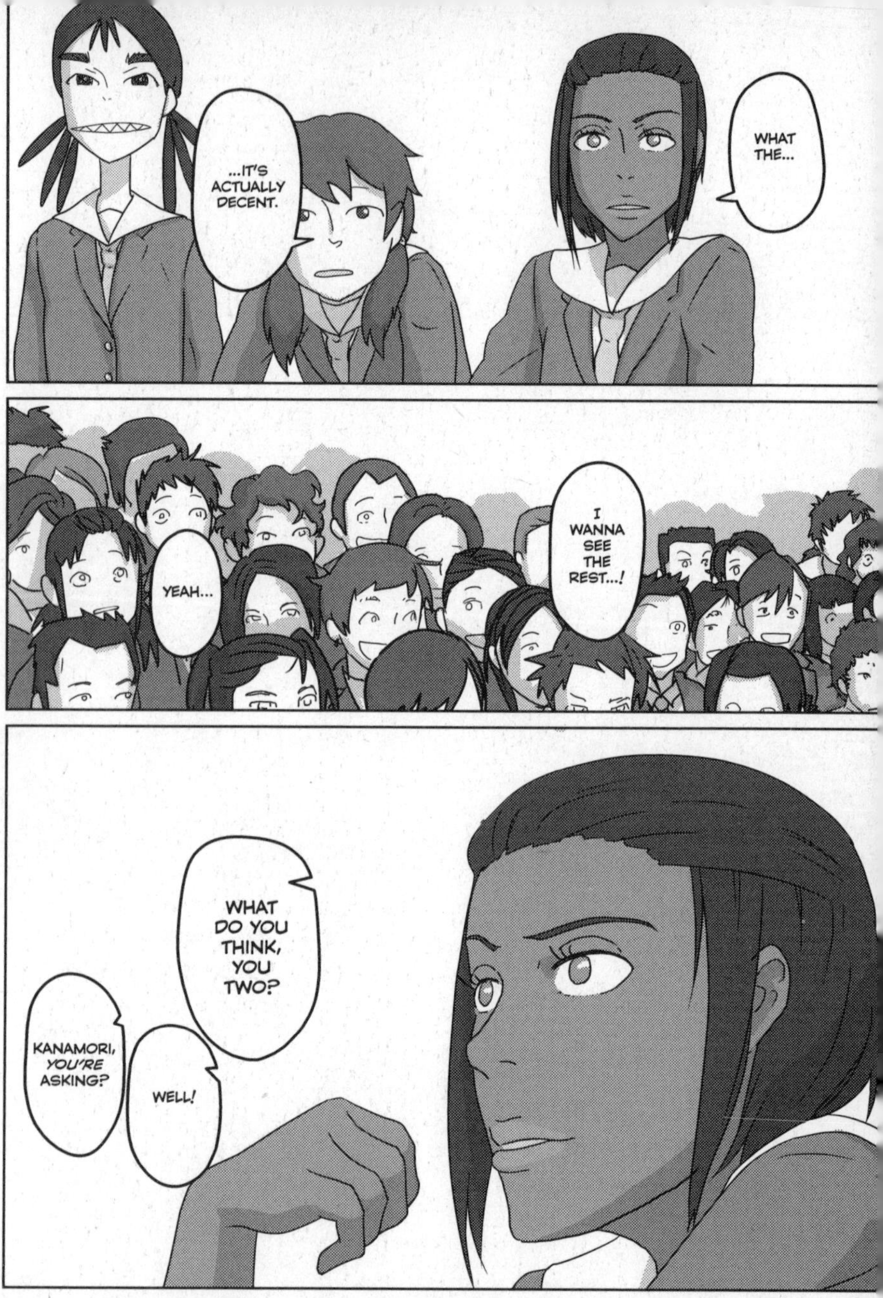
WHAT THE...
...IT'S ACTUALLY DECENT.
I WANNA SEE THE REST...!
YEAH...
WHAT DO YOU THINK, YOU TWO?
WELL!
KANAMORI, *YOU'RE* ASKING?

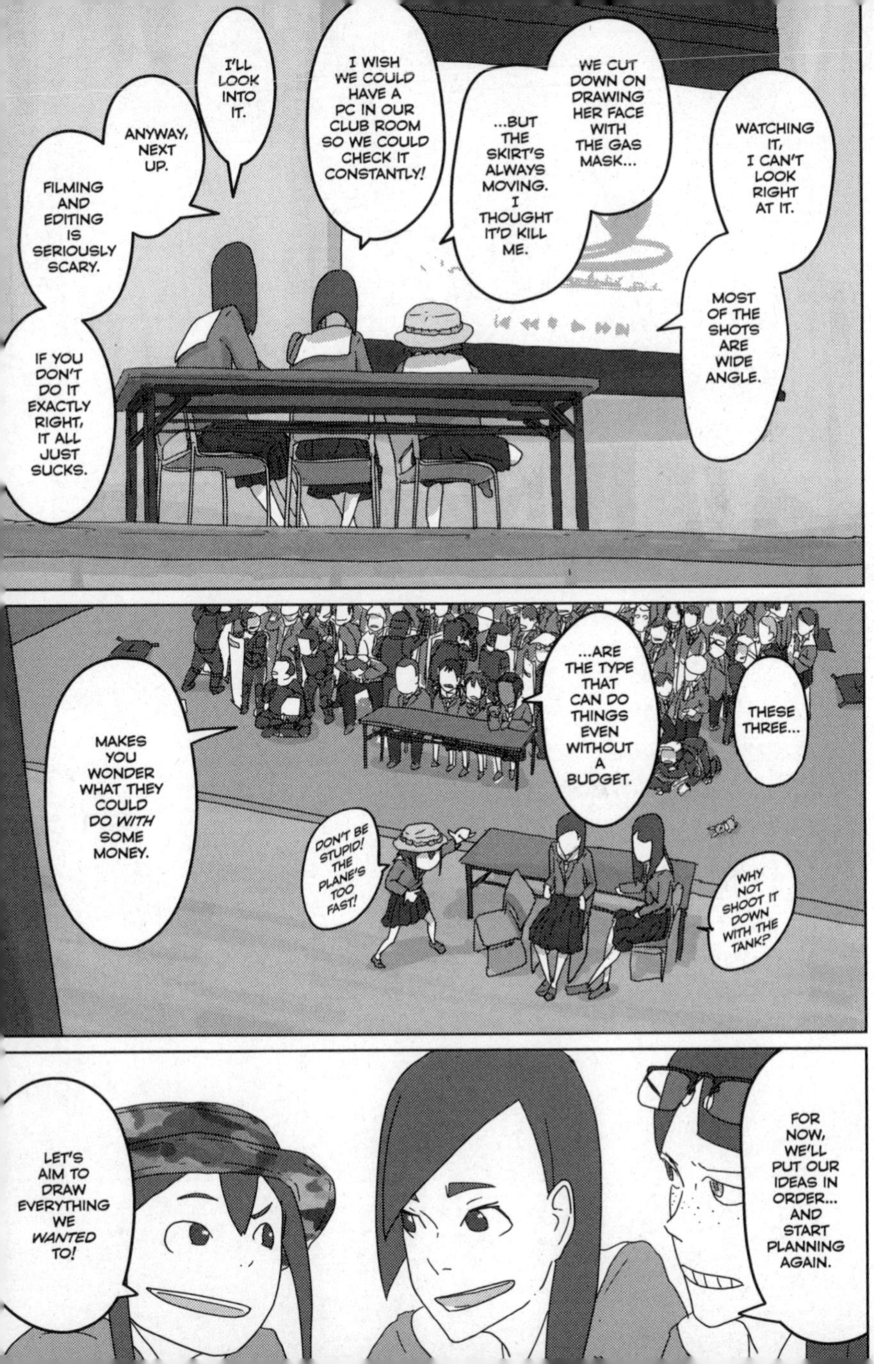
WATCHING IT, I CAN'T LOOK RIGHT AT IT.
MOST OF THE SHOTS ARE WIDE ANGLE.
WE CUT DOWN ON DRAWING HER FACE WITH THE GAS MASK...
...BUT THE SKIRT'S ALWAYS MOVING. I THOUGHT IT'D KILL ME.
I WISH WE COULD HAVE A PC IN OUR CLUB ROOM SO WE COULD CHECK IT CONSTANTLY!
I'LL LOOK INTO IT.
ANYWAY, NEXT UP.
FILMING AND EDITING IS SERIOUSLY SCARY.
IF YOU DON'T DO IT EXACTLY RIGHT, IT ALL JUST SUCKS.
THESE THREE...
...ARE THE TYPE THAT CAN DO THINGS EVEN WITHOUT A BUDGET.
MAKES YOU WONDER WHAT THEY COULD DO *WITH* SOME MONEY.
WHY NOT SHOOT IT DOWN WITH THE TANK?
DON'T BE STUPID! THE PLANE'S TOO FAST!
FOR NOW, WE'LL PUT OUR IDEAS IN ORDER... AND START PLANNING AGAIN.
LET'S AIM TO DRAW EVERYTHING WE *WANTED* TO!

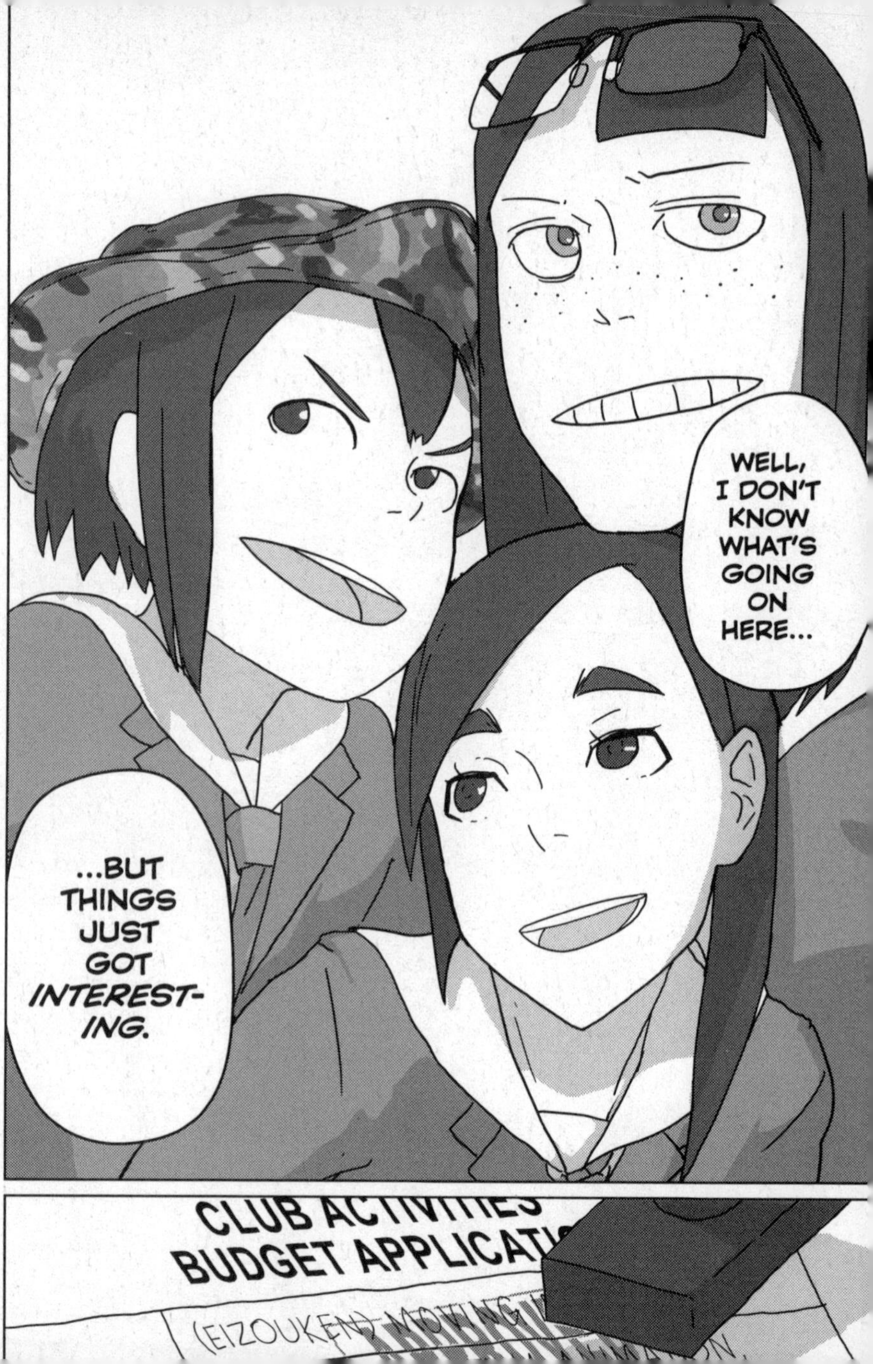
WELL, I DON'T KNOW WHAT'S GOING ON HERE...
...BUT THINGS JUST GOT *INTERESTING.*
CLUB ACTIVITIES
BUDGET APPLICATI
(EIZOUKEN)

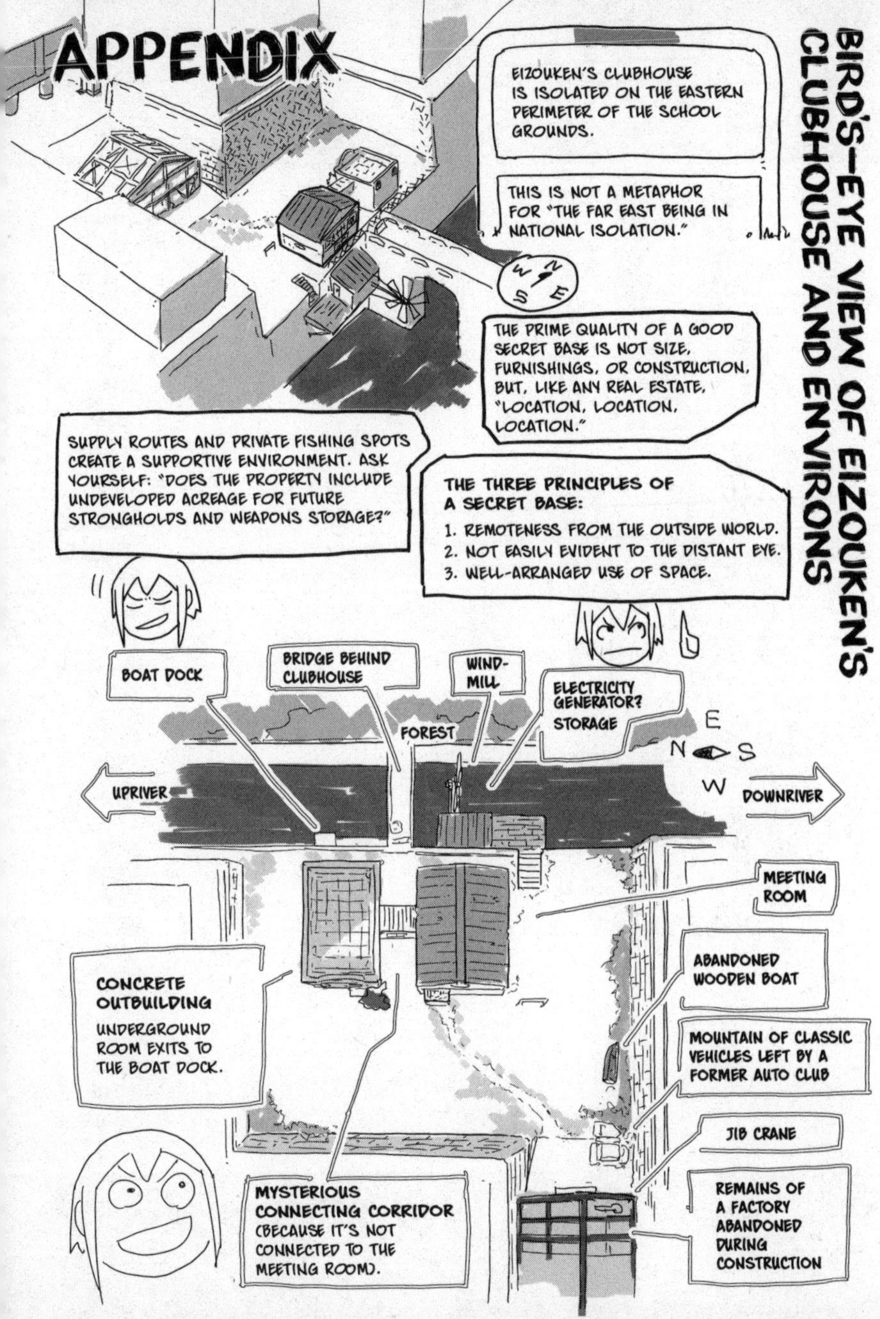
APPENDIX
BIRD'S-EYE VIEW OF EIZOUKEN'S CLUBHOUSE AND ENVIRONS
EIZOUKEN'S CLUBHOUSE IS ISOLATED ON THE EASTERN PERIMETER OF THE SCHOOL GROUNDS.
THIS IS NOT A METAPHOR FOR "THE FAR EAST BEING IN NATIONAL ISOLATION."
N
W
S
E
THE PRIME QUALITY OF A GOOD SECRET BASE IS NOT SIZE, FURNISHINGS, OR CONSTRUCTION, BUT, LIKE ANY REAL ESTATE, "LOCATION, LOCATION, LOCATION."
SUPPLY ROUTES AND PRIVATE FISHING SPOTS CREATE A SUPPORTIVE ENVIRONMENT. ASK YOURSELF: "DOES THE PROPERTY INCLUDE UNDEVELOPED ACREAGE FOR FUTURE STRONGHOLDS AND WEAPONS STORAGE?"
THE THREE PRINCIPLES OF A SECRET BASE:
1. REMOTENESS FROM THE OUTSIDE WORLD.
2. NOT EASILY EVIDENT TO THE DISTANT EYE.
3. WELL-ARRANGED USE OF SPACE.
ELECTRICITY GENERATOR? STORAGE
WIND-MILL
BRIDGE BEHIND CLUBHOUSE
BOAT DOCK
FOREST
E
N
S
W
UPRIVER
DOWNRIVER
MEETING ROOM
ABANDONED WOODEN BOAT
CONCRETE OUTBUILDING
UNDERGROUND ROOM EXITS TO THE BOAT DOCK.
MOUNTAIN OF CLASSIC VEHICLES LEFT BY A FORMER AUTO CLUB
JIB CRANE
REMAINS OF A FACTORY ABANDONED DURING CONSTRUCTION
MYSTERIOUS CONNECTING CORRIDOR (BECAUSE IT'S NOT CONNECTED TO THE MEETING ROOM).

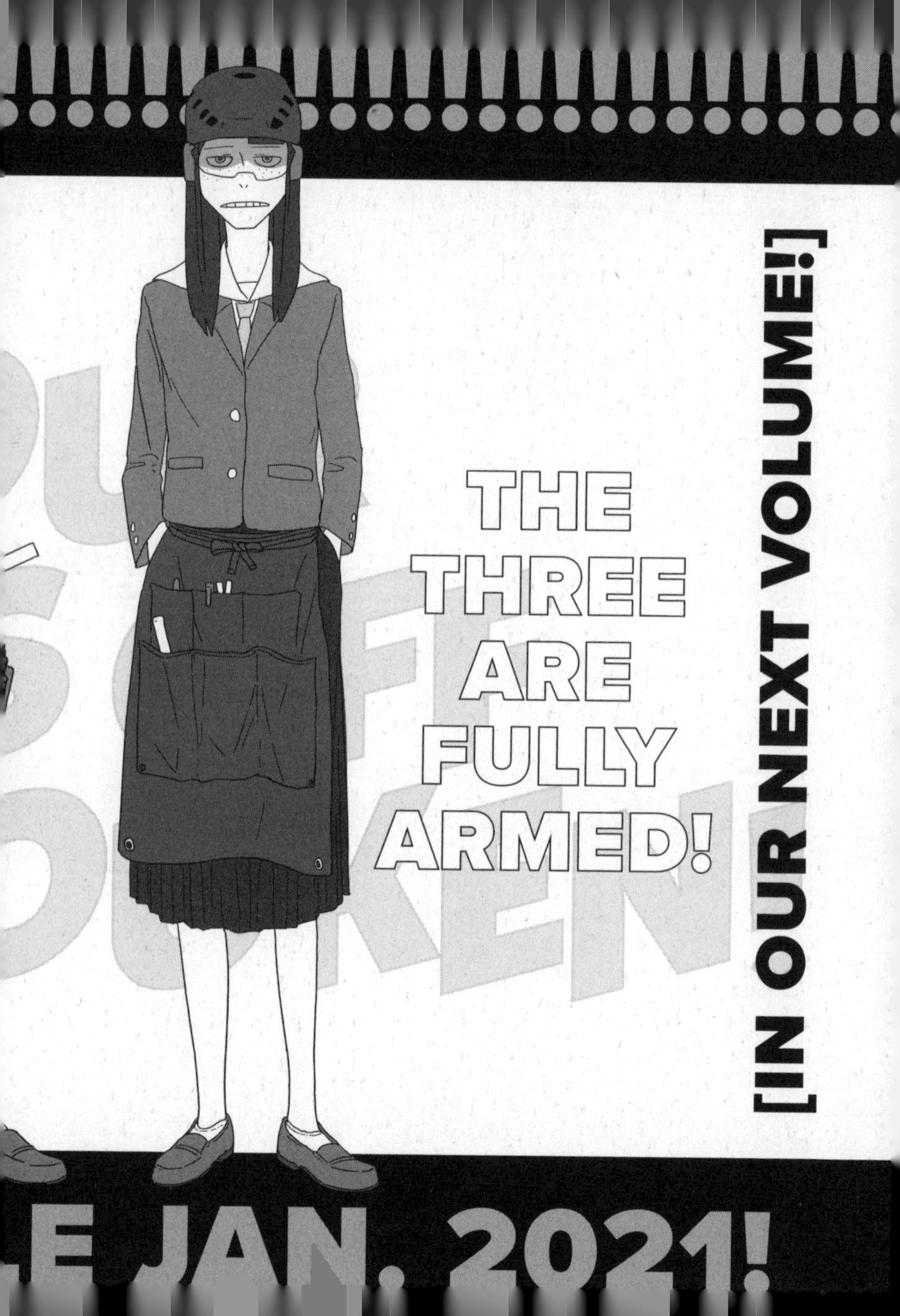
[IN OUR NEXT VOLUME!]
THE THREE ARE FULLY ARMED!
E JAN. 2021!

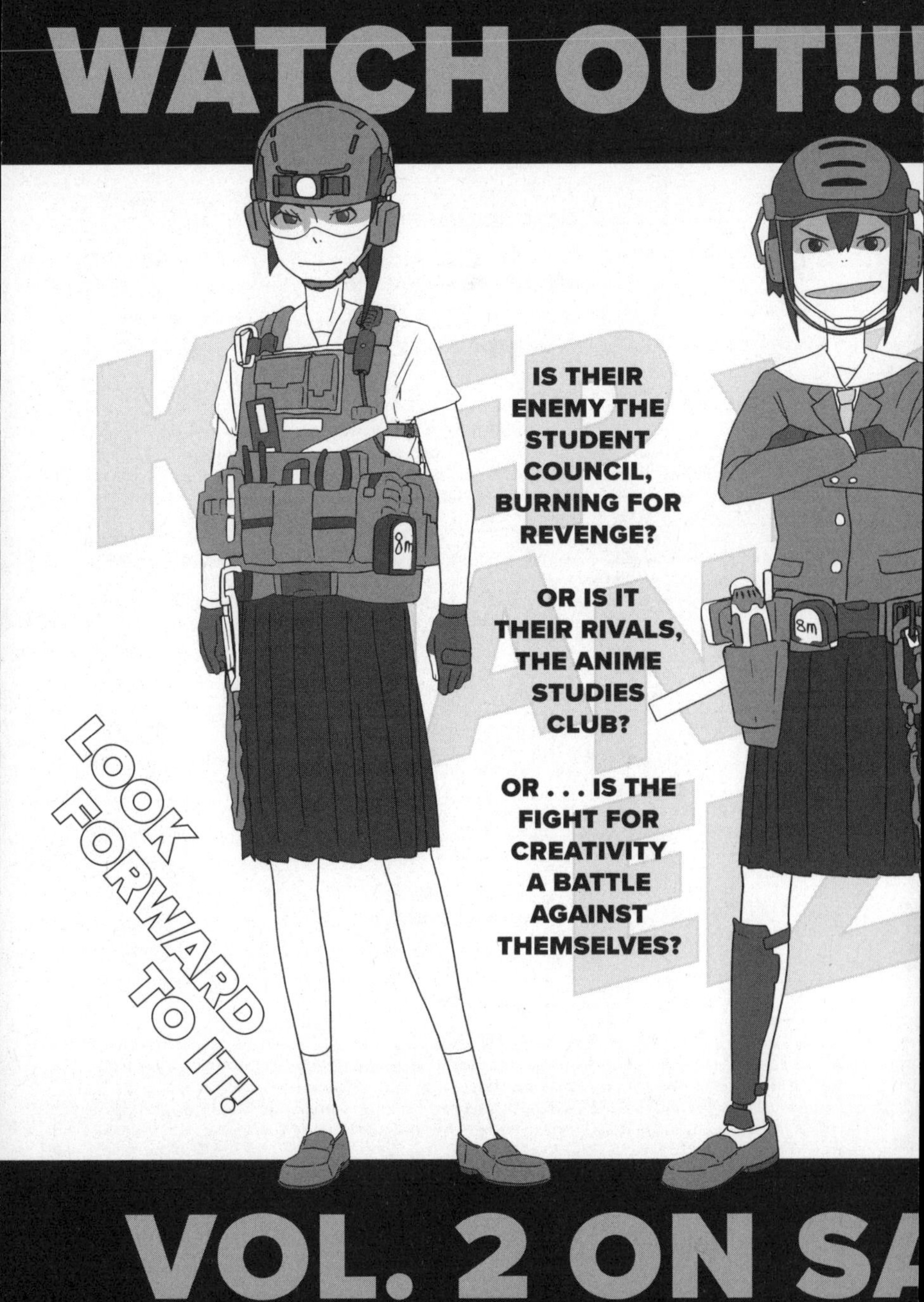
WATCH OUT!!!
IS THEIR ENEMY THE STUDENT COUNCIL, BURNING FOR REVENGE?
OR IS IT THEIR RIVALS, THE ANIME STUDIES CLUB?
OR . . . IS THE FIGHT FOR CREATIVITY A BATTLE AGAINST THEMSELVES?
LOOK FORWARD TO IT!
VOL. 2 ON SA

President and Publisher
MIKE RICHARDSON

Editor
CARL GUSTAV HORN

Designer
SKYLER WEISSENFLUH

Digital Art Technician
CHRIS HORN

English-language version produced by Dark Horse Comics

KEEP YOUR HANDS OFF EIZOUKEN!

Published by
Dark Horse Manga
A division of Dark Horse Comics LLC
10956 SE Main Street
Milwaukie, OR 97222

DarkHorse.com

To find a comics shop in your area, visit comicshoplocator.com.

First edition: November 2020
ISBN 978-1-50671-897-2

3 5 7 9 10 8 6 4 2

Printed in the United States of America

NOTES ON VOL. 1 BY THE TRANSLATOR AND EDITOR

Thank you for reading vol. 1 of the original manga version of *Keep Your Hands Off Eizouken!* by writer and artist Sumito Oowara. We became excited about this manga at Dark Horse even before vol. 1 came out in Japan, first discovering it with chapter 3 of the story in the magazine in which it is originally serialized, Shogakukan's *Monthly Big Comic Spirits* —a spinoff publication of the more famous *Weekly Big Comic Spirits* from which many well-known seinen manga titles have come, including Dark Horse's *I Am a Hero* by Kengo Hanazawa. We didn't know at that time *Eizouken* was going to be made into an anime, but were very excited when the news came that Masaaki Yuasa, who had already captivated so many viewers with works like *The Tatami Galaxy* and *Devilman Crybaby*, was going to direct an animated adaptation of the manga.

You'll have seen just from this first volume that creator Sumito Oowara already laid down a distinctive, detailed and quirky visual and storytelling style that provided an excellent launching pad for the anime. Readers will have noticed that many of the lines of dialogue in the manga are at a skew—for example, in page 18, panel 2. Whenever this skew appears, it's an instance where the same visual effect was used by Sumito Oowara in the original

Japanese version of this manga, so the effect has also been reproduced here in English. *Eizouken* is full of movement, as befits Mizusaki, but it is also a place for world-building, as befits Asakusa, and letterer and retouch artist Susie Lee has worked to adapt the signage and various excerpts in this volume from Asakusa's design books into an English version of Oowara-sensei's styles.

In reading *Eizouken* the editor (who, for reasons of height, must take on the Kanamori role) was reminded of another famous student trio of anime makers— *Daicon III*'s Hiroyuki Yamaga, Takami Akai, and Hideaki Anno, whose exploits at art school in the early 80s were woven into their classmate Kazuhiko Shimamoto's manga memoir *Aoi Honoo*, made into the live-action 2014 Japanese comedy known as *Blue Blazes* (or *Blue Fire*). But the most obvious influence for Mizusaki and Asakusa's expression is Hayao Miyazaki— and particularly his earlier works as a director from the 1970s and 80s, when his original fanbase was more hardcore anime fans than it was the general public (for more on this topic, please see the afterword to Dark Horse's manga *Seraphim: 266613336 Wings* by Satoshi Kon and Mamoru Oshii). You can see some translated pages out of Miyazaki's own design scrapbooks from the early 1980s within the book *Starting Point: 1979~1996* from Viz Media, and their spirit is very much in Asakusa's (and of course, Oowara's) drawings.

Some comments on the English version. *Eizouken* is rendered here as "moving image studies," to reflect the broader scope of the term in Japanese, where *eizou* can encompass not only films, but videos, TV shows, or any type of analog or digital image moving on a screen. The use of "moving image" to convey this in English was inspired by the example of the Museum of the Moving Image in New York City, which has also regularly featured animation (Japanese and otherwise) within its programming. In the original manga (for example, on page 9, panel 1), Asakusa uses the English letters "GHQ" to refer to the period of US military administration in Japan following the Second World War. Although this is a common nickname that was used in Japan during the actual occupation, and is still learned in Japanese schools today (GHQ is short for "General Headquarters" and is much shorter than the formal Japanese name for the period, *Rengoo kokugun senryoo-ka no Nihon*, "Japan Under Allied Forces Occupation"), it's not as common in English-language histories of the period, where the more frequently employed acronym is SCAP (Supreme Commander for the Allied Powers, which was occupation chief Gen. Douglas MacArthur's title). However, even this is a bit obscure when you're just trying to make a joke work ^_^ so the English version simply refers to what these terms represented, that is, the U.S. occupation.

On page 65, panel 4, Asakusa is looking at some audiocassette tapes. The date October 6, 1974, and the fact this is an old-fashioned animator's desk, would suggest it's referencing the first episode of the famous anime series *Space Battleship Yamato*, which made its debut on that date (readers may have seen the 2010s remake of the series, released here as *Star Blazers 2199*—also a manga from Dark Horse!). On the second tape, Asakusa in the original Japanese is only able to make out the words ". . . *pan tantei mu* . . ." which suggests this may be a recording of *Chinpan Tantei Musshu Barabara* ("Monsieur Mixed-Up, Chimp Detective"), which was in fact the Japanese name of the 1970-71 US live-action TV series *Lancelot Link, Secret Chimp*, a spy parody cast with chimpanzees dubbed over by human voice actors. Home videotape systems existed in the early 1970s, but they were uncommon and expensive, so it was not unknown for fans instead to record shows they liked on the much cheaper audiocassettes, even if that meant they could only capture the sound portion of the program—it of course can also be presumed that the animator needed something to listen to (rather than watch) while they drew.

An amazing in-joke from Oowara-sensei can be spotted just in front of Asakusa and Mizusaki's faces on page 67, panel 2. That object that looks like an old urinal turned on its side is exactly that—in fact, it is Marcel Duchamp's 1917 installation piece *Fountain*, voted in a 2004 British survey as the most influential single artwork of the 20th century. It's hard to see clearly at manga size, but looking at the original art file, Duchamp's signature "R. Mutt 1917" can be made out on the bottom rim. In addition to all the interpretations inherent in the work itself, there's an extra level in *Eizouken*, as the original of *Fountain* was lost shortly after its debut; even one of the replicas authorized by Duchamp in the 1950s and 60s has sold for $1.7 million. If only the trio recognized it as a great work of art rather than as an old urinal turned on its side, their budget worries would be over.

The PGT gripped by Asakusa on page 92, panel 4 is indeed a real computer-controlled power tool specifically developed by NASA and Swales Aerospace for the microgravity, vacuum, and temperature extremes of space; it was used not only to fix the Hubble Space Telescope, but to assemble the International Space Station in orbit, and remains a regular part of its maintenance on spacewalks. The large lunch ordered by Kanamori (she's obviously still growing) on page 98, panel 2 includes a *koshi anpan*, which is a bun filled with sweet paste made from beans with their seed coats removed, as opposed to *tsubu anpan*, made from beans with the coats left on. Although the taste of anpan is nothing like peanut butter, the two styles are sometimes compared to the smooth-vs.-chunky debate.

On page 101, panel 4, the "Hold on a sec . . ." was a bit of wordplay in the original Japanese, where Asakusa said *matsutake* (a variety of mushroom) instead of *matsu* (wait). The "slideshow" Kanamori refers to on page 108, panel 6, was in the original Japanese *kamishibai*, a form of street theater where a performer would set up a picture frame on a stand and tell a story by sliding different illustrations in and out while providing narration and sound effects; some postwar manga artists, including the famed Shigeru Mizuki (*Onward Toward Our Noble Deaths, Showa: A History of Japan*), got their start painting images for the *kamishibai* trade; it was also an old joke in the anime business that the limited number of drawings used (compared to American cartoons) keeps up the proud traditions of *kamishibai*.

Asakusa's reminiscence on page 116, panel 6 of transferring schools "before the last summer vacation of elementary school," references the fact that unlike in the US, the summer break occurs within a Japanese school year, which begins in April. On page 119, panel 2, her mother's remark about watching anime on "Dyao" is a play on GyaO, a Japanese video streaming site run by Yahoo!; one of the pioneering web services companies founded during the original 1990s dot-com era, it remains a major presence in Japan. The anime show she chooses to watch in panel 6 (and which is represented by various scenes on pages 120-121) is Hayao Miyazaki's 1978 series *Shonen Mirai Conan* (*Future Boy Conan*) and interestingly, it is called by its real name in the manga, whereas the anime version of this scene (near the beginning of the first episode) calls the series *Nokosarejima no Conan* (*Conan of Remnant Island*), a reference to the title of the first episode of the real show.

It may be that Oowara-sensei found it easier to use the original name in the manga version, whereas the co-producer of the *Eizouken* anime, Eunyoung Choi, has noted the difficulties getting clearance to use actual clips from the 1978 anime series; in the end, they were obliged to literally *trace* the 1978 clips, so what's shown in *Eizouken* is sort of a "cover version" of the original show! English-speaking anime fans can be sympathetic to the producer's troubles, as despite the fact *Future Boy Conan* is the only TV show ever directed in its entirety by Miyazaki (he has directed individual episodes of other series), it has never had a licensed home video release in English, although it has shown on TV in a number of different countries, and could sometimes be seen in the United States on Spanish-language channels. The advertisement for the Japanese Blu-ray sets at the bottom of page 121 was in the original manga, and if you're interested, you can buy them at a 15% discount from CD Japan.

We'll hope to see you again for *Eizouken* Volume 2! The anime series may be over, but the manga series is ongoing, so with strong reader support we can continue to follow the *Eizouken* cast all the way as they make an adventure out of their creative struggles. The editor would like to dedicate the English version of this manga to the memory of Zac Bertschy, who as executive editor of Anime News Network was a passionate supporter of the *Eizouken* anime series. I was honored to know Zac for many years, and just a few weeks before his passing, I told him how much we were looking forward to releasing the manga of the series he had championed. He got to see what it inspired, and now here we have the inspiration.

—CGH

the KUROSAGI corpse delivery service
黒鷺死体宅配便

OMNIBUS EDITIONS

Five young students at a Buddhist university find there's little call for their job skills in today's Tokyo. . . among the living, that is! But their studies give them a direct line to the dead—the dead who are still trapped in their corpses, and can't move on to the next incarnation! Whether death resulted from suicide, murder, sickness, or madness, the Kurosagi Corpse Delivery Service will carry the body anywhere it needs to go to free its soul!

"Nobody does horror-comedy comics better than Otsuka and Yamazaki"

—Booklist

Each 600+ page omnibus book collects three complete volumes of the series!

Vol. 1:
Contains vols. 1–3, originally published separately.
ISBN 978-1-61655-754-6 $19.99

Vol. 2:
Contains vols. 4–6, originally published separately.
ISBN 978-1-61655-783-6 $19.99

Vol. 3:
Contains vols. 7–9, originally published separately.
ISBN 978-1-61655-887-1 $19.99

Vol. 4:
Contains vols. 10–12, originally published separately.
ISBN 978-1-50670-055-7 $19.99

REPENT, SINNERS!
THEY'RE BACK!

Miss the anime?
Try the *Panty & Stocking with Garterbelt* manga! Nine ALL-NEW
stories of your favorite filthy fallen angels, written and drawn by TAGRO,
with a special afterword by *Kill La Kill* director Hiroyuki Imaishi!
978-1-61655-735-5 | $9.99

LOOK AT THIS
(the other way)

Sayaka Kanamori would like to thank you for your purchase of *Keep Your Hands off Eizouken!* and reminds all customers that this manga reads in the traditional Japanese style, right-to-left. To get your money's worth, please flip the book around and begin reading.

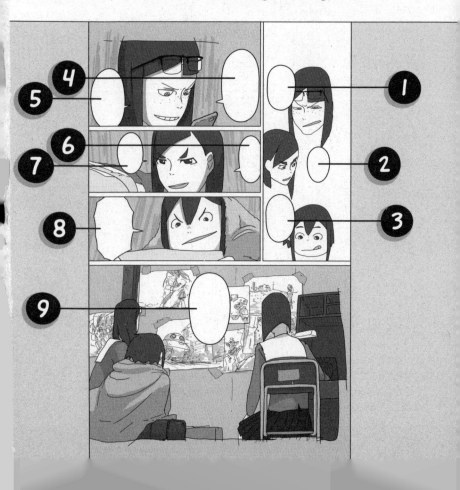